HINDU CIVILIZATION

HINDU CIVILIZATION

(From the earliest times up to the establishment of the Maurya Empire)

BY

RADHA KUMUD MOOKERJI

GYAN

Published by

GYAN

Gyan Publishing House
5, Ansari Road
Daryaganj, New Delhi-110002
Phone: 011-47034999, 9811692060
E-mail: books@gyanbooks.com

Distribution Network
gyanbooks.com
India, USA, Canada, UK, Australia

ISBN: 978-93-6208-484-2 (HB)
First Published, 1936

2nd Impression 2024

Printed at: Gyan Press, Delhi.

HINDU CIVILIZATION
Author: RADHA KUMUD MOOKERJI

HINDU CIVILIZATION

Works by the same Author

1. *A History of Indian Shipping* (Longmans, Green & Co., Ltd., London).
2. *The Fundamental Unity of India*, with Foreword by the Right Hon. J. Ramsay MacDonald, M.P. (Longmans, Green & Co., Ltd., London).
3. *Nationalism in Hindu Culture* (Asian Library Series, London).
4. *Local Government in Ancient India*, with Foreword by the Marquess of Crewe (Oxford University Press).
5. *Harsha* (Rulers of India Series, Oxford University Press).
6. *Men and Thought in Ancient India* (Macmillan & Co., Ltd., London).
7. *Asoka* [Gaekwad Lectures] (Macmillan & Co., Ltd., London).

INTERIOR OF HALL AT MOHENJO-DARO (c. 3250-2750 B.C.).

Frontispiece.]

HINDU CIVILIZATION

(From the earliest times up to the establishment of Maurya Empire)

By

RADHA KUMUD MOOKERJI, M.A., PH.D.

Professor of Indian History, University of Lucknow

LONGMANS, GREEN AND CO.

LONDON . NEW YORK . TORONTO

To

My Darling

PRABUDDHA KUMUD MOOKERJI

(June, 1920–September, 1931)

PREFACE

The present work has been suggested by the needs of study and teaching at the Universities of a subject which, for the period dealt with, is necessarily somewhat nebulous, indefinite, and, sometimes, speculative and highly controversial. It intends to bring together the results of specialized study of the different aspects of a vast subject as parts of an organic whole. The task of writing such a work has been considerably lightened by the publication of the *Cambridge History of India*, to which my obligations are both general and specific.

But perhaps I may claim that the Indian point of view has received its due scope in the work and constitutes its chief justification. That has naturally suggested the value and use of some neglected texts, some new points of interest in known and familiar documents, or some new relations of old facts. The work has also followed its own method of building up history, as far as possible, in terms of original sources or texts, on the basis of what may be called the "key-words" in which are locked up its essence, its vital elements, its characteristic features. Such "key-words" are the clues to forgotten national traditions. They open up the buried past and breathe life into its dead bones. They give body and form, flesh and blood, to the dry skeleton of history. The past is thus seen in its proper setting, in its true colours and perspective. It speaks through its own language, wherever possible.

The system of transliteration adopted in the work has been somewhat simplified, as may be understood from the following examples: *Kṛishṇa, Mahāvaṁśa, Vasishṭha, Lichchhavi, Aṅga.*

I owe the illustrations numbered II–XII to the Archæological Department to whom belongs their copyright. My thanks are due to Messrs. Macmillan and Co., Ltd., for their kind permission to reproduce in this work maps numbered 1 and 3 from my work *Men and Thought in Ancient India* published by them. Map No. 2 is based on that of Pargiter for his article in the *JRAS.*, 1908, pp. 309–336. The abbreviations of the names of texts cited are generally those adopted in all standard oriental works.

RADHA KUMUD MOOKERJI.

THE UNIVERSITY,
LUCKNOW.
January, 1936.

CONTENTS

ILLUSTRATIONS

MAPS

CHAPTER I

INTRODUCTION

History as a Subject.—History deals with the past of a people or country and not with its present or future. It deals with what has been, and not with what is, or what ought to be. It records realities, actual events, or accomplished facts, and has nothing to do with ideals, with which are concerned subjects like Ethics or Poetry, Art, and Literature. But though it deals with what may be regarded as the dead past, it is not without its lessons or value for the problems of the present or the prospects of the future. It supplies the data upon which are based the social sciences like Economics or Politics. Politics has even been defined as the fruit of the tree of which History is the root. All reform, whether social, economic, or political, must not be by a violent or complete break with the past, but should be along the lines of least resistance in consonance with the national traditions and aptitudes of the people concerned, as reflected in their history, if such reform is to take root and not to be flourished in the air.

Scope and Method.—The character of History as a subject of study determines the method proper for its study. As it records and recalls the past, it must do so faithfully like a mirror or a photograph, showing in its true contours and colours the object it brings before the eye. In dealing with the events or facts of the past, it must first ascertain them correctly and let them speak for themselves. This means that history is entirely bound by its material. It cannot modify or improve upon it. A chemist can get the material he needs by means of artificial manipulations and experiments with which he proceeds to find positive or objective proofs of the hypothesis or theory suggested by his scientific and constructive imagination. But a historian must not manipulate his material. He must take the facts as he finds them. He cannot create them. The facts are external to him, and are beyond and independent of him. He cannot, like the philosopher, spin out of his inner consciousness an ideal system, or, like the poet or artist, enthuse on " the light that never was on sea or land ". He must be always true to his facts with all their imperfections in point of precision or definiteness, quality, reaction, effects, or consequences. History cannot be made to order. Its materials are beyond control. They are fixed with a dead certainty. When these are found, the historian must take a detached view of them.

Sometimes it is difficult to get at the correct facts of the past from the different accounts given of them in the sources or records from which they are derived. In such cases, the historian will require the critical spirit of a scientist in dealing with his material or the discrimination and impartiality of a judge in tracing the truth through a maze of conflicting and contradictory accounts and evidence. His views and judgments of the past must not be influenced by any personal bias or pre-conceived theories. He must accept as inevitable the conclusions to which the evidence leads, and bow to the picture of the past which his facts call up. That picture may, or may not, be to his taste, may be agreeable or painful, may feed or hurt his national pride, but he must present it as it is. He must not touch up the picture. He must also place the picture in its proper setting. He must not interpret the past in terms of the present, or read into old texts modern notions.

Thus the ideal historian must possess the objective attitude of the scientist towards the facts and phenomena of his study, the mechanical precision and perfection of the mirror in reflecting and reproducing the past, the dialectical skill of the lawyer in sifting and interrogating the evidence, the impartiality of the judge in finding the way to truth through its different or conflicting accounts, and, lastly, the insight and vision which lead to the discovery and exploration of new sources or untrodden fields.[1]

[1] Benedetto Croce has summed up the requirements of a historian in his own inimitable way. According to him, the historian must have " a point of view ", " an intimate personal conviction regarding the conception of the facts which he has undertaken to relate. The historical

Limitations.—History is thus limited by, and to, the facts that are found. But the facts of the past cannot all or always be found. Some of them may be lost in oblivion. Much of the past is dead and buried; it can only be preserved if records are kept of it. Where there are no records kept of the facts and events of the past, there can be no history. History begins with recorded time. Besides the limitation of ascertained facts, history has thus the further limitation imposed upon its scope by the sources of such facts. The exploration of the sources is thus the first task of the historian. His second task is the extraction of facts from the sources.

Treatment.—The treatment of the facts thus recovered will depend on their nature. Firstly, the sequence of facts may be traced in time, in the order of chronology. There is a view that history proper must be limited to chronology, that the facts and events of a distant or obscure past for which the precise dates are not available should be beyond the province of history. Such a limited view of history will make it merely political history made up of definite and concrete events and measures connected with the succeeding sovereigns of a country. But the sequence of

work of art cannot be achieved among the confused and discordant mass of crude facts, save by means of this *point of view*, which makes it possible to carve a definite figure from that rough and incoherent mass. . . It suffices to read any book of history to discover at once the point of view of the author, if he be a historian worthy of the name and know his own business. There exist liberal and reactionary, rationalist and catholic historians, who deal with political or social history. . . . Absolutely historical historians do not and cannot exist. Can it be said that Thucydides and Polybius, Livy and Tacitus, Machiavelli and Guicciardini, Giannone and Voltaire, were without moral and political views; and, in our time, Guizot or Thiers, Macaulay or Balbo, Ranke or Mommsen? . . . If the historian is to escape from this inevitable necessity of taking a side, he must become a political and scientific eunuch; and history is not the business of eunuchs. . . Historians who profess to wish to interrogate the facts, without adding anything of their own to them, are not to be believed. This, at the most, is the result of ingenuousness and illusion on their part; they will always add what they have of personal, if they be truly historians, though it be without knowing it, or they will believe that they have escaped doing so, only because they have referred to it by innuendo, which is the most insinuating and penetrative of methods." And yet this subjective element or factor, which is necessary and inevitable "in every narrative of human affairs", is "compatible with the utmost objectivity, impartiality, and scrupulosity in dealing with historical data and materials" (*Æsthetic*, pp. 220–3, in Ainslie's translation).

facts may be traced not merely in time but also in ideas. Facts may be so arranged and presented as to exhibit the order of development, a process of organic evolution from origins and in successive stages. Or the facts may follow a logical order of ideal sequences and connections. By the application of both these methods, chronological and logical or philosophical, the horizon of history may be considerably widened. It will not be confined only to political history within the rigid limits of an immutable chronology, but will include much other matter of considerable interest and importance. It will include social history, the history of institutions, of culture and civilization, which is of more consequence to a people's national history and of more *abiding* value to the general culture of mankind than purely political, chronological history, treating only of particular and dated facts and events. For these form but a small and comparatively unimportant part of a people's history which should concern itself not so much with its rulers, government, or administration as with its development in culture and civilization, and those formative forces, agencies, or movements which shape that development. It will be evident that for such history, the history of thought, of ideals and institutions, of manners, customs, and beliefs, the merely datable facts, facts which are studied individually and piecemeal, do not count as much as they do for purely political history. For the history of civilization, of a nation's development through the ages in the different spheres of thought and action, facts are to be viewed in the mass, in their general and broader bearings and effects, in their tendencies, as comprising or exhibiting the stages or processes of that development.

Application to Indian History.—Indian history based on chronology dates approximately from 600 B.C., the time of the great religious leader, Gautama the Buddha, whose date is the earliest date that can be ascertained with some degree of precision in Indian history. Yet, surely, the rise of Buddhism was not the first fact of Indian history. There was a long period of previous history and development of which Buddhism was a product. For this earlier history, it is not possible to trace any dates for the facts and movements that make it up. In reconstructing that history of the remote past, the chronological method breaks down. We have to fall back upon the other methods which will be very fruitful for the purpose. If the earlier pre-Buddhistic history of India is devoid of chronological data, it is rich in other kinds of data on the basis of which we can build up, instead of a political history presenting events in their chronological sequence in relation to sovereigns, a history of civilization presenting the broad movements in thought and morals, - the evolution of institutions, the progress achieved through the ages in social organization, economic life, literature, and religion.

Sources.—All history, however, whether cultural or chronological, is limited by its sources. The sources, or the evidence and records left of a people's life in the past, may be either in writing or in the form of material remains; they may be either literary or monumental in their character. There is an evolution of sources with the evolution of history. The earliest evidence of man's life was not in any written record or literary text, for writing, learning, or literature must come with considerable progress in civilization. According to many scholars, writing was not developed in India before about 800 B.C., though this view is not universally accepted. It is not, however, doubted that literature in India was much older than writing and was conserved and transmitted from teacher to pupil, from generation to generation, by a system of oral tradition. Texts in this Indian system of learning passed from ear to ear, and constituted what was technically called *śruti* (literally, what is revealed by *hearing*). All knowledge was thus stored up in the memory. The learned men were the travelling libraries of those days. This system of oral learning and teaching was valued highly in ancient India for its intrinsic merits and efficiency as an educational method and continued in vogue long after writing was in common use. Some of the primary religious texts, like the Veda especially, are carefully treasured up in the heart for meditation, and considered to this day too sacred by devotees to be consigned for their conservation to external agencies like writing or books. But even granting that literature in India was older than writing and had lived long from mouth to mouth, it could not be the earliest source of Indian history. That has to be found in some of the material remains and vestiges left of the earliest life of man in India in what may be called the prehistoric ages. These are in the form of tools, implements, and traces of dwelling sites and habitations that were in use in those early days. Later, with progress in culture and civilization, the evidence of man's life grows in volume and variety till, in the historic periods, the sources of history are to be found not merely in literature, folklore, and tradition, but in such material remains of diverse kinds as works of architecture, sculpture, painting, inscriptions found on stone or copper, and coins conveying historical information in their marks, symbols, legends or writings, weight, or standard, fabric, and material. Thus history has to be built up on the basis of all these sources wherever available, literary, epigraphic, numismatic, and artistic or monumental. Sometimes these sources may have to be found far afield, even in foreign and distant countries. The history of countries with which India had intercourse will throw light on her own history. Some of the sources of Indian history are thus found in the writings of Greek and Roman authors. An inscription discovered in Mesopotamia throws light on the antiquity of the Rigveda, the earliest literary work of India and perhaps of the world. There are many old monuments in the islands of the Indian Archipelago such as Java, Sumatra, and Bali, or countries like Siam and Cambodia, comprising what has been conveniently called Indonesia, which owe their origin to Indian ideals and craftsmanship and throw light on the "expansion" of India, the growth of a Greater India beyond her boundaries.

Chapter II

PREHISTORIC INDIA

Geological Formations.—Prehistoric India is to be viewed both in its physical and human aspects. The geographical form of India, as we see it on the map, was not built up in a day. It is the outcome of a long course of geological evolution or earth-formation. Originally, the earth itself was one burning and moving mass like the sun, not showing on it any separate countries like India, nor supporting any life or organic form. Geologists distinguish four main ages of the earth, each with a number of sub-ages, with reference to life-development. These ages are: (1) *Azoic*, when there was no life on earth; (2) *Palæozoic*, when life first appeared in the form of Invertebrates, such as seaweeds, sponges, or jelly-fish, and later, as fish, reptiles, and birds, together with gigantic trees and forests, the sources of our coal-seams; (3) *Mesozoic* (middle life); and (4) *Cainozoic* (recent life), during which evolved different types of mammals out of which developed Man.

Life developed as the earth cooled and solidified into a crust. Through earthquakes, volcanic eruptions, atmospheric and climatic changes, the earth has attained to its present form. So also has India. She has been built up in parts and by stages. Some of her parts are very old, parts of the earth's earliest crust. She has a rocky foundation or backbone as old as creation, running right through from north to south. What is called Peninsular India, the Deccan as well as southern India, is also a chip of this old block, compared with which the plains of northern India are very recent. Peninsular India was at first a part of a different continent to which the name Gondwana is given by geologists. It extended from South Africa through Australia as far as South America, as shown by the identity of fossil remains, animal and vegetable, in all this area.

The Western Ghats formed the watershed separating the eastern from the western part of Gondwana. That is why we find the rivers of Peninsular India flowing from sources in sight of the Arabian Sea in the opposite direction till they fall into the Bay of Bengal. In the north, an extensive Eur-Asiatic Ocean called the *Tethys* engulfed the whole area from Central Europe through Asia Minor to northern India and Burma. In India, it was only the Aravallis that looked down upon this ocean. To the free migration in this ocean are to be traced the affinities found in the fossil contents of places so far apart as China, Central Himalayas, and Burma. After a long interval, the first tremors of mountain-building were felt. The Tethys retreated westward with its floor rising, and the lands on its opposite sides approaching each other. The soft deposits of the sea that separated them were folded and crushed to form the Himalayas in India,[1] the mountains of Persia, the Carpathians, and the Alps. The chief movement was that of Asia coming southward and driving the sea deposits against the stable block of India, namely, the northern part of Peninsular India, which bore the brunt of the shock, broke somewhat, and was involved in the folding. Traces of this folding are noticed by geologists in the central part of the Himalayas, including the highest peaks, and the foothills around Simla, just as the folded sediments of the sea are traced in the northern part of the Dehra-Dun-Simla-Spiti zone. There was also the simultaneous consequence of a subsidence of the land between the Himalayas and the Deccan plateau. The plains of northern India were formed ages later by the gradual filling up of this depression or sea with material washed down from the northern highlands.

[1] The importance of the Himalayas to human history cannot be overstated. The growth of Man is itself traced to that momentous geological formation. Barell first suggested that Man and the Himalayas arose simultaneously, towards the end of the Miocene Period, over a million years ago. According to Sir Arthur Smith Woodward, "as the land rose, the temperature would be lowered, and some of the apes which had previously lived in the warm forest would be trapped to the north of the raised area." "As the forests shrank and gave place to plains, the ancestors of Man had to face living on the ground. If they had remained arboreal, or semi-arboreal like the apes, there might never have been men" (Thomson and Geddes in *Outlines of General Biology*, vol. 2, p. 1164).

Even when India thus attained to her present geögraphical form and configuration, there had been a long interval before Man appeared in India to make her history. Human history began long after the physical history of the country had accomplished itself, creating conditions calling for the advent of Man.

Prehistoric Cultures: *Ages of Stone.*—The different stages in the early history of Man are marked by the different materials used by him for the satisfaction of his elementary needs. These materials are traced mainly in tools, weapons, pottery, and tombs. First were devised implements of stone, chipped and rude in form, usually found in association with fossils of animals now extinct. Thus the earliest period of civilization is called the Old Stone, or Palæolithic, Age. Then came the New Stone, or Neolithic, Age, marked by the evolution of improved stone implements, ground, grooved, and polished, and usually associated with remains of fauna not extinct. It was further marked by the use of pottery, at first hand-made, and later turned on the wheel, and by the practice of honouring the dead by giving them burial in tombs of massive stones. It will thus appear that a wide gulf and distance of time separated the two Stone Ages. The subsequent stages of development came on more rapidly and imperceptibly—those characterized by the use of Copper, Bronze, and Iron.

India, like other countries, has passed through these stages of development, except that she seems to have missed the Bronze Age (except in certain areas), instead of which she had something like the Copper Age.

Palæolithic remains are rather rare in India. They are mainly found in the Deccan and southern India, as being geologically the oldest parts of India. They are found in laterite beds and ossiferous gravels south of 25° north latitude, and made generally of quartzite, whence the Palæolithic men are sometimes called Quartzite men. Numerous quartzite implements have been found near Madras city and Ongole in Guntur district, and more in Cuddapah, which was the home of Palæolithic culture for its quartzite rocks, just as Bellary was the home of Neolithic culture. Isolated palæolithic remains have been found in a few other places. A well-made ovate instrument of chipped quartzite was found in the Narmadā valley in post-tertiary gravels containing the bones of hippopotamus and of other animals now extinct. An agate flake was found in similar gravels in the Godāvarī valley. The Kon ravines of Mirzapur have yielded some implements considered to be neolithic from their locality. A serrated fish-bone resembling an arrow-head was excavated in Gangetic alluvium in Ghazipur district below a stratum containing polished neolithic tools.

While the Palæolithians practically confined themselves to quartzite areas like Cuddapah or Madras coast, the Neolithians spread all over India. Their remains are broadly classified as follows: (1) "*Pigmy Flints*" or miniature stone implements varying in length from half to an inch and a half and shaped like arrow-heads, crescents, or jointed forms. These were apparently meant to be fitted into wooden holders and handles for a variety of uses. They were found in shoals in the Vindhya hills, in Baghelkand, Rewah, Mirzapur, generally on the floors of caves or rock-shelters, along with the ashes and charcoal of hearths, or in tumuli, along with entire skeletons and rude pottery. A peculiar chisel-shaped, high-shouldered celt is found in Chota Nagpur, Assam, and more abundantly in Burma, Indo-China, and the Malay Peninsula. (2) *Implement Factories*: Sites of several neolithic settlements and implement factories have been discovered in southern India. The implements seem to have been polished on gneiss rocks exhibiting grooves 10–14 inches long and about 2 inches deep. High-class wheel-made pottery is also found in abundance at these settlements, together with stone beads and pieces of hæmatite for manufacturing pigments. (3) "*Cinder-mounds*" found in the Bellary district of southern India. These are supposed to be the results of wholesale holocausts of animals and have yielded neolithic implements. (4) "*Cup-marks*" or sculpturings on stone and rock found in many places in India. (5) "*Ruddle or hæmatite drawings.*" These are found (*a*) in the Mirzapur district Vindhyan hills,

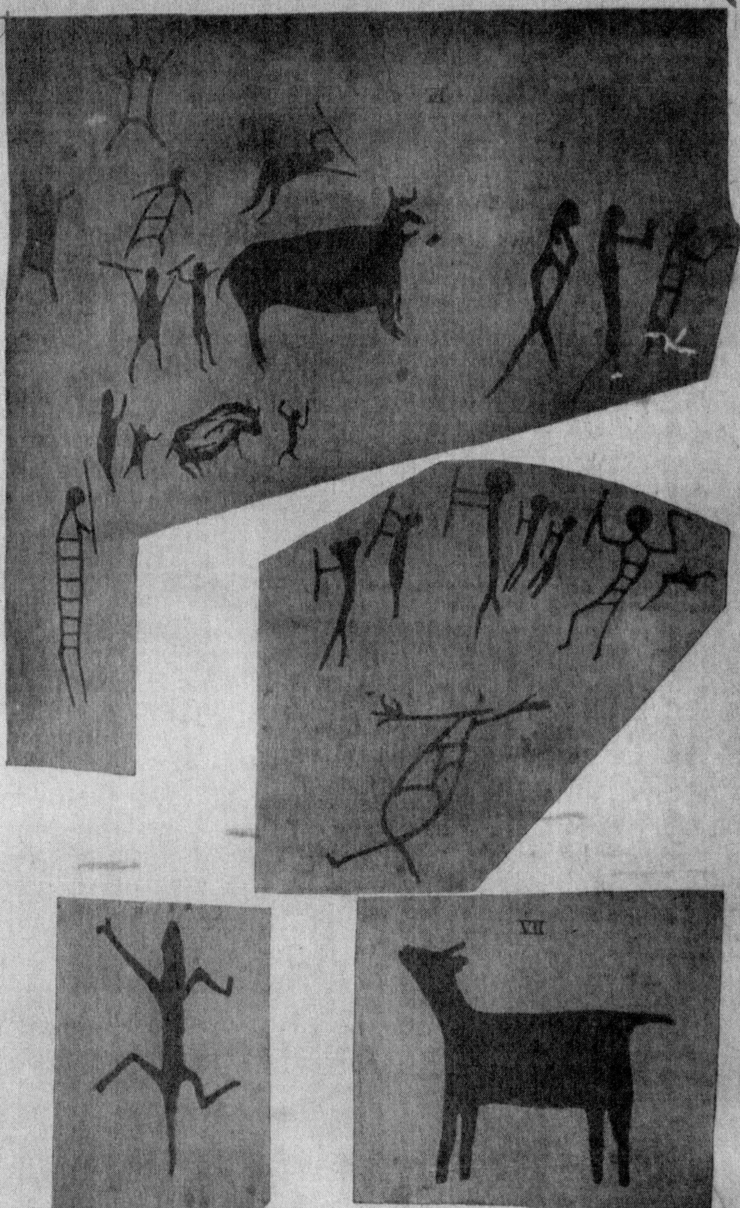

EXAMPLES OF NEOLITHIC RUDDLE (HÆMATITE) Drawings showing Stag, Crocodile, Boar, and Hunters (S. C. Roy's collection).

[*To face p. 10.*

representing hunters with barbed spears attacking a rhinoceros, now extinct; (*b*) in caves in Hoshangabad district, representing a giraffe; (*c*) in the Kaimur hills, showing stag-hunts; and (*d*) at Singanpur, showing representations of an animal resembling a kangaroo, and also of horse and deer, which are very like the Spanish drawings of the same age. These prehistoric paintings are found along with neolithic tools. (6) *Tombs*: while palæolithic men deserted their dead in the forests, the neolithics disposed of them by the more civilized practice of giving them burial. Neolithic sepulchres are, however, rarely found in India. The skeleton of an adult male was found with vessels of glazed pottery and glass in a grave in Mirzapur. A neolithic cemetery containing fifty-four tombs was discovered in the Kolar district, together with piles of pottery. At Pattavaram, near Madras city, have been found earthen mounds covering terra-cotta coffins, oblong for females and pyriform for males, who were buried in a contracted position. In other Madras districts, such as Chingleput, Nellore, and Arcot, similar oblong terra-cotta sarcophagi have been discovered, but sometimes associated with iron implements. *Megalithic tombs* in various forms occur throughout Madras, Bombay, Mysore, and the Nizam's Dominion, but are mostly post-neolithic for the iron implements they contain. They also show evidence of cremation. There was also the practice of *Urn-burial* in the neolithic age. The urns did not contain cremated ashes but whole bodies reduced in bulk by pounding or by dissection. A vast cemetery covering an area of about 114 acres, each acre accommodating about 1,000 urns buried underneath, has been found at Adichanallur, in Tinnevelly district along the Tāmraparṇī River. Parts of this necropolis must have been neolithic for the stone implements they contain, but much of it is recent for the implements of iron, ornaments of bronze and even of gold found. Examples of urn-burial have been also found in Brahmanabad in Sindh.

Copper Age.—The Age of Stone was followed by the Age of Iron in southern India but by an Age of Copper in northern India. There seems to have been no Bronze Age preceding the Iron Age in India, except in Sind, as will be seen later. Bronze is an alloy made up of nine parts of copper and one of tin. The many bronze objects brought to light in the archaic tombs of southern India are articles of luxury like bowls and regarded as later in date or as imports. The most important find of copper came from a village called Gungeria in central India. It comprised 424 copper implements, very closely resembling Irish copper celts, considered to be as old as 2000 B.C. The hoard also contained 102 silver plates comprising circular discs and figures of a bull's head with horns. This silver must have been rare in India and might have been even an import. But copper was indigenous to India and is taken to be the red *ayas* mentioned in the Rigveda. Besides the Gungeria hoard of copper implements, fine celts, harpoons, swords, and spear-heads of the same material have been found in the Cawnpore, Fatehgarh, Mainpuri and Muttra districts, and indeed all over northern India, "almost from the Hooghly to the far side of the Indus, and from the foot of the Himalayas to the Cawnpore district".

Use of Iron.—Iron was used earlier in northern than in southern India, as it was used earlier in Babylonia than in Egypt. It is referred to in the *Atharvaveda*, which is not later than about 2500 B.C. Herodotus states that the Indian soldiers who fought in Europe under the Persian emperor, Xerxes, against Greece in 480 B.C. used iron-tipped cane arrows for their bows. Later, at the time of Alexander's campaigns in India, the Indians, according to the Greek writers, were as well versed in the use of iron and steel as the Greeks themselves. They further record that a present of 100 talents of steel was made to Alexander by some of the Panjab chiefs.

The Indus Civilization, *c.* 3250–2750 B.C.—While we have mere scraps of evidence scattered throughout India for these prehistoric cultures, recently quite a mass of conclusive and concentrated evidence has been unearthed by archæological excavation in one region, that of the Indus, at two sites, viz. Harappa, between Lahore and Multan, and Mohenjo-daro ("the Mound of the Dead") in the

PLATE II

REMAINS OF INDUS CIVILIZATION (*c.* 3250-2750 B.C.):
DRAINS AT MOHENJO-DARO.

[*To face p.* 12.

Larkana district of Sind. The evidence points to the development of an entire civilization which may be designated as the Indus Civilization in a region which was then more watered and wooded than now. Sind had in those early days a heavier rainfall, as indicated by the use of kiln-burnt bricks for the exposed parts of its ancient buildings, and of sun-dried bricks for its foundations and infillings protected against the elements; by the seals showing animals which were denizens of dense forests, or by the elaborate drainage system of its city. It was also then watered not merely by the Indus (with its affluents and branches) but also by a second river, the Great Mihran, which existed up to the fourteenth century A.D. These two rivers between them divided the vast volume of water from the five rivers of the Punjab and were mainly responsible for the growth of this most ancient civilization in Sind. Similarly, in the neighbouring region of southern Baluchistan, now dessicated, Sir Aurel Stein has discovered remains of large and prosperous prehistoric settlements. The prosperity of Sind continued up to the time of the Achæmenid emperor of Persia in the fifth century B.C. (under whom it was a satrapy), and of Alexander the Great, who saw it as the most flourishing part of India under its chief called Mousikanos (=Mūshika or Muchukarṇa ?). The region was then even exposed to floods, as pointed to by the particularly solid basements and high terraces provided for the Mohenjo-daro buildings.

The surface of the Mohenjo-daro site is covered by mounds whose heights vary from 70 to 20 feet. Between the summits of these mounds and the level of the subsoil water have been unearthed seven strata of remains, of which the first three belong to the Late Period, the next three to the Intermediate Period, and the seventh to the Early Period. Below the seventh, at a depth of about 40 feet from the surface, there must be earlier layers, now submerged beneath the subsoil water, for the layers already brought to light reveal a full-fledged civilization whose roots and origins must be traced to much older times, at least 1,000 years older.

Its remains: Buildings.—These were dwelling-houses, shrines, and public baths, for both secular and religious purposes.

The houses vary from the smallest ones of two rooms to a large one like a palace, showing a frontage of 85 feet and a depth of 97 feet, wide entrance hall and doorway, porter's lodge, courtyard 32 feet square, surrounded by chambers on both ground and upper floors, paved with brick and provided with a covered drain which was connected with vertical drains discharging into small earthenware vessels sunk beneath the courtyard pavement for purposes of the upstairs privies. There are unearthed some exceptionally large and elaborate structures which might have been temples. A hall of twenty brick piers, about 90 feet square, of the Intermediate Period, has also been found.

But the most singular structure is the Great Bath, a regular hydropathic establishment with several annexes. It consisted of (*a*) an open quadrangle with verandahs backed by galleries and rooms on all sides; (*b*) a swimming bath 39 feet by 23 by 8 feet (deep) in the middle of the quadrangle, with flights of steps at the ends; (*c*) wells from which the bath was filled; and (*d*) an upper storey of timber indicated by charcoal and ashes found. The construction of the swimming-bath reflects great credit on the engineering of those days. To make it watertight and its foundations secure, "the lining of the tank was made of finely dressed brick laid in gypsum mortar, about 4 feet thick; backing this was an inch-thick damp-proof course of bitumen" further stabilized "by another thin wall of burnt brick behind it; then came a packing of crude brick and behind this again another solid rectangle of burnt brick encompassing the whole". This is how this tank, about 5,000 years old, is still so well preserved.

One of the accessories to this Great Bath is supposed to be a ***hammam*** or hot-air bath, showing traces of a series of dwarf walls supporting the floor and vertical flues for heating the room, "evidence of a hypocaustic system of heating."

THE GREAT BATH [ditto].

Other Antiquities, Arts, and Crafts.—The growth of these early cities depended on agriculture and trade. There are unearthed specimens of wheat and barley[1] then cultivated, and of muller and saddle-quern by which they were ground, but not of the circular grindstone. Date palm was also cultivated, from the seeds found.

The *food* of the Indus people comprised beef, mutton, pork, and poultry, flesh of the ghariyāl, turtles, and tortoises, fish from the river or brought from the sea. The bones or shells of all these have been found among the ruins.

Skeletal remains testify to the following *animals* being then *domesticated*: the humped bull, buffalo, sheep, elephant, camel, pig, and fowl, and possibly dog (of which several terra-cotta figurines have been found) and horse.

Remains of the following wild animals have been found, viz. mongoose, shrew, black rat, and deer, and also figurines of bison, rhinoceros, tiger, monkey, bear, and hare.

Metals and Minerals.—There was use of gold and silver, of copper, tin, and lead, but iron was absolutely unknown. The gold used has been found to contain an alloy of silver known as electron, and must have come by trade from places like Kolar and Anantapur in the south, where such gold is found. Gold was used for making ornaments.

The copper used along with lead must have come from Rajputana, Baluchistan, or Persia, where lead is found in association with copper ores. Copper had now taken the place of stone for manufacture of weapons, implements, and domestic utensils such as lance-heads, daggers, knives, axes, chisels, or ornaments like bangles, ear-rings, etc. Copper is found here in the earliest stratum, earlier than 3000 B.C. That it was extensively worked in India in very early times is proved by the find of 424 hammered copper implements at Gungeria already noticed.

[1] Expert examination has revealed this *wheat* to be of the species still cultivated in the Punjab. It is not certain whether wheat or barley was the first cereal cultivated by man. Both have been found in the earliest graves of Egypt. The *barley* found at Mohenjo-daro is of the species found in pre-Dynastic graves in Egypt. It is believed that both wheat and barley are Asiatic in origin. (Cf. Peake's presidential address in *J.R. Anthrop. Inst.*, 1927.)

Tin was not used by itself but as an alloy with copper so as to form bronze containing 6 to 13 per cent tin. Bronze was preferred to copper for producing sharp edges or finer finish. Being found in the earliest stratum, it must have been in use before 3000 B.C. This disposes of the theory held that there was no Bronze Age in India at all. The sources of tin or bronze used in Sind must have been outside India, North Persia, and Western Afghanistan, from which they came by way of the Bolan Pass. The only Indian source was Hazaribagh district, which could not be tapped in those days by the Indus people from that distance.

Various stones were used for building and other purposes and came from places far and near. The Sukkur limestone was used for covering drains. The Kīrthar hills supplied gypsum used as a mortar and alabaster for making lattice screens, vessels, and statues. Harder stones of the neighbourhood, like gneiss and basalt, were used to make saddle-querns and mullers, door sockets, or weights. Chert was chipped and ground into weights and polishers, or flaked for use as knives. Steatite was used in the making of seals and statuettes. The yellow Jaisalmir stone is the material found in statues and cult objects like *liṅgas* and *yonī* rings. Many varieties of semi-precious stones were used for beads and ornaments, such as rock crystal, hæmatite, carnelian, jasper, agate, or onyx. The fine green amazon stone came from Doddabetta in the Nilgiris as its only source in India, and amethyst from the Deccan trap. Lapis lazuli came from Badakshan, turquoise from Khorasan, and jadeite (hard jade) from the Pamirs, Eastern Turkestan, or Tibet.

Other materials were also used such as bone, ivory, shell, or faience. Shell came from the coasts of India, and Persian Gulf or the Red Sea.

Numerous spindle-whorls found in the houses of Mohenjo-daro testify to the common practice of *spinning* and that among the rich and poor alike, as shown by costly whorls of faience and cheaper ones of pottery or shell. The material for textiles was both *wool* and *cotton*. Scraps of cotton found adhering to the side of a silver vase have been found by expert examination to resemble the present-day coarse Indian cottons with its typical convoluted structure. Thus this indigenous Indian cotton was known to the Babylonians as *sindhu* and to the Greeks as *sindon*, and was a true cotton and not a product of the cotton-tree as hitherto believed.

The *dress* of the days included a long shawl as shown in two statues found. The men wore short beards and whiskers, with upper lip sometimes shaven as in Sumer. The hair was taken back from the forehead and then clipped or coiled in a knot with a fillet to support it at the back of the head. Sometimes there is seen a skull-cap curling into a point behind, or a taller cap with a rolled brim. Three bronze figures of dancing girls show the hair coiled in a heavy mass taken above the left ear to fall over the right shoulder.

Ornaments included chiefly necklaces, fillets, armlets, and finger-rings for both sexes, and girdles, ear-rings, and anklets. For the rich these were of gold, silver, faience, ivory, or semi-precious stones; for the poor, shell, bone, copper, and terra-cotta. Carnelian was skilfully bored to form beads for girdles.

That the Indus civilization was of the Chalcolithic Age is shown by the fact that *arms* and *utensils* of stone were used side by side with those of copper or bronze. The weapons of war and the chase are the bow and arrow, spear, axe, dagger, and mace, but the sword was not yet evolved, nor defensive bodily armour. Among the other implements may be mentioned hatchets, sickles, saws, chisels, and razors, made of both copper and bronze; knives and celts of these metals, as also of chert or other hard stones. Some stone objects like dishes, bowls, vases, toilet-boxes, palettes, burnishers, or weights have, however, left far behind the typical artefacts of a Stone or Chalcolithic Age.

Judging from the paucity of finds of offensive and defensive weapons, it may be held that the people of Mohenjo-daro were not very military or much troubled by fears of invasion.

The Indus *weights* are interesting. The small ones are cubes of chert or slate, the larger ones conical in form. The weights show " greater accuracy and consistency than those of Elam and Mesopotamia ". The sequence of their ratios was at first binary like that of the Susa weights, but later decimal, viz. 1, 2, 4, 8, 16, 32, 64, 160, 200, 320, 640, 1,600, the weight most in use was the ratio 16, weighing 13·71 gm.

Domestic *vessels* were generally of earthenware of various kinds and shapes, offering stands, goblets, heaters, store-jars, and the like. Vast numbers found of goblets or drinking cups show the Indus practice, still the Hindu practice, of throwing away the cups once used for drinking.

The Indus *pottery* was generally wheel-made and was painted red-and-black ware. Some of it was also " incised ", " polychrome ", and " glazed ". The " glazed " Indus pottery is " the earliest example of its kind in the ancient world ", and that, too, as a fine fabric. It appeared in Mesopotamia about 1000 B.C. and much later in Egypt.

Terra-cotta *toys* were produced in great variety, such as rattles, whistles (shaped like birds), figures of men, women, birds, and carts. Birds were mounted on wheels and oxen yoked to carts. The carts are the earliest known specimens of their kind, like the chariot figured on a stone slab at Ur (dated 3200 B.C. by Woolley).

The Indus people had invented *Writing*, for which they employed a script which belongs to the same order as other quasi-pictographic scripts of the period, such as the Proto-Elamitic, Early Sumerian, Minoan, or Egyptian. There are found 396 Signs of the script, accompanied by inscriptions on seals, sealings, pottery fragments, copper tablets, and even bangles of vitrified clay. *Signs* are also found in combination, while characters are modified by the addition of accents, or strokes. There are also seen groups of strokes, never exceeding twelve in number, which have perhaps a phonetic rather than a numerical value. The direction of the writing is seen generally to be from right to left, except for continuation. The large

A YOGI [ditto].

To face p. 19.]

number of Signs again rather shows that the script was not an alphabetic one but phonetic.

The remains and antiquities show that lack of ornament in which *art* originates. But the smaller objects, like *seals* and *amulets,* show some art. The humped bull, buffalo, or bison engraved on seals may be taken as examples, as also the powerfully modelled young bull of terra-cotta, a mastiff-like hound in steatite, seated ram, squirrel, or monkey, figured on amulets. There is here realism tempered with restraint.

Examples of artistic human form are not numerous, the many terra-cotta figurines hardly showing any art. Of *stone images,* few as they are, three are worthy of mention. One is that of a *Yogī* with meditative eyes fixed on the tip of the nose. Another is a portrait head showing prominent cheekbones, wide, thin-lipped mouth, but ugly saucer-like ears. There is a third seated image showing a shawl worn. We may also note in this connection the bronze figurine of a dancing girl, showing disproportionately long arms and legs and beating time to music with her feet. There are two remarkable *statuettes* found at Harappa, one of which, of red stone, imported from a distance, shows faithful modelling of fleshy parts, and the other of dark grey slate, the figure of a male dancer, standing on his right leg, with the left leg raised high, the ancestor of Śiva Naṭarāja. Both these statuettes anticipate Greek artistry by their striking anatomical truth, just as the seals already referred to anticipate the Greek delineation of animal forms.

Religion.—The data discovered so far both at Mohenjodara and Harappa are meagre.

A large number of female figurines of terra-cotta has been discovered, akin to those discovered in Baluchistan, though these latter are not full-length images.

Female statuettes akin to these from the Indus Valley and Baluchistan are also found in large numbers in countries of Western Asia and around the Ægean coasts, in Elam, Mesopotamia, Transcaspia, Asia Minor, Syria, Palestine, Cyprus, Crete, the Cyclades, the Balkans, and Egypt.

The accepted view is that these are representations of the Great Mother- or Nature-Goddess. It is in keeping with the religious tradition of India, the home of worship, from time immemorial, of the divine Mother, *Ādyā-Śakti* or *Prakṛiti*, the *Pṛithvī* [*Rv.* vi, 12, 5; x, 187, 2], or *Pṛithivī* [*Rv.* v, 85, 1-5; vii, 7, 2–5], or *Aditi*, the mother of the Ādityas of the *Rigveda*, down to the *Grāmadevātās* or village goddesses of modern times, figuring as the national deities of the masses of India, Aryan or non-Aryan.

A striking oblong sealing found at Harappa represents the Earth or Mother Goddess, with a plant growing from her womb, and a man, knife in hand, and a woman with raised hands, who was probably to be sacrificed.

A male deity, "the prototype of the historic *Śiva*," is portrayed on a seal with three faces and eyes (the *ṭrimukha* and *ṭrinayana* of Śiva), seated on a low Indian throne in the typical posture of a *Yogī*, with animals on each side, elephant and tiger on right and rhinoceros and buffalo on left, and two horned deer standing under the throne, justifying the title of Rigvedic Rudra and of Śiva as *Paśupati*, Lord of Animals. The deer indicative of the forest anticipate the Buddhist sculptures representing the deer-park where the Buddha had delivered his first sermon. There is also the last characteristic of the historic Śiva in this figure, a pair of horns crowning his head to denote the deity and anticipating the *triśūla* or trident of the Śaivas, or the *ṭriratna*, the three jewels, of the Buddhists.

It is to be noted that a deity in the same posture of a *Yogī* with a Nāga kneeling in prayer to him with uplifted hands on either side of him, is also found portrayed on a faience sealing from Mohenjo-daro, while another seal portrays the deity in the same posture but with only one face. A reference has also already been made to the stone portrait head of a *Yogī* with the eyes fixed on the tip of the nose.

Mr. R. P. Chanda (in the *Modern Review* for August, 1932) takes the standing four-armed figure occurring among the Signs of the Indus script (e.g. No. 383 of the Sign Manual) to be that of a deity and indicating that four-armed deities

Śiva Paśupati ("Lord of Animals") [ditto].

[*To face p. 20.*

were included in the Indus pantheon, anticipating the later four-armed Hindu gods like Brahmā, Vishṇu, or Śiva.

He also points to the figures of standing deities on some six seals [plate xii and plate cxviii, fig. 7 of Sir John Marshall's work on Mohenjo-daro] of Mohenjo-daro as those of deities in the posture of *yoga* known as *Kāyotsarga*, a standing posture peculiar to the Jain *Yogīs* as illustrated, for instance, in the famous statue of Jina Ṛishabhava of about second century A.D., on view at Muttra Museum. The name *Ṛishabha* itself means the bull, which is also the emblem of the Jina. It is curious that seals numbered (*f*), (*g*), (*h*) of plate ii [*Ib.*], also show a standing deity with a bull in the foreground. Can it be the forerunner of *Ṛishabha*? If so, Jainism also, along with Śaivism, must take its place as one of the oldest religions of Chalcolithic origins, thus helping over the hiatus between the Indus and subsequent Indian civilizations as phases in a common cultural evolution.

Along with this worship of Śakti and Śiva was also that of *liṅga* and *yonī*, as evidenced in the realistically modelled and unmistakable figures in stone of both found in the Indus Valley and Baluchistan, together with numerous ring-stones. Indeed, three types of cult stones are brought to light at Mohendo-daro and Harappa, the bœtylic, the phallic, and the *yonī* ring-stones, of which the smaller specimens carried and worn as amulets are more numerous than the larger ones which were objects of worship. Some smaller specimens probably served as gamesmen.

There is also evidence found of tree-worship in two forms. One was the worship of the tree in its natural form, as illustrated in certain sealings from Harappa. In the other case, what was worshipped was not the tree but its indwelling spirit. A most remarkable seal found at Mohenjo-daro represents the deity, a standing nude figure, between two branches of a tree, showing it to be the pipal-tree (*ficus religiosa*) made famous as the Bodhi-tree, the Tree of Knowledge of the Buddha. The worship of the deity is indicated by a line of seven figures with plaits of hair falling down the back, indicating that these were female officiants or ministrants of the goddess, and also by the figure of a half-kneeling suppliant with long hair, behind whom is a composite animal, part bull, part goat, with human face, perhaps the *vāhana* or vehicle of the goddess of the pipal-tree. There are found a few other seals, one showing a tree springing from the jugate heads of two unicorns, others (from Harappa) showing a goat or other horned animal, along with the deity and her suppliant. The continuance of this religious tradition is found in the sculptures of Bharhut and Sanchi showing the *Yakshīs* as dryads but in a subordinate place in the pantheon.

Evidence of *Zoolatry* (animal worship) is also found at Mohenjo-daro in the animals represented on seals and sealings, or in terra-cotta, faience, and stone figurines. Firstly, there are represented mythical and composite creatures; e.g. human-faced goat just described, or creatures which are part ram or goat, part bull and part elephant, three-headed chimeras, semi-human semi-bovine creature attacking a horned tiger (closely resembling the Sumerian Eabani or Eukidu of the fourth millennium B.C.), use of horns for deities, and Nāgas. Secondly, there are represented creatures not completely mythical, such as unicorns and two-horned beasts, accompanied with incense-burners or animals figuring as officiant genii. Thirdly, there are represented the real, natural animals, such as (1) the water buffalo, (2) the gaur or Indian bison, (3) the Indian humped bull or zebu, (4) the Indian rhinoceros, (5) a short-horned humpless bull, (6) the tiger, and (7) the Indian elephant. Some of them, especially the tiger, rhino, and bison, are shown as feeding from troughs, indicative of food-offerings to beasts deified, which could not be domesticated beasts. Lastly, there are the figurines and engravings of other animals and birds, ram, pig, dog, monkey, bear, hare, squirrel, parrot, and other birds, of which some were toys, but some sacred, such as sheep and ram, exquisitely modelled in faience for use as amulets; as also squirrels and the mastiff similarly modelled. Some of these animals still figure as the vehicles of Hindu deities, e.g. the bull of Śiva, the lion of Durgā, the buffalo of Yama,

A

A. SEALS [ditto] showing—(*a*) Antelope; (*b*) Tiger; (*c*) Elephant; (*d*) Humped Bull with Jungle Fowl; (*e*) Ram; (*f*) Bull; (*g*) Buffalo; (*h*) Bison; (*i*) Crocodile; (*j*) Humped Bull; (*k*) Rhino.

B. A Dancing Girl in bronze [ditto].

[*To face p. 22.*

the ram of Brahmā, the elephant of Indra, the monkey worshipped as Hanumān, or the wild boar of Gaurī.

Lastly, purification by bath or ceremonial ablutions formed a feature of this religion. This explains the elaborate bathing arrangements marking the city of Mohenjo-daro and distinguishing it from all other cities of antiquity.

Summary.—Thus the religion of the Indus people comprised: (1) the worship of the Mother Goddess or *Śakti*; (2) the worship of a male deity, the ancestor of Śiva; (3) worship of animals, natural, semi-human, or fabulous; (4) worship of trees in their natural state or of their indwelling spirits; (5) worship of inanimate stones or other objects, of *liṅga* and *yonī* symbols; (6) Chrematheism as illustrated in the worship of the sacred "incense-burners"; (7) faith in amulets and charms indicative of *demonophobia*; and (8) practice of *Yoga*. It will be seen from these characteristics that this religion, in spite of a few foreign elements already noticed, was mainly an indigenous growth and "the lineal progenitor of Hinduism", which is still marked by some of these features, the cults of Śakti and Śiva, of the Nāgas, of Animal-, Tree-, and Stone-worship, of Phallism and *Yoga*.

Disposal of the dead.—The Indus people disposed of their dead by cremation. This is proved by the discovery of many cinerary urns, or other receptacles, containing calcined human bones and ashes, together with vessels of burnt and other offerings and sundry articles for use of the dead in after-life. Other urns are also discovered containing vessels for offerings and other articles for the dead, but not any human bones, probably because the calcined bones which remained over after cremation were ground to powder and cast off, as is still done in the Punjab. Sir Aurel Stein has also discovered many such cinerary and cenotaphic urns at different sites in Baluchistan. Cases of burial, whether fractional (where only a fraction of the bones was collected and buried after the body had been exposed to beasts and birds) or complete, were rare. Examples of complete burial are found in twenty-one skeletons discovered at Mohenjo-daro, seven in public streets and the rest in a room, betokening three distinct racial types, proto-Australoids, Mediterraneans, and Alpines. The layers in which the skeletons were found show that the burials belonged to the age of the decline of Mohenjo-daro. A few examples of complete burial are also found at Harappa and in Baluchistan, but these are later in time.

Extent.—The antiquities unearthed at the two sites of Mohenjo-daro and Harappa point to a common and uniform civilization that had already struck its roots deeply throughout Sind and Punjab. Quite a number of other sites has also been discovered in these regions belonging to the Chalcolithic Age. There is also an earlier stratum of culture traced in Sind in numerous Neolithic artefacts, such as cairns, burrows, and other rough stone structures, together with flint flakes and cores, mostly found among the Rohri and Kirthar hills. Thus, Mohenjo-daro was preceded by Neolithic culture in Sind.

Origins and affiliations.—The development of this Indus civilization was part of a larger movement which manifested itself in the growth of similar early civilizations along the broad Afrasian belt up to Western Persia and Mesopotamia, in the Chalcolithic Age, as the offspring of the great rivers, the Nile in Egypt, the Euphrates and the Tigris in Mesopotamia, the Karun and the Karkheh in Western Persia, and the Helmand in Seistan. It is, therefore, not at all surprising if the richer and broader river valleys of Sind and Punjab also became the seats of this early civilization, or if further exploration reveal proofs of its extension even in the more promising valleys of the Jumna and Ganges.

These several civilizations are marked by individual peculiarities, as well as certain common elements. For instance, each country devised its own Signs to record its speech. The hieroglyphs of Egypt differ from those of Crete, the Cretan from the Sumerian, the Sumerian from the Elamite, and so on. But though the scripts differ, they are based on a common idea, that of using pictured Signs to record not only objects or concepts, but actual sounds. A similar example is found in spinning and weaving. The

Indus people used cotton where flax was used on the Nile. But the art of spinning and weaving was known in both regions as the common property of the then civilized world. The same remark applies to painted pottery. Each region had its own designs and shapes for its ceramic wares, but the potter's wheel and the art of fixing the colouring on the vessels by firing were common knowledge. In spite, however, of these common ideas and inventions, the Indus civilization is as distinctly individual and national as any of the other great and contemporary river civilizations.

These specifically Indian features of the Indus civilization have been already indicated and may be summed up here. They comprise (1) the use of cotton for textiles not known to the Western world until two or three thousand years later; (2) a higher standard of urban life and amenities, as seen in the commodious houses, baths, wells, and systems of drainage meant for the ordinary citizens, and not known in prehistoric Egypt or Mesopotamia or any other country in Western Asia, where architecture is chiefly aristocratic, being marked by magnificent palaces, temples, and tombs, without spending much thought on the dwellings of the poor or the masses; (3) a high level of achievement in glyptic art, as illustrated in the faience models or the intaglio engravings on seals of animals like bulls, or in the exquisitely supple modelling of human statuettes already noticed; and (4) religion, which is easily seen as the ancestor of modern Hinduism in its several features already described.

Age.—The age of the Indus civilization is inferred from certain general resemblances, already noticed, between it and the other early civilizations of known dates, the proto-historic civilization of Sumer, and the later prediluvian civilizations of Elam and Mesopotamia. Certain specific resemblances are also disclosed in a variety of objects recovered from the Indus, Elamite, and Mesopotamian sites, and these cannot be explained away except as the outcome of active intercourse between these regions at the close of the fourth milennium B.C.

The most important of these objects are *Five Seals* bearing the unmistakable " Indus " pattern (the script and humped bull), which were discovered at different sites in Elam and Mesopotamia. Of these, two found at Ur and Kish are definitely assigned to the pre-Sargonid Period, i.e. to an age before 2800 B.C., although similar seals have been found in even earlier layers at Mohenjo-daro. If a period of 500 years is allowed for the seven different layers of remains at Mohenjo-daro as being subject to a speedier process of decay and renewal due to frequent inundations, the period of its civilization may be rightly placed between 3250–2750 B.C., allowing for still earlier times for its previous history and origins.

Besides seals are found several other objects and *motifs* betokening an intimate contact between these civilizations. Of these, the most noteworthy are (1) certain fragments of vases of Indian potstone found at Al-Ubaid; (2) the trefoil patterning on the robe of the Yogī's statuette already noticed, which is supposed to be Sumerian; (3) horned figures on seals identified with the Sumerian hero-god Eabani; (4) etched beads of carnelian showing the identical technique of beads from pre-Sargonid graves at Kish; (5) types or shapes of jars, offerings stands, stone-weights, etc., and so forth.[1] The painted pottery of Mohenjo-daro, from the general style of its decoration, is assigned by Mr. Ernest Mackay to a later period than that of Susa I (*c.* 4250 B.C.) or even Susa II (*c.* 4000 B.C.), to the period *c.* 3250–2750 B.C., to which is also to be assigned the painted pottery of Baluchistan, as discovered by Sir Aurel Stein.

Recently (1932), Mr. Woolley has discovered at Ur another Indian seal in a tomb-shaft ascribed by him to the Second Dynasty and dated at about 2800 B.C. But he himself doubts its date and importance, as it was an isolated object found in the filling of a tomb. A similar chronological uncertainty attaches to the five other seals mentioned above.

We are, however, on more definite ground in respect of

[1] A writer in *JRAS.*, 1931, pp. 593–6, points out three links of connection between India and Mesopotamia, viz. script, painted ware, and rectangular brick. Of these, the Indian script on introduction was abandoned in favour of the indigenous Sumerian script, while after 3500 B.C. the Indian rectangular brick also disappears, being replaced by the clumsy plano-convex brick.

certain objects discovered by the Iraq Expedition of the Chicago Oriental Institute in a well-defined archæological stratum at Tell Asmar (ancient Eshnunna) in the desert near Baghdad. On the very surface of this site were found cylinder seals, pots, and tablets of the reign of Sargon of Akkad (about 2500 B.C.), one seal impression actually mentioning Shu-dur-ul, the last king of that dynasty. There were also found some definitely Indian objects, indubitable importations from the Indus Valley of which the civilization can thus be dated without doubt. A seal is found, depicting the animals, elephant, and rhinoceros, foreign to Babylonia, and marked by the Indus convention by which the feet and ears and the folds in the elephant's skin are represented, and also in the peculiar rendering of the ears of the rhinoceros. We may recall in this connection the Mohenjo-daro seal showing a procession of animals in which the elephant and rhinoceros are placed side by side. Thus there cannot be any doubt that this particular seal was imported from the Indus Valley and reached Eshnunna about 2500 B.C. Other similarly Indian objects found at this new site include square stamp seals with pierced knobs on the back and bearing a design of concentric squares not found in Mesopotamia but common at Mohenjo-daro; beads of etched carnelian, definitely Indian, introduced among the ordinary Akkadian beads of necklaces; or kidney-shaped inlays of bone identical in shape with some in shell from Mohenjo-daro and not found in Mesopotamia.

Excavations at this Baghdad site have brought to light remains of five successive periods, viz. (1) Larsa Period (2186–1931 B.C.), (2) post-Sargonid Period of invading mountaineers, (3) and (4) Sargonid Period traced in inscribed tablets and seals, and (5) the earliest period marked by houses built of plano-convex bricks contemporary with the tombs of Ur. Thus the Ur finds are earlier than the Baghdad finds by 1,000 years, according to Mr. Woolley, i.e. of about 3500 B.C. In that case, Babylonia gains priority over Egypt, where the early dynastic period is not older than 3000 B.C. This view will also antedate further the Indus civilization.

Finally, it is to be noted that these Indian objects found in houses in Eshnunna of the time of Sargon (as definitely stated in inscriptions) do not bear the same close resemblance to the Mohenjo-daro finds as the six seals mentioned above. There may be chronological or geographical reasons for this difference. The seals from the Baghdad site may belong to a later or earlier stage of Indus civilization than that found at Mohenjo-daro; or they might have come from some other site of the same civilization. Perhaps the second assumption is nearer the truth. At any rate, the Mohenjo-daro phase of this early Indus civilization is not its only or earliest phase, as already shown. [Dr. H. Frankfort, Field Director of Iraq Excavations, in a letter dated 5th March, 1932, to *The Times*.]

Authors.—Who were the authors of this civilization? The human remains found at Mohenjo-daro bring to light four ethnic types, viz. the proto-Australoid,[1] Mediterranean,[2] Mongolian branch of the Alpine and the Alpine.[3] The proto-Australoids must have come from the Indian sub-continent, the Mediterranean from along the southern shores of Asia, the Alpines and the Mongoloid Alpines from Western and Eastern Asia respectively. Thus the population of Sind was already cosmopolitan in that early age. The evidence of skulls is also confirmed by that of sculptures. The sculptured heads and figures unearthed at Mohenjo-daro point to the blending of diverse racial types. But all this evidence is to be treated with caution. After all, the artists were not anthropologists, and were not out to produce faithful transcripts of the originals, the exact shapes of heads. The number of skulls found is also too small to warrant a safe generalization regarding the composition of the civic population at Mohenjo-daro. Harappa also has brought to light but a few skulls, of which only three have so far been examined by experts. The entire skeletal material from both the places is thus too scanty.

The next question that may be raised is, Were the Indus

[1] Now represented by the Kols, Bhils, etc.

[2] As seen in the modern long-headed Hindusthanis.

[3] Represented in the modern broad-headed Gujaratis, Marathas, Bengalis.

people Dravidians, in view of the theory held that the Sumerians with whom they had such intimate relations are believed to belong to the same ethnic type as the Dravidians? The presence of the Dravidians up in these northern regions in remote ages is also proved by the language of the *Brahuis* of Baluchistan. But the difficulty of the problem is that it is not possible precisely to define either the Sumerian or the Dravidian type, as they are themselves mixed types. Thus even if the Dravidians had come from the West to India as invaders, their original racial type was transformed by their intermarriage with the aboriginal Indians, the proto-Australoids. Again, if they are considered as being native to India, they must have been originally proto-Australoids and acquired their Dravidian character in course of natural evolution and by intermingling with foreign elements. In either case, whether they came from West to East or East to West, the few skulls examined at Mohenjo-daro cannot be identified as Sumerian or Dravidian.

Links with Vedic Civilization.—Lastly, there is the question as to whether the Indus people and their culture were known to India's earliest literary record, the Rigveda, or whether the Indus culture had preceded or followed the Vedic culture, and that, as its ancestor, or descendant.

A study of Rigvedic India is to follow later. A critical consideration of the evidence of the Rigveda will lead to the conclusion that the references it contains to the non-Aryans and their civilization may be taken to refer to the Indus people. As will be explained later, the antiquity of the Rigveda itself is now established by certain inscriptions of the Hittite capital of the fifteenth century B.C. invoking specifically Rigvedic deities, so that the Rigveda itself must have originated earlier to have its culture migrate from India to Mesopotamia in that early age; while a proper view of the evolution of Sanskrit Language and Literature antecedent to the rise of Buddhism in about sixth century B.C. cannot place the Rigveda later than about 2500 B.C., when it was also already a finished product. Considering these chronological probabilities,

Professor Langdon has concluded that "It is far more likely that the Aryans in India are the oldest representatives of the Indo-Germanic race". He is further confirmed in this view by his belief that the Brahmī script itself derives from the Indus script.

Regarding the non-Aryan or the aboriginal peoples of India, the Rigveda shows considerable acquaintance. It calls the non-Aryan as Dāsa, Dasyu, or Asura and in one passage [i, 133, 4] refers to "ruddy" *piśāchas* and *rākshasas* uttering fearful noise and yells in battle. It also mentions the names of individual non-Aryan leaders and peoples [cf. references given later.] It mentions some significant characteristics of non-Aryan culture which recall and resemble those of the Indus. Thus the non-Aryan is described as speaking a strange language (*mṛidhravāk*), not following Vedic rituals (*akarman*), gods (*adevayu*), devotion (*abrahman*), sacrifices (*ayajvan*), or ordinances (*avrata*), but following their own system (*anyavrata*). And besides these negative characterizations, the Rigveda also mentions a positive characteristic of the non-Aryan, viz. that he was a phallus-worshipper (*śiśnadevaḥ*) [vii, 21, 5; x, 99, 3].

There is thus nothing in this Rigvedic description of non-Aryan culture which goes against its identification with the Indus culture. We have already seen how the religion of the Indus people was characterized by the worship of the phallus, while their language, not read and understood to this day, very well deserved the description given of it by the Rigveda, viz. that it was radically different from Sanskrit.

As regards the material aspects of non-Aryan civilization, the Rigveda refers to towns and forts, broad (*pṛithvī*) and wide (*urvī*), full of kine (*gomatī*), of 100 pillars (*śatabhujī*), built of stone (*aśmamayī*), to autumnal (*śāradī*) forts as refuge against inundations, and to 100 cities in a non-Aryan kingdom. Even the Vedic god Indra is designated for the occasion as Purandara, "sacker of cities"! Does not all this seem appropriate reference to the city civilization of the Indus valley? The Rigveda again knows of a mercantile people it calls *Paṇis* and refers to the Vedic peoples, Turvasa and Yadu, as hailing from the sea.

Some of the Mohenjo-daro skulls are, again, found to be proto-Australoid, while this particular aboriginal population the Rigveda describes as *anāsa,* "snub-nosed," and "a dusky brood" (*kṛishṇa-garbha*).

Most of the animals known to the Indus people are also known to the Rigveda, such as sheep, goats, dogs, or bulls [iv, 15, 6; viii, 22, 2; vii, 55, 3]. The animals hunted down by the Rigvedic people were antelopes [x, 39, 8], boars [x, 86, 4], buffalo (gaura) [x, 51, 6], lions [x, 28, 10], and elephants [viii, 2, 6], and these are also familiar to the Indus people. Horses, however, were domesticated in Rigvedic India, but not in the Indus Valley.

As regard metals, the Rigveda knows ornaments of gold (hiraṇya) [i, 122, 2]. These gold ornaments comprised ear-rings, necklaces, bracelets, anklets, and garlands [*karṇa-śobhana*, vii, 78, 3; *nishka-grīva*, ii, 33, 10; *khādi*, i, 166, 9, and v, 54, 11; *rukma-vaksha*] and jewels for the neck [*maṇi-grīva*, i, 122, 14]. We have seen how most of these ornaments were also in use in the city of Mohenjo-daro.

Besides gold, the Rigveda knows of another metal called *ayas*, of which vessels were made [*ayasmaya*, v, 30, 15]. This metal was also hammered [*ayo-hata*, ix, 1, 2]. It is probable that the *ayas* of Rigveda means copper. In the later Atharvaveda, however, iron is known and called *śyāma-ayas* and is distinguished from copper called *lohita* (red) *ayas* [xi, 3, 1, 7]. The Rigveda also knows of implements of stone, such as *aśmachakra*, stone pulley [x, 101, 5, 6], or *adri* [i, 51, 3] or *aśani* [vi, 6, 5], i.e. sling-stones.

The Rigveda, however, knows of some kinds of armour not known in the Indus Valley, such as the coat of mail (*varma*) made up of metal plates sewn together (*syūta*) [i, 31, 15] and close fitting (*surabhi*) [i, 122, 2] or helmet (*śipra*) [vi, 75, 14], made of *ayas* [iv, 37, 4], or of gold (*hiraṇya*) [ii, 34, 3]. The treatment of hair by the men and women of the Rigveda also bears some resemblance to Mohenjo-daro practice. The hair was combed and oiled.

Women wore it plaited. There is mention of a maiden wearing her hair in four plaits (*chatush-kapardā* in *Rv.* x, 114, 3). Men also sometimes wore their hair in coils. The Vasishṭhas had it coiled on the right [i, 173, 6; vii, 33, 1]. Men also grew beards (*śmaśru*) [ii, 11, 17].

But the most singular feature of the Indus civilization, namely, the cotton industry, is also an established industry in Rigvedic India. The Rigveda calls the weaver *vāya* and his loom *veman* [x, 26, 6], the shuttle *tasara*, the warp *otu*, and the woof *tantu* [vi, 9, 2].

All this Rigvedic evidence is not, however, cited to prove that the Rigvedic civilization was the ancestor or the descendant of the Indus civilization. What is sought to be proved is that the Rigveda, from the very nature of its geographical and historical background (to be discussed fully later), shows wide acquaintance with the non-Aryan world, the conditions of its life and culture, some of which, as described in the Rigveda, tally with those indicated by the remains unearthed at Mohenjo-daro. Thus the non-Aryan of the Rigveda may in a sense be taken to be the non-Aryan responsible for the Indus civilization. This supposition fits in also with the widely accepted view of the age of the Rigveda to be not later than 2500 B.C. and thus practically contemporary with this early history of the Indus Valley.[1]

Pre-historic Peoples.—We have now to connect as far as possible these successive prehistoric cultures with the races responsible for them, to link up archæology with anthropology. The determination of racial elements, origins, and affinities depends on the study of physical, linguistic, and cultural features. Such a study cannot be attempted except in a special treatise.

Cranial Material.—The prehistoric cranial material for the study of Race in India is rather meagre. It is found but in a few places: Adichanallur and a few other places in Southern India, Sialkot, Bayana near Agra, Nal in Baluchistan, and Mohenjo-daro. These exhaust the whole

[1] **Reference**: *Mohenjo-daro and the Indus Civilization*, in three volumes, by Sir John Marshall and other writers.

field of prehistoric craniology in India. The skulls found at these places are of different types, proto-Australoid, Mediterranean, and Alpine, dolicho-cephalic as well as brachy-cephalic.[1] The citizens of Mohenjo-daro were thus already not a homogeneous but a mixed population.

We have also to admit the existence of both dolicho-cephalic and brachy-cephalic elements in the earliest population of India, as shown by these skulls.

The differentiation of human skull into these two forms is first seen in the Anthropoid stock out of which man arose, the ancestral form being normally brachy-cephalic and the longer form of skull a later development, though a certain proportion of individuals at the outset showed the long head.

Negritos.—The earliest people to occupy India are supposed to belong to the Negrito race, traces of whom are still found in the Andamans, and perhaps also in the forests of the extreme south of India among the Kadars and Uralis, with their dwarfish stature and frizzly hair. The Negrito contribution to culture is the invention of the bow.

Proto-Australoids.—The Negritos were followed by what are called proto-Australoids, a dolicho-cephalic type. Its origin is now considered to have been in Palestine and not Australia, as was hitherto supposed. These proto-Australoids are to be regarded as the true aborigines of India on the ground that their racial type, with its special features and characteristics, came to be ultimately fixed in India, although the type came to India by a very early migration from the West. The type is seen in its purest form in the Veddas. It is this type which is primarily responsible for the platyrrhine and dark-skinned elements found in India in all castes except the highest.

[1] Race-types are classified with reference to two main standards. These are (1) the *Cephalic Index*, i.e. the proportion of the maximum breadth of the skull (measured above the ears) to its maximum length (measured from the glabella to the back of the head). The *dolicho-cephalic* begins with the index being 75 per cent and below. The higher index points to the *brachy-cephalic* type. (2) The *Nasal Index*, which is the proportion of the breadth of the nose to its height. Narrow-nosed (leptorrhine) types show the index to be below 70 per cent and broad-nosed (platyrrhine) types show it to be 85–100 per cent.

Melanesian.—The Melanesian represents a stabilized type derived from mixed Negrito and proto-Australoid elements. The type is seen in the hilly tracts dividing Assam from Burma, in the Nicobars, and also on the Malabar coast. It is traced by certain cultural features, such as disposal of the dead by exposure or the canoe cult. But it does not exist in India as a distinct or isolated type with a culture of its own.

Proto-Australoid Contributions to Culture: Muṇḍā.—The proto-Australoids are responsible for the introduction of Neolithic culture and pottery in India. But their linguistic legacy is more enduring and important. They are known as the speakers of Austro-Asiatic languages distributed over the widest area from the Panjab to New Zealand and from Madagascar to Easter Island. The Indian variety of these languages is known as the Muṇḍā, which, accordingly, is to be considered as the earliest language spoken in India. A consideration of the Muṇḍā linguistic areas in India throws light on the course of proto-Australoid migrations. These may have been from east to west or from west to east. Muṇḍā survives now in the inner Himalayan ranges between Ladakh and Sikkim, in the west of the Central Provinces, and southwards among the Ganjam and Vizagapatam hills, but not beyond the Godāvarī. Muṇḍā shows affinity not merely with the languages of south-east Asia and the Pacific, but also with the agglutinative Sumerian language. Thus it is considered that the various branches of the Austro-Asiatic family of languages originated at some common centre in central or south-east Asia, from which it spread in a more or less southerly direction.

The Muṇḍā-speaking peoples are called by the generic names of Muṇḍās, Kolarians, or Kols, and number over six millions, comprising *Sontals* (numbering about 23 lacs), *Bhils* (about 18 lacs), *Kurumbas* (9 lacs), *Muṇḍās* (6 lacs), *Savaras* (5 lacs), *Hos* (4 lacs), and other minor tribes like the *Korwas* (of Sirguja and Mirzapur), the *Juangs* (of Dhenkanal) or the *Korkus* (of Panchmarhi hills). The vast region comprising the Sontal Parganas and Chota Nagpur, together with parts of the Central Provinces, Orissa, and

Madras is the seat of a separate, primitive Muṇḍā or Kolarian civilization continuing through the ages in its special features such as free village communities, collective hunting and fasting, absence of caste-system, worship by each clan of its own presiding spirit in trees by sacrifice, special codes of law, punishment of minor offences by fines in the shape of tribal feasts and of serious ones by expulsion, agriculture, and the like.[1]

Mongolian.—This element is traced in the non-Dravidian languages known as Mon-Khmer spoken by peoples inhabiting the Khassi hills of Assam, the hills of Upper Burma and parts of Lower Burma, Malay Peninsula, and Nicobar Islands. These languages came to India with the invaders from the East, the Mongolians, coming partly from Tibet down the valley of the Brahmaputra, and partly from China through Burma by the Mekong, the Salween and the Irrawady. It may also be noted that further invasions from the east have introduced to India two languages of what is called the Tibeto-Chinese family, viz. (1) the Tibeto-Burman spoken by the Tibetans of Almora and Garhwal, the Daflas, Abor-Miris and Mishmis of northern Assam, the Garos of western Assam hills, the Kuki-chins of Naga hills, the Bodos or Kochs of Cooch-Behar, Nowgong, Kamrupa and Goalpara in Assam, and the Kachins or Singhphos on the upper Irrawady and the Burmese; and (2) the Siamese-Chinese prevailing in the Shan States of eastern Burma.

[1] According to Dr. Haddon, the Muṇḍā-speaking peoples belonged to a great Indonesian race which had spread up to Polynesia from its home in the Ganges Valley and Western Bengal. Its cultural unity is traced in certain forms like the outrigger canoe found on the west coasts of India and Ceylon, or the coconut palm, but chiefly the "shouldered celt" found in parts of Indian Archipelago, Indo-China, Burma, and India. Square-shouldered adzes abound in the Irrawady Valley. They are distinct from the usual India type found in the Sontal Parganas and in central and south India, and allied to the unshouldered copper and bronze types found at Mohenjo-daro. Shouldered copper celts are also found in pre-historic cemeteries in Chota Nagpur areas. Thus it is not certain if the polished shouldered stone adze of the Irrawady region had preceded or followed the copper celts of India. If the copper celt is later, the shouldered stone celt of India must have been intrusive from Indonesia. If the copper form was the original type (as seen in Mohenjo-daro), the stone form must have come to India or Indonesia from the west. It is more probable that the square-shouldered and highly polished Irrawady adze copied a metallic model rather than stone.

The Mongoloid thrust into India from the east has extended farther towards the west than the range of its linguistic occupation. Mongolian features are noticed in some of the terra-cotta figurines and skulls of Mohenjo-daro.

Earliest Languages.—It will thus be noted that these early peoples of India have given to India her earliest languages, the Muṇḍā, Mon-Khmer, and Austronesian and Tibeto-Chinese languages. As will be shown below, these languages were pushed to the south-east by Dravidian, which was in its turn supplanted by the Indo-Aryan tongues.

Mediterraneans and Armenoids.—The proto-Australoids were followed by the Mediterraneans who came to India in successive waves of migration. An early branch came with its agglutinative tongue, migrating down the Ganges valley, mingling with the proto-Australoids, and influencing their Austro-Asiatic languages, as already stated. They introduced navigation, agriculture, and architecture of rude stones. Later Mediterranean immigrants came with a more advanced culture and civilization which they had built up in Mesopotamia in association with the Armenoids. The Mediterraneans were dolicho-cephalic, while the Armenoids of the Alpine stock were brachy-cephalic. While typical of Armenia and Anatolia, they spread themselves all over Asia Minor and Mesopotamia and mingled with the Mediterraneans in varying proportions, forming the most important element in the population of Sumer. Thus the Sumerians were a mixed race made up of dolicho-cephalic Mediterranean and brachy-cephalic Armenoid.

These peoples thus appear to be the most important of the prehistoric peoples of the world, as the first makers of civilization, which probably originated in the "Fertile Crescent" skirting the hills north of Mesopotamia from Syria to the Persian Gulf. This civilization was, as we have seen, in full swing by the end of the fourth millennium B.C., achieving a high standard of comfort, art, and sanitation in city life. Its language was ***Dravidian***, and it used a pictographic script like that used in prehistoric Mesopotamia.

A combination of Armenoid and Mediterranean is also

found in India, particularly among the Tamils. There were probably direct contacts by sea between southern India and Mesopotamia. Land contacts between Mesopotamia and Indus Valley are also proved by the discovery of objects of common type in these two regions, and also by the existence of Brahuī in Baluchistan. The Brahuī gives evidence pointing to speakers of Dravidian languages as the ancient inhabitants of Mohenjo-daro and perhaps the givers of culture to India.

Alpines.—The brachy-cephalic leptorrhine seen in Bengal in the east and more markedly in the west of India can only be explained by the theory of an invasion of another people, the Alpines, from the Pamirs. This brachy-cephalic stock, an Eurasiatic Alpine stock, must have entered the Indus Valley, dislocating the Mohenjo-daro civilization, and spreading down the West Coast of India to become the ancestors of the Prabhus, the Marathas, etc., and also introducing the brachy-cephalic element into the Brahuī. They went down farther to the south across the Mysore plateau, but missing the Malabar coast, where is thus preserved at its best the ancient civilization of Dravidian-speaking India. They spoke an Indo-European language, of which traces are still to be found in the Indo-Aryan Dardic language spoken by the people of Chitral, who are also brachy-cephalic. Later, these brachy-cephals, pushed by the Vedic Aryans, carried the round-headed element down the Ganges valley eastward to Bengal.

Dravidians.—It will thus appear that the civilization of the Indus Valley was associated with the speakers of Dravidian languages of Mediterranean race with an Armenoid admixture and a developed culture derived from the near east. This early culture of the Mediterraneans and Armenoids in India may be best described as pre-Vedic Hinduism, anticipating some of the characteristics of later Hinduism already explained. As we have already seen, it was vigorous enough to have influenced Vedic civilization. The Rigveda [i, 6] speaks of its strength in cities, castles, wealth, and of its women bathing in milk. The "noseless" non-Aryans of the Rigveda could refer only to the proto-Australoids, in which case tribes like the Bhils or the Chodhras would be then lingering in hills and forest areas in spite of the Mediterranean and Alpine migrations, or they might have been in occupation of the Indus Valley with the decline of its pre-Vedic civilization. Again, the Rigvedic story of conflict between Vasishṭha and Viśvāmitra is that of conflict between two cultures, of which the amalgamation is indicated by the Kshatriya becoming a Brahman. There is also reference to non-Aryan Ṛishis in later traditions. Lastly, the Brāhmī script of later Vedic civilizations is itself traced to the Indus Valley pictographs. As early as 1867, Mr. E. Thomas suspected that the Aryans invented no alphabets of their own in the course of their wanderings, but depended on the country in which they settled for the script by which they could reduce their speech to writing. This theory for long received no acceptance, and the Brāhmī script was traced to Semitic origins and considered to have been imported from Phœnicia in the first millennium B.C. It remained for Professor Langdon to prove after more than six decades that the Brāhmī characters derive from the Indus signs, the symbols used on their seals by the pre-Aryans of the Indus Valley. Thus, as he points out, " the Aryan Sanskritists gave values derived from their own language to these characters. In other words, they knew their ideographic meaning, translated them into Sanskrit, and derived the syllabic values from the Sanskrit words."

It will thus appear that the Dravidian speakers were the latest occupants of India before the Indo-Europeans arrived. They came from the north-west, where they left traces of their language among the Brāhuī (who themselves regard the remains of Mohenjo-daro as the work of their ancestors), and brought with them the ancient cultures of Mesopotamia, Asia Minor, and the eastern Mediterranean. Dravidian place-names are sometimes traced in Mesopotamia and Iran, while an ancient language spoken in Mittani (Kharian) reveals striking similarities to modern Dravidian of India.

Thus the fact seems to be that India was not an isolated welter of Australoid tribes prior to the coming of the

Aryans or Indo-Europeans in the second millennium, B.C., as was so long supposed, but had already a civilization comparable to and in communication with the ancient Mesopotamian civilizations in the valleys of the Indus, and possibly of the Ganges too.

Marks of their Migration from North to South.—The Dravidians retreated before the Aryans, leaving notable marks of their strength in the north and of their march from the north to the south, where they found their final home. Dravidian elements are to be found alike in Vedic and classical Sanskrit, in the Prakrits, and even in the modern vernaculars of Northern India. It is found by linguists that Indo-European, on its introduction to India, suffered a change which could only have come from the Dravidian source. This is the presence of a second series of dental letters in the language of the Rigveda, by which it is distinguished from that of the *Avesta* and from all other languages of the Indo-European family. Further marks of the course of Dravidian migration from the north to south are to be found in other islands of Dravidian speech and culture preserved among certain kindred peoples they left behind in the north, such as the Mal and Sauria Paharis of Rajmehal hills, the Oraons of Chota Nagpur (numbering about 8 lacs), the Gonds (numbering about 30 lacs), and the Kandhs of Orissa and tributary states.

The Dravidian-speaking peoples present three racial types or elements, viz. (1) Dolicho-platyrrhine or Vedda-Australoid type, (2) Dolicho-leptorrhine or Mediterranean type, and (3) Brachy-leptorrhine or Alpine type. Generally speaking, the Deccan is brachy-cephalic, while the region south of it, including the two coastal strips, is dolicho-cephalic. There is also to be found an increasing association of brachy-cephaly with leptorrhiny, and also of leptorrhiny with Sanskrit language, as is the case with Kanarese, Malayalam, Marathi, and Telugu, while Tamil, the least Sanskritic of these, is spoken by the dolicho-platyrrhine peoples.

The brachy-cephalic Alpine type is spread along the western littoral from Gujarat to Coorg, and also from

Benares to Bihar, and markedly in Bengal where it is associated with leptorrhiny, most in its central and deltaic parts, and in decreasing degrees in the north and east. There is thus a continuity of type from Bombay to Bengal. For the origin of the Bengalis we have thus to look to the west rather than to the east, or the Mongolian source, some of whose chief characteristics they lack, such as absence of bodily hair[1] [Dr. B. S. Guha, in his presidential address to the Anthropological Section of the Indian Science Congress for 1928.]

[1] This chapter is largely based on the up-to-date material presented by Dr. J. H. Hutton in pages 357–369 and 439–460 in vol. i, part i, of the Census Report for 1931.

Some unexpected light is thrown on the origins of civilization by the new science of Plant Genetics. Civilization depends not merely on man but also on plants and animals. To trace civilization to its source, we must find out where cereals and cattle were first domesticated. This task is being undertaken by Russian Scientists led by Vavilov, who is the head of U.S.S.R. Department of Applied Botany and Plant-Breeding. They have found that there are two distinct groups of wheat which cannot be hybridized easily. Each of these groups can be traced to a definite centre. One such centre is in Abyssinia, and the other, from which the more important group of wheats is derived, lies somewhere near south-eastern Afghanistan, the fold between the Hindukush and the Himalayas, embracing parts of the Panjab and the neighbouring hill-country. Abyssinia, accordingly, is taken to be the original home of the agriculture that led up to the Egyptian Civilization. The other region is the original home not only of Indian and Mesopotamian wheat but also of its more important varieties grown in Europe and North America to-day, and of many cultivated plants besides the bread-wheats, such as the small-seed types of flax and leguminous plants, old-world cottons, the turnip, carrot, apricot, and peach.

Of course, civilization might have started with other cereals, such as maize, but maize is very poor in Vitamin B_2. Populations living mainly on maize develop a skin-disease called Pellagra. That is one reason why the maize-civilizations of Central America could not attain the level of the wheat, barley, and rice-civilizations of the old world. On these grounds, India can be considered as the very cradle of civilization. [J. B. S. Haldane's *Inequality of Man*, pp. 46–8, 71–6.]

Chapter III

GEOGRAPHICAL AND SOCIAL BACKGROUND

Indian history proper begins with the advent of the Aryans to India. It is, however, necessary to study at the outset the physical basis of that history in the geographical conditions influencing its course through the ages. We may remember the old saying of Richard Hakluyt: "Geographie and Chronologie are the Sunne and the Moone, the right eye and the left eye of all history."

The principal features in the geography of India that have bearings on her history are (1) Isolation, (2) Intercourse, (3) Vastness, (4) Variety, and (5) Unity.

Isolation.—There is hardly any part of a continent that is so clearly separated and marked out by Nature as a region by itself as India. Mountain-guarded in the north and sea-girt in the south, India is indisputably a geographical unit, and is effectively isolated by sharply-defined boundaries from the rest of the world. The Himalayas present a double wall running unbroken for a distance of about 1,600 miles from east to west and presenting an average width of 250 miles throughout this length. On the Tibetan side of the northern wall rise the three rivers, Indus, Sutlej, and Tsan-po (Brahmaputra in its Indian part), and on the Indian side of the southern wall the Ganges and its northern tributaries. The Himalayan barrier at its eastern extremity throws out spurs forming the Patkoi, Naga, and Lushai hills, densely forested, separating the Irrawady Valley of Burma from the plains of India and obstructing the direct way from China to India. At its north-western end the barrier is taken up by an angle of the loftiest mountain ridge made up of the Karakoram, with its second highest peak in the world, Mount Godwin Austen, and of the Hindu Kush, and enclosing within it the Valley of Leh, Gilgit, and Chitral, forming the northernmost outposts of the Indian

Empire. Beyond, or south of, the Hindu Kush, lie the Sufed Koh and Sulaiman ranges separating India from Afghanistan, and Kirthar hills separating it from Baluchistan.

Towards the south, the ocean in the olden times operated as a formidable isolating barrier, except for such peaceful, periodical trading intercourse as could be carried on by sail shipping and the slow and timid coasting voyages of those times. It served as an ample protection against overseas invasion until the Europeans rounded the Cape of Good Hope. It was the arrival in 1498 of the three small ships of Vasco da Gama at Calicut that first opened up the country to bold adventurers coming by way of the sea, a path of conquest which was subsequently followed successively and successfully by the four European Powers, the Portuguese, the Dutch, the French, and the English. The science of navigation has now transformed the ocean into a highway of intercourse and invasion and made the control of the country depend on command of the sea. The sea-coast cities of Bombay and Karachi, Madras, Calcutta, or Colombo, have now acquired a new strategic importance in the defence of India. Colombo, upon which now converge four streams of traffic, from the Mediterranean, the Cape of Good Hope, Australia, and Singapore and the Far East, has become the strategical centre of British sea-power in the Indian Ocean. It is, however, to be noted that on the west coast the barrier of the Western Ghats, and on the east coast the want of natural harbours, the shallow depth of water along the coast, and the unruly surf, constitute natural and permanent obstacles to intercourse by way of the sea with foreign countries. The character of the coast-line of India is not also favourable to her growth as a sea-power. Much of the country is deeply inland and the majority of its people are naturally land-locked. There are few indentations, few of those deep bays, gulfs, or river-mouths opening up the inland areas, as is the case with Norway or the British Isles, of which no part is far from the sea. Even the few bays and gulfs which India has are not suitable sites for harbours. The only natural harbour in India is Bombay. Madras and Colombo are artificial harbours, while Calcutta is on a river-mouth. Owing to this natural handicap, Indian shipping and seamanship have played a very small part in Indian history.

While India is thus as a whole isolated from the outside world, some of her parts, again, are isolated from one another. The ranges of the Vindhya system, with their almost impenetrable forests, have in all ages formed the great dividing line between northern and southern India. It was at this barrier that Aryan colonization had stopped for a long time, according to older Sanskrit texts. The two halves of India offer to this day striking contrasts in race, language, and social customs. For instance, in an old law book, that of Bodhāyana of about 500 B.C., the outstanding social custom dividing the south from the north is stated to be the southern practice obtaining to this day of a man's marriage with his maternal uncle's daughter. The south has had, in fact, an independent history, with but few points of contact with the history of northern India. Very few were the sovereigns whose dominion had embraced both the north and the south, like that of Chandragupta Maurya and Asoka, Akbar or Aurangzeb. The comparative isolation of the south was responsible for its immunity from Moslem invasions to which northern India had been subjected for several centuries. The Vindhyan system, including the Satpuras, and enclosing within it the valleys of the Narmadā and the Tapti, runs from the Gulf of Cambay to Rajmahal in Bengal. Towards the centre of India, the Vindhyas and Satpuras converge to form the highlands of the Central Provinces. Towards the east, up to the Eastern Ghats, the region between the Godavari and the Mahānadi, extending northward to the Valley of Son, is again isolated by hills and fever-haunted forests, the abode of aboriginal peoples beyond the pale of civilization, in tracts like the Sontal Parganas, the hills and forests of Central India, or on the Nilgiris, as already described. Even in the time of the Vedic text, *Aitareya Brāhmaṇa* (not later than about 2000 B.C.), non-Āryan peoples like the Andhras, Puṇḍras, Śabaras, Pulindas, and Mūtibas, are mentioned as living in the outskirts of Aryan civilization in the Vindhyan jungles towards the east. In the farther south, again, the Anamaloi, Palni, and Cardamum hills isolated the kingdom of Kerala, which in modern times gave rise to the two states of Cochin and Travancore. The effects of their isolation are seen in the prevalence of peculiar social customs like polyandry or matriarchal system of inheritance (by which a man's heir is his sister's son), which are foreign to the Aryan social system and the rest of India. Another striking example of isolation is that of the two most densely-peopled regions of southern India, viz. the Carnatic plain from Madras to Tanjore, and the Malabar coast between Cochin and Calicut. The isolation from each other of these two populous regions is only breached by what is called the Gap of Coimbatore, or Pālghāt, giving to the Carnatic markets the much-needed access to the many natural harbours and ports on the Malabar coast. The surf of the Coromandel coast, coupled with the barrier presented by the Western Ghats behind the Malabar coast, accounts for the comparative isolation of southern India, only relieved by the Gap of Coimbatore, which has thus a great importance.

Intercourse.—With all this physical isolation, India presents an extraordinarily composite and heterogeneous social complex, the undoubted outcome of her intercourse with the world outside, of immigrations and invasions from without. The history of India to some extent thus belies her geography. World-movements of thought and population have impinged upon her isolation through the ages and introduced to her civilization a variety of racial and cultural elements which may be broadly distinguished as (1) pre-Dravidian, (2) Dravidian, (3) Aryan, (4) Iranian, (5) Greek, (6) Roman, (7) Scythian, (8) Hun, (9) Islamic, and (10) European.

The question is: How was all this influx of foreign influence possible? What were precisely the ways through which it penetrated into India? The north-eastern frontiers present but few gaps, and these do not admit of movements on a large scale. The three passes, the Jelap, the Natu, and the Donkia, which lead from Sikkim into Tibet, are too high and permit only of small traffic. In the east, passage is offered by the course of the Brahmaputra from Tibet, and from China by the three rivers, Mekong, Salween, and Irrawady, but immigration on a large scale by this way is impeded by the dense growth of jungle and its wild denizens, and by the British occupation of Upper Burma. The defence of India in this quarter is thus practically left to nature.

The whole of the northern bulwark for well-nigh 1,500 miles is practically impenetrable. There are a few passes leading from the Pamirs by way of Gilgit, and from Tibet by Leh, and the gorge of the Sutlej into India. By the three passes known as the Muztagh ("Snowy Mountain"), the Karakoram ("Black Mountain"), and the Changchenmo, which are all over heights of 18,000 feet, some small traffic is carried on between the Panjab and eastern Turkestan, and Tibet on the other side. But these are fit for the passage of traders and not for migrations or invasions. These were not considered suitable by the medieval Buddhist pilgrims from China like Yuan Chwang who first travelled westward by the desert routes north of Tibet, as far as Oxus, and then southward over the Hindu Kush.

In the south, India has been always open to foreign influence by way of the sea, and of peaceful commercial intercourse, first with Egypt and Babylon, and later with the Roman Empire. Indian products like indigo, tamarind-wood, or muslin, in which were wrapped the mummies, have been detected in the tombs of Egypt. The booty which Pharaoh carried in his vessel to Egypt included elephants' teeth, gold, precious stones, sandal-wood, and monkeys, which came from India. Some scholars find in the Bible evidence of Indian trade in the mention of articles which India alone could supply in those days, such as precious stones, gold, ivory, ebony, peacocks, and spices, forming part of the merchandise carried by Solomon's ships. Indian teak is traced in the ruins of Ur, and the Babylonian word for muslin is *sindhu*. The Indian Pali work, the *Baveru-Jātaka* of about 500 B.C., definitely mentions Indian traders taking peacocks to Babylon. The specifically Indian products—rice, peacocks, and sandal-wood—were known to the Greeks only by their Indian, Tamil, names. As direct intercourse between India and Babylon had ceased after 480 B.C., these products must have been imported to Babylon much earlier so as to have reached Greece by about 460 B.C., and become familiar at Athens in the time of Sophocles (495–406 B.C.) who mentions them. The chief centres of all this ancient trade, according to old Indian texts, were at Sūrpāraka-Sopara and Bhārukachchha-Bhroach on the Bombay coast. The later Indian trade with Rome which developed most between the times of Augustus and Nero, had its chief centres at Muziris (Cranganore) on Malabar coast and at Kāviripaddanam (Puhar) on the Coromandal coast from which were shipped the Indian goods greatly prized in Rome, viz. spices and perfumes, silk, muslin and cotton, pearls and precious stones. The centre of the pearl trade was the old Pandya capital of Korkai (Tinnevelly), now buried in sand. Of precious stones, beryl, most in demand, was found in the mines of Coimbatore and Salem districts. Roman coins are also mostly found in Coimbatore and Madura. Old Tamil texts refer to "powerful Yavanas" and "dumb Mlechchhas" as being in the service of the Tamil kings. The word *Yavana* itself came into Sanskrit from Indian intercourse with the Ionians (Greeks). To this intercourse was also due the deposits of two small settlements of Jews and Christians on the Malabar coast. After Egypt, Babylon, and Rome, the merchants of Yemen in south Arabia came into this Indian trade. After the rise of Islam in A.D. 622 the Arabs controlled all the harbours of the Arabian sea and African coasts, and the maritime route from the Persian Gulf to India and China. Up to the end of the fifteenth century A.D. the Indian contact with the west was confined only to coasting trade on the western side of India. Then the sea yielded to the science of navigation and paved the way of European incursions to India, where previous invaders and conquerors found their way by the land routes on the north-western frontiers.

The north-western frontier, though apparently mountain-guarded, is really the most vulnerable frontier in the whole

British Empire,[1] requiring constant and costly preparations for its defence. What further increases its insecurity is that it is an extensive frontier passing through turbulent tribal territory up to Afghanistan, beyond which again is the menace of the continental powers of Europe.

To understand the full significance of the north-west frontier, we must look beyond the immediate boundaries of India and study the features of the Iranian plateau comprising the three adjoining countries of Afghanistan, Baluchistan, and Persia. This plateau rises to the inaccessible heights of the Pamirs in the north-east and of Armenia in the north-west, but is easy of access on other fronts towards the Persian Gulf and the Arabian Sea, India, and Turkestan or Turan to the north. The defence of India, therefore, needs control of the Persian Gulf and Arabian Sea and absence of alien bases of power on the Iranian plateau towards the south and east. The access to India is easy from Afghanistan by way of the Kabul River and from Seistan, and from both it is agreed that foreign powers are to be excluded. The Hindu Kush, separating the basin of the Oxus from that of the Indus, is easy of access from both sides and offers several ways into India along river valleys, of which the most famous and frequently trodden is the Khyber route. The Khyber leads from Kabul down the valley of the Kabul River to Peshawar. The Kurram River flows from Afghanistan into the Bannu district through the Kurram Pass and then falls into the Indus. The Tochi valley leads from Ghazni into India;

[1] The land frontier of 3,000 miles separating Canada from the United States does not require to be defended by a single fort or a gun, while the other Dominions of the empire, Australia, New Zealand, Newfoundland, and Ireland are islands. The Union of South Africa is equally free from the danger of foreign invasion. Of their total revenues, the expenditure on defence amounts to 2·4 per cent for Australia, 2·9 per cent for Canada, 7·2 per cent for Irish Free State, 3·9 per cent for Newfoundland, and 2·4 per cent for South Africa. But India has to spend on her defence more than 60 per cent of her central revenue and nearly a third of her total net central and provincial revenues taken together. This is due to the perpetual menace of raids by the independent tribes living beyond the north-west frontiers. The period of 72 years from 1850 to 1922 saw as many as 72 expeditions, an average of one a year, being sent against these tribes! This heavy burden of anxiety which India has to carry for her security is a serious obstacle to her internal development, being a permanent drain and strain on her resources.

through it flows the Tochi River, which rises on the slopes of the Waziristan Mountains and falls into the Kurram. The Gomal lies between Afghanistan and Dera Ismail Khan. Farther away, where the Afghan Mountains subside towards the west, lies another way round their fringe over the open plateau from Herat to Kandahar, and not far from Seistan, and leading south-eastward from Kandahar through a rocky district into the lowland of the Indus. This is called the Bolan route after the last gorge towards India. A last line of communication connecting Persia with India passes through the inhospitable region of Makran along the coast of Baluchistan. This route is famous in history as being chosen (probably on the precedents of previous conquerors, Semiramis and Cyrus) by Alexander the Great, with disastrous consequences to his army on its return journey from India in 325 B.C. This route was later much frequented by Arab traders. There is, again, a lateral connection between the two more important routes, the Khyber and Bolan, following a chain of valleys between Kandahar and Kabul, through Ghazni. This route has been made famous in history by Alexander's march to his Bactrian and Indian campaigns and in recent times by the march of General Roberts from Kabul to the relief of Kandahar in the Afghan war of 1882. Several passes also lead from the Kabul-Kandahar road into the mountainous belt of the Indian frontier.

All this geography thus supplies the key to much of Indian history, ancient and modern. The breaches in the north-western barrier of mountains just discussed have served in all ages as highways of peaceful intercourse and violent invasions, of extensive racial movements and immigrations. By these ways came some of the prehistoric peoples, and the Aryans who have made Indian history, and, in historical times foreign invaders like Cyrus and Darius, Alexander, Seleucus, and Demetrios, the Scythians, Parthians and Kushans, under whom India entered into active commercial intercourse by land with the Roman empire, and, in the medieval age, the Moslems. The only exception is in the case of the most important factor of

Indian history, the European, which came into India from the south by way of the sea.

The defence of India in modern times has been organized with reference to the two vulnerable points of Khyber and Bolan. The Indian defensive forces are grouped into a northern army distributed from Calcutta past Allahabad and Delhi to Peshawar, in support of the Khyber front, and a southern army distributed through the Madras and Bombay Presidencies with reference to the garrison city of Quetta guarding the Bolan route, which can be further reinforced by sea through Karachi directly from Britain. The defence of India has been further strengthened by the North-Western Railway from Karachi, with branches towards the Bolan and the Khyber, and backed by the barrier of the Rajputana Desert.

The military or strategic importance of the Rajputana Desert to the defence of India through the ages can hardly be overstated. This waterless waste running from the Rann of Cutch north-eastward to a distance of about 400 miles, with a width of 150 miles, with the Aravalli range in its rear as a further bulwark, forms a second line of fortifications against hostile incursions by way of the Bolan and Makran routes. Once the Khyber route is passed, the way is open up to Delhi, which may be called "the historical focus of all India". Standing at the northern extremity of the Aravallis, where the invading forces from the north-west come through to the navigable waters, it commands the gateway which leads from the Panjab plains to the interior, the heart of India, comprising the plains of the Jumna and Ganges. This gateway was not reached by the Persian invader Darius, in the sixth century B.C., nor by Alexander, whose progress was stopped at the Beas. It was only left to the Moslems to pass this gateway and thereby effect a permanent settlement in India. But they took nearly five centuries, from the date of the Arab conquest of Sind in A.D. 712 to that of the first Sultan of Delhi, A.D. 1193, to spread from the confines of India through the Delhi gateway into the heart of India. During all this time it was the Rajputs, who, aided by the natural advantages of their country, held in check the Moslem invaders on the direct road to Delhi from the north-west and posted themselves on the southern flank of their advance. The conquest of Delhi made the Moslems the predominant power in India. "We may think of the Indus basin—lying beyond the Rajputana Desert, low beneath the uplands of Afghanistan—as having an antechamber to India Proper. In this antechamber, for more than 900 years the Moslems have had a majority. Northwestward of Delhi, in the gateway between the desert and the mountains, the ground is sown over with battlefields—ancient battlefields near the Jumna, where the incoming Moslems overthrew the Indian resistance, and modern battlefields near the Sutlej, where advancing British power inflicted defeat upon the Sikhs. It is by no accident that Simla, the residence of the British Viceroy during half the year, is placed on the Himalayan heights above this natural seat of empire and struggle for supremacy." [*Cambridge History of India*, I, 24.]

Vastness.—India, though geographically distinct as a single and separate country, is more like a continent than a country in its size and dimensions. It is as large as the whole of Continental Europe without Russia, more than twenty times the area of Great Britain. Among its divisions or provinces, the Punjab, the United Provinces, and the Central Provinces, each exceed Great Britain in size; the area of each of the provinces of Bengal and Bihar and Orissa approximates to that of England and Scotland together; the Presidencies of Bombay and Madras are each bigger than Italy, while Assam is of the size of England alone. Nor does India suffer in greatness if estimated not in area but in terms of population. British India alone has a population nearly 2½ times that of the United States; the Indian States, making up a third of the area of India, absorb a fourth of its total population, which is as much as a fifth of that of the whole world. Even provinces like Bengal, U.P., or Madras are each more populous than Great Britain, while the small province of Assam has the population of countries like Belgium, Sweden, or Holland.

Variety.—The vastness of India has produced a corresponding variety in respect of both physical features and social conditions for which India has been aptly described as " the epitome of the world ".

(*a*) *Physical.*—In India is to be found an assemblage of geographical conditions which are distributed among other countries of the world. In the wide range of her latitudes and longitudes, she offers all the three types of climate, the Arctic or Polar, in the vast areas above 15,000 feet among the Himalayas, and the Temperate and the Tropical climates in her lower levels down to the sea. In the matter of moisture or rainfall, she offers an equally wide range, from the world's highest record of 480 inches at Cherapunji to less than 3 inches per annum in parts of Sind and Rajputana. These wide varieties of climate again have produced corresponding varieties of products. According to Hooker, the flora of India is more varied than that of any other country of equal area in the eastern hemisphere, if not in the globe. According to Blandford, the variety of fauna in India far surpasses that of Europe, although Europe is about twice the size of India. Indeed, as Lilly puts it, the products of India include everything needed for the service of man. India is thus endowed by nature with a singular capacity for economic self-sufficiency and independence which it is left to man to realize.

(*b*) *Social: Peoples, Languages, and Religions.*—The immensity of the population of India, making up a fifth of mankind, embraces the widest variety in culture and social life. Here meet all the three primary ethnological types of mankind, the Caucasian or white type, with its subdivisions of blonde and dark, the Mongolian or yellow type, and the Ethiopian or black type (in the Andamans). These broad divisions include ethnographically the following physical types, most of which were first suggested by Sir Herbert Risley in the *Census Report* for 1901 :—

(1) The *pre-Dravidian* aboriginal type, marked by short stature, broad (platyrhine) nose, and other characteristics already discussed and illustrated in the various jungle-tribes of India.

(2) The *Dravidian* type, marked by short stature, dark complexion, plentiful hair, long head, and broad nose; found practically all over the region lying to the south of the U.P. and east of longitude 76° E.

(3) The *Indo-Āryan* type found in Kashmīr, the Punjab, and Rajputana, marked by tall stature, fair complexion, plentiful hair on face, long head, and narrow and prominent nose.

(4) The *Turko-Irānian* type found in the N.W. Frontier Province, Baluchistan, and the regions to the west of the Indus, characterized by "stature above mean, complexion fair, head broad, nose very long though narrow". "The Indus is thus the ethnographical boundary between the Turko-Irānian and Indo-Āryan types, as it is the political boundary between Irān and India." [*CHI*, p. 44.]

(5) The *Scytho-Dravidian* type found in Sind east of the Indus, Gujarat, and western India, marked out from the Turko-Irānian type by "a lower stature, greater length of head, a shorter nose", and the like. Its name assumes that the foreign broad-headed element of the type was due to the Śakas (Scythians) who ruled in western India between c. A.D. 120–380. But the Śakas, as their history shows, could not have affected the race when they themselves, instead of affecting its culture, became gradually Hinduized. The foreign element must have come from the broad-headed Alpine race of western Asia, including Irān, which found its way into western India, like the Dravidians, ages before the way of migration was blocked by desiccation.

(6) The *Āryo-Dravidian* or Hindustāni type of east Punjab, U.P., and Bihar, with "head form long, complexion ranging from brown to black, and nose from medium to broad, stature below the average, 5 ft. 3 in. to 5 ft. 5 in". It is traced to the mixture of the Indo-Āryans with the Dravidians whom they conquered. It first appears as a separate type about the longitude of Sirhind. The Rigveda also shows that Āryan colonization did not extend in its time beyond Sirhind, the valley of the Sarasvatī. The Rigveda is associated with the country of the seven rivers (*Saptasindhavaḥ* [viii, 24, 27]). Later Vedic Literature

of *Brāhmaṇas* and *Upanishads* is associated with the more easterly region between the Jumna and the Ganges and up to Muttra District, called *Brahmarshideśa*, which included *Kurukshetra*, the land on which the fate of India has been determined from the days of the Mahābhārata to those of the battles of Panipat. The evidence of literature thus supports that of ethnology in regard to the boundary between the two physical types following naturally the line of division between two phases and periods of history, that of Indo-Āryan tribal migration succeeded by that of Indo-Āryan colonization, a much slower process involving conquests[1] and fusion of races and cultures.

(7) The *Mongoloid* type in Burma, Assam, and the sub-Himalayan tract comprising Bhutan, Nepal, and fringes of the U.P., Punjab, and Kashmir, marked by " broad head, dark, yellowish complexion, scanty hair on face, short stature, flat face, and oblique eyelids." This type is due to Mongolian invasions from Tibet and China.

(8) The *Bengali* type in Bengal and Orissa, marked by " broad head, dark complexion, plentiful hair on face, medium stature, and medium nose with a tendency to broad ". Risley termed this type as Mongolo-Dravidian, as he thought it was a blend of Dravidian and Mongoloid elements. It has been already shown that it is really the brachy-cephalic Alpine type. The line of division between Bengal and Bihar is both political and ethnographical, and is also indicated in literature. In the *Atharvaveda*, for instance, the *Māgadhas* and the *Aṅgas* are mentioned as peoples outside the pale of Āryan civilization, while the *Śatapatha Brāhmaṇa* has a legend telling of the spread of Brāhmanism from the west eastwards up to Videha or Tirhut.

This ethnological variety is, however, accompanied by a wider variety of languages in India. The last *Census Report* counts the living languages of India to be as many as 225, representing between them four of the great families

[1] The Rigveda mentions only once [vii, 18, 19] the Jumna in a manner showing that a battle was won on its banks. But the region between the Upper Jumna and Ganges was occupied later as a result of conquests indicated in the *Śatapatha Brāhmaṇa* [xiii, 5, 4, 11–14], the triumphs celebrated by Bharata Dauḥshanti after his victories on the Jumna and the Ganges.

of human speech, viz. the Austric, the Tibeto-Chinese, the Dravidian, and the Indo-European. The Dravidian languages are stabilized in the south in Telugu and Tamil, Kanarese, and Malayālam, each with a great literature. Beyond them in the north, Indo-Āryan holds its sway, driving before it the spoken languages which have not yet been stabilized and stereotyped by literature. The present distribution of Indo-Āryan languages is on lines adumbrated in old Sanskrit texts. The *Śatapatha Brāhmaṇa* [iii, 2, 3, 15] locates the home of speech, i.e. Indo-Āryan, in the land of the Kuru-Pañchālas from which it spread in different directions. Later, Manu locates the home of Indo-Āryan culture in what he calls *Āryāvarta*, i.e. the region between the Himalayas and the Vindhyas from the Bay of Bengal to the Arabian Sea, with *Brahmarshideśa*, the land of the Kurus and Pañchālas, Matsyas and Śūrasenas, still leading in that culture and supplying its teachers [ii, 22]. So, in modern times, we find the central region of Midland languages represented by western Hindī, with an Inner Band of languages like Punjābī, Rājasthanī, and Gujaratī on the west, Pahārī on the north, and Eastern Hindī on the east, and an Outer Band comprising Kāshmīrī, Lahndā, Sindhī, and Kachchhī on the west, Marāthī on the south-west, and Bihārī, Bengali, Assamese, and Oriyā on the east. It is as if we are following the spread of Indo-Āryan culture from Brahmarshideśa corresponding to the Midland linguistic area along the course of Jumna–Ganges through Kosala to Videha and Vaṇga, embracing the areas of the Inner and Outer Bands of languages.

The linguistic relations between Brahmarshideśa and the earlier Āryan settlements in the land of the Seven Rivers must have been affected by the invasions of the Persians (Achæmenids) in the sixth century B.C. from Bactria as their base. The result of this contact between Irānians and Indo-Āryans was the rise of a group of mixed languages called *Piśacha* languages, still containing many archaic Vedic words, and spoken in the districts about the Kabul (*Kubhā*) and Swāt (*Suvāstu*) rivers referred to in the Rigveda. Beyond the Piśācha languages and the Outer Indo-Āryan

Band on the west are Irānian languages like *Pashto* and *Baloch.*[1]

India also presents the largest diversity in its religious aspect. Here are to be found all the world-religions. *Hinduism* alone is the religion of about 240 millions of people, of two-thirds of the people of India, of one-half of the total population of British India, and of one-eighth of that of the globe. A religion that suits so many millions must be very catholic and cosmopolitan in its principles. By the synthetic comprehensiveness and universality of its system; its undefined character, vagueness, and elasticity; by the protean form of its mythology, its ceremonies and its ordinances, it has become the common religion of peoples differing widely in race, language, and political and social traditions and interests. *Islam* counts as its followers nearly 78 millions of people distributed through the different provinces of India in different proportions to their total populations, forming majorities in the North-West Frontier Province, the Punjab, Sind, and Bengal, and minorities elsewhere. Then there are *Buddhists* numbering over 12 millions, *Christians* over 6 millions, *Sikhs* over 4 millions, *Jains* over 1 million, and a lac of *Parsis*. India also presents human evolution in all its states and stages from the lowest to the highest. She may be described as a museum of cults and creeds, customs and cultures, faiths and tongues, racial types and social systems, but it is a museum not of dead things and material objects, but of living communities and spiritual systems, each evolving along its own lines.

Unity.—The character of India as a single country is thus easily missed and lost in her continental extent and diversity. The whole is too large to be grasped as a unit and is realized only in parts. It is just like the blind men seeing the elephant in the old adage, each taking one of its limbs he could feel by his touch, for the whole animal. Or we are reminded of the story in one of the *Upanishads* of the quarrel for supremacy among the different members of man's bodily organism, not realizing the common life by

[1] See Chapter II of *Cambridge History of India*, vol. I, upon which I have freely drawn.

which each is sustained. It is difficult, indeed, to discover the One in the Many, the Individual in the Aggregate, the Simple in the Composite. Mere variety is, however, no proof against unity. It is, on the contrary, a sign of vitality, richness, and strength.

The geographical unity of India is, however, patent on the map showing how the country is sharply separated from the rest of the world by almost inviolable boundaries, very unlike the disputed frontiers artificially settled between most of the countries of continental Europe.

And yet the question remains : How far is this fundamental unity of India realized by her people or exemplified in her history ? Nature's gifts are of no consequence unless they are harnessed to the service of Man who must know how to explore, exploit, and take advantage of them.

The first condition of the progress of a people in political life and civilization is its possession of a fixed and definite piece of territory which it can call and serve as its own mother country. A people that has not found a home for itself but lives in unstable and unsettled conditions, in unrest and uncertainty, lacks the conditions in which culture and civilization can take their rise. The nomadic is one of the lowest stages of civilization. A great handicap to the political development of the Jews has been that they have not united to build up a fatherland for themselves. The country is to a nation what the body is to the individual. It is necessary for its self-expression. The growth of a nation, no doubt, depends upon several unities, such as those of language, religion, government, common history and tradition, manners, and customs. But all these are secondary factors which have their roots in a common life in a common country.

The early progress of the Indians in culture and civilization was owing to their first grasp of India as their common motherland. Accordingly, they applied to the whole of India the designation of *Bhāratavarsha*. The *Purāṇas* expressly define the term *Bhāratavarsha* as "the country that lies north of the ocean (i.e. the Indian Ocean) and south of the snowy mountains (Himalayas), marked by seven main chains of mountains, viz. Mahendra, Malaya, Sahya, Śuktimat, Ṛiksha (mountains of Gondwana), Vindhya, and Pāripātra (western Vindhyas up to the Aravallis); where dwell the descendants of the Bharatas, with the Kirātas (barbarians) living to its east, the Yavanas (Ionians or Greeks) to its west, and its own population consisting of the Brāhmaṇas, Kshatriyas, Vaiśyas, and Śudras (i.e. the Hindus)". [See Wilson's *Vishṇu Purāṇa*, ii, 127–9.] The modern name *India* for the country is not an indigenous appellation but a foreign import. India was known to foreigners in olden times by its river *Sindhu*, which the Persians pronounced as *Hindu* and the Greeks as *Indos*, dropping the hard aspirate. But the name *Bhāratavarsha* is not a mere geographical expression like the term *India*. It has a historical significance, indicating the country of the Bharatas, of Indo-Āryan culture of which the Bharatas were the chief bearers. Once their country was settled, the Indo-Āryans built it up with all their devotion. It engaged their deepest sentiments of love and service as expressed in their literature. One of the commonest prayers for a Hindu requires him to recall and worship the image of his mother country as the land of seven sacred rivers, the Gaṅgā, Yamunā, Godāvarī, Sarasvatī, Narmadā, Sindhu, and Kāverī, which between them cover its entire area. Another prayer calls up its image as the land of seven sacred cities, Ayodhyā, Mathurā, Māyā (modern Hardwar), Kāśī, Kāñchī (Conjeeviram), Avantikā (Ujjain), Dvarāvatī (Dwarka), representing the important regions of India. The spirit of these prayers is further sustained by the peculiar Hindu institution of pilgrimage. It expects the Hindu to visit in his life the holy places associated with his faith. Each of the principal Hindu faiths or sects has its own list of holy places, Vaishṇava, Śaiva, or Śākta, and these are distributed throughout the length and breadth of India and not confined to a single province. Thus the different sects are at one in enjoining upon their respective votaries a pilgrimage to the different and distant parts of India and thereby fostering in them a live sense of what constitutes their common mother country. In the same spirit, Śaṅkara established his four *Maṭhas* (religious schools) at the four extreme points of the country, viz. Jyotirmaṭha in the north (near Badri-Kedar on the Himalayas), Śāradāmaṭha at Dwarka in the west, Govardhana-maṭha at Puri in the east, and Śriṅgerī-maṭha in Mysore. Sectarianism is thus an aid to nationalism in Hindu culture. In some of the sacred texts like the *Bhāgavata Purāṇam*, or *Manu-Smṛiti* are even found passages of patriotic fervour describing Bhāratavarsha as the land fashioned by the gods themselves (*devanirmitaṁ sthānam*) who even wish to be born in it as heaven on earth, for the spiritual stimulus of its environment, and above these is the culminating utterance—" Mother and Mother-country are Greater than Heaven ! " (Jananī janmabhūmiścha svargādapi garīyasī).

All these prayers and passages show that the Hindu has elevated patriotism into a religion. In the words of a distinguished British critic,[1] " the Hindu regards India not only as a political unit naturally the subject of one sovereignty—whoever holds that sovereignty, whether British, Mohammedan, or Hindu—but as the outward embodiment, as the temple—nay, even as the goddess mother—of his spiritual culture. . . He made India the symbol of his culture ; he filled it with his soul. In his consciousness it was his greater self."

But besides religion, the political experiences of the ancient Hindus also aided them in their conception of the mother country. The unity of a country is easily grasped when it is controlled by a single political authority. The ancient Hindus were familiar with the ideal and institution of paramount sovereignty from very early times. It is indicated by such significant Vedic words as Ekarāṭ, Samrāṭ, Rājādhirāja, or Sārbabhauma, and such Vedic ceremonies as the Rājasūya, Vājapeya, or Aśvamedha, which were prescribed for performance by a king who by his *digvijaya* or conquests made himself the king of kings. Some of the Vedic works and later texts like the *Mahābhārata*

[1] The ex-Prime Minister, Mr. J. Ramsay MacDonald, in his Introduction to the writer's book, *The Fundamental Unity of India* [Longmans, London].

or the *Purāṇas* contain even lists of such great kings or emperors. And apart from these prehistoric emperors, there have been several such emperors in historical times, such as Chandragupta Maurya, Asoka, Samudragupta, Harsha, Mihira Bhoja, and, in later times, Akbar and Aurangzib. Some even performed the horse-sacrifice in declaration of their paramount sovereignty, such as Pushyamitra, Samudragupta, Kumāragupta I, Ādityasena and Pulakesin I. Thus the institution of paramount sovereignty has had a long history in India. Its conception was quite consistent with the ideals set in their sacred works for kings who were encouraged to cherish as quite legitimate and laudable the ambition, which became them as Kshatriyas, of extending the area of their authority up to the limits of their mother-country.

The unity of the country also manifests itself in the impress of a distinctive culture stamped upon it. That culture has been developed by its predominant people, the Hindus, numbering nearly 240 millions. The Persians had already defined India as the land of the Hindus, *Hindusthan*. Indeed, " India and Hinduism are organically related as body and soul " [J. Ramsay MacDonald already cited]. Hinduism has imparted to the whole of India a strong and stable cultural unity that has through the ages stood the shocks of political revolutions, being preserved in its own peculiar system of social self-government functioning apart from, and offering but few points of contact with, the State, indigenous or foreign. India is predominantly a land of villages, and these villages were recognized as self-governing republics, with a complete apparatus of local institutions for the conservation of indigenous culture, unaffected by political changes at the top or in the central government. What are the characteristic features of this indigenous Indian culture called Hinduism ? These are indicated in the indigenous definition of Hinduism as *Varṇāśrama-dharma*, the religion based upon the two-fold division of *Varṇas* (castes) and *Āśramas* (stages of life), the most distinguishing and unifying feature of Hinduism. In its origin, as seen in

Vedic literature, it rested on the division of society into four castes or self-contained social groups, the Brāhmaṇa, the Kshatriya, the Vaiśya, and the Śūdra. These in course of time became subdivided into any number of sub-castes. Now the Hindus all over India are divided into hundreds of castes and sub-castes. The principle of the caste-system, which is an outstanding peculiarity of India, is much misunderstood. It chiefly concerns one's private, domestic, and religious life, and not public life. It only interdicts marriage between different castes (mainly on grounds of eugenics) and interdining, especially eating from the same plate or eating the food that has been contaminated by unclean touch. Eating is recommended as the individual's private act, an act of prayer to God " the Giver of our daily bread." But the division into castes is only a part of the Hindu system. The other part is the division of the individual's life into well-defined stages or *Āśramas* through which it should pass in its normal course. These *Āśramas* are those of (1) the *Brahmachārī* or the student, (2) the *Gṛihastha* or the householder, (3) the *Vānaprastha* or the hermit, and (4) the *Sannyāsī* or the ascetic absorbed in contemplation. The third stage of life should begin at fifty, when a householder should retire from the world and family life and devote himself to wider and higher interests of life and to the service of others. The last stage of life is meant as preparation for its end through the severing of all possible earthly ties. As has been already pointed out, Hinduism in its external social aspect is thus made up of two limbs, the caste-system and the *āśrama*-system. Unfortunately, more emphasis has come to be laid on the caste than on the *āśrama*. Caste divides, and that on the basis of birth. But the *āśrama* system unites, binding all castes in its common rules to lead life along a regulated course of development by natural stages.

The vehicle of this Hindu culture is *Sanskrit*. The unifying influence of Sanskrit can hardly be overstated. This has been well pointed out by Monier Williams [*Hinduism*, p. 13] : " India, though it has more than five hundred spoken dialects, has only one sacred language, and only one sacred literature, accepted and revered by all adherents of Hinduism alike, however diverse in race, dialect, rank, and creed. That language is Sanskrit and that literature is Sanskrit literature—the only repository of the Veda or 'knowledge' in its widest sense; the only vehicle of Hindu theology, philosophy, law, and mythology; the only mirror in which all the creeds, opinions, customs, and usages of the Hindus are faithfully reflected; and (if we may be allowed a fourth metaphor) the only quarry whence the requisite materials may be obtained for improving the vernaculars or for expressing important religious and scientific ideas."

This distinctive Indian culture in course of time so far unified the country that the country and the culture came to be identified and became synonymous terms. The country was the culture and the culture the country, the kingdom of the spirit, transcending territorial limits. Since its introduction to India at the time of the Rigveda, this Indo-Āryan culture had accordingly spread through the ages in ever-widening circles and regions known successively as *Sapta-Sindhu*, *Brahmarshideśa*, *Brahmāvarta*, *Madhyadeśa*, *Āryāvarta*, *Jambudvīpa*, or *Bhāratavarsha*, till in its abounding vitality it ultimately travelled beyond the limits of India to other lands and built up a Greater India beyond her frontiers across the seas. Indian thought and institutions are to this day traced in literature, monuments, folk-lore, tradition, manners and customs still extant in countries like Siam and Cambodia on the mainland, and in the islands of Java, Sumatra, Bali, and Borneo, as a result of the work of Indian colonists. Some of these countries have even received their religion from India: Tibet, Nepal, China, following *Mahāyāna* Buddhism, and Burma, Ceylon, Siam, and Cambodia adopting *Hīnāyāna* Buddhism. Colonization springs from an active and aggressive nationalism fed by the consciousness of a common mother country and of its distinctive culture.

Effects on History.—In spite of this fundamental unity of India, the vastness of its size, and the variety of its physical features and social conditions, had their own natural consequences to its history and political development. It has been always difficult to organize the whole of India as a unit and have it governed from one centre under a common sovereign or political authority. The result has been that what may be strictly called Indian History as an organic whole or a unified development like English History or the history of France has been rarely achieved. More often the history of India has resolved itself into a number of subsidiary, subordinate, and unconnected histories, without continuing as a common history for the whole of India. Instead of developing from one centre under a common direction, it has developed very often from different, and even mutually independent centres, losing its unity in the variety of separate and local histories of different peoples and regions, evolving along their own independent lines and offering but few points of contact or agreement and more of conflict between them. Thus the political history of India has to be often traced and studied in parts and fragments, in interruptions and isolated restorations, and in many missing links. It has been shaped through the ages by so many different peoples and governments such as Maurya, Kushan, Andhra, Gupta, or Gurjara, for the north, and Pallava, Chālukya, or Chola in the south, or Moslem, Maratha, Sikh, and British in later times, functioning from different and changing centres like Pāṭaliputra, Purushapura, Paithan, Nasik, Ujjain, Kanauj, Bādāmi, Kanchi, Kalyānī, and Tanjore; or Delhi, Poona, Lahore, and Calcutta, the headquarters of different political authorities in different epochs of Indian History. It was only once in Hindu India that the whole of India had a common history under the control of a common government, the Maurya empire under Asoka who made his authority felt all over the country, and even Afghanistan and Baluchistan as parts of an extended India, of which he became the paramount sovereign.

It must, however, be noted that apart from its size, the conditions of ancient times, the difficulties of communication in the pre-mechanical ages, which have now yielded to the power derived from coal, electricity, or oil, did not permit the establishment of a large empire or a centralized administration. A government to be effective, to get its authority habitually obeyed in the different and distant parts of a large area, had to be very much decentralized, giving full scope to local self-government. Thus there was inevitably more of local life and history throwing into background the general life and history of India. Indian history thus becomes a mere collection of local and disconnected histories and but seldom the record of one common political development affecting India as a whole.

The effects of this physical immensity of India have left indelible marks on its history and are still to be seen in spite of modern facilities of communication abridging so much both space and time. The whole of India still lacks a common government. A large part of it, almost a third, is divided up into a number of what are known as the Indian States, the relics of a political system marked by the growth of local history at the expense of a unified one for the whole country. At present the number of these separate States exceeds six hundred. As regards British India, it is no doubt under a common government, a unitary State, but the needs of efficient and effective government of an extensive territory marked by a wide variety of social conditions have called for a number of local administrations or Provinces which equal some of the countries of Europe in size. The whole of India, the Greater India of two parts, British and Indian, remains to be unified in a comprehensive federation which should mark the next stage in her political evolution.

It is, however, to be noted that behind this diversity of local history, there has always been in the background a kind of an all-Indian history which is from the nature of the case not political, but cultural in its character, the history of thought which transcends local limits and administrative boundaries. The whole of India bears the impress of certain common movements of thought and life, resulting in the development of certain common ideals and institutions which distinguish the civilization of India from all other civilizations of the world, and marks it out "as a unit in the history of the social, religious, and intellectual development of mankind" [V. A. Smith's *Early History of India*, 4th ed., p. 5].

Chapter IV

THE ARYANS IN INDIA: RIGVEDIC CIVILIZATION

Rigveda on Aryan Origins.—The history of India is generally taken to be the history of the Aryans in India. It thus begins with the advent of the Aryans to India. Its earliest source is the work known as the *Rigveda-Saṁhitā*, which is the earliest work not only of the Indo-Aryans, but of the entire Aryan race. The work thus throws light not merely on the beginnings of Aryan history in India, but on Aryan history elsewhere, on prehistoric phases of language (such as inflexion, accent, and metre), of religion, and of civilization in general.

Common Aryan Language and Home.—Linguists have found that the language of the Rigveda shows its affinity in forms of grammar and roots of verbs to Persian, Greek, Latin, Teutonic, Celtic, and Slavonic, as if they are descendants of a common ancestor. They have in common words expressive of primary relationship or experience in life such as those for father, mother, son, daughter, God, heart and tears, axe and tree, dog and cow; e.g. Sanskrit ***mātar***, Latin ***mater***, English ***mother***; Sanskrit ***Sūnu***, Lithuanian ***Sūnū***, old High German ***Sunu***, English ***son***.

This linguistic evidence is evidence of some important primitive history. The languages thus related point to their common origin from a common language spoken in a common home by the ancestors of their present speakers. The speakers of these languages became separate peoples migrating from their original common home, but their ancestors were one Aryan people whom we may call the *Wiros* after the word *Wiros* for men occurring in the majority of the languages in question.

The question is, Where was this original Aryan home, the country of the Wiros? It can only be inferred from certain data found in these Indo-European or Indo-Germanic languages. Firstly, the Wiros did not live in an island or even near the *sea*, for which they had no word. Secondly, they lived in a temperate climate, knowing the oak, the beech, the willow, and some coniferous trees. Thirdly, they were a settled people, growing corn with the care of months, domesticating animals like the ox and cow, sheep and horse, dog and pig, but not the ass, or camel, or elephant. The horse and the cow, again, point to diverse conditions. The horse is a native of the open plain with its foal following the mother in her wanderings. But the cow must keep close to its calf in its grazings. Thus the original Aryan home must have combined pastoral and agricultural conditions, horse-breeding steppes and high ground for pasturing of sheep.

According to Dr. P. Giles [*Cambridge History of India* vol. I, chap. iii], these data for flora and fauna should rule out the following places suggested for the common Aryan home: (1) India, (2) the Pāmirs, a notoriously inhospitable region for early settlement, (3) the northern plains of Europe which in early times were too densely forested, (4) the southern steppes of Russia, or (5) the Arctic regions. He would suggest for it the region in Europe now comprising Hungary, Austria, and Bohemia.

Aryan Migrations.—The Aryans who migrated from this original home towards the east (with whom Indian history is concerned) in search of fresh woods and pastures new must have followed the easy route along the Danube to Wallachia and farther south towards the Bosphorus and the Dardanelles. Crossing these and the Plateau of Asia Minor, they must have struck the upper waters of the Euphrates and Tigris, avoiding the region between them as the then seat of a powerful civilization, before they reached Persia by the route between Tabriz and Tehran, or proceeded farther towards Mashad, Herat, and Bactria.

Similarity between Rigveda and Avesta.—In this region lived these Aryans who were the ancestors of the Indians and Irānians. Accordingly, their respective religious books, the Rigveda and the Avesta, show closer affinity in language and thought than with Greek, Latin, or other Indo-Germanic works. " Not only single words and phrases but even whole stanzas may be transliterated from the dialect of India into the dialects of Irān without change of vocabulary or construction " [ibid., p. 74]. This may be illustrated by the following examples :—

1. Stanza

Avestan.	*Vedic Equivalent.*
Tat thwā	Tat tvā
perśa ers	pṛichchhā
moi vochā	ṛiju ma
Ahurā	vach Asura
Tā Chīt	Tā Chit
Mazdā	medhishṭha
vaśmī	Vashmi
anyāchā	anyāchā
vīdye	vide

2. Gods

Avestan.	*Vedic.*
Indra	Indra
Vāyu	Vāyu
Mithra	Mitra
Nāonhaithya	Nāsatya
Verethraghna	Vṛitraghna

It will thus be seen that the ancestors of the Hindus and the Persians had lived longer together than their other Aryan kinsmen who had migrated towards the west. They were probably the last to leave the original Aryan home because their language carried off the largest share of the common Aryan inheritance as traced in roots, grammar, words, myths, and legends.

Age of Rigveda : *Foreign and Indian evidence.*— The question now is, What was the probable age of these momentous migrations ? An unexpected light comes from a source outside India. Some inscriptions of about 1400 B.C. discovered at Boghaz-Koi in Asia Minor recording contracts concluded between the king of the *Hittites* and the king of *Mitani* mention some gods as protectors of these contracts, whose names are thus given :—

" ilāni Mi-it-ra aś-śi-il (ilāni) U-ru-w-na-aś-śi-il (ilu) In-dar (ilāni) Na-śa-a (t-ti-ia-a) n-na . . ." The names are considered to correspond to the names of the Rigvedic gods, Mitra, Varuṇa, Indra, and the two Nāsatyas. As these gods are also known to *Avesta*, some scholars think they were the common gods of the undivided Aryan people prior to their separation as Indians and Irānians. But the spelling of the names in the Mesopotamian inscription points clearly to their Rigvedic origin. In that case, we must assume that the Rigveda and its culture must have established themselves in India much earlier than 1400 B.C. to have been able to influence the culture of Asia Minor at that time.

Of the same time as the Boghaz-Koi inscriptions are the famous letters from Tel el-Amarna in which some Mitāni princes are mentioned with names of Sanskrit form, such as Ārtatama, Tusratta, and Suttarna. Some of the princes of the Kassites, too, who ruled over Babylonia between *c.* 1746–1180 B.C., also bear Sanskritic names like *Shurias* (*Sūrya*), *Marytas* (Vedic *Marutas*), etc. In the library of Assurbanipal of about 700 B.C. was found a list of deities worshipped in Assyria, which includes the name Assara-Mazas equivalent to Avestan chief god, *Ahura-Mazda*, though the form *Assara* is nearer Sanskrit *Asura* than Avestan *Ahura*.

The same antiquity of the Aryan migration to India and of the Rigveda is pointed to by Indian literary evidence. If Buddhism rose in India in *c.* 600 B.C., the Brahminical literature and culture it presupposes must be of earlier age. We have to allow for adequate time for the growth of such different types of Brahminical literature as the Sūtras, the Āraṇyakas, the Upanishads, the Brāhmaṇas, the four Vedic Saṁhitās preceded by the original material which was later edited in the Rigveda Saṁhitā. On a modest computation, we should come to 2500 B.C. as the time of the Rigveda.

The Rigveda *reveals an advanced Civilization.*—The Rigveda itself, however, does not contain a single allusion to these migrations. It points to a settled people, an organized society, and a full-grown civilization. According to the orthodox Hindu view, the Rigveda shows not the early streak or dawn of Indian culture but rather its zenith. It is like Minerva born in panoply. The Rigveda is the root of the entire tree of Hindu Thought with its ramifications into so many sects, schools of philosophy, and systems of worship. It is still the only acknowledged source of prayers like the Gāyatrī *mantram* which is uttered verbatim to this day by millions of Hindus believing in the mystical potency of every accent, syllable, and word it contains, and forbidding its replacement by any other human composition.

Rigvedic India: *Its rivers, scenery, and peoples.*—We see in the Ṛigveda the Āryans already in possession of a wide extent of territory in which they worked out their destiny and culture. The limits of Rigvedic India are indicated by certain geographical details found in the Rigveda. On the west are mentioned the rivers Kubhā (Kabul), Krumu (Kurrum), Gomatī (Gomal), Suvāstu (Swāt), pointing to the Indian occupation of Afghanistan in those days. Next are mentioned the five rivers of the Panjab—Sindhu (Indus), Vitastā (Jheelum), Asiknī (Chenab), Parushṇī (Irāvatī or Rāvi), Vipāś (Beas), as also Śutudri (Satlej) and Sarasvatī (Sarsūti). The Yamunā and the Gaṅgā are also mentioned. A part of the Rigveda, the hymns to Ushas, recalls the splendours of dawn in the Panjab, but a larger part refers to the strife of the elements, thunder and lightning, rain bursting from the clouds, and mountains, which are not seen in the Panjab, but in the region called Brahmāvarta watered by the Sarasvatī, the Dṛishadvatī and the Āpayā, where the bulk of the Rigveda must have been composed.

The whole of this territory was divided up among a number of Vedic peoples, the more important of which are named as the Gandhāris (noted for their woollen industry), the Mūjavants (on the south bank of the Kubhā), the Anus, Druhyus, and Turvaśas (along the course of the Parushṇī), the Pūrus and the Bharatas of Madhyadeśa.

Its political evolution: *Battle of Ten Kings.*—The process of political unification of Rigvedic India was already in full swing. The Rigveda tells of the Battle of Ten Kings, *Dāśa-rājña* [vii, 33, 2, 5; 83, 8], against Sudās, King of the

Bharatas, which was a contest for supremacy between the peoples of the earlier settlements of the north-west and of the later ones of Brahmāvarta. It appears that the whole of Rigvedic India including the non-Aryan peoples was involved in this great Vedic war. There were five peoples to the west of the Indus, the Alinas (of modern Kafiristan), the Pakthas (recalling Afghan Pakhthun), the Bhalānases (probably of the Bolan Pass), the Śivas (from the Indus) and the Vishāṇins. There were also the five peoples of the interior, viz. the Anus, the Druhyus, the Turvaśas, the Yadus, and the Pūrus. The coalition also comprised three eastern peoples on the Yamunā who are believed to have been non-Aryans, viz. the Ajas, Śigrus, and Yakshus, led by their leader Bheda. Another non-Aryan king in the coalition was Śimyu. Other Aryan kings mentioned were Kavasha, Śambara, and two Vaikarṇas who themselves brought into the coalition their following of twenty-one peoples. The Ṛishis as Purohitas or royal preceptors figure as leaders in this war. Viśvāmitra was leading the coalition against Sudās who was following Vasishṭha. The Anus were led by the Bhṛigus. The victory of Sudās established his overlordship in Rigvedic India.

Among other Rigvedic peoples of importance, along with the Bharatas, may be mentioned the Pūrus who with the Bharatas became later merged in the Kurus, the Krivis allied to them, and the Sṛiñjayas.

This struggle for supremacy among the different Aryan peoples was a part of the evolutionary process tending towards the formation of larger political aggregates and the unification of Rigvedic India under a paramount sovereign or overlord. A no less important part of that process was the achievement of Aryan supremacy over the aboriginal peoples, the non-Aryans. Glimpses of this fundamental conflict between the Aryan and the non-Aryan are amply given in the Rigveda. The causes of the conflict were both cultural and political.

The non-Aryan in Rigveda.—The Rigveda calls the non-Aryan as Dāsa, Dasyu, or Asura. Individual non-Aryan chiefs are named, such as Ilibisa, Dhuni, Chumuri, Pipru,

Varchin, and Śambara, and non-Aryan peoples, the Śimyus, Kīkaṭas, Ajas, Yakshus, and Śigrus already referred to. In Rigveda, i, 133, 4, there is a reference to ruddy Piśāchas and Rākshasas uttering fearful yells in battle.

The distinction between the Aryan and the non-Aryan is also defined. It is both physical and cultural. The non-Aryan is dark-skinned as well as noseless (*anāsa*) or snub-nosed (like the Dravidian). He is (1) of hostile speech (*mṛidhravāk*), i.e. speaking a language radically different from Vedic Sanskrit; (2) devoid of Vedic rituals (*akarman*); (3) not worshipping the Vedic gods (*adevayu*); (4) devoid of devotion (*abrahman*); (5) non-sacrificing (*ayajvan*); (6) lawless (*avrata*); (7) follower of strange ordinances (*anyavrata*); (8) a reviler of Vedic gods (*devapīyu*); and (9) a phallus-worshipper (*Śiśnadevaḥ*) [1] [vii, 21, 5; x, 99, 3].

The Aryans drove the non-Aryans to forests and mountain fastnesses or made them slaves. The *dāsī* or female slave

[1] Some of these epithets are also applied to Āryans. In *Rv.*, vii, 83, 7, all the ten kings and their allies who were the enemies of Sudās are branded "non-sacrificers" (*ayajyavaḥ*) and in vii, 18, 16, as *anindra*, "not worshipping Indra." In another passage, vii, 104, 14–15, Ṛishi Vasishṭha himself is condemned as "worshipping false gods" (*anṛitadevaḥ*). From these data and the other fact that the coalition against Sudās included non-Aryan chiefs and peoples, Rai Bahadur R. P. Chanda concludes that Rigvedic history is concerned more with the civil wars among the Aryans or Indra-worshipping kings and clans than with the supposed wars between the Aryans and non-Aryans and that the age of the Rigveda was not one of migrations and conflict with the aborigines but an age when the *Ārya* and the *Dāsa* had already been reconciled to each other as citizens of a common mother country. His further conclusions, which are controversial, are: (1) That the religion of the Ṛishis, worshippers of Indra, Varuṇa, Agni, and other gods, was accepted by the kings and the people of the Indus Valley whose culture and civilization were then in decline. (2) That the Vedic Kshatriya clans like the Bharatas, Pūrus, Yadus, Turvaśas, Anus, Druhyus, and the like were the representatives of the indigenous chalcolithic population. (3) That there was a fundamental cultural difference between the Ṛishi or the Brāhman, and the Kshatriya or other castes favouring human sacrifice, *anumaraṇa* (custom of the *Satī*), and other customs, contrary to Brahman usage. (4) That the diversity of castes was thus due to that of cultures. (5) That the contact between Vedism and the indigenous religion of the Indus Valley modified both (*a*) by making the cult of *yoga* acceptable to Vedism, which formerly believed only in sacrifice, and (*b*) by the retention of non-Vedic elements in popular religion. As to the cult of *yoga*, its indigenous origin is seen in certain stone statuettes discovered at Mohenjo-daro showing ascetics with eyes half-shut in contemplation and fixed on the tip of the nose. These, according to Mr. Chanda, supply the missing links between the prehistoric Indus Valley civilization and the later civilization of India, Buddhist, Jain, or Brahmanical. [*Memoir No.* 41 *of Arch. Survey.*]

is frequently referred to in Vedic literature. In the Rigveda, in its famous Purushasūkta describing the creation of the four castes out of the universal body of the Lord (*Virāṭ-purusha*), the fourth caste is formed by the Śūdra, including the slaves. There was also inevitably at work a process of fusion between the Aryan and the non-Aryan by inter-marriage or by alliance. Instances of such alliance were seen in the Battle of Ten Kings already described. Thus the Aryan had to face a three-fold mission in India, to conquer, to colonize, and to civilize. He had to subdue or to assimilate the aboriginal element.

But the overthrow of the black skin was by no means an easy task for the Aryan. The non-Aryan of the Rigveda was fully fortified in the strongholds of his own civilization which was materially quite advanced. The Rigveda tells of his towns and forts (*pura* and *durga* [i, 41, 3]) made of iron (*āyasī* in ii, 58, 8) or stone (*aśmamayī* in iv, 30, 20); of forts "broad" (*pṛithvī*) and "wide" (*urvī* in i, 189, 2) and "full of kine" (*gomatī* in *Av.*, viii, 6, 23); to forts of hundred pillars (*śatabhuji* in *Rv.*, i, 166, 8; vii, 15, 14); and to autumnal (*śāradī*) forts as refuge against inundations.

Remnants of this civilization are traced in the ruins of cities unearthed at Harappa and Mohenjo-daro already described. The principal non-Aryan opponents of the Aryans in the Rigveda are the *Paṇis*, a merchant-people according to Yāska (*Nirukta*, vi, 27), who must have been the builders of this commercial civilization of the Indus Valley, of which many of the antiquities unearthed are coins and articles of conch-shell derived from sea-trade. Thus the Aryans had to contend against an advanced civilization in the Indus Valley [1] with its many cities which they had to reduce. Accordingly, their god, Indra, was called *Purandara*, "sacker of cities." [2] [*Rv.*, i, 103, 3].

[1] That the Rigveda knew of a civilization existing in the region south of the Panjab is perhaps indicated by a solitary passage, vi, 20, 12 (repeated in i, 174, 9), in which it is stated that Indra safely brought Turvaśa and Yadu over the *samudra* or sea. This shows that while most of the Rigvedic peoples hailed from the north-west, the Yadus and Turvaśas were immigrants from the south and considered worthy of admission to the society of the Āryas. [Rai Bahadur R. P. Chanda in *Memoir No. 31 of Arch. Survey of India.*]

[2] Ibid.

A few select passages of the *Rigveda* will throw light on this Aryan–non-Aryan conflict. In i, 174, 7–8, the earth is described as the burial-ground of the *Dāsas*; ii, 20, 6–7 describes Indra storming towns and destroying the troops of the black *Dāsas*; iv, 16, 13, refers to the slaughter of 50,000 black-complexioned enemies on the battle-field, and iv, 30, 21, to the slaughter of 30,000 *Dāsas*; i, 53, 8, refers to the blockade of 100 cities of the non-Aryan Vaṅgṛida by Rijiśvan in his fight against the "dusky brood" (*kṛishṇagarbhāḥ*). Many passages refer to the destruction of the forts of the Dāsa Highlander, Śambara, of which the number is given as 90 [i, 130, 7], 99 [ii, 19, 6], and 100 [ii, 14, 6]. The Aryan prayer to Indra in x, 22, 8, sums up the situation thus: "We are surrounded on all sides by Dasyu tribes. They do not perform sacrifices; they do not believe in anything; their rites are different; they are not men! O destroyer of foes! Kill them. Destroy the Dāsa race!"

Society: *Marriage and Family.*—Rigvedic society was well organized. Its unit was the family which was patriarchal. It was primarily monogamic, while polyandry was unknown. The husband was the master of the household with his wife as its mistress. Sexual morality was very high. Incest, or marriage between father and daughter or between brother and sister, was not permitted.[1] Child marriage was also unknown, though usual in later times [x, 85, 21–2]. Freedom of choice in marriage was given [x, 27, 12]. Girls lived under the protection of their parents, and after their death, of their brothers [ii, 17, 7, and iv, 5, 5].

Dowry at marriage was usual [i, 109, 2]. The Rigvedic Marriage Hymn, x, 85, shows that the bride after marriage was conveyed from the house of her father to that of her husband and that in her new home she had an honoured place as mistress with authority over her aged father-in-law, mother-in-law, her husband's brothers and sisters. It also shows that Vedic marriage was indissoluble by human

[1] *Rv.*, x, 10, 10, refers to "*past* ages (*uttarā yugāni*) when sister *did* (*Kṛiṇavan* = *akṛiṇavan*) what is unbecoming (*ajāmi*) to them", i.e., married their brothers.

action and that the remarriage of a widow was not contemplated, though there is a reference [x, 40, 2] to the widow married to the brother of her husband who died without issue. The wife was the husband's partner at religious ceremonies [viii, 31].

Inheritance.—The father's property was inherited by his son and not by his daughter, unless she was the only issue [iii, 31]. The right of adoption was recognized [vii, 4, 7–8].

Property.—The right of property was known. It was allowed in movable things like cattle, horses, gold, ornaments, and slaves. It was also allowed in land which was divided into different fields carefully measured off, called *kshetra*, with strips of land between them held in common and called *khilyas* [x, 33, 6; i, 110, 5; vi, 28, 2; x, 142, 3].

Economic Life: *Pasture and Agriculture.*—Economic life centred round the cattle. Bulls and oxen served for ploughing and drawing carts. Horses were used to draw the chariot and also for races. Other animals domesticated were sheep, goats, asses, and dogs used for hunting, for guarding and tracking cattle, and for keeping watch at night [iv, 15, 6; viii, 22, 2; vii, 55, 3].

The cattle grazed on pastures called *Goshṭha* [i, 191, 4] under the herdsman, Gopāla, armed with a goad [x, 60, 3], who had to see that they did not fall into pits, or break limbs, or were not lost or stolen. There were forays for cattle, *Gavishṭi* [i, 91, 23]. The ears of cattle were marked for ownership [vi, 28, 3].

The Rigveda attached great importance to agriculture (*Kṛishi*) which in the Pañchaviṁśa Brāhmaṇa [xvii, 1] distinguishes the Ārya from the *Vrātya*, i.e. a Hindu outside the pale of Brahminism.

The plough land was called *urvarā* or *kshetra*. The plough was drawn by oxen in teams of six, eight or even twelve [*Rv.*, viii, 6, 48; x, 101, 4]. The ripe grain was cut with a sickle (*dātra, sriṇi*), collected in bundles (*parsha*) [viii, 78, 10; x, 101, 3; 131, 2] and beaten out on the floor of the granary (*khala*) [x, 48, 7]. The grain was then separated from the chaff by a sieve (*titau*) or a winnowing fan (*śūrpa*) [x, 71, 2]. The winnower was called *Dhānya-Kṛit* [x, 94, 13] and the grain was measured in a vessel called *Urdara* [ii, 14, 11].

There was also use of manure called *Śakan* or *Karīsha*. The agricultural operations are neatly summed up as "ploughing, sowing, reaping, and threshing" (*kṛishantaḥ, vapantaḥ, lunantaḥ*, and *mṛiṇantaḥ*) in *Śatapatha Brāhmaṇa* [i, 6, 1, 3].

Irrigation.—There is mention of wells for men and wells for cattle [x, 101, 7]. Water was drawn out of a well in buckets (*kośa*) tied to leather strings (*varatrā*) pulled round a stone-pulley, *aśmachakra* [Ib., 5–6]. The water thus raised was led off into broad channels (*sūrmī sushirā*) for irrigation [viii, 69, 12]. The water for irrigation also came from lakes (*hrada*) and canals (*kulyā*) [iii, 45, 3 ; x, 99, 4].

Pests.—Agricultural pests such as insects, birds, and locusts are mentioned [x, 68, 1]. Excess of rain or drought is mentioned as damaging the crops [cf. *Atharvaveda*, vi, 50, 142].

Grain.—The grain grown is called *yava* and *dhānya* [i, 117, 21 ; vi, 13, 4]. The later Vedic work, *Bṛihadāraṇyaka Upanishad* [vi, 3, 22], mentions ten cultivated (grāmyāṇi) kinds of grain : rice and barley (*vṛīhi-yavāḥ*), sesamum and beans (*tila-māshāḥ*), maize (*godhūmāḥ*), lentils (*masūraḥ*), and the like.

Wealth.—Wealth was counted in cattle [v, 4, 11], in horses [vi, 41, 5], in heroes (*vīra*) or "good sons" [ii, 11, 13].

Hunting.—Besides pastoral pursuits and agriculture, the Rigvedic Indians indulged in hunting for livelihood, sport, and protection of flock from wild beasts. The means employed included the arrow [ii, 42, 2], nets called *pāśa* [iii, 45, 1], *Nidhā* [ix, 83, 4], *Jāla* [*Av.*, x, 1, 30], or *Mukshijā* [i, 125, 2] used by the fowler called *Nidhā-pati* [ix, 83, 4]. Antelopes (*ṛiśya*) were caught in pits called *ṛiśya-dā* [x, 39, 8]. The boar was chased with dogs [x, 86, 4], and the buffalo (*Gaura*) by a lasso [x, 51, 6]. The lion was captured in pitfalls [x, 28, 10] or caught by ambuscade and led into a hidden pit [v, 74, 4] or surrounded and slain by hunters [v, 15, 3]. Wild elephants were captured by tame ones [viii, 2, 6].

Handicrafts.—The carpenter, *takshan* [ix, 112, 1], was

foremost, making the chariot, *ratha*, for war or sport, as also the draft wagon, *anas* [iii, 33, 9], which had sometimes a covering, *chhadis* [x, 85, 10]. He worked with the axe, *paraśu*, as his tool [i, 105, 18], and also produced fine carved work [x, 86, 5]. Next came the worker in metal, *karmāra* [x, 72, 2], who smelted the ore in fire (*dhmātṛi* in v, 9, 5), using bellows of birds' feathers [ix, 112, 2], and made vessels of metal (*gharma ayasmaya* in v, 30, 15) and also of hammered metal (*ayo-hata* in ix, 1, 2). The goldsmith, *hiraṇyakāra*, made ornaments of gold, *hiraṇya* [i, 122, 2]. The gold was derived from the bed of the river like the Indus, a "golden stream" [vi, 61, 7], and also from the earth [i, 117, 5]. The leatherer made articles of leather like bowstring, slings, thongs to fasten part of the chariot, reins, lash of the whip, or bags. The art of tanning leather was also known [*Vedic Index*, i, 234, 257]. There was also the weaver called *Vāya* [*Rv.*, x, 26, 6] working with his loom called *veman*. The shuttle used for weaving was called *tasara*. The warp was called *otu* and the woof *tantu* [vi, 9, 2]. Weaving was generally left to women [i, 92, 3]. We may note an interesting passage [ix, 122] referring to the father of a Ṛishi being a physician (*bhishaj*) and his mother a grinder of corn (*upala-prakshiṇī*).

Trade and Money.—The trader, *Vaṇik*, was known to the Rigveda [i, 122, 11]. Barter was in vogue: ten cows are quoted as price for an image of Indra [iv, 24, 10]. The haggling of the market was known as well as the obligation of a contract: "One sells a large quantity for a small price and then goes to the purchaser and denies the sale and asks for a higher price. But he cannot exceed the price once fixed on the plea that he has given a large quantity. Whether the price was adequate or inadequate, the price fixed at the time of sale must hold good" [iv, 24, 9]. The conception of money may be traced in the mention of a gift of 100 *nishkas* and 100 steeds [i, 126, 2]. Indebtedness was known [ii, 27, 4]. It was chiefly due to dicing [x, 34, 10]. There is mention of an eighth and a sixteenth being paid either as interest or part of the principal [viii, 47, 17].

Sea-borne trade was known. *Samudra* is unmistakably used in the sense of ocean in *Rv.*, vii, 95, 2. There are references to the treasures of the ocean [i, 47, 6; vii, 6, 7; ix, 97, 44], perhaps pearls or the gains of trade [i, 48, 3; 56, 2; iv, 55, 6] and the story of Bhujyu, being shipwrecked on the main "where there is no support, no rest for foot or hand", and rescued in a hundred-oared galley, points to marine navigation [i, 116, 3].

Dress.—The dress of the people (*vāsas* in i, 34, 1; also called *vasana* [i, 95, 7] and *vastra* [i, 26, 17]) consisted of the under-garment (*nīvi*), a garment, and an over-garment called *adhīvāsa* [i, 140, 9]. It was generally woven of sheeps' wool, called *ūrṇā* [iv, 22, 2], for which the Parushṇī country was famous (ib.), as Gandhāra was for its sheep [i, 126, 7]. There are also references to embroidered garments called *peśas* [ii, 3, 6] made by the female embroiderer (*peśas-kārī*), and also to mantles adorned with gold (*hiraṇyayān atkān* in v, 55, 6). Ascetics wore skins called *ajina* [i, 166, 10] or *mala* [x, 136, 2].

Ornaments.—Ornaments of gold were used by both sexes, such as ear-rings, *karṇa-śobhana* [viii, 78, 3], necklaces (*nishka-grīva* in ii, 33, 10), bracelets and anklets, *khādi* [i, 166, 9, and v, 54, 11], and garlands (*rukma-vaksha*). Jewels were also worn (*maṇigrīva*, "with bejewelled neck," in i, 122, 14).

The hair was combed and oiled. Women wore it plaited. Sometimes men wore it in coils. The Vasishṭhas had it coiled on the right [i, 173, 6; vii, 33, 1]. There is mention of a maiden wearing her hair in four plaits (*chatush-kapardā*, in x, 114, 3). Beard was worn (*śmaśru* in ii, 11, 17) but shaving was also practised. There is mention of razors (*kshura*) sharpened on stone [viii, 4, 16]. The barber was called a *vaptā* [x, 142, 4].

Food and Drink.—Milk was the most important food [*kshīra* in i, 109, 3], together with its products, butter [*ghṛita*, i, 134, 6] and curd [*dadhi*, viii, 2, 9]. There is also mention of "mess of grain cooked with milk" (*kshīra-pākam-odanam*) and of a kind of cheese [vi, 48, 18]. Cake of rice or barley was eaten mixed with ghee [x, 45, 9].

Porridge was also made of grain (*yava*) which was unhusked, parched, and then kneaded [i, 187, 16]. As regards meat, it was generally that of the animals which were sacrificed, viz. sheep and goats. The cow was already deemed *aghnyā*, "not to be killed" [viii, 101, 15-16]. Spirituous liquor, *surā*, was condemned [vii, 86, 6]. It gave rise to broils in the *sabhā* or assembly [viii, 2, 12]. There was also the *soma* drink as a religious offering extolled in the entire ninth *maṇḍala* of the Rigveda and in six other hymns. The plant grew on the mountains like the Mūjavants [i, 93, 6], or in the country of the Kīkaṭas [iii, 53, 4]. It was treated to an elaborate process, the details of which it is difficult to follow. It was placed on a skin, *tvak* [ix, 65, 25], and on a *vedi* or *dhishaṇā* [i, 109, 3], platform, and then pressed with stones, or with pestle (*manthā*) in a mortar (*ulūkhala*) [i, 28] to yield its juice which was received in a *chamū* [ix, 99, 8], the cup for the gods, or in *kalaśa* and *chamasa*, the cups for the priests. Sometimes it was steeped in water (*āpyāyana*) to yield more juice [ix, 74, 9]. The plant has been sought to be identified as the Afghan grape or the sugar-cane or a species of hop, but not with certainty. Its exhilarating and exciting effects are alluded to [viii, 18].

Amusements.—These included chariot-racing, horse-racing, dicing, dancing, and music. The race was called *āji* [v, 37, 7], the race-course, *kāshṭhā* [viii, 80, 8] or *saptya* [viii, 41, 4], and was broad, *urvī*, and of measured distance [viii, 80, 8]. *Viśpalā* was the name of a swift steed or racer [i, 116, 5]. Dicing, *aksha* [i, 41, 9], was played with stakes, *vij* [i, 92, 10], and led to ruin and slavery for paying the debts incurred [x, 34, 2]. The gambling son was chastised by his father [ii, 29, 5]. Dancing was indulged in by both sexes to the accompaniment of music from cymbal (*āghāṭi*) [x, 146, 2], and the three types of musical instrument, operated by percussion, string, and wind, were already known, viz. the drum, *dundubhi* [i, 28, 5], lute, *karkari* [ii, 43, 3], or lyre or harp, *vāṇa*, with its seven notes recognized and distinguished [x, 32, 4], and the flute (of reed) called *nāḍī* [x, 135, 7].

Polity.—The political evolution of Rigvedic India may

be traced in the following ascending series of formations or groups :—

(1) The Family (*Gṛiha* or *Kula*).
(2) The Village (*Grāma*).
(3) The Canton or Clan (*Viś*).
(4) The People (*Jana*).
(5) The Country (*Rāshṭra*).

Family.—The unit of social formation was the family comprising several members living under a common head, the father, or eldest brother, called the *Kulapa* [x, 179, 2], in the same house called *Gṛiha* [iii, 53, 6 ; ii, 42, 3], which was large enough to accommodate not merely the entire undivided family but also their cattle [vii, 56, 16] and sheep [x, 106, 5] at night, returning from their grazing grounds, *vraja* [ii, 38, 8]. The house with its several rooms could be shut up [vii, 85, 6].

Village.—An aggregate of several families made up the *Grāma* [i, 44, 10] or village, which is contrasted with the forest, *araṇya*, with its wild animals and plants [x, 90, 8]. The term *grāma* was sometimes used to denote the village folk [*gavyam grāmaḥ,* " the horde seeking cows," in iii, 33, 11]. A village had its head man called *Grāmaṇī* [x, 62, 11 ; 107, 5].

Clan.—The next larger formation was called the *Viś* [iv, 4, 3 ; 37, 1], implying a settlement, from the root *viś*, to " enter " or " settle ", under the head called *Viśpati* [i, 37, 8]. It is, however, difficult to state whether the *Viś* of the Rigveda was a local subdivision, a canton, or a blood-kinship like a clan, and in what exact relation it stood to the *Grāma* or to *Kula* and *Gotra*.

The People (*Jana*).—Larger than the *Viś* was the *Jana* [x, 84, 2]. In ii, 26, 3 we have the series—" *Putra, Janma, Viś,* and *Jana,*" " family, canton, or clan, and the people." In x, 91, 2, the *Gṛiha* or family is contrasted with the *Viś* and *Jana*. Regarding *Jana*, we have mention of the famous five peoples, " pancha janāh," and of the peoples called the Yadus [*Yādva-jana, Yādvāḥ* in viii, 6, 46, 48] and the Bharatas [*Bhārata-jana* in iii, 53, 12]. The king is also called the protector of the Jana or people [*Goptā janasya* in iii, 43, 5].

The Country.—The term for the country or kingdom was *Rāshṭra* [iv, 42, 1].[1]

The King.—The Vedic kingship was the natural outcome of the conditions surrounding the Āryans as invaders in a hostile country. "War begat the king" in Vedic, as in Teutonic, history generally. Rigveda, x, 124, 8, refers to the sad plight of a people not choosing a king to lead them against the enemy. The king was thus the leader in person of war of aggression and also in defence. He was called "the protector of the people" (*gopā janasya*), as we have already seen, and a "sacker of cities" (*purāṁ bhettā*).

In return for these services, he received the obedience of his people, sometimes voluntary, but sometimes compelled [ix, 7, 5], and also contributions made by them for the maintenance of royalty (called *bali* [i, 64, 4]); *bali-hṛit*, "receiving tribute," in vii, 6, 5, and x, 173, 6]. Tribute also came to the king from hostile tribes subdued [vii, 6, 5; 18, 19].

In return he performed the duties of judge, probably as a court of final appeal in civil justice, while in criminal justice he exercised a wide jurisdiction [i, 25, 13; iv, 4, 3]. Himself above punishment (*adaṇḍya*), he wielded the rod of punishment (*daṇḍa*) as the chief executive of the people, employing spies for his work [viii, 47, 11].

The marks of royalty were the pomp of dress [i, 85, 8], the possession of a palace [ii, 41, 5], and of a retinue. There is mention of palaces with 1,000 pillars [ii, 41, 5] and 1,000 portals [vii, 88, 5].

His Ministers.—The foremost was the *Puro-hita*, literally "placed in front" [i, 1, 1]. His office was called *Purohiti* and *Purodhā* [vii, 60, 12; 83, 4]. He was the sole associate of the king as his preceptor, or guide, philosopher, and friend. Examples of Purohitas in the Rigveda are *Viśvāmitra*

[1] A few other political formations are indicated in the terms *Vrājapati*, who is described as being attended by the family heads, *Kulapas*, like the leader of the village contingent of the clan [x, 179, 2], and *Śardha*, *Vrāta*, and *Gaṇa*, used to denote a Vedic host, fighting "according to clan, village, and family" [v, 53, 11].

or Vasishṭha, in the service of the Bharata king, Sudās, of the Tṛitsu family [iii, 33, 53; vii, 18]; the Purohita of Kuruśravaṇa [x, 33]; and Devāpi, the Purohita of Śāntanu [x, 98]. His chief function was that of the domestic priest of the king. He was the *alter ego* of the king in all religious matters. But he also assumed leadership in matters political. He accompanied the king to battle and strengthened him by his prayers for his safety and victory [vii, 18, 13]. It was the predominance of the Brāhmaṇa in politics which is significant in all ages of Indian history.

The king's *entourage* also included the *Senānī*, "leader of the army" [vii, 20, 5; ix, 96, 1], and the *Grāmaṇī*, the leader of the village [x, 62, 11; 107, 5] for both civil and military purposes. There must have been many *Grāmaṇīs* in a kingdom, but the texts seem to contemplate only one as being in the royal *entourage*, possibly as a representative of the rural interests and population. The king's personal following was also called *upasti* (dependents) [x, 97, 23] and *ibhya* [i, 65, 4].

Assemblies.—The king's autocracy was somewhat limited by the popular bodies called the *Sabhā* and the *Samiti*, through which the will of the people expressed itself on important matters affecting their welfare, including the election of the king himself.

The *Sabhā* is mentioned in many passages of the Rigveda [vi, 28, 6; viii, 4, 9; x, 34, 6], which, however, do not define its exact character and functions. It is used in the sense of an assembly as well as of the hall or meeting-place for social intercourse and discussion of public matters like cows, and for dicing. A person "eminent in the Assembly" is called *sabhā-saha* [x, 71, 10]; "worthy of the Assembly" a *sabheya* [ii, 24, 13]; there is mention also of the *Sabhā* being attended by persons of noble birth, *su-jāta* [vii, 1, 4], and of "wealth worthy of the *Sabhā* (*rayiḥ sabhāvān* in iv, 2, 5). These terms probably indicate that the Rigvedic *Sabhā* was a Council of Elders or Nobles.

The *Samiti* is also mentioned in many passages in the Rigveda without throwing light on its exact character. There is a reference to the king being a familiar figure in the *Samiti* [x, 97, 6,] and to his duty of attending it [ix, 92, 6]. One passage represents the king meeting the *Samiti* with power invincible and capturing their minds and their resolutions [x, 166, 4]. Another emphasizes the fact that concord between the king and the *Samiti* was essential for the prosperity of the realm [x, 191, 3: a prayer for union of *Mantra* (Policy), Gain, Minds (*Manaḥ*), Hearts (*Chittam*) and Endeavour between the king and Assembly (*Samiti*)].

Justice.—Evidence is meagre on this subject. The system of *Wergeld* (monetary compensation to relatives of the man killed) was in force. A man is called a *Śata-dāya* [ii, 32, 4], as the price of his blood was a hundred cows. But the niggardly and unpopular *Paṇi* was called a *Vaira-deya* [v, 61, 8], deserving "the requital of enmity". The fixing of such prices shows an improvement upon the primitive system of "eye for eye and tooth for tooth", and a restriction of the sphere of private revenge. Terms like *Ugra* [vii, 38, 6] and *Jīva-gṛibh* [x, 97, 11], literally "seizing alive", are taken to indicate police officials. The arbitrator of disputes was called *Madhyama-śī*, "lying in the midst" [x, 97, 12]. The village judge is called *Grāmya-vādin* in the later *Taittirīya-Saṁhitā* [ii, 3, 1, 3].

War.—The Rigvedic wars were those for defence and conquests, and also expedition into neighbouring territory for the sake of booty [x, 142, 4]. A battle was called a *yuddha* [x, 54, 2] or a *raṇa* [i, 61, 1, 9]. The army, *pṛit* or *pṛitanā* [vii, 20, 3], comprised foot-soldiers, *patti* [*Av.*, vii, 62, 1], and charioteers going together to battle [ii, 12, 8]. We also read of chariots opposing troops (*grāma*) of infantry [i, 100, 10] or of hand to hand fight, *mushṭi-hatyā* [i, 8, 2] carried on by the foot-soldier against the charioteer [v, 58, 4]. The equipment of the warrior, *Yodha* [i, 143, 5], is described in the account of *Dāśa-rājña* in vi, 75. He was armed with the following weapons: (1) bow, *dhanus* [viii, 72, 4] and arrow, *bāṇa* [vi, 75, 17]. The bow was made of a strong staff bent into a curved shape (*vakra*) with its ends joined by the bow-string, *jyā*, made of a strip of cowhide [vi, 75, 11]. The arrow was discharged from the ear and aptly called *karṇa-yoni* [ii, 24, 8], i.e. "having the ear as its point of origin." The quiver was called *ni-shaṅgin* [v, 57, 2: *Sudhanvān ishumanto nishaṅginaḥ* ("warrior well-equipped with bow, arrow, and quiver").

(2) Coat of mail, *varma*, made up of parts, metal plates, sewn together (*syūta*) [i, 31, 15; x, 101, 8]; also called *atka*, described as being woven (*vyuta*) and close-fitting (*surabhi*) [i, 122, 2; vi, 29, 3].

(3) Handguard, *hastaghna*, as protection against friction of bowstring [vi, 75, 14].

(4) Helmet, *śiprā* [ib.] of iron (or copper) [iv, 37, 4: *ayaḥ-śiprā*] or of gold [ii, 34, 3: *hiraṇya-śiprā*]. The helmeted warrior was a *śiprin* [i, 29, 2].

Other weapons referred to are *asi*, sword, with its sheath, *aśi-dhāra* and the attached belt, *vāla* [i, 162, 20]; *srakti*, spear [vii, 18, 17]; *srika*, lance [i, 32, 12]; *didyu*, missile [i, 71, 5]; and *adri* [i, 51, 3] or *aśani* [vi, 6, 5], sling-stones. The weapons lent themselves to skilled use [i, 92, 1].

The chariot was drawn by two, three [x, 33, 5], or four horses [ii, 18, 1], whicn were controlled by the driver, *sārathi* [i, 55, 7], by means of reins, *raśmi*, and whip, *kaśā* [v, 83, 3]. His companion-warrior was seated to his left and hence called *savyashṭhā* [ii, 19, 6; x, 102, 6].

Other accompaniments of war were banners, *dhvaja* [vii, 85, 2], drums, *dundubhi* [i, 28, 5], and war-cries, *kranda* [ii, 12, 8].

Military operations included the storming of defences, earthworks or dikes, thrown up against attack [vi, 47, 2] or siege of forts (*Pur*) by fire [vii, 5, 3].

Learning.—The Rigvedic civilization was based on plain living and high thinking. It is lacking in great monuments of material progress like the Egyptian or Assyrian civilization but not in proofs of intellectual and spiritual progress. Life was simple, but Thought high and of farthest reach, wandering through eternity. Some of the prayers of the Rigveda, like the Gāyatrī Mantram, touch the highest point of knowledge and sustain human soul to this day, while no Hindu, however modernized, will permit a single alteration of their original accents, syllables, or words.

The history of Rigveda is the history of the culture of the age. The Rigveda in the form in which it is now extant is a composite work made up of different parts and chronological strata, comprising not merely the hymns proper in praise of the gods, invocations, and sacrificial songs, but also ballads, fragments of secular poetry, and hymns conveying the highest philosophical speculation. The Rigveda itself refers to older and later poetry and to older and later Ṛishis, the authors of its hymns [i, 1, 2; 109, 2, etc.]. Its material had been building through the ages. Each Ṛishi was the "seer" of the hymns revealed to him as the result of his contemplation based on the practice of *tapas* or austerity [x, 109, 4; 154, 2]. He confined them to his son and pupil, his family. Each particular Ṛishi-Kula or family thus functioned as a Vedic school where its own stock of hymns was conserved and transmitted from sire to son, or preceptor to pupil. The work of all these families of Ṛishis or Vedic schools resulted in a large output, a general, national stock of hymns. Out of this general body or floating mass of hymns, a handy selection was necessary for purposes of worship. Thus arose the selection called the Rigveda Saṁhitā, out of which arose on similar principles the other three Vedic Saṁhitās of Sāma, Yajus, and Atharvan. We have thus here four stages in the growth of Vedic learning: (*a*) the growth of the earliest hymns; (*b*) multiplication of hymns at different centres or schools, the different priestly families; (*c*) selection of hymns in the Rigveda Saṁhitā; and (*d*) growth of the other three Vedic Saṁhitās out of the original material preserved and presented in the Rigveda Saṁhitā.

All this development recorded in the Rigveda points to a long history. "Some hundreds of years must have been needed for all the hymns found in the Rigveda to come into being" [Macdonell]. "Centuries must have elapsed between the composition of the earliest hymns and the completion of the Saṁhitā of the Rigveda" [Winternitz]. And, accordingly, when we come to the Rigveda, we come to a high degree of linguistic and philosophical development. The Rigvedic Sanskrit shows no trace of a growing language. Its entire grammatical mechanism is perfected; every tense, mood, every number and person of the verb, is fixed, and all the terminations of the cases are firmly established, pointing to the later and more advanced inflectional stage in the life-history of a language. As remarked by Bunsen, "even these earliest specimens of Vedic poetry belong to the modern history of the human race."

The principles on which the selection and arrangement of hymns were made in the Rigveda Saṁhitā and the methods of their conservation show considerable literary skill and originality of design. First, six of the Rigvedic Ṛishis were chosen as the most representative ones whose work was worthy of conservation. These were Gṛitsamada, Viśvāmitra, Vāmadeva, Atri, Bharadvāja, and Vasishṭha. The hymns attributed to them were arranged in six separate "family" books, the Maṇḍalas II–VII of the Rigveda, which form its nucleus. To these were added (1) the group of hymns by other families to form the second part of Maṇḍala I (51–191); (2) the hymns making up the first part of Maṇḍala I; (3) the hymns attributed to the family of Ṛishi Kaṇva making up Maṇḍala VIII; (4) the collection of Soma hymns in one place, Maṇḍala IX, instead of leaving them mixed up with the hymns making up the other Maṇḍalas; and (5) a collection of supplementary hymns of the same number (191) as the number of hymns of Maṇḍala I, to form Maṇḍala X, exhibiting some special features in its language, metrical form, and contents comprising philosophical hymns and those bearing on miscellaneous topics like marriage or burial.

The Saṁhitā thus compiled contained 70,000 lines out of which 5,000 are found to be repetitions. This was because there was already in the country a floating mass of hymns upon which the Ṛishis composing the later hymns had drawn as common literary property. It is also to be noted that a high standard of verbal authenticity was maintained in the long interval between the rise of the hymns and the constitution, by grammatical editors, of the extant phonetic text called the Saṁhitā. These editors have scrupulously preserved in the Saṁhitā text the actual words used by the ancient seers and the most minute irregularities of accent or alternate forms without any attempt at modernization, except where changes are called for in phonetic forms by the rules prevailing in the later phase of the Sanskrit language when the sacred text was edited. Thus the word *sumna* was not replaced by *dyumna*, but the old form of the words *tvam hi Agne* would appear as *tvaṃ hy Agne*, " for thou, O Agni."

When the Saṁhitā text was constituted, other devices were evolved for its own conservation in turn against possible changes or corruption in time. These may be considered in this connection, though they were considerably later in time. The first was the formation of a new text of the Saṁhitā itself in which every single word is shown in its independent and phonetically unmodified form and compounds are separated into their elements. This is called the *Pada-pāṭha* or " word-text ". The other device was the *Krama-pāṭha*, " step-text," in which every word of the *Pada-pāṭha* appears twice to be pronounced both after the preceding and before the following one. Thus *a b c d* as representing the first four words would be read as *ab, bc, cd.*

The scheme of protecting the purity of the sacred text was further elaborated by the composition of special treatises like the *Prātiśākhyas*, presenting, with examples, the euphonic modifications necessary for turning the Pada into the Saṁhitā text, and the *Anukramaṇīs*, or Indexes, stating the number of the hymns, verses, words, and even syllables of the sacred text by way of checking its integrity. " These devices have secured a faithfulness of tradition unparalleled in any other ancient literature " [*India's Past* by Macdonell].

Education.—Now as to the methods of learning and education in that age. As has been already indicated, the home of the teacher was the school where he taught the particular sacred texts for which he was responsible, to his pupils, mostly his sons or nephews. The texts were in the first instance learnt by rote. The Rigveda [vii, 103, 4] refers to the repetition by the pupil of the words taught by his teacher. A great importance was attached to enunciation and pronunciation. There is mention of seven forms of utterance and four grades of speech [i, 164, 3, 5; *Taitti. Saṁ.*, vi, 4, 7, 3] and also of the skill of Viśvāmitra in recitation [*Rv.*, iii, 53, 15]. But the fundamental educational method was *tapas* or practice of penance and austerity as a process of self-realization [x, 109, 4; 154, 2; 190, 1; 167, 1] by which was produced the *Muni* of divine afflatus (*deveshita*) [x, 136, 2, 4, 5], or *Vipra*, the "inspired singer" [i, 129, 2, 11; 162, 7; iv, 26, 1] (from root *vip*, "quiver"), or the *Manīshi* [vii, 103], comprehending all knowledge of which only a part is said to be revealed in human speech (*vāk*). We have thus here stated the profound philosophical position attained in the Rigveda that what is rendered explicit in the creation is but a fragment of the Implicit or the Absolute. Another interesting passage [vii, 103] refers to a period of intense subjectivity and concentration followed by Enlightenment (*parjanya* from *pṛi*, to become perfect) by which the pupil becomes qualified to be an expounding teacher (*vāchamavādishuḥ*), just as frogs, after a season of slumber, are quickened into activity by the clouds (*parjanya*).

Religion and Philosophy.—The Rigvedic simplicity of life contrasts itself with the elaboration of its religious side as shown in the magnitude of the pantheon.

First, we have a group of deities standing for the principal phenomena of nature, viz. (*a*) *Dyaus* (sky); (*b*) *Pṛithivī* (earth) [cf. *dyāvā-pṛithivī*, "heaven and earth" in i, 143, 2; 159, 1; etc.]; (*c*) *Varuṇa* (the sky-god proper, the subject of some of the noblest hymns of the Rigveda. Varuṇa is also given the epithet *Asura*, corresponding to the Irānian god Ahura Mazda. In the more philosophical hymns of the Rigveda, Varuṇa typifies *Ṛita*, indicative of the cosmic, and later the moral, order; (*d*) *Indra*, the god of thunderstorm, who causes rain. Indra gradually acquired supremacy over Varuṇa in Rigvedic worship as the Āryans left the dry regions of the Panjab and advanced eastward to the holy land of Brahmāvarta noted for rain and storm; (*e*) the

Sun was worshipped in no less than five forms as (1) *Sūrya* (2) *Savitṛi*, representing the quickening power of the sun; (3) *Mitra* more famous in Irān than in India, where he is associated with Varuṇa; (4) *Pūshan*, symbolizing the power of the suṇ in its effects on the growth of herbs and vegetation, (5) *Vishṇu*, representing the swift-moving sun in the Rigveda, though later he is worshipped as an independent god; (*f*) *Rudra*, or storm-god, the precursor of later Śiva; (*g*) the two *Aśvins*, representing the morning and evening star; (*h*) the *Maruts*, storm-gods attending on Rudra; (*i*) *Vāyu* and (*j*) *Vāta*, the wind-gods; (*k*) *Parjanya*, the the god of rain, the waters and the rivers; (*l*) *Ushas*, the god of dawn, inspiring some of the most beautiful Rigvedic poetry.

Next, we have a group of domestic deities, viz. (*a*) *Agni*, the god of fire in his three forms, the sun in the heavens, the lightning, and the terrestrial fire; (*b*) *Soma* (draught of immortality), who has inspired the most mystical hymns of the Rigveda and is identified with the moon.

We have also a group of abstract deities, viz. (*a*) *Śraddhā*, faith, and (*b*) *Manyu*, wrath.

There were also some minor deities like (*a*) the *Ribhus*, aerial elves; (*b*) the *Apsaras*, water-nymphs; and (*c*) the *Gandharvas*, aerial sprites.

Sometimes, the gods are conceived of as animals, e.g. Indra as bull, the Sun as a swift horse. But this does not indicate any animal worship in the Rigveda. Nor is there in the Rigveda any trace of what is known as *Totemism*, i.e. belief in an animal ancestor with the consequent treatment of that animal as sacred and divine, or of snake-worship, although the snake figures as the god of abyss, or as the demon producing drought whom Indra destroys, though there may be a trace of *Fetishism* as seen, for instance, in the use of the image of Indra as protection against one's enemies. The Rigvedic gods had also their enemies who are designated as *Asuras* and *Rākshasas*.

The Rigvedic religion consisted principally in worship being offered to the gods whose favours or boons are expected by the performance of prescribed sacrifices by which these could be secured or controlled. The sacrifice consisted of offering of milk, grain, ghee, flesh, and Soma. But it is the Soma-sacrifice alone which is elaborated in the Rigveda. The ceremonial religion was so far developed as to have given rise to seven different classes of priest necessary for its performance, viz. the *Hotṛi* priests reciting hymns, the *Adhvaryu* performing manual functions connected with worship, the *Udgātṛi* singing the Sāman chants, together with their assistants. Some sacrifices were elaborate and costly and could be performed only by the king or the nobles (the *Maghavans*). The Rigveda is thus distinctly aristocratic in its outlook and has very little of popular religion suitable for the masses.

All this ritualistic religion, however, culminated in a profound philosophy which finds expression chiefly in the tenth *Maṇḍala* of the Rigveda, and also in other passages. The multiplicity of the gods is frankly and boldly questioned and the ultimate unity of the universe is asserted as the creation of one God to whom different designations are applied, such as *Viśvakarmā*, *Hiraṇya-garbha*, *Prajāpati*, or *Aditi*, the primæval mother. The creation is also presented as the outcome of the sacrifice made by the *Virāṭpurusha* (Oversoul) or of evolution from non-being manifested in the form of water or heat. The Rigvedic passage [i, 164] pointedly refers to "the One Reality (*ekaṁ sat*) whom the sages speak of in many ways, calling it Agni, Yama or Mātariśvān".

Lastly, the Rigveda believes in the life after death in the world controlled by Yama.[1]

[1] References: *Vedic Index* by Macdonell and Keith; and Chh. iv and v of *CHI*.

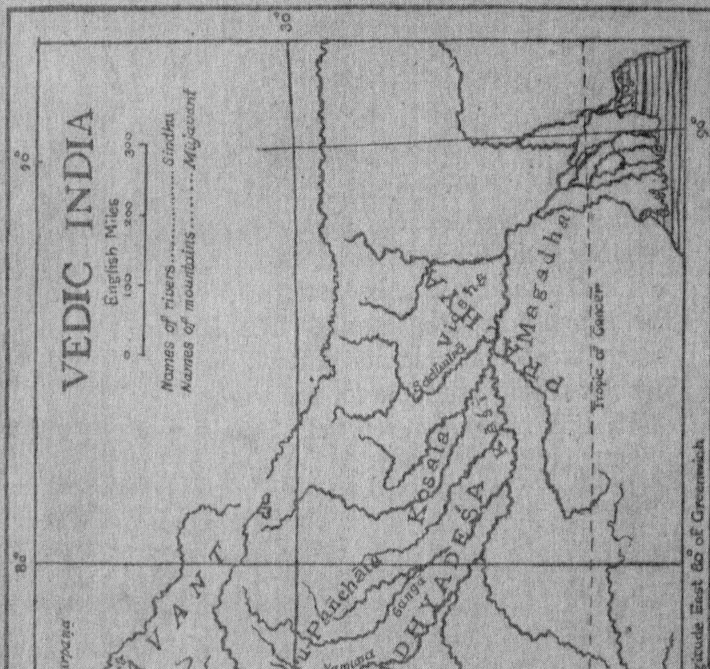
VEDIC INDIA
English Miles
0 100 200 300
Names of rivers.........Sindhu
Names of mountains.........Mūjavant
Longitude East 80° of Greenwich
Tropic of Cancer
Magadha
Kosala
Videha
Kāśi
Pañchāla
MADHYADEŚA
Yamunā
Gangā
Sarasvatī
Sṛñjaya
Uttara-Kuru
Uttara-Madra
Druhyu
Turvaśa
Anu
Yadu
Sindhu
Pakthas
Bhalānas

To face p. 89.]

CHAPTER V

LATER VEDIC CIVILIZATION

Sources.—The Rigvedic civilization is to be distinguished from the civilization revealed in the later Vedic works, such as the later Vedic *Saṁhitās*, the *Brāhmaṇas*, the *Āraṇyakas*, and the *Upanishads*.

We may note at the outset how the different branches of Vedic literature had grown out of one another. The *Saṁhitā* of the Rigveda was the primary work. The *Sāma-Veda Saṁhitā* was made out of it. But the two Saṁhitās of the *Yajur-Veda*, Black and White, contain new matter, the formulæ and prayers for the Adhvaryu priest-in-charge of the actual performance of the sacrificial acts. The Black Yajur-Veda is so called because it combines into one whole its contents of both verse and prose, whether the formulæ and prayers or their prose explanations or comments. The White Yajur-Veda, however, confines the verse and prose formulæ to the Saṁhitā called the *Vājasaneyi Saṁhitā* and relegates the prose explanations to a *Brāhmaṇa*, called the *Śatapatha Brāhmaṇa*. Lastly, there was the *Atharva-Veda Saṁhitā* meant for the priest called *Brāhman* who superintended the whole sacrifice. It contains 731 hymns and about 6,000 verses, some of which are even older than the Rigveda, and some give interesting secular details. These are (1) Songs and Spells for healing of diseases [e.g. v, 22, describing fever]; (2) Benedictions for farmer, shepherd and merchant; (3) Spells for harmony (with master, or at Assembly or Court of Law); (4) Songs of marriage and love; (5) Songs in aid of Royalty, and the like.

The *Saṁhitās* were followed by the *Brāhmaṇas*, the *Āraṇyakas* and the *Upanishads*.

The *Brāhmaṇas*, the earliest Indo-European prose literature, are theological treatises, explaining in minute detail the Vedic sacrificial ceremonial and illustrating its value by numerous stories and speculations on its origin. They are attached to the Vedas, e.g. the *Aitareya Brāhmaṇa* of the Rigveda dealing with Soma sacrifices and royal inauguration ceremonies; the *Pañchaviṁśa* of the Sāmaveda which contains the famous *Vrātyastoma* by which non-Aryans could be admitted to Aryan society; the *Śatapatha* of the White Yajurveda, the most valuable work of the Vedic age in the variety of its contents; and the *Gopatha Brāhmaṇa* of the Atharva-Veda.

The *Āraṇyakas* are the concluding portions of the *Brāhmaṇas* and are so called because the philosophical and mystical character of their contents required that they should be studied in the solitude of the *araṇya* or forest. The extant *Āraṇyaka* works are the *Aitareya*, the *Kaushītaki*, and the *Taittirīya*, which are appendages to the Brāhmaṇa works of those names, and of which the first two are associated with the Rigveda and the third with the Black Yajurveda.

The *Āraṇyakas* form a transition to the *Upanishads* which are usually their final form and, indeed, mark the last stage in the development of Brāhmaṇa literature and, from their language, closely approximating to classical Sanskrit, emerging about 500 B.C., represent the latest phase of Vedic literature. The contents of the Rigveda broadly reveal twofold character, philosophical (*jñāna-kāṇḍa*), and ritualistic (*karma-kāṇḍa*), of which the latter is developed and elaborated in the *Brāhmaṇas* proper, and the former in the *Upanishads*. The Upanishads thus do not believe in the sacrificial ceremonial but in the saving knowledge by which deliverance is obtained from mundane existence through the absorption of the individual soul in the world-soul (*ātmā*). The two oldest and most important of the Upanishads are the *Chhāndogya* of the *Sāmaveda* and the *Bṛihadāraṇyaka* of the White *Yajurveda*. Among other Upanishads of note may be mentioned the Kāṭhaka, Īśā, Śvetaśvatara, Maitrāyaṇīya, Taittirīya, Muṇḍaka, Praśna, Māṇḍūkya, and Kena, but except the Kāṭhaka, these are not believed to be much older than Buddhism.

Later Vedic history and civilization are to be studied in all this vast and varied literature indicated above.

Extension of Territory.—In the period of the Rigveda, the centre of civilization was shifting from the west, the land of the famous five peoples (*pañchajanāḥ*) in the Punjab, to the east, the land between the Sarasvatī and the Dṛishadvatī, the home of the Bharatas. But now, the localization of civilization in the more eastern regions has been definitely achieved. Its centre is Kurukshetra, bounded on the south by Khāṇḍava, on the north by Tūrghna and on the west by Parīnaḥ. In relation to this centre, the later *Madhyadeśa*, the land of the Kurus and Pañchālas, with the Vaśas and Uśīnaras, are located the Satvants to the south, and the Uttara-Kurus and the Uttara-Madras to the north beyond the Himalayas, by a famous geographical and ethnological passage found in the *Aitareya Brahmāṇa*. While the west recedes into background, the regions east of the Kuru-Pañchāla country come into prominence, like Kosala (Oudh), Videha (north Bihar), Magadha (south Bihar), and Aṅga (east Bihar), while to the south about the Vindhyas, which are not mentioned by any Vedic text, are located imperfectly Brāhmanized outcast tribes like the Andhras and Pulindas (mentioned in Asoka inscriptions), Mūtibas, Puṇḍras and Śabaras (who still live on the Madras border of Orissa and speak a Muṇḍā dialect) and the Naishadhas, as well as the region called Vidarbha mentioned in the *Aitareya* [vii, 34, 9] and *Jaiminīya* Upanishad Brāhmaṇas [ii, 440]. Evidently the Āryan civilization had not yet overstepped the Vindhya.

New States and Peoples: The Kuru-Pañchālas.—An extended territory brought with it new States and Peoples, new centres of life. We hear no longer of the Anus and Druhyus, the Turvaśas, the Krivis and Kurus, the Pūrus and the Bharatas of the Rigveda, but of new tribal formations and amalgamations led by the Kuru-Pañchālas who in the texts figure as the best representatives of Vedic culture, models of good form, speakers of the best Sanskrit [*Śatapatha Br.*, iii, 2, 3, 15], performers of sacrifices with perfection, having the best of kings, running the best Academy, and leading in other ways. The *Kaushītaki Brāhmaṇa* refers to people going to the north in search of pure speech [vii, 6]. The Pañchāla king, Pravāhaṇa Jaivali, is mentioned as daily attending the *Pāñchāla-Parishad* [*Chh. Up.*, v, 3; *Bṛiha. Up.*, vi, 2, 1–7]. The hostility between the Kurus and Pañchālas as depicted in the *Mahābhārata* is not known in the Vedic texts, which tell of the confederate kingdom of the Kuru-Pañchālas as being a seat of culture and prosperity, though the independent history of the Kurus seems to have been chequered. They had their zenith of prosperity under Parikshit and Janamejaya, whose capital was Āsandīvant [*Śata. Br.*, xiii, 5, 4, 2] with two other towns, Mashṇāra [*Aita. Br.*, viii, 23, 3] and Kārotī [*Sat. Br.*, ix, 5, 2, 15]. The *Atharvaveda* [xx, 127, 7–10] describes this prosperity by stating that in the *rāshṭra* of Parikshit the husband asks the wife what he should bring her, "curds, stirred drink, or liquor," so "thriving" were the whole people there. But the *Chhāndogya Upanishad* alludes to a hailstorm or perhaps a shower of locusts afflicting the Kurus, and the *Bṛihadāraṇyaka* to some catastrophe in which they perished. But the confederate Kuru-Pañchāla kingdom continued in prosperity for a long time with an extensive territory indicated by its chief towns like Kāmpīlya, the capital, Kauśāmbī, and Parichakrā [*Śat. Br.*, xiii, 5, 4, 7].

Kosala, Kāśī, and Videha.—The Aryan expansion towards the east is indicated in a legend of *Śatapatha Brāhmaṇa* [i, 4, 1, 10, 17] describing how Māthava the Videgha[1] (i.e. King of Videha) migrated from the Sarasvatī, the land of Vedic Culture, crossed the Sadānīrā, the eastern boundary of Kosala (modern Gandak), and came to the land of Videha. The texts in fact testify to the growth of three kingdoms as seats of Vedic culture, viz. Kosala, Kāśī, and Videha, which sometimes confederated themselves. Para, son of Aṭṇāra, figures as a king of both Kosala

[1] It is, however, to be noted that the priest and guide in this adventure was Gotama Rāhugaṇa, a Rigvedic Ṛishi, and this rather establishes the fact that this eastward extension of Aryan civilization was achieved in the time of the Rigveda. Therefore, we find Videha already leading in Vedic culture under King Janaka and Ṛishi Yājñavalkya, though it was its easternmost outpost and farthest from its headquarters.

and Videha [*Śāṇkhāyana Śrauta Sūtra*, xvi, 9, 11], while Jala Jātūkarṇya as a Purohita of the Kosalas, Kāśīs, and Videhas [ib. xvi, 29, 6]. The most famous kings of the times were the two philosopher kings, Ajātaśatru of Kāśī, and Janaka of Videha, who were leaders of thought, in association with the Brahman scholars, Yājñavalkya, and Śvetaketu.

Magadha and Aṅga—Beyond the pale of Āryan civilization lay *Magadha* which along with *Aṅga* is indicated as a distant land in the *Atharvaveda* [v, 22, 14] which is also familiar with the Bengal tiger and makes the king at his consecration step upon a tiger skin. The expression *Aṅga-Magadhāḥ* occurs in the *Gopatha Brāhmaṇa* [ii, 9]. A *Māgadha* is dedicated in the *Yajurveda* [*Vāj. Saṁhitā*, xxx, 5, 22] to loud noise (*ati-krushṭa*), suggestive of minstrelsy. A *Māgadha* in later literature denotes a minstrel. The dislike to Magadha is as old as the Rigveda if the Kīkaṭas it mentions were Magadhans, as some believe. The dislike is more explicit in the Atharvaveda where evil things like fever are wished away to the distant westerners like the Gandhāris, Bahlikas, and Mūjavants [v, 22, 7] and to easterners, Aṅgas and Magadhas. It was due to the imperfect Brahmanization of these regions, the home of the aborigines, and later of Buddhism which did not believe in the caste-system. The native Magadhans are also dubbed as *Vrātyas* in the Vedic texts [*Atharvaveda*, xv, 2, 1–4], regarded as outcasts and nomads, speaking a Prakritic dialect as indicated by the remark that "they called what was easy of utterance (i.e. Sanskrit) hard to speak" [*Pañchaviṁśa Br.*, xvii, 1, 9]. The Prakrits find it hard to accommodate the harsh consonantal combinations which Sanskrit affects. But the *Vrātyas* were not strangers to Sanskrit when they are described as *dīkshita-vāch*, speaking the language of the initiated [ibid.]. It was open to them to acquire admission to Brahminical society by performance of prescribed rites [*Āpastamba Śrauta Sūtra*, xxii, 5, 4–14]. It is best to regard them not as non-Aryans but as Aryans outside the pale of orthodox Brahmin culture. The *Aitareya Āraṇyaka* [ii, 1, 1] refers to the

Vaṅgas, Vagadhas, and Cheras as birds, i.e. non-Aryans, speaking language not intelligible to the Aryans. The Vagadhas might be a misreading for the Magadhans, while the Cheras were a wild tribe in the Vindhya region. The Kaushītaki Upanishad [vi, 1] sums up the situation by describing Aryan India as represented by the Uśīnaras, Vasas, Matsyas, Kurus, Pañchālas, Kāśīs, and Videhas.

Social System.—While the Rigveda knew of a hereditary priesthood and nobility, and even refers to the threefold [viii, 35, 16–18] or fourfold division [i, 113, 6; x, 90, 12 (the Purusha-sūkta)] of the people, this period saw the development of the full-fledged caste-system due to differentiation of occupations growing in number and variety with progress of settled life and due also to contact with aborigines raising questions of purity of blood and the colour bar.

The system, however, is not yet seen to be as rigid as in the succeeding period of the *Sūtras*. It was a midway between the laxity of the Rigveda and the rigidity of the *Sūtras*. In the Rigveda, the restrictions on intermarriage applied only to incest, such as marriage between brother and sister, father and daughter. In the *Śatapatha Brāhmaṇa* [i, 8, 3, 6], the restriction is extended to marriage with relations of the third or the fourth degree, while Brāhmaṇa and Kshatriya could intermarry with the lower castes, including Śūdra. Sukanyā, daughter of Kshatriya King Śaryāta, is mentioned as marrying Brāhmaṇa Chyavana [ib., iv, 1, 5, 7].

Change of caste was very unusual but perhaps not impossible in that age. The Rigveda describes Viśvāmitra as a Ṛishi, but the *Aitareya Brāhmaṇa* as a Kshatriya. Certain Rigvedic hymns are even ascribed to royal Ṛishis. In the Upanishads we have certain remarkable examples of kings leading in learning, and teaching Brāhman pupils, such as King Janaka of Videha, King Aśvapati of the Kekayas, King Ajātaśatru of Kāśī, and King Pravāhaṇa Jaivali of Pañchāla. But these cases do not prove interchange of castes but of occupations. They only show that some of the kings of the times were individually devotees and patrons of learning. Again, there is not a single instance in the entire Vedic Literature of a Vaiśya being promoted to the rank of a priest or a prince, Brāhmaṇa or Kshatriya. Only the two upper castes cultivated closer relations.

The lines on which the caste system was developing in this period are well indicated in a passage of that representative work, the *Aitareya Brāhmaṇa* [vii, 29]. The Brāhmaṇa is described as a receiver of gifts (*ā-dāyī*), a drinker of Soma, being always on the move (*avasāyī*), and moving at will (*yathākāma-prayāpya*), showing that he attached himself to kings at will. The Vaiśya is tributory to another (*anyasya balikṛit*), to be lived on by another (*anyasyādyaḥ*) and to be oppressed at will (*yathākāma-jyeyaḥ*), i.e. removable at the king's will from his land. The Śudra is the servant of another (*anyasya preshyaḥ*), to be expelled at will (*kāmotthāpyaḥ*) and to be slain at will (*yathākāmavadhyaḥ*), showing that he had no rights of property or life against the Kshatriya or king. This passage points to the spiritual authority of the Brāhmaṇa who was subject in secular matters to the authority of the king as the temporal sovereign. It also shows that the Vaiśya, or the commoner, was not given the right of property or landholding except on the basis of tribute or tax payable by him in return for his protection by the Kshatriya. The Kshatriyas, or nobles, were the landholders and the Vaiśyas the tenantry. Grants of lands and slaves came to the Kshatriyas as gifts for their conquests of the aborigines from the king.

Economic Life.—The growth of economic life is indicated in the many prayers (*paushṭikāni*) contained in the Atharvaveda for the success of the farmer, the shepherd, or the merchant. There are prayers for ploughing, sowing, growth of corn, for rain, for increase of cattle, exorcisms against pests, wild animals, and robbers, and the like. There was continued progress in agriculture and pastoral pursuits. The plough (*sīra*) became large and heavy enough to require a team of twenty-four oxen [*Kāṭhaka Saṁhitā*, xv, 2] to drag it. The furrow was called *sītā* [*ib.*, xx, 3]. The *Śatapatha Brāhmaṇa* classifies agricultural operations as "ploughing, sowing, reaping, and threshing" [i, 6, 1, 3]. It also refers to the use of cowdung (*karīsha*) as manure [ii, 1, 1, 7], while the *Atharvaveda* [iii, 14, 3, 4; xix, 31, 3] refers to the value of the natural manure of animals. Many kinds of grain were grown, such as rice (*vrīhi*), barley (*yava*), beans (*mudga, māsha*), sesamum (*tila*), and grains called *godhūma, masūra*, etc., of which a list is given in the *Vājasaneyi Saṁhitā* [xviii, 12]. Their seasons are also mentioned: barley, sown in winter, ripened in summer; rice, sown in the rains, ripened in autumn, but beans and sesamum ripened later, in winter [*Taittirīya Saṁhitā*, vii, 2, 10, 2]. There were also two harvests a year [*ib.*, v, 1, 7, 3].

There was a striking development in industry and occupations, of which a list is given in the *Yajurveda* [*Vājasaneyi Saṁhitā*, xxx, 7]. We hear of such new occupations as those of fishermen, fire-rangers, ploughers, washermen, barbers, butchers, footmen, messengers, makers of jewels, baskets, ropes, dyes, chariots, bows, smelters, smiths, potters, and so forth. Architectural skill is indicated in the construction of the Fire-altar with 10,800 bricks and shaped like a large bird with outspread wings [*Vājasaneyi Saṁhitā*, xi–xviii (on Agnichayana)]. There is mention of professional acrobats (*Vaṁśa-nartin*) and players on drum and flute; of the boatman, *Nāvāja* [*Śata. Br.*, ii, 3, 3, 5], ferryman or poleman, *Śambī* [*Atharvaveda*, ix, 2, 6], rudders (*naumaṇḍa* in *Śata. Br.*, ii, 3, 3, 15), and oars, *aritra*, handled by the *aritā*, and even of a ship of a hundred oars (*śatāritra*) [*Vājasaneyi Saṁhitā*, xxxi, 7] used for sea-voyages. The *Atharvaveda* [v, 19, 8] compares the ruin of a kingdom to a ship sinking by leaking (*bhinnā*). There is mention of merchant and his trade, *vaṇijyā* [*Śata. Br.*, i, 6, 4, 21], and of the moneylender, *kusīdi* [ib., xiii, 4, 3, 11]. The word *Śreshthī* occurs in several texts [*Aita. Br.*, iii, 30, 3; iv, 25, 8–9; vii, 18, 8; *Br. Up.*, i, 4, 12, etc.] in the sense of a merchant-prince and possibly the "headman of a guild", while the word *śraishṭhya* is also interpreted in a technical sense implying the presidency of a guild.

Woman figured in industry as the dyer (*rajayitrī*), the embroiderer (*peśaskārī*), the worker in thorns (*kaṇṭakī-kārī*), or the basket-maker (*bidala-kārī*).

The advance of civilization is noticed in the extended use of metals. A passage in the *Vājasaneyi Saṁhitā* [xviii, 13] mentions these as *hiraṇya* (gold), *ayas* (bronze), *śyāma*, i.e. swarthy (iron), *loha* (copper), *sīsa* (lead), and *trapu* (tin). *Ayas*, somewhat undefined in the Rigveda, is now differentiated as *śyāma ayas* to indicate iron [*Av.*, xi, 3, 1, 7 ; ix, 5, 4] and *lohita ayas* [ib., xi, 3, 1, 7] or *lohāyasa* [*Śat. Br.*, v, 4, 1, 2], red *ayas* or copper.

Copper was used to make bowls [*Av.*, viii, 10, 22].

Sīsa, lead, is mentioned as being used as a weight by weavers [*Vāja. Saṁhitā*, xix, 80].

Rajata, silver, was used to make ornaments (*rukma*) [*Śata. Br.*, xii, 8, 3, 11], dishes, *pātra* [*Taittirīya Br.*, ii, 2, 9, 7 ; iii, 9, 6, 5], and coins, *nishka*. [*Pañcha. Br.*, xvii, 1, 14].

Gold, *hiraṇya*, was widely used and obtained from the bed of rivers like the Indus [*Rv.*, x, 75, 8], or extracted from the earth [*Av.*, xii, 1, 6, 26, 44], or from ore by smelting [*Śata. Br.*, vi, 1, 3, 5], or from washings [ib., ii, 1, 1, 5]. It was used to make ornaments for neck and breast, *nishka*, ear-rings, *karṇa-śobhana*, and cups [*Śata. Br.*, v, 1, 2, 19 ; 5, 28]. There were also known definite weights of gold indicating a gold currency, e.g. (*a*) *Ashṭā-prūḍ* [*Kāṭhaka Saṁhitā*, xi, 1] and (*b*) *Śatamāna* = " weight of 100 *Kṛishṇalas* " [*Śata. Br.*, v, 5, 5, 16].

Another sign of the new era is the domestication of the elephant, *hastī* or *vāraṇa*, noted for its strength and virility [*Av.*, ii, 22, 1, 3 ; iii, 22, 6 ; vi, 70, 2]. The keeper of the elephant was called *Hastipa* [*Vāja. Saṁhitā*, xxx, 11].

Polity : Kingship.—Kingship was consolidating itself as the normal form of government with the States growing in both number and size.

The theory of the origin of kingship is quaintly stated in the following passage of the *Aitareya Brāhmaṇa* [i, 14] :

" The Devas and Asuras were fighting . . . The Asuras defeated the Devas . . . The Devas said : ' It is on account of our having no king (*a-rājatayā*) that the Asuras conquer. Let us elect a king.' All consented (*rājānaṁ karavāmahā iti tatheti*)."

Imperialism.—There was also emerging the king of kings, the conception of paramount power and imperial sovereignty expressed in such technical terms as *adhirāj, rājādhirāja, saṁrāṭ* and *ekarāṭ* used in most of the texts. The *Aitareya Brāhmaṇa* [viii, 15] defines *Ekarāṭ* as the sole ruler of the territory up to the seas, while the *Atharvaveda* [iii, 1, 4, 1] defines *Ekarāṭ* to be the sole paramount sovereign such as that of the people of the eastern regions (*prāṅ viśāṁ patiḥ*).

There were also developed special ceremonies for the anointment of emperors, such as the *Vājapeya*, the *Rājasūya*, and the *Āśvamedha*, as described in the texts. The last ceremony, according to *Āpastamba Śrauta Sūtra* [xx, 1, 1], was to be performed only by a *sārvabhauma* sovereign, i.e. by one ruling the whole country. According to the *Gopatha Brāhmaṇa*, one became a *Rājā* by performing the *Rājasūya*, while the *Vājapeya* was for the *Samrāṭ*, *Aśvamedha* for *Svarāṭ*, *Purusha-medha* for *Virāṭ*, and *Sarva-medha* for *Sarvarāṭ*.

Nay, more: the texts even preserve the names of kings who by their conquests had achieved the eligibility for these imperial inaugurations. Both the *Aitareya Brāhmaṇa* [viii, 2, 3] and the *Śatapatha Brāhmaṇa* [xiii, 5, 4], for instance, extol the world-wide conquests of the two Bharata kings, Dauḥshanti, who defeated the Satvants and won victories at Mashṇāra in the Kuru country, at Sāchīguṇa, and on the Yamunā and Ganges at a place called Vṛitraghna; and king Sātrājita Śatānīka who had defeated the king of the Kāśīs. "The great deed of Bharata neither men before or after have attained, as the sky a man with his hands." No less than twelve such great kings are named in the two texts aforesaid. The ideal set before them in the sacred text [*Aita. Br.*, viii, 20] is to "win all victories, find all worlds, attain superiority (*śreshṭhatā*), pre-eminence (*pratishṭhā*) and supremacy (*paramatā*) over all kings, and achieve overlordship (*sāmrājya*), paramount rule (*bhaujya*), self-rule (*svārājya*), sovereignty (*vairājya*), supreme authority (*pārameshṭhya*), kingship (*rājya*), great kingship (*mahārājya*) and suzerainty (*ādhipatya*), encompassing all, ruler of all territory (*sārvabhauma*), the sole single sovereign (*ekarāṭ*) of the earth up to its limits in the ocean."

Democratic Elements.—Though monarchy thus established itself on firm foundations, it was not absolute but limited in several ways. Within the framework of autocracy, there were operative certain democratic elements the significance of which should not be missed. These were : (1) the people's voice in choosing their king; (2) the conditions imposed on the king's autocracy at his coronation ; (3) the king's dependence on his Ministry; and (4) the Assemblies of the people, the *Sabhā* and the *Samiti*, as checks upon the king's absolutism.

Election of the King.—The *Atharvaveda* has several passages indicative of the people choosing their king. The passage vi, 87, 88, appears to be a complete song of election of the king. The king's anxiety to secure the people's support and loyalty is expressed in *Av.*, vi, 73, and viii, 94. It was necessary against his rivals, brothers and kinsmen [vii, 34 ; i, 29 and 30]. *Av.*, iii, 3, contains spells in the interests of royalty. *Av.*, iii, 3, 5, refers to a king in exile (*anyakshetre aparuddhaṁ charantam*) being recalled and being welcomed alike by his friends and foes (*pratijanāḥ* and *pratimitrāḥ*). *Av.*, iii, 8, 2, refers to the re-election of a king after he had been once deposed. *Av.*, viii, 10, refers to a king expelled from his kingdom and seeking support for its restoration. Other texts also contain references to kings being expelled from their realms and their efforts to recover their lost sovereignty [*Taittirīya Saṁhitā*, ii, 3, 1 ; *Śata. Br.*, xii, 9, 3, 3, etc]. The *Pañchaviṁśa Brāhmaṇa* [xix, 7, 1–4] refers to a special ceremony called the *Rāḍ-Yajña* by which a deposed king should get back his kingdom or a reigning king the lost loyalty of his subjects. The *Vājasaneyi-Saṁhitā* [xix–xxi] recommends a ceremony for a banished king seeking to regain his throne.

This new position of the king resting on the suffrage of

his people is indicated by appropriate titles. He is called the prince of princes (*kshatranām rājendraḥ*), the lord of the people (*viśāṁ viśapatiḥ*), the sole lord of the exchequer (*dhanapatir dhananāṁ*), the sole lord and leader of the people (*ekavṛisham janānām*), of the entire country and creatures (*vṛishā viśvasya bhūtasya*), the highest of the people (*kakud manushyānām*), and co-equal with the gods (*devānāṁ arghabhāk*) [*Av.*, vi, 86].

Conditions of Coronation.—These may be gathered from the rituals prescribed for the *Rājasūya* and best described in the *Śatapatha Brāhmaṇa*. One of these requires the king-elect to seek the *Anumati* or approval of the earth, i.e. the mother country, in the following words : "Mother Pṛithivi! Injure me not nor I thee!" "This is performed," says the interpreter, "lest she should shake him off (*meyaṁ nāvadhūnvīta*)." The commentator explains that the metaphor shows that king and country must enter into friendly relations like son and mother [v, 4, 3, 20]. Then there are offerings to the Divine Quickeners, to Savitā Satyaprasava for righteous energy, Agni Gṛihapati for mastery of the household, Soma Vanaspati for protection of forests and agriculture, Bṛihaspati Vāk for power of speech, Indra Jyeshṭha for pre-eminence in administration, Rudra Paśupati for protection of cattle, Mitra Satya for truth, ending with the offering to Varuṇa Dharmapati, which brings out the true character of the king as the upholder of the Dharma. The Hindu theory regards *Dharma*, or law, as the real sovereign, and the king as *Daṇḍa* or the executive to support and enforce Dharma. The above offerings symbolize the manifold qualifications and obligations of sovereignty. In Vedic tradition there is no theory of the divine right of kings, but only attribution of divine virtues to kings by means of prayers. Next comes the sprinkling of waters collected from seventeen different sources, river, of which the representative chosen is the Sarasvatī of sacred memory, sea, whirlpool, flood, well, and even a stagnant pool. The Sarasvatī symbolized Speech, the flowing river Vigour, flood stood for Plenty, sea for Dominion, and the pond for the Loyalty of the people to the king, which should be steady and harmless like the waters of a stagnant pool (*sthāvarāmanapakramaṇīṁ karoti*, v, 3, 4, 14). The sprinkling is done jointly by the Brāhmaṇa (*adhvaryu*), a Kshatriya, and also a Vaiśya, representing the three estates of the realm. The next important feature of the ceremonies was the bath administered to the king before he is seated on the throne, He must be first *dhṛita-vrata*, established in the *vrata* or vow [*Ait. Br.*, viii, 18]. He must be loyal to religion, law and truth (*satya-sava, satyadharma* in *Taitti. Br.* i, 7, 10, 1–6), and then take the following oath :

"If I play thee false, may I lose the merit of all my religious performances and gifts, of my good deeds, my place, my life, and even my progeny" [*Ait. Br.*, viii, 15]. The ascent to the throne (*āsandī*) is accompanied by exhortation to the four estates of the realm (the Brāhmaṇa, Kshatriya, Vaiśya, and Śūdra) for protecting the king-elect as "the precious treasure". Then the king is proclaimed with the words : "This man, O ye People! is your king, but of us, Brāhmaṇas, Soma is the king" [*Sat. Br.*, v, 3, 3, 12 ; v, 4, 2, 3]. This emphasizes the theory already explained that *Dharma* as represented by the Brāhmaṇa has precedence over the king who rules in secular matters. The *Śatapatha Brāhmaṇa* [v, 4, 4, 5] further explains that the king and Brāhmaṇa stand together as upholders of the *dharma* among men, being both incapable of any speech or deed that is not right. In another passage [ii, 2, 2, 6], it is stated that "the Brāhmaṇas who have studied and teach the sacred lore are the human gods". Then there is the further proclamation : "To thee this State is given, for agriculture (*kṛishyai*), for the common weal (*kshemāya*), for prosperity and for progress (*poshāya*)." It implies that (*a*) the kingdom is entrusted to the king as a trust ; (*b*) the condition of his holding it is the promotion of the people's well-being and progress. The coronation is followed by another very significant rite. It is that of the *Adhvaryu* and his assistants striking the king on the back by the rod (*daṇḍair ghnanti*). Thereby the king is rendered *adaṇḍya* and placed beyond the reach of judicial destruction (*enaṁ daṇḍavadhamatinayanti*) [*Śat. Br.*, v, 4, 4, 7]. This also symbolizes the doctrine that the king, who can do no wrong and is above punishment, *adaṇḍya*, is himself the wielder of the rod of justice, the *daṇḍa* which upholds the *dharma*. He is not the source of law but its sanction.

Ministers.—The king's dependence on his ministers is brought out in the part assigned to them in his consecration. For purposes of this function they are called *Ratnins*, i.e. receivers of the jewels which are offered by the king-elect to each of them at his house at the ceremony called *ratna-havis*. The significance of the ceremony is indicated in the prescribed formula to be uttered by the king : " For it is for him that he is thereby consecrated, and him he makes his faithful follower " [*Śata. Br.*, v, 3, 1, 6]. It was to win for the king the consent of the ministers to his consecration and their loyalty. Each of these *Ratnins* is also described as a jewel in the crown of sovereignty (*asyakam ratnam*, ib.).

The constitutional character of this ceremony of *ratna-havis* is also indicated in the terms *Rāja-kartṛi* and *Rāja-kṛit* applied in the *Atharvaveda* [iii, 5, 7] and the *Brāhmaṇas* [*Aita.*, viii, 17, 5 ; *Śata.*, iii, 4, 1, 7 ; xiii, 2, 2, 18] to those who, " not themselves kings," aided in the consecration of the king. In the *Aitareya Brāhmaṇa*, the " king-makers " are made to proclaim the king formally to the people.

The *Atharvaveda* mentions these king-makers to be : (1) the *Sūta*, bard ; (2) the *Ratha-kāra*, the chariot-maker ; (3) the *Karmāra*, artisan ; (4) the *Grāmaṇī*, the village head-man ; and (5) *Rājās*. The last comprised the nobles, the king's kinsmen, whose support of his election is mentioned as necessary in several passages. For instance, *Av.*, i, 9, 3. 4, are prayers for the king's supremacy over his kinsmen (*sajātā*), and iii, 4, refers to these kinsmen welcoming him as king, while i, 19, and 20 refer to them as a menace to his authority. In fact, these kinsmen and nobles, called *rājās*, encircled the king, who had always to reckon with them and make them friends.

These " king-makers " grow in number in the later texts.

The *Taittirīya* texts mention twelve *Ratnins*, viz. (1) Brāhmaṇa (i.e. the Purohita); (2) Rājanya (noble); (3) Mahishī (chief queen); (4) Vāvātā (favourite wife); (5) Parivṛiktī (discarded wife); (6) Sūta (charioteer); (7) Senānī, commander of the army; (8) Grāmaṇī, village headman; (9) Kshattṛi, chamberlain; (10) Saṁgrahītṛi, treasurer; (11) Bhāgadugha, collector of taxes, and (12) Akshāvāpa, superintendent of dicing. The Śatapatha Brāhmaṇa [v, 3, 1, 1] includes the huntsman (*gonikartana*) and the courier (*pālāgala*), while the Maitrāyaṇī Saṁhitā [ii, 6, 5] adds the Takshan (carpenter), Rathakāra (chariot-maker) called the *Rājanya Rājā* and the Grāmaṇī as *Vaiśya-grāmaṇī*. The *Pañchaviṁśa Brāhmaṇa* [xix, 1, 4], however, gives an older and shorter list of what are called *vīras*, or heroes, as forming the king's entourage, comprising brother, son, Purohita, Mahishī, Sūta, Grāmaṇī, Kshattṛi, and Saṁgrahītṛi.

There was an order of precedence among these *Ratnins*. It was shown in the order in which the king visited them for *Ratna-havis*, his offering of jewels. The first to be so visited was the Senānī followed by the Purohita, or Brāhmaṇa, and others, except Kshatra or Rājanya, Go-nikartana, and Akshāvāpa, whom the king offered the jewels at his own palace. An order of precedence is also indicated in a Rājasūya ceremony at which the sacrificial sword which is made over to the king is passed on by him first to his brother and then to the Sūta, Sthapati, Grāmaṇī, and Sajātā (royal kinsman) [*Śata. Br.*, v, 4, 4, 15–19].

It is not, however, certain whether these various names indicated the king's courtiers and private servants, or public functionaries. The *Sūta* usually taken to be the charioteer, *Sārathi*, or master of the horse, might also be the minstrel or court poet, in view of the epithets *ahanti*, non-fighter [*Vāja. Saṁhitā*, xvi, 18], *ahantya* [*Taitti. Saṁ.*, iv, 5, 2, 1] or *ahantva* (= *ahanya*, "inviolable") [*Kāṭhaka*, xvii, 2] applied to him in the texts. In the Epics, he definitely figures in this capacity. The *Grāmaṇī* similarly appears as a military official already in the Rigveda. The position is described as the summit of prosperity for a

Vaiśya [*Taitti. Saṁ.*, ii, 5, 4, 4] and as such must have meant the headship of the village in matters both civil and military. The *Grāmaṇī* proper or *par excellence*, who was one of the kings entourage, was probably regarded as representing rural interests in the ministry just as the industrial interests were represented by the *Karmāra*, the military by the Senanī, Rathakāra, and Sūta, and financial by the Saṁgrahītṛi and Bhāgadugha. The *Askāvāpa* may be also similarly taken as "a public officer who superintends the gambling halls of the State and collects the revenue (due therefrom), as was regularly done later on" [*Vedic Index*, ii, 200 n]. Kauṭilya, for instance, mentions the *Dūtādhyaksha* as one of the chief officers of the State. The fact was that the officers of the royal household were developing into ministers of State, as is seen in early English history too.

An officer not mentioned among the Ratnins was the *Sthapati*. We read of the Sthapati named Chākra who was powerful enough to help his master, Dushṭarītu, to the throne, from which he was expelled by his rebellious subjects, the Sṛiñjayas [*Śata. Br.*, xii, 8, 1, 17]. Thus Sthapati is taken to mean a local governor, as in the expression Nishāda-Sthapati, used in the Sūtras [Āpastamba Śrauta Sūtra, ix, 14, 12]. But as he ranks below the Sūta, he is more usually taken as "chief judge", exercising both executive and judicial functions.

Popular Assemblies: The Sabhā.—The popular Assemblies known as the *Sabhā* and the *Samiti* are described in the *Atharvaveda* [vii, 12, 1] as the twin daughters of God Prajāpati to indicate that they were the original and earliest institutions of Indian polity. A member of a *Sabhā* is called a *sabheya*, *sabhāsad*, or *sabhāsīna*. The Speaker of the *Sabhā* was called *Sabhāpati* [*Vāja. Saṁ.*, xvi, 24]. The Sergeant of the Assembly was called the *Sabhā-pāla* [*Taitt. Br.*, iii, 7, 4, 6].

The *Sabhā* was so important to the king that even God Prajāpati could not do without it [*Chhāndogya Upanishad*, viii, 14, 1]. We read of Ṛishi Gautama going to the *Sabhā* to meet the king there [ib., v, 3, 6]. The *Śatapatha Brāhmāṇa* [iii, 3, 5, 14] tells of a king of kings holding his *Sabhā* to which the subordinate kings flock together.

The *Sabhā* functioned as a parliament for disposal of public business by debate and discussion. Accordingly, eloquence and debating skill were greatly valued and prayed for [*Av.*, vii, 12]. There is a prayer that one may " speak agreeably to those assembled " (*chāru vadāmi saṁgateshu*) ; " that the members of the *Sabhā* be of one voice with the speaker " (*ye te ke cha sabhāsadaste santu savāchasaḥ*) ; " that the speaker may hold the *Sabhā* spell-bound by drawing unto himself (*ādade*) the enlightenment (*varchaḥ*) and the wisdom (*vijñanam*) of all its members (*sabhāsīnānām*) " ; " that the attention of all the members of the *Sabhā* may be riveted on one's speech, the delight of all " (*mayi vo ramatāṁ manaḥ*) [ib.].

There were rules of debate, of which violation is referred to in a passage in the Vājasaneyi Saṁhitā [iii, 45 ; repeated in xx, 17]. " Rebuke administered to the great men of the *Sabhā* " (*mahājana-tiraskārā-dikaṁ*) is instanced by the commentator as an example of such violation, of " sins against the assembly ".

Decision by the vote of the majority was known, as is indicated by the term *Narishṭā* applied to the *Sabhā* in the *Atharvaveda* [vii, 12, 3], which Sāyana explains as " inviolable, not to be overridden " (*ahimsitā parairana -bhibhāvyā*), because in the *Sabhā*, " the many meet and speak with one voice which is binding on others " (*bahavaḥ saṁbhūya yadi ekaṁ vākyaṁ vadeyuḥ tat hi na paraiḥ ati-laṁghyaṁ*).

Lastly, the *Sabhā* seems to have also functioned as a court of justice. The Vajasaneyi Saṁhitā [xxx, 6] mentions the *Sabhā-chara* as being dedicated to Dharma, or Justice. The term, therefore, may be taken to mean " one who attends the *Sabhā* sitting as a law court to dispense dharma or justice ", like the other technical term *Sabhā-sad* used in the texts [*Av.* iii, 29, 1 ; vii, 12, 2 ; xix, 55, 6 ; *Aitareya Br.* viii, 21, 14, etc.], which cannot denote any member attending the *Sabhā* but the assessor deciding legal cases in the *Sabhā*. Perhaps the term may be further differentiated to denote the Elders, or heads of families, forming the *Sabhā* which met to administer justice more frequently than for general business. In this connection may be recalled the passage in the Rigveda [x, 71, 10] which refers to a person returning from the *Sabhā* in joy, being acquitted of blame [*kilvisha* (sin)—*spṛit* (touched by) *pitushaṇiḥ* (absolved of guilt]. In the *Pāraskara Gṛihya Sūtra*, the *Sabhā* is given the names of *nādi* and *tvishi*, i.e. sounding and shining. The sound is due to proclamation of justice (*dharma-nirūpaṇāt*) and the blaze to the fire which is kept in the court house for purposes of ordeals.

The *Taittirīya Saṁhitā* [ii, 3, 1, 3] mentions the village judge (*Gramya-vādin*) and the *Maitrāyaṇī* his *Sabhā* or Court [ii, 2, 1].

The Samiti.—We have already seen how the *Atharvaveda* [vii, 12] describes both the *Sabhā* and the *Samiti* as the twin creations of Prajāpati, i.e. as primæval institutions marking the dawn of Indian civilization. This is probably the earliest reference in literature and history to democratic institutions, together with the references of the Rigveda already cited. The evidence, however, is not clear as to how the *Samiti* differed in composition and functions from the *Sabhā*. Perhaps the *Sabhā* was a smaller and select body of Elders and functioned usually as a law court, while the *Samiti* was the larger, general assembly of the people. Accordingly, it is referred to as expressing the voice of the *Viś*, or people, in the choice of theii king in several passages of the *Atharvaveda*. In one, it is the *Samiti* that chooses the king (*dhrūvāya te samitiḥ kalpatāmiha*), and in another it withdraws that choice for the king's misdeeds and tyranny (*nāsmai samitiḥ kalpate*) [vi, 88 ; v, 19]. It is also stated that the support of the *Samiti* is essential to the king to subdue his enemies and make his position firm on the throne (*dhruvochyutaḥ*) [vi, 88, 3].

Learning and Education.—The period, as we have seen, witnessed the growth of a vast and varied literature registering in some of its works, the Upanishads, the highest level of intellectual attainments and spiritual progress. It was the golden age of literature which was no doubt the outcome of schools remarkable for the efficacy and fruitfulness of their methods of teaching. These have not received the attention they deserve, nor are they directly described in any of the numerous works of the period. They are to be deduced out of stray passages, indirect allusions, or incidental illustrations contained in the texts of the period.

Rules of Studentship in the Atharvaveda and Yajurveda.—The system is first adumbrated in the *Atharvaveda* [xi, 3; also vi, 108, 2; 133, 3]. First, there is the ceremony of *Upanayana*, by which the teacher, *āchārya*, initiates the pupil, *brahmachārī*, into a new life described as a second birth, whence he becomes a *dvija*, twice-born. By *Upanayana* the *brahmachārī* is endowed with a spiritual body (*Vidyā-maya-Śarīra* as explained by Sāyana) as distinguished from the physical body given him by his parents. The new life has its own marks and rules for the pupil. He wears the skin of the black antelope (*kārshṇaṁ vasānaḥ*), the girdle (*mekhalā*) of Kuśa grass *mauñjyā*) and lets his hair grow long (*dīrghaśmaśru*). He has also to collect fuel (*samit*) to offer both morning and evening to Agni or sacrificial fire by which he himself becomes enlightened (*samidhā samiddhaḥ*, i.e. sandīpitaḥ, "illumined," according to Sāyana). Begging (*bhikshā*) is also one of his duties. He has also to practise control of the senses (*śrama*) and austerities (*tapas*). By his *tapas* he sustains (*piparti*) his teacher, who is responsible for his sins ("*śishyapāpaṁ gurorapi*"). His is thus a strictly regulated (*dīkshita*) life. There is also a reference to the pupil pleasing his preceptor by grateful gifts [xi, 3, 15]. The aims of learning are stated to be *śraddhā* (faith), *medhā* (retention of knowledge acquired), *prajā* (progeny), *dhana* (wealth), *āyuḥ* (longevity), and *amṛitatva* (immortality) [xix, 64]. They thus comprehended success in both secular and spiritual life. There is, lastly, a reference to suspension of study in certain times and places —" in cloudy (*antariksha*) or windy (*vāta*) weather, under shade of trees (*vṛiksheshu*), in sight of green barley (*ulapeshu*), or within hearing of cattle " [vii, 66].

The *Yajurveda* [*Taitti. Saṁ.* vi, 3, 10, 5] refers to *brahmacharya*, or studentship, by which the debt to Ṛishis or to culture has to be paid, just as the debt to the gods is to be paid by sacrifices (*yajñas*) and that to ancestors by progeny (*prajayā*).

The Rules in the Brāhmaṇas.—All these features of the educational system are repeated in later texts. The essence of the system was that the student had to take up residence in the home of his teacher and was hence called an *antevāsī* [*Bṛihad. Up.*, vi, 3, 15] or *āchārya-kula-vāsī* [*Chhāndogya Up.*, ii, 23, 2]. There his main duties were to beg for his teacher [*Chhāndogya Up.*, iv, 3, 5], to look after the sacrificial fires [ibid. iv, 10, 2], and tend the house [*Śata Br.*, iii, 6, 2, 15] and also his cattle [*Chhāndogya Up.*, iv, 4, 5]. According to *Śatapatha Brāhmaṇa* [xi, 3, 3, 5], begging for alms was prescribed for the pupil, to produce in him a spirit of humility, and tending fires, for "enkindling the mind with fire, with the holy lustre" [ib. xi, 5, 4, 5]. Tending cattle would give the pupil wholesome exercise in open air, training in dairy-farming, and other accomplishments. The pupil was not to sleep in day-time [ib.].

Domestic Schools.—The age at which studentship commenced, and its period are not always the same. Śvetaketu commenced study at twelve and continued it for twelve years [*Chhāndogya Up.*, vi, 1, 2]. Upakośala also studied for twelve years under his teacher, Satyakāma Jābāla [ib., v, 10, 1]. Longer periods of study, such as thirty-two years, and study for whole life, are also mentioned [ib., viii, 7, 3; 15].

Charakas.—Besides these domestic schools or small homes of learning run by an individual teacher who would choose his own pupils, the texts refer to other educational agencies. The end of formal studentship was not the end of education. The *Taittirīya Upanishad* [i, 11] contains a remarkable exhortation addressed by the teacher to his parting pupil (anticipating a modern University Rectoral or Convocation Address) in which the pupil is asked "not to neglect the study, learning, and teaching of the Veda". There were many educated men who as householders carried on their quest of knowledge by mutual discussions or seeking the instruction of distinguished specialists and literary celebrities at different centres. These wandering scholars are called the *Charakas* [*Bṛihad. Up.*, iii, 3, 1], who were the real educators of the country [*Śata. Br.*, iv, 2, 4, 1]. The texts mention many typical examples of these. Uddālaka Āruṇi of the Kuru-Pañchāla country goes to the north, where in a disputation to which he challenges the northern scholars, he has to yield to their leader, Śaunaka [ib., xi, 4, 1, 24]. He also spent some time in the land of the Madras in the north to receive instruction from their learned philosopher, Patañchala Kāpya [*Bṛi. Up.*, iii, 7, 1]. "Five great householders and theologians came out together and held a discussion as to what is our Self and what is Brahman," and then went together to the sage Uddālaka Āruṇi and to the King Aśvapati Kaikeya for instruction on the subject of Vaiśvānara [ib., x, 6, 1, 12 ; *Chhāndogya Up.*, v, 11]. Nārada, after completing the study of all the sciences and arts of his times, seeks further instruction from Sanatkumāra [*Chhāndogya Up.*, vii, 14].

Parishad.—We also read of regular organizations for such advanced study, like the Pāñchāla Parishad, an Academy patronized by the king of the country, Pravāhaṇa Jaivali, who daily attended its meetings [ib., v, 3 ; *Bṛihad. Up.*, vi, 2, 1–7].

Learned Conferences.—Besides these residential schools, academies for advanced study, and circles of philosophical disputants, a great impetus to learning came from the assemblies of learned men gathered together by kings. A typical example of these was the Conference organized by King Janaka of Videha in connection with his horse-sacrifice, to which he invited all the learned men of the Kuru-Pañchāla country. The leading figure in that Conference was Yājñavalkya, to whom difficult metaphysical problems were put by eight leading philosophers of the times, viz. (1) Uddālaka Āruṇi, who was the centre of a circle of scholars contributing most to the philosophy of the Upanishads ; (2) Aśvala, the Hotṛi priest of king Janaka ; (3) Ārtabhāga ; (4) Bhujyu, a fellow-pupil of Āruṇi senior ; (5) Ushasta ; (6) Kahoḍa ; (7) Śākalya ; and (8) Gārgī, the learned daughter of Vachaknu. The satisfactory solutions which Yājñavalkya gave to all the problems put to him won him the palm of supremacy among the philosophers of his times and the king's reward of 1,000 cows with their horns hung with gold coins (5 pieces or *pādas* to each) [*Bṛi. Up.*].

An Example of Education: Yājñvalkya.—Indeed, the life of Yājñavalkya very well illustrates the educational agencies and conditions of the times. He started as the pupil of Uddālaka Āruṇi whose son, Śvetaketu, was one of his fellow-disciples. Next we find him wandering through the country with his companions, Śvetaketu, and Soma Śushma, till they meet on the way King Janaka of Videha who defeats them in argument. While the other two hold back, Yājñavalkya, a true seeker after Truth, drives after the king and has no hesitation in receiving instruction from him, a Kshatriya. After instruction, the Brāhmaṇa pupil, Yājñavalkya, offered a boon to his Kshatriya teacher, the king, who answered: " Let mine be the privilege of asking questions of thee when I list, O Yājñavalkya! " [*Śata. Br.*, xi, 6, 2]. We next find Yājñavalkya figuring in the Philosophical Congress called by Janaka, as described above, and establishing his superiority to his teacher, Uddālaka. We then find him teaching King Janaka, another of his former teachers, on three occasions. Janaka was taught six different definitions of Brahman by six teachers named Jitvan, Udaṅka, Barku, Gardabhī-vipīta, Satyakāma, and Śākalya. Yājñavalkya taught him the Upanishads or hidden attributes behind those definitions. On the next occasion, King Janaka sought his instruction on the question, " Whither will you go after death? On Yājñavalkya's reply to this question, Deussen says: " Nor have we even to-day any better reply to give " [*Philosophy of the Upanishads*, p. 90]. The king was so much moved by it that he offered his preceptor his entire kingdom as a gift, with himself as slave! On the third occasion, Yājñavalkya delivers to the king his last discourse on Brahman, to attain Whom one must free himself from desire. " Knowing this, the people of old did not wish for offspring. What shall we do with offspring, they said, we who have this Self and this world of Brahman ?" Again: "The Ātman is that which is without and above hunger and thirst, sorrow and passion, decay and death. Realizing that Ātman, Brāhmaṇas conquer the desire for progeny, for wealth, and possessions, and even for heaven, and embrace the life of renunciation as homeless mendicants, subsisting by the strength which the knowledge of Ātman alone gives; then they devote themselves to contemplation till they are ultimately merged in the Brahman" [*Br. Up.*].

Yājñavalkya was not slow to apply to himself his teachings. He had two wives, Maitreyī and Kātyāyanī, whom he called one day, and said: "Verily, I am going away from this my house into the forest. Let me make a settlement between you!" Maitreyī, however, asked him: "My Lord, if this whole earth, full of wealth, belonged to me, tell me, should I be immortal by it or no?" "No," replied Yājñavalkya, "there is no hope of immortality by wealth." Then Maitreyī said: "What should I do with that by which I do not become immortal? What my Lord knoweth of Immortality, tell that clearly to me." Yājñavalkya then gave to his wife, Maitreyī, instruction on Brahma and then retired to the forest [*Br. Up.*, iv, 6].

The learning or culture of ancient India was chiefly the product of her hermitages in the solitude of the forests. It was not of the cities. The learning of the forests was embodied in the books specially designated as *Āraṇyakas*, "belonging to the forests." Indian civilization in its early stages had been mainly a rural, sylvan, and not an urban, civilization.

Women and Kshatriyas in Education.—Two features in this educational system should not be missed. The first is the part taken in intellectual life by women like Gārgī who could address a Congress of philosophers on learned topics, or like Maitreyī, who had achieved the highest knowledge, that of Brahma. The Rigveda shows us some women as authors of hymns, such as Viśvavarā, Ghoshā, and Apālā. The second feature is the part taken by Kshatriyas in intellectual life, by kings as patrons and devotees of learning. The most famous of these was

King Janaka of Videha, whose contributions to learning have been already indicated. There was also the Pāñchāla king, Pravāhaṇa Jaivali, who taught Brāhmaṇa scholars like Śilaka, Dālbhya [*Chhāndogya Up*., i, 8], Śvetaketu, and his father Uddālaka [ib., v, 3]. King Aśvapati Kaikeya was another learned king teaching Brāhmaṇa pupils [ib., v, 11]. So also was King Pratardana (*Kaushi. Br.*, xxvi, 5] or King Jānaśruti [*Chhān. Up.*, iv, 1–3]. Nārada, the foremost Brāhmaṇa scholar, with all his learning, had to seek the instruction of Sanatkumāra on Ātman [ib., vii, 1]. Sanatkumāra told Nārada that what he had hitherto studied was mere words, that he was a *Mantravit* but not an *Ātmavit*. The Āruṇis, father and son, once sought the teachings of King Chitra-Gāṅgāyani [*Kaushītaki Up*., i, 1]. Another learned king mentioned is Jānaśruti Pautrāyaṇa [*Chhāndogya Up*., iv, 2, 3]. Another was King Bṛihadratha [*Maitrāyaṇī Up*.]. Ajātaśatru, King of Kāśī, was another very learned king whose superiority and pupilage were acknowledged by that distinguished Brāhmaṇa scholar, Dṛipta-Bālāki Gārgya, whose fame for learning was known all over the country, to the Uśīnaras, Satvat Matsyas, Kuru-Pañchālas, and Kāśī-Videhas [*Bṛihad. Up*., ii, 1, 1].

Recitation of Texts.—The methods of education addressed themselves to the conservation of sacred texts by oral tradition. The need of recitation was paramount. It was started by students before birds announced break of day [*purā-vayabhyaḥ*, i.e. *pakshādīnāṁ vāgvadanā-raṁbhāt prāk*; *T.S.*, vi, 4, 3, 1; *A.B.*, ii, 15]. The *Aitareya Āraṇyaka* [viii] recalls the Rigvedic passage of frog-like (*māṇḍūkya*) mode of recitation, and refers to three ways of reciting the Rigveda, *pratṛiṇṇa*, *nirbhuja*, and *ubhayamantareṇa*, by taking the words singly or in pairs or in a continuous way, corresponding respectively to the *Saṁhitā*, *Pada*, and *Krama pāṭhas* already explained. There was developed a sound system of phonology. The Aitareya and Śatapatha *Āraṇyakas* already distinguish sounds as *ghosha*, *ūshman*, and *vyañjana*, dental and lingual *n*, and the sibilants *ś*, *sh*, and *s*, and discuss rules of *Sandhi* or combination of sounds. The Upanishads go further by recognizing phonological factors like *mātrā* (quantity), *balam* (accent), *sāma* (euphony), and *santāna* (relations of letters) [*T.U.*, 1, 1, 2]. Prayers were offered for memory, *medhā*: " May the Lord endow me with *medhā*; may we learn much and learn by the ear and may we retain what we have thus learnt " [ib., i, 4]. Texts were recited loudly at noon [*T.A.*, ii, 11, 15]. Purity of speech was a mark of culture. An Aryan family was barred out of priesthood for its *apūta* (impure) speech [*A.B.*, vii, 2, 7; *S.B.*, iii, 21].

Literature explanatory of Texts.—Mere recitation of texts without knowing their meaning is condemned in the Rigveda [x, 71, 5] which describes it as " bearing speech without fruit or flowers ", and also in Yāska's *Nirukta* [i, 18], which compares it to a pillar (*sthāṇu*) supporting a hall, or to a bearer of burden (*bhārahāra*).

There was thus a great growth of literature explanatory of the Vedic texts, of subjects like the six *Vedāṅgas* and the *Upavedas* like the *Dhanurveda, Gandharvaveda* (evolved from the *Sāman* chanting), etc. These were associated with one or other of the four schools of Vedic interpretation pointed out by Yāska, viz. *Aitihāsika* (historical), *Ādhyātmika* (spiritual), *Ādhiyājñika* (ritualistic), and *Svābhāvika* (natural).

Interpretation through Discussion.—Interpretation of texts was the outcome of discussion depending on (*a*) the *Praśnin* (questioner), (*b*) the *Abhi-praśnin* (cross-questioner), and (*c*) the *Praśna-vivāka* (answerer), as stated in the *Taittirīya Brāhmaṇa*. The *Atharvaveda* refers also to the *Prāvāchika* (cf. *Nirvachana*, whence *Nirukta*).

Various Subjects of Study.—The texts mention the subjects of study then developed. A good list of these is given in *Chhāndogya Upanishad* [vii, 1]. It includes (1) *Rigveda*, (2) *Yajurveda*, (3) *Sāmaveda*, (4) *Atharvaveda*, (5) *Itihāsa* and *Purāṇa*, described as the fifth Veda, (6) *Vyākaraṇa*, described as the Veda of Vedas, (7) *Pitrya*, dealing with Śrāddha or funeral rituals, (8) *Rāśi*, or science of numbers, (9) *Daiva*, or science of portents, (10) *Nidhi*, explained as mineralogy, (11) *Vākovākya*, i.e. Tarka-Śāstra or science of logic, (12) *Ekāyana*, i.e. Nīti-Śāstra or science of ethics, (13) *Deva-vidyā*, explained as Nirukta or exegetics, or as the science of worship of gods, (14) *Brahma-vidyā*, the knowledge relating to Brahma or the three Vedas and hence explained to mean the Vedāṅgas like Śikshā (phonetics), Kalpa (ritualism), and Chhandas (prosody), (15) *Bhūta-Vidyā*, biology, (16) *Kshatra-vidyā*, military science, (17) *Nakshatra-vidyā*, astronomy, (18) *Sarpa-vidyā* or *Gāruḍa-vidyā*, the science dealing with poisons, (19) *Deva-jana-vidyā*, the arts affected by the lesser gods such as perfumery, dancing, singing, playing on musical instruments (*vādya*), and other fine arts and crafts (*śilpādi-vijñāna*). Some split up the compound into *Deva-vidyā* or musical arts and *Jana-vidyā* or *Āyurveda*, medicine.[1] Valuable medical material is found in the *Atharvaveda* verses describing diseases like fever [v, 22].

Different Texts and Schools.—It is to be noted that all this literature was the outcome of the various schools of Vedic study and interpretation functioning all over the country. Firstly, the sacred texts were preserved and propagated by various families in different parts of the country, which were known as the *Kulas* and *Gotras*. Next, there were other institutions in which teachers and students came together in a different relationship which was not that of blood. These were known as *Śākhā* and *Charaṇa*. The *Śākhā* was the Vedic school of students studying the same text of the Veda. The Rigveda was studied in a variety of Śākhās, each of which adhered strictly to its own text of the Rigveda. As the text of the Vedas differed in different schools or Śākhās, so also, and more widely, did the texts of the corresponding *Brāhmaṇas* studied in

[1] Some of these subjects of study are ascribed to contact with the non-Āryans, subjects like *Sarpa-vidyā*, *Devajana-vidyā*, *Bhūta-vidyā* in the sense of *Piśācha-vidyā* [as explained in Āśvalāyana Gṛihya Sūtra], *Daiva-vidyā*, the art of hypnotizing and mesmerizing, in which the Nāgas excelled, as stated in the *Taittirīya Brāhmaṇa* [ii, 4], or *Asura-vidyā* mentioned in the *Śatapatha Brāhmana*. The *Gopatha Brāhmaṇa* [i, 10] mentions *Sarpa-vidyā*, *Asura-vidyā*, and *Piśācha-vidyā*, along with *Itihāsa* and *Purāṇa*, as the five newly created Vedas. This only indicated the cultural fellowship of the Āryan and non-Āryan. This is also shown by the mention in connection with *purusha-medha* in the *Taittirīya Brāhmaṇa* [iii, 4, 2, 13] of non-Āryans like the *Sūta*, *Māgadha*, *Ṛitula* (narrator of tales of kings and countries) who were the educators of the masses, along with the wit, the buffoon, the dancer, engineer or architect.

the schools called Charaṇas. Each such Charaṇa had its own arrangement of texts, its own manner of application of the texts to rituals, and its own rules of conduct and discipline for its members. These Śākhās and Charaṇas, based on slightly different texts, were very useful in preserving the purity of their respective texts.

Supreme Knowledge.—The Muṇḍaka Upanishad classes all these subjects of study under *Aparā-vidyā*, including in it even the four Vedas and the six Vedāṅgas, Śikshā (phonetics), Kalpa (ritualism), Vyākaraṇa (grammar), Nirukta (exegetics), Chhandas (metrics), and Jyotisha (astronomy). It reserves the term *Parā-vidyā* for the highest knowledge, the knowledge of the Ātman, the real subject-matter of the Upanishads, which is *sarva-vidyā-pratishṭhā*, the foundation of all sciences and arts, the *vedānta*, the final and highest stage of Vedic wisdom [*Muṇḍaka Up.*, i, 1, 2, 3; iii, 2, 6]. Nārada regretfully acknowledges that all his learning in the Vedas and other subjects has left him ignorant of the true knowledge, that of the Ātman, by which he can cross the ocean of suffering [*Chhāndogya*, vii, 1]. The Kaṭha Upanishad plainly states that "not by the Veda is the Ātman attained, nor by intellect, nor by much knowledge of books", and condemns all *aparā-vidyā* in which the Vedas are included as *a-vidyā*, as not true knowledge. The Vedic religion of sacrifice has been accordingly valued very little in some of these Upanishads. The *Muṇḍaka* [i, 2, 7] brands as fools those devoted to mere rites and ceremonies. In the same strain the *Bṛihadāraṇyaka* [i, 4, 10] likens those offering sacrifices to gods to animals ministering to the comforts of their owners. In the *Aitareya Āraṇyaka* [iii, 2, 6] we read: "To what end shall we repeat the Veda, to what end shall we sacrifice? For we sacrifice breath in speech or in breath speech."

How it can be attained.—Thus Education aimed at the highest knowledge, the knowledge of the Ātman or the absolute, or self-realization. Such knowledge was not attainable within the limits of formal pupilage, of the first *āśrama* or stage of life. It depended on a dedicated life. Its foundations were laid in the life of *brahmacharya*. Its attainment required much further and longer effort. As stated in the *Bṛihadāraṇyaka* [iv, 4, 22], "Brāhmaṇas seek to know him by the study of the Veda, by sacrifice, by gifts, by penance, by fasting, and he who knows him becomes a *Muni*. Wishing for that world (of Brahman) only, mendicants leave their homes. Knowing this, the people of old did not wish for offspring and they, having risen above the desire for sons, wealth, and new worlds, wander about as mendicants." In the Kaṭha [ii, 15], all the Vedas, all the practices of *tapas* and *brahmacharya*, are described as means by which the One is to be attained, and in the *Muṇḍaka* [ii, 1], *tapas*, *śraddhā*, *satya*, *brahmacharya*, and *vidhi*. The *Maitrāyaṇī Upanishad* [iv, 3, 4] describes *Jñāna* as the result of *vidyā*, *chintā*, and *tapas*. The *Taittirīya Upanishad* [iii] declares: "By *tapas* seek to know Brahman." Yājñavalkya, as we have seen, even after achieving fame as the greatest philosopher, renounced the world and retired into forest to practise *tapas* for knowing the Brahman. All these passages indicate that while the aim of education was the knowledge of the highest truth and ultimate reality, it could not be ordinarily realized except by the consecrated efforts of a whole life in all its four Āśramas of the Student, the Householder, the Anchorite, and the Sannyāsī.

In the *Kaṭhopanishad*, Yama did not impart to Nachiketas the highest knowledge before testing his zeal for it. He tried to wean him away by offering him all a mortal could desire: "Sons and grandsons who shall live a hundred years, herds of cattle, elephants, horses, gold, sovereignty of the earth, fair maidens, and even control over death." But Nachiketas answered: "Keep thou thy horses, keep dance and song for thyself. No man can be made happy by wealth." Then Yama admitted: "I believe Nachiketas to be one who desires knowledge, for even many pleasures did not tear him away." King Jānaśruti brought to Raikva a present of 600 cows, a necklace, and a carriage with mules, but Raikva snubbed him: "Fie, necklace and carriage be thine, O Śūdra, together with the cows" [*Chhān.*, iv, 2].

These stories are typical of the inner development required for a knowledge of the highest truths.

Religion: *Growth of Rituals and Priesthood.*—The *Brāhmaṇas* record a great growth of ceremonial religion and the consequent growth of priesthood. From the simplest Soma sacrifice occupying one day, there were now many others culminating in the Sattras lasting from twelve days to a year or years. The Rigveda knows of seven priests, Hotṛi, Potṛi, Nestṛi, Agnīdh, Praśāstṛi, Adhvaryu and Brahman [ii, 1, 2], and the other two Sāman priests called Udgātṛi and his assistant, the Prastotṛi [viii, 81, 5]. Now the sacrifices required seventeen priests classified as under:

(1) Hotṛi, with Maitrāvaruṇa, Achāvāka, and Grāvastut.

(2) Udgātṛi, with Prastotṛi, Pratihotṛi, and Subrahmaṇya.

(3) Adhvaryu, with Partishṭhātṛi, Nestṛi, and Unnetṛi.

(4) Brahman, with Brāhmaṇāchchhaṁsin, Agnīdhra, and Potṛi. The seventeenth Ṛitvij was the Sadasya who superintended the whole sacrifice as its presiding priest. The Adhvaryu had three other assistant priests of lower rank, viz. the Śamitṛi (the slayer), the Vaikarta, and the Chamasādhvaryu.

Symbolism of Rituals.—Some of the rituals are informed by a new spirit of symbolism and spirituality. This is evident in connection with the building of the altar for sacrifice and for the sacred fire. The building is elaborated in the texts out of all reason and utility, because it was to symbolize the constitution of the unity of the universe. The symbolism was originally suggested by the Purusha hymn of the Rigveda presenting the conception of the creation of the universe from the Virāṭ Purusha. In the *Brāhmaṇas*, Prajāpati stands for Purusha and "the sacrifice is conceived as constantly recurring in order to maintain the universe. To render this possible is the end of the fire-altar, the building of which is the reconstruction of the universe in the shape of Prajāpati. Prajāpati, again, is identified with Agni, the fire of the altar, and both Prajāpati and Agni are the divine counterparts of the human sacrificer. But Prajāpati is himself Time, and Time in the long run is Death, so that the sacrificer himself becomes Death, and by that act rises superior to Death, and is for ever removed from the world of illusion and trouble to the world of everlasting bliss. In this the true nature of Prajāpati and of the sacrificer is revealed as Intelligence and the Śatapatha Brāhmaṇa urges the seeker for truth to meditate upon the Self, made up of intelligence and endowed with a body of spirit, a form of light and an ethereal nature " [*Cambridge History of India*, I, 142].

Doctrines of Māyā, Karma, Transmigration, Mukti, and Ātman in the Upanishads.—This same doctrine has been taken up and elaborated in the Upanishads, which deal with Brahman or Ātman as the only, underlying, and ultimate Reality, as stated above. Indeed, the Upanishads really expound a new religion which is opposed to the sacrificial ceremonial and represents the philosophic aspect of Hinduism for about 2,500 years. They aim at the achievement of deliverance from mundane existence by the absorption of the individual soul (*ātmā*) in the world-soul (*brahma*) by virtue of correct knowledge. For such an aim, ritual is useless and saving knowledge all-important. Earthly rewards or heavenly blisses are not thought of at all in this scheme. The identity of the individual *ātman* with the world *ātman* is asserted in statements like *Tvat tvam asi*, " That art thou " [*Chhāndogya*]. " Brahma or the Absolute is grasped and definitely expressed for the first time in the history of human thought in the *Bṛihadāraṇyaka Upanishad* " [Macdonell in *India's Past*, p. 46]. The conception of the material world as *Māyā* or illusion first finds expression in the later *Śvetāśvatara* Upanishad, though it is inherent in the oldest also. Lastly, the doctrine of transmigration also appears first in the *Śatapatha Brāhmaṇa* where it is stated that retribution follows in the form of repeated births and deaths and is elaborated in the Upanishads which offer to the ascetic, possessed of true knowledge, " the path of the gods " leading to absorption in Brahma, and to pious householders, lacking that supreme knowledge, " the path of the fathers," followed by rebirth on earth in various forms depending on their *karma*. Thus we find that in this age were enunciated the leading doctrines of Hinduism, those of transmigration, karma, māyā, and mukti or final release by absorption in Brahma.

Emergence of deities, Rudra and Vishṇu.—Parallel with the development of this philosophy, there was also in progress, the movement which leads to the religions of modern India, the emergence of Rudra and Vishṇu as the great gods. Prajāpati was now yielding to Rudra, figuring as a popular deity already in the Yajurveda, while the Aitareya Brāhmaṇa brings up the Bhūtapati, representing the dread forms of the gods, and an aspect of Rudra's activities as the slayer of Prajāpati. The growing position of Vishṇu is indicated by his identification with sacrifice, a sign that he counted for much in Vedic life.

Chapter VI

CIVILIZATION AS REVEALED IN POST-VEDIC LITERATURE: THE SŪTRAS, EPICS, AND LAW-BOOKS

Age.—These three classes of works, making up later Brāhmaṇa literature, date roughly from 800 B.C.,[1] though some of their representative works in their extant form belong to much later dates. The material is much older than the works in which it is transmitted and, broadly speaking, this post-Vedic literature gives a picture of ancient Hindu civilization as it was fixed in its normal form before the rise of Jainism and Buddhism.

Sūtras.—The *Sūtras* were manuals of instruction in the form of brief rules strung together (*sūtra* = thread). They conveyed the maximum of matter in the minimum of words and helped to preserve the vast sacredotal literature by giving its essence in a form convenient to memory. The first Sūtra works were the *Vedāṅgas*. comprising the six subjects of Kalpa (religious practice), Śikshā (phonetics), Vyākaraṇa (grammar), Nirukta (etymology), Chhandas (metre), and Jyotisha (astronomy). All of these aim at explaining, preserving, or practically applying the sacred texts. The most important of these works are the linguistic works which deal with phonetics, derivation, and grammar. Of these the most valuable and still extant are Yāska's *Nirukta*, the earliest specimen of classical Sanskrit prose, and Pāṇini's *Ashṭādhyāyī*, the starting point of post-Vedic Sanskrit literature, and dominating its entire course, though it bases itself on the usage of the *Brāhmaṇas*, Upanishads, and Sūtras and not that of classical Sanskrit,

[1] "Although the chronology of the legal literature is uncertain, it can be assumed with probability that the older Dharma Sūtras belonging to the Vedic schools date from between 800 and 300 B.C." [Macdonell, *India's Past*, p. 161.]

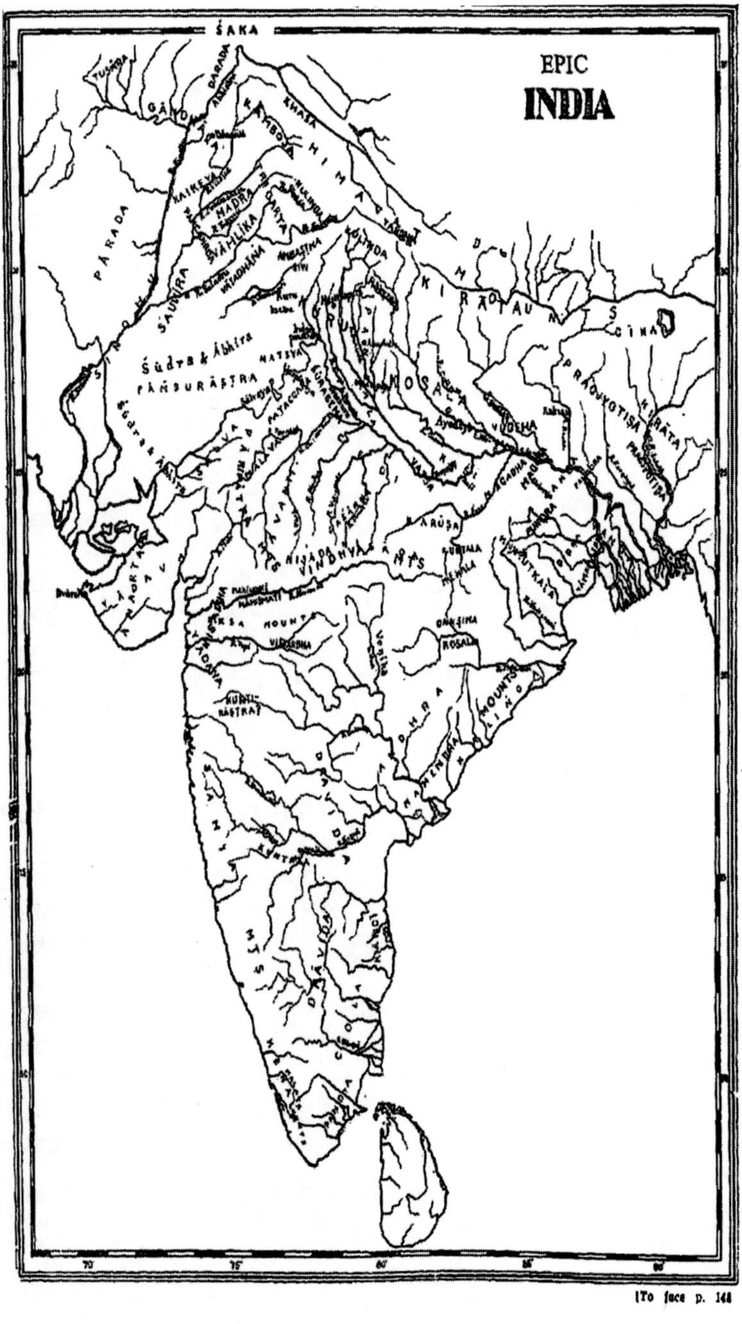
EPIC
INDIA
ŚAKA
TUṢĀRA
DARADA
KHAŚA
KAMBOJA
KAIKEYA
MADRA
TRIGARTA
VĀHLĪKA
PĀRADA
SAUVĪRA
Śūdra & Ābhīra
MATSYA
PAÑSURĀṢṬRA
KURU
KOSALA
VIDEHA
KIRĀTA
CĪNA
PRĀGJYOTIṢA
MAGADHA
KARŪṢA
NIṢĀDA
VINDHYA MOUNTS
ṚKṢA MOUNTS
VIDARBHA
DAKṢIṆA KOSALA
UTKALA
ANDHRA
KALIṄGA
Dvārakā
70°
75°
80°
85°
90°

[To face p. 148

and deals with Vedic grammar in the form of exceptions to classical Sanskrit.

The other Sūtras works arise out of the Vedāṅga called Kalpa, and fall into three classes: (*a*) the *Śrauta* Sūtras dealing with the great ceremonies involving for their performance a number of priests; (*b*) the *Gṛihya* Sūtras dealing with the domestic sacrifices and rites performed by the gṛihī or householder; and (*c*) the *Dharma* Sūtras which enunciate customary law and practice.

Picture of Civilization in Pāṇini's Grammar : *Its Date.*—Pāṇini's grammar throws some light on the history of its times. His date was thought to be earlier than 700 B.C. by Goldstucker on the ground that he was acquainted only with the three Vedic Saṁhitās and the *Nighaṇṭu* (Yāska's *Nirukta*). Sir R. G. Bhandarkar was for the same date on the ground that Pāṇini does not show much acquaintance with the Deccan. According to Macdonell [*India's Past*, p. 136], "the date of Pāṇini is usually assumed to be about 350 B.C., but the evidence for this is very doubtful; it is perhaps safer to say that he lived after, probably soon after, 500 B.C."

Geographical Horizon.—Pāṇini's geographical horizon extended to Kaliṅga [iv, 1, 70] in the east, to Sind [iv, 3, 32] and the Cutch [iv, 2, 133] in the west, and to Taxila [iv, 3, 93], Aśmaka [iv, 1, 173], and the Swat Valley [iv, 2, 77] in the north-west. The different regions or States were called *Janapadas*, of which he mentions twenty-two, including Kekaya [vii, 3, 2], Gāndhāra [iv, 1, 169], Kāmboja [iv, 1, 175], Madra [iv, 2, 131], Avanti [iv, 1, 176], Kuru [iv, 1, 172; 2, 130], Śālva [iv, 1, 173], Kosala [iv, 1, 171], Bhārata [iv, 2, 118; viii, 3, 74], Uśīnara [iv, 2, 118], Yaudheya [iv, 1, 178], Vṛiji [iv, 2, 131], and Magadha [iv, 1, 170]. Besides these, Pāṇini refers to *Prāchya Janapadas* [iv, 1, 178] or eastern States which, according to *Kāśikā*, comprised Pañchāla, Videha, Aṅga, and Vaṅga.

Administrative Divisions.—These States were named after their Kshatriya peoples [iv, 1, 168]. The Kshatriya rulers were called *Jānapadins* [iv, 3, 100]. The citizens of the same State, or *Janapada*, were called *sajanapadāḥ* [vi, 3, 85]. As the State was represented in the ruler, loyalty to the State was synonymous with loyalty to its ruler [iv, 3, 100]. There was thus a lively sense of patriotism in those days.

The different *Janapadas*, or States, were separated by well-defined boundaries [iv, 2, 124].

Below the *Janapada* were the administrative divisions called *Vishaya* [iv, 2, 52], *Nagara*, and *Grāma*. A village was named after its *Grāmaṇī*. [v, 2, 78].

Literature then known.—Pāṇini refers to Rigveda [vi, 3, 55] Sāmaveda [i, 2, 34] and Yajurveda [ii, 4, 4]; to the Śākala Śākhā of the Rigveda [iv, 3, 128], its *pada-pāṭha* [iv, 2, 61] and its divisions into Sūktas, Adhyāyas, and Anuvākas [v, 2, 60]; to the Kāṭhaka recension of the Black Yajurveda [vii, 4, 38].

He knows of *Brāhmaṇa* works and refers to two containing thirty and forty *adhyāyas* [v, 1, 62], supposed by Keith to be the Aitareya and Kaushītakī Brāhmaṇas.

He mentions Chhandas works of Ṛishis like Tittiri, Varatantu (whose disciple, Kautsa, was of Yāska's time), Kaśyapa and Kauśika, Śaunaka, of Kaṭha and Charaka, Kalāpi and Chhagalin, of the pupils of Kalāpi and Vaiśampāyana [iv, 2, 101–9].

As regards *Sūtras*, he knows of *Kalpa Sūtras* [iv, 3, 105] of ancient authors [*purāṇa-prokta*) and mentions recent works like the Bhikshu-Sūtras of Parāśara and Karmanda and the Naṭasūtras of Śīlālin and Kṛiśāśva [iv, 3, 110, 111].

He knew of a wide variety of secular literature comprising drama [e.g. Śiśukrandīya in iv, 3, 88], *Śloka* [iii, 1, 25], *Gāthā*, *Kathā* [iv, 4, 102] or *Mahābhārata* [vi, 2, 38].

He knew of the literature of *Vyākhyāna* or commentary such as works giving details of *puroḍāśa* [iv, 3, 70], grammatical works dealing with nouns (*nāma*) and verbs [iv, 3, 72], Chhāndasa works and those called *Ārchika* (relating to hymns) or *Ādhvarika* (relating to sacrifices).

All these various works are classified by Pāṇini under (1) *Dṛishṭa* ("revealed", i.e. *Śruti*), (2) *Prokta* ("compiled", "enounced", i.e. secondary works), (3) *Upajñāta* and

Kṛita ("originated" and "composed"), and (4) *Vyākhyāna* or "explanatory" works.

Education.—The ceremony of initiation was called *āchārya-karaṇa* [i, 3, 36]. The pupil was called a *chhātra* because he was protected from all evil by his teacher [iv, 4, 62]. Pupils of the same teacher were called *satīrthyas* and *sabrahmachāriṇas* [vi, 3, 86]. They are named after their teachers, e.g. Pāṇinīyas [vi, 2, 36], or after their subjects of study, such as Vedic Kratus, Ukthas, and Sūtras [iv, 2, 59, 60].

The ordinary term for a teacher was *Adhyāpaka.* The specialist in Vedic recitation was called a *Śrotriya* [v, 2, 84] and in Vedic discourse and interpretation (*pravachana*) a *Pravaktā.* One *Charaṇa* might follow the system of recitation of another *Charaṇa* [ii, 4, 3]. A teacher usually repeated the text five times. A pupil learning it from a single recitation was called an *Ekasandhagrāhī* [v, 1, 58]. Pupils were graded according to the number of mistakes they committed in such Vedic recitation, the limit allowed for such mistakes being fourteen [iv, 4, 63–6].

Girls were admitted to Vedic schools or *Charaṇas.* A *Kaṭhī* denoted the female student of the *Kaṭha* school. There were hostels for female students, called *Chhātrī-śālā* [vi, 2, 86].

Each *Charaṇa* had an inner circle of teachers and advanced scholars, which was called *Parishad,* whose decisions on doubts about readings and meanings of Vedic texts was binding on the *Charaṇa.* The Prātiśākhya literature was the product of these Parishads.

Economic Life: Occupations.—Paṇini gives evidence of advanced economic life. He refers to the professions or unproductive occupations called Jānapadī Vṛitti [iv, 1, 42] depending on pay for livelihood [*Vetanādibhyojīvati* in iv, 4, 12], as in government service. Men in service were called *Adhyakshas* and *Yuktas* [vi, 2, 66, 67]. There is mention of profession of arms [iv, 4, 14]. He also refers to labourers, *karmakāra,* employed on wages, *vṛitti* [i, 3, 36] under stipulated terms, *parikrayaṇa* [i, 4, 44]. Wages were paid both in cash and kind [ii, 2, 22].

Trade ; Interest.—There is mention of trade and commerce *Kraya-Vikraya* [iv, 4, 13] and of the necessary money-lending [iv, 4, 31]. The rate of interest is stated to be 10 per cent, whereby ten rupees lent out were to return as eleven [ib. *Kusīda-daśaikādaśāt*]. The debt was called after the month in which it was due for repayment [iv, 3, 47], e.g. *Āgrahayāṇika* [iv, 3, 50] or *Sāṁvatsarika* [ib.] and it could be repaid in kind, e.g. barley [iv, 3, 48].

Agriculture.—As regards agriculture, the plough was called *hala* or *sīra* [iv, 3, 124]. Methods of ploughing and of sowing are indicated [v, 4, 58, 159]. Crops were called after the name of the month in which they were sown [iv, 3, 44, 45], and fields after the name of the crop grown, e.g. fields of *vrīhi* (rice), *śāli*, *yava*, *shashṭika*, *tila*, *māsha*, *umā* (linseed), *bhaṅgā* (hempen flax), etc. [v, 2, 2–4]. There is also a reference to *uñchhavṛitti*, picking up grains from the fields by ascetics [iv, 4, 32].

Arts and Crafts.—A variety of arts and crafts is mentioned. Weaving is implied in the terms *goṇī* (small sack for carrying grain), *āvāya*, and *pravāṇi* [v, 4, 160]. There is mention of cloth fresh from the loom—" *tantrādachirāpahṛite* " [v, 2, 70]. *Āvāya* is explained by Patañjali as the place where the weavers came and wove the cloth. Woollen cloth is mentioned (*ūrṇā*) [iv, 3, 158]. There was also dyeing with indigo (*nīla*) [iv, 1, 42], *lākshā* (shellac), and yellow ointment produced from potsherds and black mud (*gorochanā*) [iv, 2, 2]. The potter was called *kulāla* [iv, 3, 118]. The leatherer was known [v, 1, 14, 15]. The fowler was called *Śākunika*, and mention is made of hunting deer and fish [iv, 4, 35].

Music.—Music was in vogue. There is mention of players on *mṛidaṅga* [iv, 4, 85], *maḍḍuka* and *jharjhara* [iv, 4, 56], and of concerts, *tūryāṅga* [ii, 2, 2]; of vocalists, *gāthakas*, and dancers, *nartakas* [iii, 1, 145, 146].

Guilds.—Crafts were organized in guilds, as indicated by a reference to a carpenter in the employ of the village community or working independently—" *grāmakoṭābhyāṁ* takshṇaḥ " [v, 4, 95].

Excise.—Excise was a source of revenue, *āyasthāna*

[iv, 3, 75]. There are mentioned brewery (śuṇḍikā) [iv, 3, 76] and distillery (*āsutī*) [v, 2, 112].

Weights and Measures.—Various weights and measures were known, such as *khārī* [v, 1, 33], *pātra* [v, 1, 40], *vista* (measure of length) [v, 1, 31], *śatamāna* [v, 1, 27], *ādhaka* [v, 1, 53], *āchita* [iv, 1, 22], *purusha* (man's height for measuring a ditch) [v, 2, 38], *dishṭi* and *vitasti* [vi, 2, 31].

Coins.—The following coins were known in Pāṇini's time : *kārshāpana* [v, 1, 29], *nishka* [v, 1, 20, 30], *paṇa* [v, 1, 34], *pāda, māsha* [ib., v, 4, 1], and *śāṇa* (a small copper coin). There is mention of striking or stamping of coins [v, 2, 120].

Corporations.—The growth of group-life, popular government, and democratic institutions is evidenced in the variety of terms recorded by Pāṇini to indicate their different types. These terms may be explained as follows :—

1. *Kula* and *Vaṁśa* [ii, 1, 19] ; *Kula* is the family which, continued for generations, counts as a *Vaṁśa*. But the *Vaṁśa* may be based on relationship in blood as well as learning (vidyā-yoni-saṁbamdha).

2. *Gotra* [iv, 1, 162–5] : which is a group based on relationship in blood and traced to a common ancestor after whom it is named. Thus the *Vatsa gotra* founded by Vatsa will comprise Vātsi, his son, Vātsya, his grandson, and Vātsyāyana, his great-grandson. Similarly, the term *Sapiṇḍa* includes six ancestors on the male side, together with their descendants up to the sixth degree. Pāṇini mentions the names of many old and famous *gotras* such as Atri, Bhṛigu, Aṅgiras and the like, most of which became extinct. Sometimes descendants became distinguished enough to found new *gotras*, e.g. Kapi and Bodha, who were descended from Aṅgiras *gotra* [iv, 1, 107]. Some *gotras* might also derive from the mother where the father was unknown [iv, 1, 14], or from a famous member, like the Maukhari dynasty from Mukhara, in which case the *gotra* will be called *gotrāvayava* [iv, 1, 79].

3. *Charaṇa* [iv, 3, 104] : it was a Vedic school for the study of the particular *śākhā* or recension of the Veda which was taught by the teacher who founds the *Charaṇa* named

after him. His disciples might also be the founders of new *Charaṇas*. Thus Vedavyāsa had his disciple Vaiśampāyana who arranged the Yajurveda, and Vaiśampāyana had disciples like Aruṇi and Kalāpin who themselves founded new schools.

4. *Saṁgha*, or Assembly, of which there were two classes, (*a*) *Gaṇa* and (*b*) *Nikāya* [iii, 3, 42, 86].

The *Nikāya* was a religious association in which there were no distinctions due to birth (anauttarādharya-Saṁgha).

The *Gaṇa* was the political assembly or Republic comprising all castes, and a special governing caste of Kshatriyas technically called *Rājanyas* consecrated to rulership [vi, 2, 34, and *Kāśikāś* gloss.]. Only Kshatriyas of the Rājanya rank could be on the governing body of the *Saṁgha* or its Parliament. In the Saṁgha government, there were also parties called *Vargas* [iv, 3, 64] named after their leader, e.g. Vāsudeva-Vargya, Arjuna-Vargya. There was rivalry for power, *Dvanda* [vi, 2, 34], or *Vyutkramaṇaṁ* [viii, 1, 15], between the parties, as in the Andhaka-Vṛishṇi Saṁgha. Pāṇini refers to individual *Saṁghas* or Republics like Kshudraka, Mālava [iv, 2, 45] or Yaudheya [v, 3, 117] and also to Confederations of Republics, like the Trigarta Saṁgha of six republics [v, 3, 116], or the Andhaka-Vṛishṇi Saṁgha [v, 3, 114], of which the federal executive was made up of the *Rājanya* leader of each constituent Republic with his own following or *Varga*; e.g. Śini and Vāsudeva, Śvāphalka and Chaitraka, or Akrūra and Vāsudeva, with their rival *Vargas*. The Kshudraka and Mālava Saṁghas had also a federal army called the Kshaudraka-Mālavīsenā [iv, 2, 45].

The Saṁgha as a Republic naturally comprised the whole population in all its castes admitted equally to its privileges. A Brahmin and a Kshatriya member would, however, be differently designated from a Śūdra member; e.g. a *Kshaudraka* would denote a Brahmin or a Kshatriya, and *Kshaudrakya*, a Śūdra member of the Kshudraka (Greek *Oxydrakai*) Republic.

The expression *Chhandaso Nirmite*, "passed or made by the free will of members," indicates that the Saṁgha performed its business in accordance with the votes of its members [iv, 4, 93]. The Pāli term for vote is also *Chhanda*.

The term *Pūga* or Guild is sometimes [v, 3, 112] used in the sense of the village community under the Grāmaṇī. It was known for its corporate character or organization [v, 2, 52]. Pāṇini also tells of *Kumāra-pūgas* which were like juvenile associations.

Kingship.—The king had his Council or *Parishat*, of which the members were called *Pārishadyas* [iv, 4, 44]. The *Parishat* strengthened the position of the king who was designated as *Parishadvalaḥ* [v, 2, 112]. As regards government officers, the general term was *Yukta* [vi, 2, 66]. The head of a department was called *Adhyaksha* [vi, 2, 67]. The officer in charge of rules and discipline was called *Vainayika*; in charge of law, *Vyāvahārika*; in charge of ways and means or finance, *Oupāyika* [v, 4, 34].

Civilization as presented in the Dharma Sutras [1] **:** *Age*.—We shall now consider the Sūtras proper as sources of history. These are the Śrauta, Gṛihya and Dharma Sūtras, forming parts of the whole called *Kalpa*, but differentiated later into independent works. The metrical Śāstras, for instance, were a development out of the Dharma Sūtras, with the part dealing with civil and criminal law increasing and their connection with the Veda loosening. The sacrificial Sūtras, the Śrauta works dealing with the greater sacrifices of Havis and Soma, are not so important for our purposes as the Gṛihya and Dharma Sūtras. The chief Sūtra works are those of Gautama, Baudhāyana, Vasishṭha, and Āpastamba named in the chronological order, though there is some doubt as to the priority of Vasishṭha to Āpastamba. They may be taken to belong to the period from the seventh to the second century B.C. and to represent the views of different Vedic schools and different regions from the Andhra country following Āpastamba to the countries of the north-west following the school of Vasishṭha.

Locality.—The Sūtras appear, from their geographical

[1] References: Kane's *History of Dharma-śāstra Literature*, Vol. I; Chapter XII of *Cambridge History*, Vol. I.

references, to have been operative within very limited areas and select regions. Baudhāyana [i, 1, 2, 13–15] requires a purificatory sacrifice for a visit to Kaliṅga, to the countries of the Āraṭṭas (in the Panjab), the Sauvīras (Multan), the Puṇḍras and Vaṅgas (in Bengal). He also condemns the peoples of Avanti (Malwa), Magadha (Bihar), Aṅga (western Bengal), and Surāshṭra (southern Kathiawad) as of mixed origin and hence of doubtful customs. The country of the Āryans narrows down to the area lying between Patiala [1] and Bihar [2] and between the Himālayas and the hills of Malwa,[3] while an opinion is cited which confines Āryāvarta only to the tract between the Gaṅgā and the Yamunā. Vasishṭha, however, cites the other opinion which places Āryavarta between the Himālayas and the Vindhyas and between the two oceans in east and west [i, 9].

Family Life: its Ceremonies.—The Gṛihya Sūtras dealing with family, the home life, and domestic ceremonies of the individual, assign a subordinate place to *dharma* or social matter, the wider relations of the individual to the State, which form the main subject-matter of the Dharma Sūtras. Of political and social life, they convey but little information, except as confined within the bounds of the family. They present the whole duty of man as a householder from boyhood to burial, indicating the ceremony marking every important phase of his life. There are ceremonies prescribed before birth, at birth, at the naming of the new-born child, at his first feeding with solid food, when his hair is cut, at his initiation into studentship, and at his return home (samāvartana) from his preceptor to enter upon the householder's life by marriage. Eight kinds of marriage are distinguished, viz. (1) Brāhma, (2) Prājāpatya which forbids a second wife and change of *āśrama,* (3) Ārsha, (4) Daiva, (5) Gāndharva or love-marriage, (6) Āsura or marriage determined by dowry, (7) Rākshasa or forcible marriage, and (8) Paiśācha. Of these, the first four are regarded as

[1] East of the region where the Sarasvatī disappears [*Vas.*, i, 8; *Bau.*, i, 1, 2, 9].
[2] "Kālakavana," black-forest traced in Bihar.
[3] Pāripātra hills.

lawful and the last two disapproved.[1] Every householder is enjoined to perform daily *pañcha-mahāyajñas*, the five great sacrifices, (1) to *Brahman* in the form of study and teaching, (2) to the *ancestors* by *tarpaṇa* (offering of food and water), (3) to the gods by the sacrifice of burnt oblation, (4) to the *Bhūtas* by the offering of *bali*, and (5) to fellow-men by the entertainment of guests. Next, there were prescribed seven *pākayajñas* which were small periodical sacrifices, viz. Ashṭakā (offered on the eighth day of dark fortnights of four months, Kārtika-Māgha), Śrāvaṇī (offered on the full-moon day of Śrāvaṇa), Āgrahāyaṇi (offered on the fourteenth or full-moon day of Agrahāyaṇa), Chaitrī (for the full-moon day of Chaitra), Āśvayujī (on the full-moon day of Āśvina), Pārvaṇa (on new and full-moon days) and Śrāddha (the monthly funeral offering to the manes on the new-moon days).

Varṇa (Castes) and Āśrama. The social system is established on the basis of what is called *Varṇāśramadharma*, the best definition of that vague and comprehensive complex known as Hinduism. The system rests on two factors. The first is *caste*, *varṇa* or *jāti*, " colour " and " kin ". The purity of caste depended on marriage as well as freedom from defilement by eating and touching what is unclean. Its rules interdict intermarriage between different castes, and interdining. In the earlier Sūtras, these rules are not so strict. Gautama permits a Brāhman to eat food given by any of the " reborn ", i.e. the three higher castes, and, in case of distress, even the food given by a Śūdra [xvii, 1 f.]. But food is defiled from a police-officer (*daṇḍika*), a miser, a jailer, or an enemy. Āpastamba [i, 6, 18, 1 f.] does not allow a Brāhman

[1] In *Brāhma* marriage, the bride is offered out of free will ; in *Prājāpatya*, the offer of marriage comes from the wooer ; in *Ārsha*, the bride's father receives a pair of kine as presents ; in *Daiva*, the bridegroom is a *Ṛitvij*, or sacrificial priest ; the *Gāndharva* or love-marriage, when completed by formal ceremonies, ranks as the best form of marriage, of which the classical example is that of Śakuntalā and Dushyanta ; *Āsura* marriage, through purchase of bride, was open only for Vaiśyas and Śūdras [*Manu*, iii, 24]. Āśvalāyana defines *Paiśācha* as secret abduction, while *Rākshasa* is abduction effected by force and fighting. Both are described as marriage by capture and called *kshātra-vivāha*, such as was practised by the Mahābhārata heroes like Duryodhana, Bhīma, or Arjuna. Allied to this is also *Svayaṁvara*, a romantic marriage by the bride's own choice of her husband.

to eat in the house of any one of the three castes below him. In marriage, caste is not so important as family. The marriage rules permit the marriage of a *Śūdra* girl, though only as a fourth wife [*Parāśara*, *GS*., i, 4, 11], with a Brāhman whose offspring, mixed, and not to rank as reborn (*dvija*), is nevertheless legally recognized.

But the rules of *Āśrama* were as vital to the Hindu social system as those of caste with its restrictions regarding marriage and food, on which an exaggerated emphasis is laid now. These rules require that an individual must pass through four stages in succession, viz. those of the Brahmachārī or initiated student, the householder or married state, the recluse (Vānaprastha), and the Sannyāsī or hermit. The obligations of studentship were so paramount that a member of the three higher castes not accepting them would be an outcast. " No one should imitate such men, nor teach them, nor perform sacrifice for them, nor have intercourse with them," and their descendants descend to the status of *Vrātyas* [ib., ii, 5, 40 f.]. This shows that Hinduism insists on compulsory education for its three twice-born classes making up the bulk of the community, and that this education was not necessarily and normally elementary. It was compulsory higher education.

Different Castes and their duties.—The duties of different *Varṇas* and *Aśramas* may be indicated.

The first three Castes have the following duties in common : (1) *Adhyayana* (study), (2) *Ijyā* (sacrifice), and (3) *Dāna* (charity).

The duties special to *Brāhmaṇa* are (1) *Pravachana* (teaching), (2) *Yājana* (conducting sacrifice), and (3) *Pratigraha* (receiving gifts).

The duties special to *Kshatriya* are : (1) protection of all creatures (*Sarva-bhūta-rakshaṇam*), (2) righteous administration (*Nyāya-daṇḍatvam*), (3) support of learned Brāhmaṇas (*Śrotriyas*), (4) support of non-Brāhmaṇas in distress, (5) support of non-Brāhmaṇa ascetics (*akara*) and those who directly serve the public (*upakurvāṇah*) like physicians (or students, according to some), (6) preparedness for war (*yogaśchavijaye*), (7) march through the country (*charyā = rāshṭrasyasarvato aṭanam*) with his army (*rathadhanurbhyāṁ*), (8) firm stand to death in battle without retreating therefrom (*saṁgrāme saṁsthānamanivṛittiścha*), (9) collection of prescribed taxes for defence of the realm (*tadrakshaṇa dharmitvāt*).

The duties special to the *Vaiśya* are: (1) *Kṛishi* (agriculture), (2) *Vāṇijya* (trade), (3) *Pāśupālya* (cattle-rearing), and (4) *Kusīda* (banking).

The duties special to the *Śudra* (described as *ekajāti*, i.e. devoid of a second birth from-*Upanayana*) are: (1) practice of truthfulness, humility, and purity, (2) bath without *āchamana mantra*, (3) *Śrāddhakarma* (funeral rites), (4) *Bhṛitya-charaṇam* (support of dependants, not allowed to slaves), (5) *Svadāravṛitti* (marrying in the same caste or always remaining in the householder's state), (6) service of higher castes (*paricharyā*) on wages (*vṛitti*), (7) practice of independent crafts (*Śilpavṛitti*) "like those of barber, washerman, painter, carpenter, or blacksmith".

There are a few provisions showing that the status of the Śūdra was not very degraded. For instance, his master must support him even when disabled (*kshīṇa*) for work, while he should also support his master in similar conditions, in which case the Śūdra's right to riches is recognized in aid of higher castes. The virtuous Śūdra could also utter *Namaskāra Mantra* and perform the *Pākayajñas*.

The Four Āśramas.—The four *Āśramas* are those of (1) the Brāhmachārī, (2) Gṛihastha, (3) Bhikshu, and (4) Vaikhānasa.

The *Brahmachārī* is marked by his living with his teacher (āchārya-kula-vasanam) and is of two classes; (*a*) *Upakurvāṇa* and (*b*) *Naishṭhika* (permanent student).

The *Gṛihastha* has manifold duties broadly marked out as (*a*) *yajña*, (*b*) *adhyayana*, and (*c*) *dāna*, and has to release himself from three debts: debt to gods, by *yajña*; to *pitṛis*, or ancestors, by offspring; and to *ṛishis* by observing continence on *parvan* days.

The last two stages of life are marked by *tapas*.

The *Bhikshu* (ascetic) must be (1) *Anichaya*[1] (devoid of store of articles); (2) *Ūrddhvaretā* (continent); (3) confined to one place in the rains (*dhruvaśīlo varshāshu*), (4) going to a village only for begging, and *that* only after the villagers' meals are finished, or when there was no refusal, without giving them any blessings in return, and restraining speech, eyes and action; (5) should wear clothing (*kaupīna*) or old rag (*prahīṇa*) duly washed (*nirṇijya*) to cover nakedness (*āchchhādanārtham*); (6) should not partake of fruits or leaves by plucking them and injuring plant-life; (7) should not, out of season (i.e. after rains), dwell for a second night in the same village, and (8) should not kill seeds to sustain his own life (e.g. pounding seeds like raw rice by a pestle) but should accept as alms only cooked food, in charity towards all (*samo bhūteshu*) and indifference to injury or gain.

The *Vaikhānasa* (hermit) is so called because he lives according to the rules promulgated by *Vikhanas* the sage [*Bau.* ii, 6, 14]. He should live in the forest (*vane*), subsisting on roots and fruits (and not cooked food), practising austerities (*tapaḥ śīlaḥ*), tending and offering oblations to Fire every morning and evening, as prescribed in the *Vaikhānasa Sāstra* called *Śrāmaṇaka*. As to his fare of roots and fruits, these must be of the forest and not of the village (*agrāmya-bhojī*), and in distress he may eat the flesh of animals killed by others like tigers (*baishkam*). He should still perform the five Mahāyajñas (worship of gods, manes, men, goblins, and ṛishis), using for his oblations the wild roots, fruits, and leaves, and practise penances as an Audumbara, a Varincha, or a Vālakhilya as a *sapatnīka*, i.e. when he is with his wife in the forest, or as Uddaṇḍaka, Uñchhavṛittika, or Pañchāgnimadhyaśāyī, as an *apatnīka*, when he is not with his wife. He must not live on ploughed land, nor enter a village, nor store up food for a year, should allow his hairs to grow (*jaṭila*) and wear only bark

[1] As he cannot own property, Vishṇu [96, 1] prescribes a sacrifice (*ishṭi*) which he has to offer to Prajāpati by which his whole property is given away as sacrificial fee.

and skin (*chīrājina*) [Gautama, iii and x, on Castes and Āśramas].

It may be noted that while Gautama uses the term *Bhikshu*, and that for the third *āśrama*, Baudhāyana and Āpastamba use instead the term *Parivrājaka*, and that for the fourth *āśrama*.

The use of the terms *Bhikshu* and *Śrāmaṇaka* and the provision that the Bhikshu must not move about in rains are associated with Buddhism. Baudhāyana [ii, 6, 11] also refers to *Śrāmaṇaka* and the hermit's rain-retreat (Pāli, *vasso*). He further refers to the use by the hermit or Vaikhānasa of cloth for straining water, a characteristic of the Buddhist Bhikshu [ii, 6, 11, 24].

Baudhāyana recruits the *Sannyāsī* or *Parivrājaka* (also called in texts as Bhikshu, Yati, or Pravrajita) of the fourth *Āśrama* from Naishṭhikas, widowers, childless householders, and men above 70 years, with sons already established in life. The childless householders are described as (*a*) *Śālīnas* (possessed of houses), (*b*) *Yāyāvaras* (those who are already vagrants), and (*c*) *Chakracharas*, those who go by turns to rich people for livelihood. [See ii, 10, 17].

Āpastamba mentions persons becoming ascetics without rules, meaning, according to the commentator, the Śākyas or Bauddhas [i, 18, 31].

He gives a fine description of the *Sannyāsī* or Parivrājaka as one who "abandoning truth and falsehood, pleasure and pain, the Vedas, this world and the next, seeks only the Ātman" [ii, 9, 21, 13].

But he refers to hermits being with or without wives [ii, 9, 22, 7], though living outside the village in each case.

Comparison of the four Dharma-Sūtras as to age, authority, and contents.—As has been already indicated, the four typical Dharma-Sūtras, viz. those of Gautama, Baudhāyana, Āpastamba, Vasishṭha, may be taken to belong to the period 600–300 B.C. As pointed out by Kumārila in his *Tantra-Vārttika*, Gautama was followed by the Sāmavedins, Baudhāyana and Āpastamba by the Taittirīyas and Vasishṭha by the Rigvedins. Of these, Gautama was the oldest. He is quoted as an authority by Baudhāyana himself on the question of the authority of local usages [*G. Dh. S.*, xi, 20]. Both hold that these cannot prevail against Vedic tradition and Smṛiti. The Manu-Smṛiti refers to Gautama as the son of Utathya [iii, 16]. Gautama mentions *Yavana* [iv, 17], but India had known of *Yavanas* (Ionians) since the time of Darius and Xerxes of sixth century B.C. and earlier.

As to literature known to these Sūtra writers, Gautama mentions the Vedic Saṁhitās and Brāhmaṇas, Upanishads [xix, 13], Vedāṅgas [viii, 5 ; xi, 19], Itihāsa [viii, 6], Purāṇa [ib.], Upa-veda and Dharma Sūtra [xi, 19]. And he actually borrows from Sāmavidhāna Brāhmaṇa (ch. 26) and Taittirīya Āraṇyaka (ch. 25). The reference of both Gautama and Baudhāyana to the Vaikhānasa-Śāstra and to that called Śramaṇaka recalls Pāṇini's reference to *Bhikshu-Sūtras* [iv, 3, 110–1]. Baudhāyana borrows from Taittirīya-Saṁhitā, -Brāhmaṇa, and -Āraṇyaka, as also from Śatapatha Brāhmaṇa, and mentions the following authors on *Dharma*, viz. Aupajaṅghani [ii, 2, 33], Kātya [i, 2, 47], Kāśyapa [i, 11, 20], Gautama [i, 1, 23], Prajāpati [ii, 4, 15], Manu [iv, 1, 14], Maudgalya [ii, 2, 61], and Hārīta [ii, 1, 50]. He also quotes a *gāthā* of the Bhāllavins [i, 1, 29] on the geographical limits of Āryāvarta (from a *Nidāna* work known to the Nirukta) and a prose passage from a work by Āsura Kapila to whom is curiously ascribed the institution of the *Āśramas* [ii, 6, 30]. He also refers to the profession of an actor or a teacher of dramaturgy (Nāṭyā-charya), but as an Upa-pātaka. Pāṇini also has mentioned the Naṭasūtras [ib.]. Āpastamba quotes the Brāhmaṇas frequently and mentions the Vedāṅgas as Chhandas, Kalpa, Vyākaraṇa, Jyotisha, Nirukta, Śikshā and Chhandovichiti (metrics). He mentions the following writers on *Dharma* by name, viz. Eka, Kaṇva, Kāṇva, Kuṇika, Kutsa, Kautsa, Pushkarasādi, Vārshyāyaṇi, Śvetaketu and Hārīta [i, 6, 19]. He shows singular acquaintance with the Pūrva-Mīmāṁsā of Jaimini, e.g. i, 1, 4, 8, on comparative value of Vedic text and Smṛiti=Jaimini i, 3, 3; i, 4, 12, 11=*J.*, iv, 1, 2 (stating that where an action is done for the pleasure of it, it need not be deemed as being based on Śāstra); ii, 4, 8, 13=*J*., i, 3, 11–14, referring to the convention (*samaya*) of those versed in Nyāya (i.e. Mīmāṁsā) that the Aṅgas cannot be designated as the Vedas; i, 4, 12, 9 = *J*., xii, 3, 14, stating that *anadhyāya* in Vedic study does not apply to recital of *Mantras* as sacrifices. Vasishṭha contains some new matter; e.g rules of adoption (ch. 15), or documents as means of proof (ch. 16, 10–15), or interdicting the learning of the language of Mlechchhas [vi, 41].

There are also points of both agreement and difference between these doctors of law. A few of these may be cited. Gautama, Baudhāyana, and Vasishṭha mention several secondary sons, on whom Āpastamba is silent. Gautama, Baudhāyana [ii, 2, 17, 62] and Vasishṭha approve of *Niyoga*, which Āpastamba condemns [ii, 6, 13, 1–9]. Gautama and Baudhāyana [i, 11, 1] speak of eight forms of marriage which are limited to six by Āpastamba who omits Prājāpatya and Paiśācha [ii, 5, 11, 17–20]. Baudhāyana [ii, 2, 4–6] allows a larger share to the eldest son in partition, while Āpastamba condemns this procedure [ii, 6, 14, 10–14]. Baudhāyana allows Upanayana to the *rathakāra* [Gr. S., ii, 4, 6], but not Āpastamba [i, 1, 1, 19]. Āpastamba is also silent on the mixed castes, of which long lists are given by both Gautama and Baudhāyana. The injunctions about usury are interesting in their difference. Gautama allows it to a Brāhmaṇa as a calling if it is done through an agent [x, 6], together with agriculture and trade. "These rules which thus allow Brāhmaṇas to be gentlemen farmers and sleeping partners in mercantile or banking firms managed by Vaiśyas do not occur in other Smṛitis" [Buhler, *SBE*., ii, p. 228, n.]. Āpastamba prescribes a penance against usury and forbids eating at the usurer's house [i, 9, 27, 10; 6, 18, 22]. Baudhāyana likens it to *brahmahatyā* and treats a Brāhmaṇa usurer as a Śūdra. But he allows the first two castes to practise usury towards atheists, Śūdras, and such-like persons [i, 5, 79–81].

Baudhāyana is supposed to belong to the south. He condemns the northern custom of sea-faring as a sin only less than a mortal one [ii, 1, 41]. But at the same time, he condemns Dakshiṇāpatha as the home of mixed castes. If he was a southerner, we must find him a place by restricting the denotation of the term Dakshiṇāpatha. Āpastamba is also regarded as a southerner from his special mention of a Śrāddha usage peculiar to the *Udīchyas*, northerners [ii, 7, 17, 17]. Haradatta quotes a verse which defines *Udīchya* as the region to the north of the Śarāvatī, while the *Charaṇa-Vyūha* commentary cites *Mahārṇava*, locating the Āpastambīyas to the south of the Narmadā towards south-east, i.e. the Andhra country and the region about the mouth of the Godāvarī.

There are two interesting passages in Āpastamba and Baudhāyana bearing on learning and education. Āpastamba regards the knowledge which exists traditionally among women and Śūdras as the farthest limit of Vidyā and is stated to be a supplement of the *Atharvaveda*. Here is probably a reference to the Arthaśāstra which, according to the *Charaṇa-Vyūha*, constituted an Upa-veda of the *Atharvaveda*. The other passage is from Baudhāyana Gṛihya-Sūtra [i, 7, 2–8], specifying the following grades among learned men or Brāhmaṇas :

(1) *Brāhmaṇa* who, after Upanayana and practice of vows of *brahmacharya*, has studied a little of the Veda; (2) *Śrotriya* who has studied one *Vedic śākhā* ; (3) *Anūchāna* who has studied the *Aṅgas* ; (4) *Ṛishikalpa*, who has studied the *Kalpas* ; (5) *Bhrūṇa* who has studied *Sūtra* and *Pravachana* ; (6) *Ṛishi* who has studied all the four Vedas ; (7) *Deva* who has achieved more progress.

It may also be noted that the Sūtras contemplate non-Brahmin teachers [*Ga.*, vii, 1–3 ; *Bau.*, i, 3, 41–3 ; *Āp.*, ii, 4, 25–7].

The *Dharma Sūtras* are a record of social customs and usages and the civil and criminal law based on them. The customs and usages were not uniform all over India. There was a marked difference between the north and the south of India, with the river Narmadā as the dividing line. For instance, the custom peculiar to the south, which is noticed by Baudhāyana [*DS.*, i, 17 f.] and persists to this day, is marrying the daughter of a maternal uncle or of a paternal aunt, while the peculiar customs of the north which would be sinful in the south were "to follow the trade of arms, to deal in wool, and to go to sea". According to Baudhāyana [ii, 1, 2, 2], "making voyages to sea" would cause loss of caste.

Law.—As regards law, its source was not the Sovereign who, as the executive or *Daṇḍa*, was to uphold and to enforce it. According to Gautama [xi, 19], "the administration of justice (*dharma*) shall be regulated by the Veda, the Dharma-Śastras, the Vedāṅgas, the Purāṇas, and the Upavedas." The different groups and communities were left to legislate for themselves. "The king's duty is to pay attention to the special laws of regions (*janapada*), castes (*jāti*) and clans (*kula*), and keep the four orders (*varṇas*, castes in general sense) to their prescribed duties" [Vasishṭha xix, 1–24]. Again, "the king must protect the castes (*varṇas*) and different stages of life (*āśramas*) . . . Authoritative in the realm shall be all laws of castes (*jāti*) and clans (*kula*) as well as the laws of regions (*janapada*) not opposed to Vedic tradition, while, for their respective orders (*varga*), ploughmen, traders, herdsmen, money-lenders, and artisans may make their own laws" [*Gautama*, xi, 21]. This passage shows the self-government enjoyed by the economic groups or guilds into which agriculture, industry, trade, and banking had organized themselves. Vasishṭha, in an interesting passage, states how in cases of conflicting evidence of documents, reliance was to be placed on the Guilds and Corporations of the neighbourhood (*Śreṇī*) [xvi, 15].

Civil Law is discussed in the Sūtras under the head of royal duties and the chief subjects of Civil Law in the restricted scope of royal duties were only *Taxes* and *Inheritance*. According to Gautama, the king could take one-tenth, one-eighth, or one-sixth of the produce, one day's work per month from artisans, one-twentieth on merchandise, one-fiftieth on cattle and gold, and one-sixtieth on roots, fruits, flowers, herbs, honey, meat, grass, and firewood [xi, 1 f.; x, 25 f.].

Inheritance is not yet regulated by any general state

law. It is discussed in connection with marriage, which was not permitted within the same *gotra* (*gens*, family) or within six degrees on the mother's side. Then the rules of inheritance mark out the *Sapiṇḍas* who were relations within six degrees as the heirs in place of sons. The *Sapiṇḍas* can be only males. The widow is excluded from inheritance and the daughter, according to Āpastamba, inherits only in default of sons, teacher or pupil. The king inherits in default of the others named and an opinion is cited that among the sons only the eldest inherits. Baudhāyana states that *Sapiṇḍas* inherit in default of nearer relations and *Sakulyas* (remoter relations) in default of *Sapiṇḍas*, and that the eldest son may receive the best chattel or the father may divide his property equally among his sons.

The status of women is indicated. Women on their own account could not offer the Vedic Śrauta or the Gṛihya sacrifices. They were not independent either in respect of sacrifice or of inheritance [Baudh., ii, 2, 3, 44; Gautama, xviii, 1]. Suttee is not known. Vasishṭha counts women as property [xvi, 18].

In *Criminal Law*, the chief crimes treated are assault, adultery, and theft. A Śūdra committing homicide, theft, or stealing land will suffer confiscation of his property and capital punishment [Āpastamba, *DS*., ii, 27, 16]; but a Brahman priest shall be blinded for same crimes [ib., 17] A Kshatriya abusing a Brāhmaṇa is fined 100 coins and a Vaiśya 150 coins, but a Brāhmaṇa abusing a Kshatriya will pay only 50 coins, and abusing a Vaiśya, only 25 coins (*Kārshāpaṇas*), and will get off scot-free for abusing a Śūdra [Gautama, xii, 8 f.].

Caste has influenced also matters outside of criminal law, e.g. rate of interest. This is stated to be five *māshas* a month on twenty *Kārshāpaṇas* [*Gautama*, xii, 29; *Baudh.*, i, 5, 10, 22], which is equivalent to 15 per cent per annum, but, according to Vasishṭha [ii, 48], "two, three, four, five in the hundred is declared in the Smṛiti to be the monthly interest according to caste," the rate being the less, the higher the caste. Usury, on the other hand, is permitted to the Vaiśya but not to a Brāhmaṇa or a Kshatriya [ib., ii, 40; *Baudh.* i, 5, 10, 21]. These restrictions of caste were, however, relaxed in case of extreme distress, when lower occupations were permitted to higher castes for the sake of livelihood, such as trade and agriculture for a Brāhmaṇa or Kshatriya [*Vas.*, ii, 24 f.], allowed as *āpad-dharma,* though if they persisted in such occupations, they would lose their rank [ib., iii, 3].

The life depicted in the Sūtras is the life of villages and not of cities, which are despised. Āpastamba [*DS.*, i, 32, 21] says: "Let him avoid going into towns." Baudhāyana [*DS.*, ii, 3, 6, 33] goes further: "It is impossible for one to attain salvation, who lives in a town covered with dust." Similarly, the ceremonies prescribed for ploughing, with sacrifices to Aśani (thunderbolt), Sītā (furrow) and other bucolic deities like Araḍā, Anaghā, etc., or to Parjanya, Indra, and Bhaga, and for "furrow-sacrifice" and "threshing-floor sacrifice", point to the life of the agricultural villager [Gobhila, *GS.*, iv, 4, 28 f., 30 f.]. There are, again, constant injunctions to "go out of the village" to sacrifice at a place where four roads meet, or on a hill, etc., which imply life rather in villages even for householders than in towns [ib., iii, 5, 32–5]. That is why the only architecture allowed in the Sūtras is that of a public gaming-hall or gambling place provided by the king, but it had a thatched roof because holes could be made in it.

Nor are conditions much changed in the other Dharma Sūtras. Gautama expressly forbids recitation of holy texts at any time in a town. He presents to us the king hitting a thief with a cudgel [xii, 43], and he is supported by Āpastamba [*DS.*, i, 25, 4], who says: "A thief shall loosen his hair and appear before the king carrying a cudgel on his shoulder. With that cudgel the king shall smite him." Does this not indicate a small place and a petty king, a direct government and not that by agents?

Another passage in Āpastamba [ii, 10, 25], however, shows a higher political development. It states that the king is to build a town (*pura*), and a palace equipped with a hall for guests, and an assembly-house (*sabhā*) furnished with a gaming-table. There were also houses kept by the king's servants, where took place assaults-at-arms, dancing, singing, concerts, etc. The king should appoint Āryas of good character to guard the people in villages and towns with their own staff. They were to guard a town from thieves for a league (*yojana*) in every direction and villages for 2 miles (a *kos* or quarter of a league). They were to pay back what is stolen within that jurisdiction and collect taxes for the king. This points to both urban and rural life and a larger kingship.

The general outlook of life became limited under injunctions forbidding sea-voyages, visits to foreign places, or the learning of a language spoken by barbarians [*Vas.*, vi, 41 ; *Āpastamba*, i, 32, 18].

Civilization of the Epics.—The two Epics, *Rāmāyaṇa* and *Mahābhārata*, in their present literary form, are of the age of the *Sūtras*, though their subject-matter is much older.

Age.—The geographical horizon of the *Rāmāyaṇa* shows it to be older than the *Mahābhārata*. It does not extend far beyond the Vindhyas and substitutes *Daṇḍakāraṇya* for the Deccan, while the *Mahābhārata* is acquainted with all parts of India and its division into numerous States which were flourishing seats of Aryan civilization.

As a literary composition, the Epic is made up of three elements : Story, Genealogy, and Instruction, each of which may be traced to remote origins ; to the Rigveda, which contains stories in verse on Urvaśī, Yama and Yamī, Sūryā and Gambler [x, 95 ; 10 ; 85 ; 34, etc.] ; to the Brāhmaṇas like the *Aitareya*, which gives the story of Harish Chandra in epic fullness ; to the later Gāthās (strophes) which were laudatory memorial verses in honour of great men, and *Nārāśaṁsīs* or "hero-lauds" ; while genealogy derives from the *Deva-Jana-vidyā* (knowledge of the god's race) of the Upanishads. The epics are also the literary descendants of *Itihāsa* (story) and *Purāṇa* (legend) mentioned in the *Atharvaveda*, *Brāhmaṇas* and Upanishads. Through Parāśara, the promulgator of the *Mahābhārata*, the epic becomes connected with the White Yajurveda in which that name figures prominently. Again, Janamejaya is mentioned in both *Mahābhārata* and *Śatapatha Brāhmaṇa* which the *Mahābhārata* acknowledges as the greatest of Brāhmaṇa works.

But there are allusions in other earlier works to epic characters, which only show the epic in its present form to be later. Thus the Taittirīya Āraṇyaka mentions both Vyāsa and Vaiśampāyana, but not as authors or editors of the epic. Pāṇini mentions the word Mahābhārata, not in the sense of the epic, but only as an adjective, denoting something great about the Bharatas [vi, 2, 38]. He, however, mentions Vāsudeva, Arjuna, and Yudhishṭhira, but the first two as gods.

It is also to be noted that the Pāṇḍus, whose feud with the Kurus forms the chief subject of the *Mahābhārata*, are not known to comparatively recent works like the *Brāhmaṇas*.

The great Mahābhārata teachers, Sumanta, Jaimini, Vaiśampāyana, and Paila are, however, mentioned in the Śāṅkhāyana Gṛihya Sūtra.

The *Mahābhārata* in its present form seems to have been well established at the time of Pātañjali's *Mahābhāshya*, second century B.C. That was also the time of the foreign invaders of India, the Yavanas, Śakas, and Pahlavas, who are mentioned in the epic. The fact is that the contents of the Epic were growing with additions and interpolations. The Gṛihya-Sūtra of Āśvalāyana mentions both a Mahābhārata and a Bhārata (its abridged form).

History.—The theme of the *Rāmāyaṇa* is in essence that of the conflict between Rāma and Rāvaṇa, who may be taken to be the representatives and embodiments respectively of the Āryan and non-Āryan civilization. The conflict ends with the victory, after a long and arduous struggle, of the Āryan over the non-Āryan who was difficult to defeat owing to the strength of his organization and the resources of a highly developed material civilization with its centre in distant Ceylon under its king, Rāvaṇa. Rāvaṇa is also described as an unequalled devotee of Śiva and deriving from that devotion considerable spiritual and superhuman powers. On the other hand, Rāma was the incarnation of Vishṇu and of spiritual strength. Behind him were the real leaders, the two Brāhmaṇa sages, Vasishṭha and Viśvāmitra, who had planned the conflict and brought into it Rāma as the appointed instrument to serve the Āryan cause. Rāma was aided in his struggle by monkey-leaders and their following, and if these stand for non-Āryan peoples, it only shows the growing hold of the Āryan over the non-Āryan. The *Rāmāyaṇa* thus ultimately tells of the extension of Āryan civilization to the south as far as Laṅkā or Ceylon. But popularly it is appreciated not for its supposed history but as a picture of perfect characters, the ideal father, son, brother, wife, husband, friend or devotee, appealing to millions of Hindus to this day.

The theme of the *Mahābhārata* is also a conflict, not between the Āryan and the non-Āryan, but among the Āryan peoples themselves, and involving not a part but the whole of India. The central fact of the conflict in the two epics is the same, an abuse of hospitality and abduction of the heroine, Sītā, in the *Rāmāyaṇa*, and Krishṇā (Draupadī) in the *Mahābhārata*. The Kurukshetra war of the *Mahābhārata* affected all the Āryan kings of India who ranged themselves on both sides, Kuru or Pāṇḍava. The Pāṇḍavas and their allies were of Madhyadeśa and Pañchāla, such as Kāśī, Kosala, Magadha, Matsya, Chedi, and the Yadus of Mathurā, while the allies of the Kurus comprised the King of Prāgjyotish, the Chīnas and Kirātas of north-east, the Kambojas, Yavanas, Śakas, Madras, Kaikeyas, Sindhus, and Sauvīras in the north-west, the Bhojas in the west, the King of Dakshināpatha in the south, the Andhras in the south-east, and the Kings of Māhismatī and Avanti in Madhyadeśa.

Settlements.—The basis of civilization is settled life of which the centres in an ascending series are called (*a*) *Ghosha*, or cattle-ranch, sometimes called *vraja*; (*b*) *Palli*, a small barbarian settlement [*pallighoshāḥ* in *Mbh.*, xii, 326, 20]; (*c*) *Durga* (fort) to protect the settlements; (*d*) *Grāma*, growing round the *durga* as its nucleus; (*e*) *Kharvaṭa* and *Pattana*, town; and (*f*) *Nagara*, or city. The city had special defences, battlemented towers, and seven moats, and was laid out in squares. Its streets were well-watered and lighted with lamps [iii, 284, 3; xv, 5, 16, etc.]. The *Rāmāyaṇa* mentions four [ii, 48, 19] and the *Mahābhārata* six squares. The city included the king's palace, the court of justice, the public gaming-hall, the hall for music and wrestling contests. Beyond the city proper or inner city lay the booths for traders and the like, the unpretentious houses, and the pleasure-gardens [*Mbh.*, iv, 22, etc.]. The walls of the epic city had usually four gates, but Laṅkā had eight [*R.*, vi, 93].

Polity and Administration.—The administration was planned on what may be called the decimal system. The unit was the *grāma* under its head-man, *Grāmaṇi*, who had to protect it up to a distance of one *krośa* (about 2 miles) in different directions. Above him in order were the *Daśagrāmī*, the *Vimśatipa* and *Śatagrāmī*, also called *Grāmaśatādhyaksha*, the lords of 10, 20 and 100 villages, and all under the general governor, *Adhipati*, the lord of 1,000 villages. In this gradually extending circle, these several authorities received revenue, the returns of crimes, and passed them on from one to the next higher, till revenues and reports focussed in the king, the lord of all [cf. Manu., vii, 115–125; Yājñavalkya, i, 321; Āp., ii, 10, 26, 4 ff.].

The King.—The king was no autocrat. He had to rule by right and morality. A wicked king was deposed. A king injuring his people was killed "like a mad dog". A "defective" king must lose his throne [*Mbh.*, v, 149, 25]. He was regularly consecrated and crowned as lord of the earth [ib., xii, 40; *R.* ii, 69].

Corporations.—He had to respect the laws of different regions (*Janapada*) and groups, such as *Kula* (clan), *Jāti* (caste), *Śreṇī* (guild) or *Pūga* (village community).

Republics.—The *Mahābhārata* (*Śāntiparva*) speaks of the republican form of government called *Gaṇa* (sovereignty of the many) as prevailing at that time and of confederations of republics (*Saṁghāta-gaṇa*).

The *Mahābhārata* [xii, 81] mentions five republican peoples, the Andhakas, Vṛishṇis, Yādavas, Kukuras, and Bhojas, who had formed themselves into a Confederation

(*Saṁgha*) under Kṛishṇa as the federal president, *Saṁgha-mukhya*, upon whom depended their common weal. Each of the constituent States of the Confederation was, however, an autonomous unit under its own chief called *Īśvara*. Thus the Bhojas were led by Akrūra. Akrūra's following included Baladeva [ib., 3037]. Āhuka was the chief of another people of the same name, though he was himself a Yādava [v, 86, 3041]. The Āhukas were allies of Kṛishṇa [iii, 51, 1994]. Something like the Party System seems to have been in operation in this federal government. There was a struggle for power among the party-leaders. Those mentioned in this connection are Āhuka, Akrūra, Gada, Pradyumna, Saṁkarshaṇa-Baladeva and Babhru-Ugrasena. All followed the leadership of Kṛishṇa except Babhru who organized opposition to him [xii, 81, 3040]. Kṛishṇa also had sometimes to complain about the loyalty of his own following. He complains to Nārada that Saṁkarshaṇa with his strength, Gada with his virtues, Pradyumna with his attractive presence, are leaving him helpless (*asahāya*), while all power is grasped by Āhuka and Akrūra, leaving him unsupported against Babhru. Nārada, however, advises Kṛishṇa to rise to the responsibilities of his position as the president of the whole Federation and save the *Saṁgha* from the internal (*ābhyantara*) dangers of disunion (*bheda*) to which republics succumb [xii, 81].

While *Saṁgha* was the term for a confederation of republics, *Gaṇa* was the term for an individual republic. A *Gaṇa*, to thrive, must avoid *bheda*, keep its State secrets in the custody of its Cabinet (*mantraguptiḥ pradhāneshu*), be governed by a council of leaders (*Gaṇa-mukhyas*) and its wise men (*Jñāna-vṛiddhas*), follow the Śāstras and established laws and customs (*vyavahāra*), avoid nepotism and make recruitment to public service on the basis of merit (*vinaya*), and nip in the bud all internal dissensions. These start from the sphere of the *Kula* and, neglected by its elders, the *Kula-vṛiddhas*, spread to the *Gotra* and ultimately involve the whole *Gaṇa* in ruin [xii, 107].

Checks to Absolutism.—The checks to the king's autocracy came from bodies like the *Mantri-parishad* and *Sabhā*, the

Council and the Assembly. A Parishad or Cabinet of nine is formed out of a ministry of thirty-seven, comprising four Brahmaṇas, eight Kshatṛiyas, twenty-one Vaiśyas, three Śūdras, and one Sūta [*Mbh.*, 85, 6–11]. The Prime Minister was called the Mantri [xii, 69, 52]. The king's first duty every day was to visit the *Mantra-gṛiha*, the council-hall, for consultation with his ministers individually or collectively [ii, 5, 43]. The President of the Assembly called *Sabhādhyaksha* was one of the eighteen chief officers of the State [ii, 5, 38]. The Sabhā is regarded as a judicial assembly in the passage : " that is no *Sabhā* where there are no elders ; those are not elders who do not declare the law " [v, 35, 58]. A judge is called a *Sabhāstāra* [iv, 1, 24].

Epic royalty is intimately associated with an aristocracy comprising the king's allies and relations, subject kings, military leaders or knights (called Śūras) and priests. These nobles took part in council, conducted the assemblies, led the army, and were the king's Vice-regents in all military affairs. The king was the chief of them for his qualifications for which he is really chosen, and not by virtue of heredity. His superiority lay in valour (vīrya-śreshṭhāścha rājānaḥ in *Mbh.*, i, 136, 19). It is further stated that " these three produce kings : an aristocrat (*satkulīna*), a hero (*śūra*), and he that leads forward an army (senāṁ prakarshati) " [xii, 75, 22 ff.]. These various classes of nobles are called (1) *Mantrins* or Cabinet Councillors ; (2) *Amātyas*, the general officers, eight of whom might form the king's Cabinet, viz. one charioteer, three slaves and four priests [i, 140, 2, ff.] ; *Sachivas* (comites) who were mainly military officials of the highest rank and were left in charge of the king's duties in his absence [i, 49, 23] ; (4) *Pārishadas*, or assembly men, who also guarded the realm in the king's absence [v, 38, 14–20] ; (5) *Sahāyas*, helpers of the king, who were high ministers [xii, 83, 22 ; 57, 23] ; (6) *Arthakārins*, or executive officers in charge of State business, who were generally five in number in the Cabinet [ib.] ; and (7) *Dhārmikas*, or Judges [xii, 121, 46 ; *R.*, vi, 3, 13]. It is to be noted that in the absence of a definition of the functions attaching to these different titles of ministers, it is difficult to differentiate their different values.

Lastly, we may note that the Epics distinguish eighteen chief officers of the State as heads of departments called *Tīrthas* [ii, 5, 38; *R.*, ii, 109, 45]. These are: (1) *Mantri* (Chief Councillor), (2) *Purohita* (Chief Priest), (3) *Yuvarāja* (Crown Prince), (4) *Chamūpati* (Commander-in-chief of the army), (5) *Dvārapāla* (Chamberlain), (6) *Antarveśika* (Overseer of the harem), (7) *Kārāgārā-dhikārī* (Overseer of prisons), (8) *Dravyasaṁchaya-kṛit* (Chief Steward), (9) Chief Executive Officer to finally determine what ought or what ought not to be done in public business (Kṛityākṛityeshu chārthānāṁ Viniyojakaḥ), (10) *Pradeshṭā* (Chief Judge), (11) *Nagarā-dhyaksha* (City Prefect), (12) *Kāryanirmāṇa-kṛit* (Chief engineer), (13) *Dharmā-dhyaksha* (Superintendent of Justice), (14) *Sabhā-dhyaksha* (President of the Assembly), (15) *Daṇḍa-pāla* (Chief Criminal Judge), (16) *Durgapāla* (Warden of Forts), (17) *Rāshṭrāntapālaka* (Warden of the Marches), and (18) *Aṭavīpālaka* (Chief Conservator of Forests).[1]

Indian History according to Indian Tradition: The Purāṇas.—The Purāṇas, as a class of literature, resemble the Epics and Law Books very closely in both form and substance, being written in the same style of Sanskrit and of verse. Sometimes they have even long passages in common. In their normal form, they should treat of the following five set topics, namely (1) *Sarga*, creation; (2) *Prati-Sarga*, recreation after *Pralaya*, i.e. the periodical dissolution of the universe; (3) *Vaṁśa*, genealogies of gods and Ṛishis or teachers; (4) *Manvantara*, the groups of "great ages" (*Mahāyuga*) included in a *Kalpa* or aeon; and (5) *Vaṁśānucharita*, the history of the royal dynasties ruling during the four ages (*yuga*), making up one "great age". This ideal scheme is not, however, fully followed in the extant Purāṇas. The historical material of the Purāṇas is confined to the topic No. (5), but is found only in seven out of the eighteen extant Purāṇas, so that as many as eleven are devoid of any historical value. The Purāṇas

[1] I am indebted to the comprehensive article of E. W. Hopkins on the subject in the *JAOS.*, vol. xiii.

are supposed to be narrated by the Sūta (Chronicler) named Lomaharshaṇa, or his son, the *Sauti*, Ugraśravas. This indicates that the traditional lore upon which the Purāṇas are based was not in the keeping of Brāhmins. The Vāyu Purāṇa [i, 1, 26–8] expressly states that the *Sūta* was born to sing the praises of the princes, the custodian of legends and traditions having no concern with the Vedas. Yet the Purāṇas eventually became considerably Brahmanized and utilized for religious purposes. Their underlying ethical purpose has been thus emphasized: "He who has heard of the races of the Sun and Moon, Ikshvāku, Jahnu, Māndhātṛi, Sagara, and Raghu, who have all perished; of Yayāti, Nahusha, and their posterity, who are no more; of kings of great might, resistless valour and unbounded wealth, who have been overcome by the still more powerful Time and are now only a tale: he will learn wisdom, and forbear to call either children, or wife, or house, or lands, or wealth, his own" [Vishṇu Purāṇa, trans. Wilson, iv, 240]. The history of kings is thus introduced only to illustrate the vanity of human wishes. Accordingly, there has been a large intrusion of the religious element in praise of the great gods of Hinduism, Śiva or Vishṇu, so that the Purāṇas now practically rank as scriptures of later Hinduism, just as the Vedas are of the older Brahmanism. Only they lack the sanctity and purity of the Vedic text and its consequent freedom from interpolations.

The conception of the Purāṇa is as old as the Upanishads in which the Itihāsa-Purāṇa already figures as a recognized subject of study, and is further designated as the fifth Veda, the Veda of the laity, along with the Epics.

Of all the Purāṇas, the *Vishṇu* Purāṇa appears to be the best preserved. Their differences are due to local touches. For instance, an Orissa stamp may be detected in the *Brahma* Purāṇa, while the *Padmā* is associated with Pushkara, *Agni* with Gayā, *Varāha* with Mathurā, *Vāmana* with Thanesar, *Kūrma* with Benares, and the *Matsya* with the Brāhmins on the Narmadā. The earliest reference to an existing Purāṇa is contained in the Dharma

Sūtra of Āpastamba [ii, 9, 24, 6] of about the second century B.C. citing the *Bhavishya* Purāṇa which may thus be taken to date from earlier times, about fifth century B.C. [Pargiter's *Ancient Indian Historical Tradition*, pp. 44–54].

Geographical Background.—The Purāṇas give some precise geographical data. India called Bhāratavarsha is defined as the country that lies north of the ocean and south of the snowy mountains, and is so called because it is the abode of the descendants of the Bharatas. It is known for its seven main chains of mountains, called Mahendra, Malaya, Sahya, Śuktimat, Ṛiksha, Vindhya, and Pāripātra. It is also stated that on the east of Bhārata dwell the Kirātas (the barbarians), on the west, the Yavanas, and in the centre, the Āryans classified into Brāhmaṇas, Kshatriyas, Vaiśyas, and Śūdras [Vishṇu Purāṇa, Wilson's trans., ii, 127–9]. There are also detailed lists given of the various rivers rising from the Himalayas and the seven great ranges, and of peoples belonging to different regions. Some of this material has been changed from time to time to bring it up to date. Thus there is mention of Yavanas, Śakas, and Pahlavas who came to India in the first and second century B.C., and also of the Hūṇas who overran the Gupta Empire in the sixth century A.D.

History up to Mahābhārata War.—The Purāṇas set up a primeval king named Manu Vaivasvata from whom are derived all the dynasties that ruled in India. He had a daughter, Ilā, of whom was born Purūravas Aila, who started ruling at Pratishṭhāna (modern Allahabad), the original Indian settlement.

Another son of Manu, Ikshvāku, set up in Madhyadeśa, with his capital at Ayodhyā.

Ikshvāku's son, Nimi, set up in Videha, and his son Daṇḍaka in the forest named after him in the Deccan.

A son of Manu by different origin, Saudyumna by name, set up at Gaya and eastern districts.

A son of Purūravas, Amāvasu, founded Kānyakubja, and a grandson founded Kāśī.

Aila imperialism soon established itself under Ikshvāku's descendant, Yayāti, whose five sons are called Yadu

Turvasu, Druhyu, Anu, and Pūru, all of Rigvedic fame, and thus linking up the traditions of the Vedas and the Purāṇas. The five sons divided between themselves the whole of mid-north India, along with the earlier Aila kingdoms of Kāśī and Kānyakubja. Pūru got the ancestral sovereignty of the middle region, the southern half of the Ganges-Jumna doab, with its capital at Pratishṭhāna. Yadu got the south-west, the region watered by the Rivers Charmaṇvatī (Chambal), Vetravatī (Betwa) and Śuktimatī (Ken). Druhyu planted himself in the west, in the country west of the Jumna and north of the Chambal; Anu in the north, i.e. the northern portion of the Ganges-Jumna plain; and Turvasu in the south-east, round Rewa.

The chief development took place among Yadu's descendants who increased and divided into two great branches, the Haihayas and the Yādavas, occupying the northern and southern parts of Yadu's territory.

The Yādavas forged ahead under Śaśabindu who conquered the territories of the Pauravas an d the Druhyus.

Yādava imperialism was rivalled by that ofAyodhyā under Māndhātā overrunning Kānyakubja, Paurava realm, and the Druhyus whose king, Gāndhāra, was driven to Gāndhāra country named after him. His son, Muchukunda, established himself at Māhishmatī (modern Māndhātā) and Purikā on the Narmadā.

Next followed great movements among the Haihayas, Ānavas, and Druhyus, as reactions to Māndhātṛi's conquests. The Ānavas divided into two branches. The one under Uśīnara spread through the Panjab, creating the Yaudheyas, Ambashṭhas, Śivis, Madras, Kekayas, and Sauvīras, pushing the Druhyus to Gāndhāra and the Mlechchha countries beyond. The Ānava branch under Titikshu moved eastward beyond Videha and Vaiśālī, founding the five kingdoms of Aṅga, Vaṅga, Puṇḍra, Suhma, and Kaliṅga under King Bali.

Haihaya imperialism now intervened with the conquests of Kārtavīrya-Arjuna, which drove the Bhārgava Brāhmans from their settlement on the Narmadā to seek alliance with the Kshatriyas of Kānyakubja and Ayodhyā.

The fruit of this fateful alliance was Jamadagni whose son Paraśu-Rāma destroyed Haihaya power under Tālajaṅgha, but only for a time.

The Tālajaṅghas in five branches—Vītahotras, Śāryātas, Bhojas, Avantis, and Tuṇḍikeras—established their dominion all over northern India, overthrowing Kānyakubja, and Ayodhyā, with the help of the Śakas, Yavanas, Kāmbojas, Pāradas, and Pahlavas from the north-west and extending their conquests up to Videha and Vaiśālī.

Ayodhyā revived under Sagara whose conquests established his empire over northern India, destroying Haihaya domination. The kingdoms that survived these cataclysms were Videha, Vaiśālī, Ānava kingdoms in the east, Kāśī in Madhyadeśa, Turvasu's line in Rewa, and the new Yādava kingdom of Vidarbha.

The old Paurava kingdom also revived after Sagara's death under Dushyanta, and his son Bharata, but in a new region, the north portion of the Ganges-Jumna doab, with its capital at Hastināpur replacing the old Pratishṭhāna. There was a great expansion of the Bhāratas in new kingdoms formed, such as Kṛivi or Pañchāla in two parts, northern called Ahichchhatra, and southern, Kāmpilya.

Ayodhyā had another spell of power under a succession of able kings like Bhagīratha, Dilīpa, Raghu, Aja, and Daśaratha, by whose time it was known as Kosala.

The Yādavas also rose to power under King Madhu and the Mādhavas whose territory extended from Gujarat to the Jumna.

This disposition of powers at the time of Daśaratha agrees with that presented in the Rāmāyaṇa. It shows Ayodhyā or Kosala on friendly terms with the eastern states like Videha, Aṅga, and Magadha, and the Punjab states of Kekaya, Sindhu, Sauvīra, the western state of Surāshṭra and the Dākshiṇātya states.

Ayodhyā after Rāma recedes into background. The next period shows the Yādavas and the Pauravas as the chief actors.

The Yādavas were represented in four kingdoms, the

chief of which were those of Andhaka and Vṛishṇi. Andhaka reigned at Mathurā, succeeded by his son Kukura, whose descendants, the Kukuras, ruled there up to Kaṁsa. Vṛishṇi reigned at Dvārakā in Gujarat up to Akrūra, his descendant.

Other Yādava kingdoms at the time were Vidarbha, Avanti, Daśārṇa, and a Haihaya kingdom at Māhishmatī. Most of the Yādavas except the Vṛishṇis were also known as Bhojas.

About this time, north Pañchāla was ruled by the powerful kings, Sṛiñjaya, Chyavana, and Sudās, of Rigvedic fame. Sudās drove the Paurava king, Saṁvaraṇa, out of Hastināpura and brought on the Battle of Ten Kings against him. But his empire declined after him, and the Pauravas revived and recovered Hastināpura and conquered north Pañchāla. Under Kuru, the Paurava dominion extended up to Prayāga. It suffered again a decline till it revived under Pratīpa and Śāntanu. Śāntanu's grandsons were Dhṛitarāshṭra and Pāṇḍu. Dhṛitarāshṭra's sons led by Duryodhana were called Kauravas, while Pāṇḍu's sons were the five Pāṇḍavas, Yudhishṭhira, Bhīma, Arjuna, Nakula, and Sahadeva.

Thus we arrive at the stage preparing for the Mahābhārata war in a continued history preserved in the Purāṇas.

History after the Mahābhārata War: Possible Date of the War.—The history subsequent to the Bhārata War is also indicated in the Purāṇas. They also help us to work out the date of that war. This has been done by Pargiter as follows. Taking the beginning of Chandragupta Maurya's reign to be 322 B.C. (as settled on other grounds), we can work out the dates for the dynasties of his predecessors with the help of the Purāṇas. He was preceded by nine Nandas, Mahāpadma and his eight sons, accounting for 100 years. The best reading ascribes to them a *life*, and not *reign*, of 100 years. If Mahāpadma became king at twenty, he became so in (322 + 80) 402 B.C. Now, as to the length of time between Mahāpadma and the Bhārata War, there are three versions, of which the most reasonable one states that up to the time of Mahāpadma's extermination of

Kshatriyas, there had reigned the following Kshatriya kings (since the Bhārata War), viz. 24 Aikshākus, 27 Pañchālas, 24 Kāśīs, 28 Haihayas, 32 Kaliṅgas, 25 Aśmakas, 36 Kurus (Pauravas), 28 Maithilas, 23 Śūrasenas, and 20 Vītahotras. If we allow the reasonable time of twenty years for Mahāpadma's conquests, these should have been completed by (402 – 20) 382 B.C. Besides this list of contemporary kings of ten dynasties, there is a dynastic list given of the Paurava, Aikshāku, and Bārhadratha kings, in which there is a line drawn between past and future kings. This line is drawn at the date of the Bhārata Battle. The Aikshāku list names twenty-five future kings from Divākara, as against twenty-four of the other list. The Paurava (Kuru) list mentions twenty-five future kings as against thirty-six of the other list. But there is a well-attested reading in which the figure given is twenty-six and not thirty-six. Thus there is practical agreement between the two lists as to the number of these kings and their reckoning from the same initial point up to the other point, that of Mahāpadma's conquest in 382 B.C. Correcting now thirty-six Kurus into twenty-six, we get 257 contemporary kings in ten kingdoms, giving an average of twenty-six kings for each. If we take eighteen years as the average period for each king's reign, we get for twenty-six such kings the period of 468 years from (468 + 382) 850 B.C. The dynastic list for Magadha also leads to the same result. The future Bārhadratha kings of Magadha number sixteen after Senājit, and these ruled, along with five Pradyotas, and ten Śiśunāgas, up to the time of Mahāpadma's accession in 402 B.C. Omitting the Pradyotas, who were not kings of Magadha, as shown below, we get (850 – 402) 448 years for twenty-six kings, an average of seventeen years, which is not very improbable in that age of changing dynasties.

Finally, to arrive at the date of the Bhārata Battle, we must add to 850 B.C. the times of kings preceding the three kings of the dynastic list aforesaid, viz. five Pauravas, four Aikshvākus, and six Bārhadrathas, i.e. a mean of five, for whom we can permit a period of 100 years, so that we obtain 950 B.C. as the date of the Bhārata Battle.

It is to be noted that this reckoning is based upon " averages (1) of the number of kings of eleven contemporaneous dynasties, and (2) of the lengths of reigns computed from the reliable data of fourteen historical dynasties in other countries ", and so may be accepted as a " reasonable general approximation " [Pargiter, op. cit., pp. 179–183].

The only point that can perhaps be urged against Pargiter's reckoning is that it is based on an average of eighteen years for each king, which may be considered as rather a low average for the number of kings counted in that reckoning. There are also the two other sets of data which should not be completely brushed aside. First, there is the statement that between Mahāpadma's inauguration and Bhārata Battle there reigned in Magadha twenty-two Bārhadrathas, five Pradyotas, and ten Śiśunāgas, who are said to have covered between them 1,408 or 1,498 or 938 years. Secondly, there is a statement of the Mahābhārata [*Mbh.*, xiv, 66–70] to the effect that there was a period of 1,050 (or 1,015) years between Mahāpadma's inauguration and Parikshita's birth which took place soon after the Mahābhārata Battle. These figures are rejected by Pargiter on the ground that they land us in too high averages for each reign. Perhaps a *via media* may be found by taking each king to represent a generation when it is not clear that the succession had always been from father to son. If a generation is measured by 25–33 years, as is usually done, the Mahābhārata total of 1,015 years or the lower total of 938 years will not then appear to be so extravagant. There is also another point of great chronological importance to be fitted into any scheme of reckoning that may be proposed. It is the synchronism between the following characters: Bimbisāra, Udayana, Prasenajit, Pradyota, Ajātaśatru, Buddha, and Mahāvīra, as established on the basis of both Pali and Jaina texts. Buddhist tradition fixes the time of the Buddha between 623–543 B.C., Mahāvīra pre-deceasing him by about three years. Several dynastic lists given in the Purāṇas lead up to the kings who were the contemporaries of the Buddha. Thus the Paurava list of the Matsya Purāṇa leads up to Udayana through a succession of twenty-five kings, or twenty-three generations between him and Abhimanyu, the second king in the list, who died in the Bhārata Battle. The second list is that of the Ikshvākus, which takes us to Prasenajit through a succession of twenty-four kings. If we omit from the list four names, viz. those of Śākya, the founder of the Buddha's family, his father, himself, and his son, evidently introduced by the Kosala bards to glorify the lineage of their lords, we shall have twenty-two generations between the Great Battle and the Buddha's time. The Magadhan genealogy also mentions twenty-two kings between Sahadeva killed in the Great Battle and Pradyota as successor of the last king, Ripuñjaya. Perhaps this is a mistake of the Purāṇas. The Pali texts point to Pradyota as one of Avanti, and not of Magadha, of which he was the most feared enemy. With the help of the Pali texts we can correct the mistake of the Purāṇas by omitting from the list the six Pradyotas succeeding Ripuñjaya of Magadha and introducing as his successor Bimbisāra as the founder of a new dynasty which counts Śiśunāga as one of his successors and not as the founder of the dynasty, as the Purāṇas have it. We thus find that the three contemporaries of Buddha—Bimbisāra, Prasenajit, and Udayana—belonged respectively to the twenty-second, twenty-third, and twenty-fourth generation after the Great Battle.

We have, therefore, now to consider three sets of data which have to be reconciled in a common system, if possible. This is possible if we count a generation at thirty-three years within the time-limit established for a generation. On this basis, firstly, the twenty-fourth generation from the Buddha will lead to (24 × 33 + 623) 1415 B.C. as the date of the Bhārata War. Secondly, thirty-one generations from Mahāpadma Nanda's time will establish (31 × 33 + 402) 1425 B.C. as the date of the same event. Thirdly, an interval of 1,050 years from Mahāpadma's inauguration will also make that date (1,050 + 382) 1432 B.C. Thus these sets of data derived from different sources will practically yield the same chronological result, viz. the date of about 1400 B.C. for the Bhārata War.

Āryan Origins according to the Purāṇas.—The traditional

history of India, as we have seen, starts with the three stocks (1) Aila, (2) Saudyumna, and (3) Mānava or Mānva, with their centres at Pratishṭhana, Gayā, Ayodhyā, and Mithilā. The other two stocks retreated before the expansion of the Ailas and their offshoots, who came to dominate, as we have seen, the whole of north India down to Vidarbha. Pargiter suggests the bold theory that the Ailas or Airas were the Āryans, the Saudyumnas the Muṇḍā race, and the Mānvas, the Dravidians. The original abode of the Ailas was some middle Himalayan region, some northern country which the Purāṇas called Ilāvṛita. Indian tradition knows nothing of any Āryan invasion of India from north-west and outside of India, nor of any advance of the Āryans from the west to east. On the other hand, it speaks of an Aila outflow, the expansion of the Druhyus through the north-west into the countries beyond. Accordingly, Rigveda x, 75, mentions rivers in their order from the east to the north-west, beginning with the Ganges, in accordance with the course of Aila expansion and its outflow beyond the north-west. Similarly, in the Rigvedic account of the Battle of Ten Kings against Sudās who was an Aila king of North Pañchāla, as already seen, he is described as pushing his conquests westwards into the Panjab. This is also in keeping with the view that the bulk of the Rigveda was composed in the upper Ganges-Jumna doab and plain. The Rigveda holds the Sarasvatī especially sacred, and also knows the Sarayu, the river of Oudh. This view seems to be further supported by the mention of the Vedic gods, Indra, Varuṇa, Mitra, and Nāsatyas in the Boghaz-Koi Inscription of 1400 B.C., already noticed, proving that there was an outflow of people from India before the fifteenth century B.C. bringing her gods with them, and that Āryan origins and cultures in India were much earlier still. Pargiter goes further and works out a possible date for this Indian migration beyond the north-west. It was the Druhyu expansion which is indicated fifty-five steps earlier than the Bhārata Battle in the genealogical table drawn up to illustrate the course of history from the Purāṇas. If twelve years are allowed for a step, the date of the Druhyu migration out of India would be (55 × 12) 660 years previous to the Bhārata Battle of about 1000 B.C. Thus it took place in the seventeenth century B.C. so as to explain the possibility of Vedic gods being known in Mesopotamia in the fifteenth century B.C.

Links with Vedic Chronology.—The date of the Bhārata war and of Parikshita as settled above will also help to settle some points of Vedic chronology. According to the *Mahābhārata*, Parikshita who came to rule at Hastināpura as the son of Abhimanyu, son of Arjuna, was succeeded by his son, Janamejaya, who is known for two important events. He performed a snake-sacrifice at Takshaśilā and also heard the *Mahābhārata* itself being recited for the first time by Vaiśampāyana.

It is interesting to note that certain Vedic works, the *Atharva-veda*, the *Śatapatha*, and the *Aitareya Brāhmaṇas*, and also the *Bṛihadāraṇyaka Upanishad* also know of Parikshita and Janamejaya, but with totally different traditions which show them to be different persons who had lived in much earlier times than their namesakes of the Purāṇas.

The *Bṛihadāraṇyaka Upanishad* (iii, 3) has the following question: "Whither have the Pārikshitas gone?" And also the reply: "Thither where Aśvamedha sacrificers go."

This reference shows that the Pārikshitas had already become a past history and a vanished glory by the time of this Upanishad; (2) that they must have committed some grievous sins leading to their extinction; (3) that they performed Aśvamedha sacrifices to atone for their sins but in vain; (4) that these particular Pārikshitas, by their performance of horse-sacrifice, are to be distinguished from the Janamejaya of the *Mahābhārata*, who was known for his snake-sacrifice.

It will now be seen that the story of the *Bṛihadāraṇyaka* is an echo of the earlier accounts of the Pārikshitas as given in the other Vedic works aforesaid.

The glory of a Pārikshita and the zenith of his power are first indicated in the Atharva-Veda (xx, 127, 7–10) which tells of the proverbial plenty of the Kuru kingdom under him in "curds, drinks, and barley".

The Śatapatha Brāhmaṇa (xi, 5, 5, 13) also tells of the "Palace of Janamejaya, Pārikshita", its bounty of "sweet drinks" (*pūrnān pariśruta-kumbhān*), its "prize-winning horses". The same text also tells how Janamejaya Pārikshita had "bound for the gods a black-spotted grain-eating horse adorned with a golden ornament and with yellow garland at his city of Āsandīvān" (xiii, 5, 4, 1–4).

The *Aitareya Brāhmaṇa* also has its own story to tell of the glory and the power of Janamejaya in several passages.

In one passage (vii, 27) Janamejaya Pārikshita is referred to as having performed a sacrifice from which he had excluded Brahmins of the clan of Kaśyapas. This passage gives the first hint of Janamejaya's hostility to Brahmins, which was fraught with grave consequences to the fortunes of himself and of his dynasty. In the other passage (vii, 34), he is described as a great king, who, "like Āditya in prosperity gave heat, obtaining tribute from all the quarters, whose sway was dread and unassailable."

There is again another passage (viii, 21) which tells how his priest "Tura Kāvasheya anointed Janamejaya Pārikshita with the great imperial sacrifice known as Aindramahābhisheka". Therefore, Janamejaya "went round the earth completely, conquering on every side, and offered the horse in sacrifice. Regarding this a sacrificial verse is sung :

> 'At Āsanḍīvant a horse, grass-eating,
> Adorned with gold and a yellow garland
> Of dappled hue, was bound
> By Janamejaya for the gods.' "

It may be observed here that in the *Aitareya*, "Janamejaya is described as having performed a horse-sacrifice" to celebrate his attainment of imperial status, and not for the atonement of any sin, of which it does not contain a single hint. This makes the *Aitareya* tradition older than that of *Śatapatha* or the *Bṛihadāraṇyaka*. Indeed, as Keith points out in his translation of *Aitareya* (p. 45), "the time of *Aitareya* is that of Bhāratas of Madhyadeśa, the time when the fame of Janamejaya was at its height." He further states: "The period of Janamejaya is doubtless that of the close of the earlier Vedic period of the Saṁhitās and they accord well with the position he holds in the *Aitareya*." There is in the *Aitareya* no hint of the decline of that position.

The story of the sin of Janamejaya which is hinted at in the *Bṛihadāraṇyaka* is, however, given in the *Śatapatha Brāhmaṇa* which states that "Janamejaya and his sons, grandsons of Pārikshit, the Pārikshitīyas, performing horse-sacrifices, by their righteous work, did away with sinful work one after another." In the same text, this sin is also described as that of Brahmahatyā, i.e. the slaughter of Brahmins. His sons are also named as Bhīmasena, Ugrasena, and Śrutasena, Pārikshitas. The priest employed for this expiatory horse-sacrifice is named Indrota-Daivaka Śaunaka. Janamejaya's priest in the *Aitareya* is a different person named Tura, because he was concerned with ceremonies performed for a different purpose, and not for atonement of sins.

The tradition of the sin to which Janamejaya and his sons had succumbed is carried down to the time of Kauṭilya who, in his *Arthaśāstra*, gives the following reference: "Kopaj-Janamejayo brāhmaṇeshū vikrāntaḥ," i.e. "Janamejaya lost his great power by his sin of wrath and violence against the Brahmins."

These several Vedic traditions about Parikshit and Janamejaya must make them different from, and older than, the persons of the same name who are concerned with the *Mahābhārata* tradition. This view is confirmed by the Purāṇas which know of two Parikshitas and three Janamejayas in the same dynasty. It is, therefore, reasonable to assume that, leaving out of account Janamejaya I as a very remote ancestor, Parikshita I and his son, Janamejaya II, were the subjects of Vedic tradition and Janamejaya III the subject of that of the *Mahābhārata*. Considering also that the Purāṇas place more than twenty generations between Janamejaya II and Janamejaya III and counting the date of Janamejaya III to be about 1400 B.C. we may conclude that the time of Parikshit I and Janamejaya II and of *Śatapatha* and the *Aitareya Brāhmaṇas* should be about

2000 B.C. This date for the *Brāhmaṇa* works will further push back the date of Vedic Saṁhitās and, finally, of the Rig-Veda which may thus be linked up with the time of the Indus Civilization discussed above.[1]

The Law-books.—Much light is thrown on ancient Hindu civilization by the law-books or Dharma-śāstras, of which the chief or representative works are those of Manu, Vishṇu, Yājñvalkya, and Nārada, all in verse except that of Vishṇu. All these works in their present forms include additions made to them from time to time, like the Epics.

Manu Smṛiti[2] *: Its age.*—The Dharma-Śāstra of Manu is the standard and most authoritative work on Hindu law and presents the normal form of Hindu society and civilization. The name Manu is of hoary antiquity, being that of the first progenitor of the human race, the first king, and the first law-giver ; mentioned as a Vedic Ṛishi in the Taittirīya and the Maitrāyaṇīya Saṁhitās [ii, 2, 10, 2 ; i, 1, 5] and in the Chhāndogya Upanishad [viii, 15], and as a law-giver in the Tāṇḍya Brāhmaṇa [xxiii, 16, 7]. Even Yāska [*c.* 700 B.C.] in his *Nirukta* [iii, 1, 4] cites a *śloka* of Manu as a legal authority, stating that the sons are to obtain their father's property in equal shares. The Dharma-sūtras of Bodhāyana [iv, 1, 14 ; 3, 16] and Āpastamba [ii, 16, 1] also cite Manu as a legal authority.

Thus, though the sayings or verses of Manu were very old, they were receiving additions in time till they were collected in what is now known as the Manu Smṛiti or Mānava Dharma-Śāstra, a composition of much later date. This Dharma-Śāstra must have been the work of the Mānava-Sūtra Charaṇa. This Charaṇa or Vedic school based itself on a Śākhā of the Black Yajurveda and developed its own Dharma-Sūtra, that of Manu. In those days, as indicated by Pāṇini [iv, 3, 126 ; 2, 46], each Charaṇa was known not merely for its *Āmnāya* or the Vedic text it studied, but also for its *Dharma* or its particular legal code. For example,

1 Adapted from my Presidential Address before the History Section of the Oriental Conference meeting in Mysore in December, 1935.

2 I am indebted to the thesis on the subject presented for the M.A. Degree by my esteemed pupil, Mr. Vasudeva Sharana Agrawala, M.A., LL.B., now Curator of Curzon Museum of Archæology at Muttra, U.P.

the term *Kāṭhaka* indicated the school of Kaṭhas, and also the Kāṭhaka Dharma-Sūtras, of which the present Vishṇu Smṛiti is the metrical recast. Thus arose the present Manu Smṛiti, a product of the Maitrāyaṇīya Charaṇa of Black Yajurveda.

While the Manu Smṛiti refers to the older Dharma-Śāstras [iii, 232] such as those of Atri, Vasishṭha, Gautama, and Śaunaka [iii, 16], it is itself referred to by the Dharma-Śāstras of Yājñavalkya [i, 4, 5] and Vishṇu which follow it closely, and of Nārada and Bṛihaspati, all of which are thus later works.

Geographical Horizon.—The geographical horizon of the Manu Smṛiti is confined to the north of the Vindhyas, as against that of Āpastamba, Hiraṇyakeśin, and Bodhāyana, followers of Taittirīya schools, lying to the south of the Narmadā. Manu mentions four regions of Aryan culture in the order of their size, viz. (1) *Brahmāvarta* between the Sarasvatī and Dṛishadvatī (modern Hissar district of the Panjab), (2) *Brahmarshideśa* comprising Kurukshetra, Matsya, Pañchāla and Śūrasena, (3) *Madhyadeśa* between the Himalayas and Vindhyas and Sarasvatī and Prayāga, and (4) *Āryāvarta* between the two mountains and the two oceans, the habitat of the black antelope,[1] the land of Vedic Yajñas, outside of which lay the *Mlechchhadeśa* or non-Aryan world, comprising the territory from the Sutlej to the Kabul in the north and the Drāviḍa country in the south [ii, 17; 19; 23]. Manu probably legislated for Brahmarshideśa, as may be inferred from two passages. In the first [viii, 92], it is stated that the truthful man need not visit the Gaṅgā or the Kurus. The second [xi, 77] locates a pilgrimage along the course of the Sarasvatī.

Post-Buddhist features.—That the Manu Smṛiti was a post-Buddhistic work is probably indicated by its mention of (*a*) such historical peoples as the Kāmbojas, Yavanas, Śakas, Pāradas, Pahlavas (Parthians), Chīnas, Kirātas,

[1] " It deserves to be noted that the black antelope selects for its home the well-cultivated, rich plains of India only, and is entirely wanting in the sandy, mountainous or forest districts, which are now, just as in ancient times, the portion of the aboriginal tribes." [Buhler, *SBE.*, xiv, 3, n. 13.]

Daradas, Khasas, Choḍas, and Drāviḍas [x, 44] as disqualified Kshatriyas; (*b*) Śūdra kings transgressing the Śāstras [iv, 61; 87]; (*c*) women joining heretical sects [v, 90]; (*d*) insult to Vedas and gods [iv, 163]; (*e*) Chaitya trees as haunts of bad characters [ix, 264]; and (*f*) non-Vedic Smṛitis and philosophies [xii, 95], most of which are associated with Buddhism.

Polity: Multiplicity of States.—Manu refers to *svarāshṭra* [vii, 32] and *pararājya* [vii, 68], to friendly and hostile states (mitra-śatrurāshṭra) [vii, 32], to a circle of States (*maṇḍala*) [vii, 154], in different degrees of friendliness with one another, with the *madhyama*, middlemost State, at the centre, to neutral (*udāsīna*) States, and to the *Vijigīshu* with lust for conquest [ix, 312]. This shows that Āryavarta to which Manu confines his attention was in his time split up into a number of States and was not politically united.

The State known to Manu.—The kingdom which Manu had within his purview was that for which the army was recruited from the four regions called Kurukshetra, Matsya, Pañchāla, and Śūrasena [vii, 193], i.e. the *Brahmarshideśa* as defined above. Its capital was at a distance from both Kurukshetra and the Gaṅgā [viii, 92].

Political Divisions.—A kingdom was called a *rāshṭra*, its citizens *rāshṭrikas* [x, 61], its king, the *rājā*, and his subjects, the *prajā* [ix, 226]. A *rāshṭra* was made up of different countries, *Deśas* [ix, 251], or provinces called *Janapadas* or *Vishayas* [vii, 134].

Feudatories.—The *Rājā* had his satellites or feudatory chiefs called *Sāmantas* whose loyalty was enforced [vii, 69; ix, 310], as well as military help [ix, 272].

Administrative Divisions.—The administrative divisions were organized in a decimal system made up of (*a*) the village, *grāma*, as the smallest unit, under the *Grāmaṇī* [vii, 120], (*b*) the group of ten villages under the officer called *Daśī* [vii, 115], (*c*) the group of twenty villages under the *Viṁśī*, (*d*) the group of 100 villages under the *Śateśa*, and (*e*) the group of 1,000 villages under the *Sahasreśa* in an ascending order of authority. Instead of 1,000 villages, Vishṇu speaks of the "whole country".

Payment of Officers.—These officers were paid in kind; the *Grāmaṇī* in food, drink, fuel, vegetables, etc. [vii, 118], the *Daśī* in land sufficient to support one family, the *Viṁśī* in land adequate for five families (and requiring twenty ploughs for its cultivation), the *Śateśa* in the revenues of one village and the *Sahasreśa* of one *pura* or town [vii, 119].

Council and Assembly.—The king is described as occupying the supreme position in the State and as the sole protector of his people [v, 94]. He ruled with Assistants, called *Sahāyas* or Secretaries [vii, 31, 36], with the advice of a Cabinet, *Parishad*, of seven or eight ministers, of whom the chief was called *Mukhyāmātya* [vii, 58]. The king gave audience to the people in his *Sabhā* [vii, 146].

There was no privacy for ordinary (*sāmānya*) business of administration, but the king took counsel with the Prime Minister alone on grave (*parama*) matters of State [vii, 58, 59].

Portfolios.—There were administrative departments like (*a*) Finance, in charge of the king himself. It included taxation, collection of revenue, and supervision of mines and stores [vii, 62]; (*b*) Inspection, *chārakarma*, to supervise the work of government officers of all ranks [vii, 81]; (*c*) Military and Police, under a civil minister or *Amātya*, though the commander-in-chief (*Senāpati*) and the general of the army (*Balādhyaksha*) were in power on the field [vii, 65, 189]; (*d*) Local Government under a special minister to attend to all the village and district officers of the decimal system aforesaid and to settle disputes of jurisdiction [vii, 120].

Defence.—The defence of the realm was organized by posting *Gulmas* or Garrisons for every 200, 300, or 500 villages [vii, 114]. They were practically distributed over the whole country [vii, 190].

Government Servants.—Government servants were called *Yuktas* [viii, 34]. The superior officers were called *Mahāmātras* [ix, 259].

Cities.—Cities (*Nagaras*) were in charge of special officers of high rank [vii, 121], with powers over the police and spies [vii, 122, 123] and even over district officers or lords of 1,000 villages [vii, 122], and having within his purview all matters pertaining to the city (*Sarvārthachintaka* in vii, 121). The site of a city or capital was chosen with reference to its strength of natural and artificial fortifications [vii, 70], such as ditch (*parikhā*) [ix, 289], and palisade walls (*prākāra*) with gateways. The variety of interests that had to be administered in a city will be evident from the presence in it of institutions like the assembly hall (*sabhā*), tanks (*prapā*), victuallers' shops or hotels, taverns, places for festivities and theatres (*samāja-prekshaṇāni cha*), labour colonies (*kāruka-veśana*), brothels [ix, 264–5], stores (*koshṭhāgāra*), and magazines (*āyudhāgāra*) [ix, 280].

Villages.—Village administration had similarly to look after the rural institutions like wells (*kūpa* or *udapāna*), tanks (*taḍāga*), ponds (*sara*), reservoirs (*vāpi*), fountains (*prasravaṇa*), embankments (*setu*), groves (*upavana*), parks (*ārāma*) [iii, 201–3], cowpens accommodating up to 1,000 cows and in individual or collective ownership [xi, 127], and pasture-grounds (*parīhāra*) of average width of 600 feet open to all cattle of the village [viii, 237–8].

Elements of Democracy.—The autocracy of the Hindu king admitted of a considerable degree of self-government to the people. The king's position was mainly that of the *Daṇḍa* or the executive to uphold and enforce the *Dharma* or law. The sources of Dharma are stated by Manu to be (*a*) *Veda* or *Śruti*, (*b*) *Smṛiti* or *Dharma-śāstra*, (*c*) *Śīla*, and (*d*) *Achāro*, the customs of holy men. Doubtful points of Dharma were to be settled by a body of experts, or *Śishṭas*, (well-versed in sacred lore), which was called *Parishad*. The Parishad was to be composed of members numbering from three to ten. The ten members comprised three proficient in the three Vedas, one Logician (*Tārkika*), one Mīmāṁsaka, one Nairukta, one Dharma-pāṭhaka (reciter of law), and three members of the three *āśramas* (i.e. those of the student, the householder, and the hermit) [ii, 6; xii, 110–12]. Next, the people were left to legislate for themselves through the groups to which they belonged, the *Kula* or family, the *Jāti* or caste, the *Śreṇī* or guild, or the *Jonapada*, the region.

The king's duty was to recognize and enforce the laws laid down for themselves by these self-governing groups, communities, and corporations, and the laws of different regions [viii, 41, 46].

Social Conditions.—The first social distinction was that of the *Ārya* and *Anārya* [x, 66–7], also called *Dasyu* [x, 45] and *Mlechchha* [ii, 23]. The term *Dasyu* is also applied to the Chaṇḍālas, Śvapākas, and others [v, 131 ; x, 51] who were inferior to the Śūdras [viii, 66].

Non-Aryans.—They were of nomadic habits (*parivrajyā cha nityaśaḥ*) and lived outside the village near the cremation ground or chaitya-trees, forests, and mountains. They used broken utensils. Their wealth consisted of dogs and donkeys, dress of that of dead persons, food of picked-up remnants from broken plates, and ornaments of black iron. They were not allowed to enter the village at night, and in day time only on express business and wearing their prescribed marks. They were employed to carry unclaimed corpses to the cremation ground and as hangmen [x, 51–6]. They lived by hunting [v, 131], were not eligible as witnesses in court [viii, 66], and had no property rights, for " a Kshatriya when starving may snatch the property of Dasyus " [xi, 18].

Aryan Society.—It was made up of the *Dvijātis*, the three twice-born castes of Brāhmaṇas, Kshatriyas and Vaiśyas, and the *Ekajātis*, the Śūdras. There was no fifth *Varṇa* or caste [x, 4].

There were mixed castes (*antara-prabhavāḥ*) springing from adultery, marriage with ineligible women, and violation of the duties of caste [x, 24]. Intermarriage between castes produced a crop of unclassified progeny who were all branded as Śūdras [x, 41] and described by their occupations (*svakarmabhiḥ*) [x, 40].

There was a catholic rule that " he who was begotten by an Aryan on a non-Aryan female may become an Aryan by virtue " [x, 67]. This was probably to accommodate the foreigners and the artisan classes " whose hand was always pure " (*nityam śuddhaḥ kāruka-hastaḥ*) [v, 129]. These new Śūdras were given a higher status than the *born* Śūdras and Untouchables.

Castes.—Social life was governed by the regulations of Caste and Āśrama, of what is known as Varṇāśrama-Dharma.

Brāhmaṇa.—The highest caste was that of the Brāhmaṇa [i, 100]. But his status depended not upon his material possessions but on his character and spirituality. He was known for his knowledge of the Absolute (*brahma-dhāraṇa* in i, 93), for his asceticism (*niyama-dhāraṇa* in x, 3), and for his universal good-will (*maitro brāhmaṇa uchyate* in ii, 87). He acted as teacher, priest, judge [viii, 9], prime minister [vii, 58], assessor [viii, 10, 11], and as member of the Dharma-Parishad, the standing legal commission [viii, 20].

He was punishable in law but not by capital punishment [viii, 380].

A Brāhmaṇa degraded himself by violating restrictions regarding acceptance of food and gifts, pursuit of occupations or professions [iii, 150–166; iv, 153–4], and earning livelihood on the strength of his birth or caste alone without its virtues or ideals [vii, 85 (*jātimātropajīvī*)].

Kshatriya.—The duties common to the three twice-born castes were (1) study, (2) performance of sacrifice (*yajiḥ*), and (3) charity. The special duty of the Kshatriya was the practice of arms and pursuit of a military career [x, 79].

Vaiśya.—His special duties were (1) agriculture (*Kṛishi*), (2) trade (*Vipaṇi-karma*), (3) commerce (*Vāṇijya*), and (4) cattle-rearing (*Pāśupālya*), all described by the general term *Vārtā* [ix, 326]. His wealth was the support of Brāhmaṇic institutions [xi, 12]. He was permitted sea-voyage [iii, 158 (*samudra-yāyī*)], for which he knew a variety of languages [ix, 332].

Śūdra.—Service was his portion in life [viii, 410, 413] including removal of dirt, filth, carcases, and other unclean work. He was not eligible for the sacraments (Saṁskāras) nor for hearing sacred texts except their substance [iv, 99; x, 2]. But he was not denied the rites of marriage, cooking of daily food in the *gṛihya* fire, and Śrāddha [iv, 223; iii, 197]. Manu mentions even Śūdra teachers and pupils [iii, 156], showing that the Śūdra was not prohibited from studying [ii, 238, 240]. As representing the lowest level of culture, the Śūdra majority (*Śūdra-bhūyishṭham*) in a country would spell its doom [x, 61, 125].

Slave.—He might be of seven descriptions ; a captive in war (*dhvajāhṛita*), a slave for food (*bhakta-dāsa*), a hereditary slave (*gṛihaja*), a slave acquired by purchase (*krīta*), or by gift (*datrima*), or by inheritance (*paitrika*), and a slave under debt (*daṇḍa-dāsa*). He could not change his status which was due to birth. Nor could he own property [viii, 414–17]. But the evils of the system were mitigated by the humane treatment which the master was bound to show to his slave [iv, 180 ; x, 124].

Woman.—The woman was not eligible for the study of the Veda nor for use of *mantras* in performing her sacraments (*saṁskāras*) except marriage [ii, 66 ; ix, 18]. She was to be under the guardianship of her male relations, of father as virgin, of husband as wife, and of her sons as mother in old age [v, 148 ; ix, 3]. She could not own property [viii, 416] except *strīdhana* or gifts made to her [ix, 194]. Her main work was to manage the household, including keeping and spending wealth [ix, 11].

Āśramas.—These were four in number, viz. those of the Brahmachārī, Gṛihastha (householder), Vānaprastha (hermit), and Sannyāsī (ascetic), and were obligatory on all the three higher Castes. Thus while the Castes divided, the Āśramas were the uniting and equalizing factors in society.

Studentship.—Studentship began with the ceremony of *Upanayana*, which was performed at the ages of 8, 11, and 12, for the Brāhmaṇa, Kshatriya, and Vaiśya pupils respectively. The ages might be 5, 6, and 8 for a precocious pupil [ii, 36–7]. Studentship meant living in the home of the teacher who prescribed a course of discipline and austerities as regards dress, food, and habits, based on what is called *brahmacharya*, or control over senses [ii, 93, 94 (*indriyasaṁyama*)]. The aim of education was both intellectual (*Veda-grahaṇa*) and spiritual (*vratādeśana*) development [ii, 173] on the basis of *tapas* or meditation [ii, 164 (*tapaḥ Brahmādhigamikam*)].

The students daily duties comprised (1) performance of

Sandhyā and Agnihotra [ii, 101, 108], (2) tending sacred fire [ii, 187], (3) *svādhyāya*, (4) begging for his teacher or school, (5) fetching water, fuel, earth, flowers, etc., from the field and forest, and (6) attending to the lecture (*pravachana* or *nirvachana*) of his teacher.

Subjects of Study.—These consisted of (1) the three Vedas called Śruti [ii, 10 ; xi, 264] read in their different texts called *Śākhās* cultivated in different schools called *Charaṇas* [iii, 145] ; (2) select Vedic hymns and verses [xi, 249–260] ; (3) *Atharvaveda* [xi, 33], to ward off evil ; (4) *Brāhmaṇas*, of which Manu mentions *Aitareya* [vi, 3], to be included in *Svādhyāya* [iv, 100] ; (5) *Āraṇyakas* to be studied after finishing the Veda [iv, 123] ; (6) *Upanishads* containing the *rahasya* or esoteric matter of the Veda [ii, 140] and forming the concluding parts of Āraṇyaka works, on which Manu says : " A Brāhmaṇa dwelling in the forest must study the sacred texts contained in the Upanishads in order to attain complete union with the supreme soul " [vi, 29 ; (7) *Vedāṅgas*, six in number [iii, 185], such as Nirukta and Kalpa [xii, 111 ; ii, 140] ; (8) *Darśana-Śāstras*, of which Manu mentions Mīmāṁsā, Nyāya [xii, 111], Vedānta [ii, 160], and probably Yoga, too [vi, 72] ; (9) *Dharma-Śastras* or *Smṛiti* [ii, 10 ; iii, 232] ; (10) *Itihāsa* and *Purāṇa* [iii, 232] ; (11) Vaikhānasa Sūtra for recluses [vi, 21] ; (12) Heretical Śāstras [xi, 65 ; xii, 95], and (13) *Vārtā* or secular subjects with many branches [iv, 19 ; ix, 331–2], including Ānvikshakī (dialectics) and Daṇḍanīti (politics) [vii, 43].

Specialization.—Students specialized as *Vaidikas* or *Śāstrins*. The aim of the former was mastery of the four Vedas [iii, 184] or less, up to one [iii, 2], or even of one of its Śākhās or a portion thereof. The more successful became known as Śrotriyas, Ṛitvijas, or Brahmavādis [iii, 128 ; ii, 143 ; ii, 113]. The Śāstrins specialized in the Śāstras or Vedāṅgas.

Period of Studentship.—It depended on the subject of study, and might be 36, 18, or 9 years, or the time required for the study of one Veda [iii, 1, 2]. A student might break off after completing his study but not fulfilling his vow ; or fulfilling the vow without completing his study ; or completing both study and vow; and would be known respectively as *Vidyā-*, or *Vrata-*, or *Vidyā-Vrata-Snātakas* [iv, 31]. A student devoting his whole life to study would be called a *Naishṭhika* [ii, 243].

Academic Year.—It was of two terms. Each term was inaugurated by a public ceremony called *Upākarma* and ended by another called *Utsarga.* The first term for Rigvedins and Yajurvedins began on the full moon day in Śrāvaṇa (July) and for Sāmavedins a month later [iv, 95]. It was devoted to study of the Vedas and continued for about four months and a half. It closed in the month of Pushya (December), or on the first bright day of Māgha (January) [iv, 97]. A break of three days was allowed after both *Upākarma* and *Utsarga.* If the *Utsarga* fell in Māgha, the second term would begin on the fifth day of the bright half of that month, what is now called Vasanta-pañchamī, or Sarasvatī Pūjā day. The second term was devoted to the Vedāṅgas.

The academic year had its holidays, called *Anadhyāyas,* comprising the two Ashṭamīs, two Chaturdaśīs, Amāvasyā and Pūrṇimā, in every month, the six holidays following Upākarma and Utsarga, and the last day of each of the four seasons called *Chāturmāsī* [iv, 113, 119, 26; vi, 10]. Besides these regular (*nitya*) holidays, there were also occasional (*naimittika*) holidays due to accidental circumstances such as storm, thunder, rain, fog, fire, dacoity, or eclipse.

Teachers.—They were of two classes called (1) *Upādhyāya* who took to teaching as a profession for his livelihood [ii, 141] and taught only a portion of the Veda or Vedāṅga [ib.]; (2) *Āchārya* who taught the pupil the Veda with its Kalpasūtras and Upanishads [ii, 140], and who taught him free. The pupil after completing his education could give him such presents as he could afford—field, gold, cows, horse, umbrella, shoes, grain, vegetables, or clothes [ii, 246].

The paid teacher and the paying student were condemned as unworthy of invitation to a Śrāddha [iii, 156].

Besides the ordinary teachers, Manu refers to educational experts (adhyāyajñāḥ=adhyāpanavidhijñāḥ [iv, 102]) who were proficient in pedagogy.

The Last Two Āśramas.—The third *Āśrama* was that of the *Vānaprastha*, one who took to the woods, renouncing the world, and living in a hermitage [vi, 7] where he subsisted on wild corn, fruits and vegetables, even manufacturing his own salt [vi, 12]. He was permitted to glean his stock of corn twice in the year [vi, 11]. The fourth *Āśrama* was that of the *Sannyāsī*, a wanderer, living on one meal a day [vi, 55] obtained by begging, practising Haṭha-yoga [vi, 70–2] and Dhyāna-yoga [vi, 73], and meditating on the Ātman of the Vedānta or Upanishad [vi, 83]. Manu mentions women ascetics of heretical sects who must have been Buddhist nuns [v, 90 ; viii, 363].

Economic Life.—Manu knows of both urban and rural life, of cities (*nagara*), towns (*pura*), and villages (*grāma*).

Building.—Houses were constructed of mud, brick, stone, and timber [viii, 250], and in rows [viii, 392] with lanes and roads between them [iv, 45 (*patha*) ; ix, 282 (*rājamārga*)], and also of several storeys [iii, 91 (*prishṭha*)]. The art of building was called *Vāstusaṁpādana* [iii, 255] and the architect or the building engineer *Gṛiha-saṁveśaka* [iii, 163]. Houses were separated by defined boundaries on which the neighbours' verdict was final on disputes [viii, 262].

Temples were built in the outskirts to serve as boundary marks [viii, 248].

The public works of utility of both towns and villages have been already noticed.

Agriculture.—It depended on a knowledge of seeds, of varieties of soil, and of its qualities [ix, 330]. The genuineness of seeds was guaranteed by penalty [ix, 291]. Areas sown were called *kedāras* [ix, 38]. The crops grown included cotton, barley, wheat, rice, mudga-beans, sesame, māsha, sugar-cane, and vegetables [ix, 39]. Two harvests were usual, spring and autumn [vi, 11].

The agricultural implements included wooden plough tipped with iron [x, 84], yoke for cattle, rope and leathern vessel for irrigation from wells [ix, 293].

Cultivation was by the Śūdra labourer and on the basis of stipulated terms, such as half the share of the produce to the cultivator [iv, 253 (*ārdhika*)] who supplied also the seeds [ix, 53]. The royal share was one-fourth, one-eighth, or one-twelfth, according to soil [vii, 130]. The king was to ensure proper cultivation by penalties [viii, 243].

The live-stock included buffalo, cow, sheep, and goat, tended by professional herdsmen (*paśupālāḥ*) who were responsible for their protection from wild beasts and thieves [viii, 232–5].

Dairying, selling of milk and ghee was known [iv, 253; viii, 231 (*kshīrabhṛit*)]. There is also mention of dealers in sheep [iii, 166] and wood (*ūrṇā*).

Arts and Crafts.—There were artisans (*śilpinaḥ*), craftsmen (*kārukāḥ*) [x, 100] and mechanics (*yantra-pravartakāḥ*) [xi, 64], who were socially higher than Śūdras [x, 99]. Every artisan had to contribute to the king a day's labour every month [vii, 75, 138].

Among individual arts and crafts are mentioned those of the goldsmiths [ix, 292 (*hemakāra*)] not known for any special honesty [ib.]; the blacksmith [iv, 215 (*karmāra*)] who smelted iron rods in the furnace [iii, 133 (dīptaśūla) and made the plough (sītā), spade [xi, 133], spear [iii, 133] (*ṛishṭi*)], spike [viii, 315 (*śakti*)], iron staff [ib., (*āyasadaṇḍa*)], weapons [ix, 293; x, 79], long nails [viii, 271 (*śaṅku*)], iron balls [iii, 133], hollow iron image [xi, 103 (*sūrmi*)] and iron bed [viii, 372 (*āyasa-śayana*)]; the dyer [iv, 216]; the launderer [ib.], who used soap-berries for washing blankets, alkali for silk and woollen clothes, and white mustard for linen [viii, 396]; the oilman [iii, 158], working with a press [iv, 85 (*chakra*)]; the tailor [iv, 214 (*tunnavāya*)]; the weaver [viii, 397 (*tantuvāya*)], who ginned cotton and separated the seed [iv, 78 (*kārpāsāsthi*)], then spun yarn (*sūtra-tantu*) and wove it into cloth of cotton, silk, linen, and wool, producing eleven *palas* of cloth out of ten of yarn [viii, 397] and also fine cloth for export [viii, 321]; the potter [viii, 327]; the worker in cane and bamboo [ib.]; makers of bow and arrow [iii, 160]; brick-kilners [viii, 250]; the leather-worker [x, 36, 49 (*charmakāra*)], making bags (*jīna*), shoes (*upānaha*), whips (*śīphā*) [viii, 369], and the like; and the distiller (*śauṇḍika*).

Trade.—There were both money economy and barter [x, 94]. Prices were fixed by government in consultation with traders with reference to the following points, viz. export (*āgama*), import (*nirgama*), period of storage in shop (*sthāna*) and changes of demand and supply [viii, 401]. There is also mention of Syndicates of traders (*Kulāḥ*= Vyavahartṛi-Samūhāḥ [viii, 201]) who controlled the market and its transactions. Adulteration was punished by law [viii, 203] as well as use of false weights and measures [ix, 286–7].

The trade-routes led through forests, marshes, and jungles, [vii, 185]. The transport was by men, animals, and wheeled carts [viii, 405].

Riverine traffic was by boats, for which fares were determined by distance and local rates [viii, 406].

For sea-borne traffic the shipping charges were not fixed, " as the distances could not be measured " [ib.].

The owners of boats or ships were liable for loss caused by their own errors of navigation but not for loss caused by accidents over which they had no control [viii, 408–9]. There was thus an idea of Insurance in this provision. These boatmen and shippers carried on their business as partnership concerns, of which the loss and profit were distributed according to shares contributed [viii, 408].

The export trade was controlled by the government. " The property of a trader was confiscated if he exported goods of which the king had a monopoly or the export of which was forbidden " [viii, 399], e.g. " elephants in eastern countries; saffron, silks, and woollens in Kāśmīra; horses in western countries; precious stones, pearls, etc., in the southern countries "; " generally articles that are rare in other countries had their exports restricted " [Medhātithi]. As to forbidden exports, Medhātithi instances export of food grains during famines which were known to Manu [viii, 22].

Taxes on Trade.—Trade had to pay customs, excise, and octroi, called by the general name of *Śulka*. The duties were levied on the principle that both Trade and the State should receive their due shares of profit [vii, 128]. They were fixed with reference to buying and selling rates, distance of transport (*adhvānam*), principal and subsidiary charges, and risk in transit [vii, 127] by the Octroi officers in consultation with the merchant representatives [viii, 398] and amounted to a twentieth of the sale-price [ib.]. The collection of the tolls was duly organized by building stations on recognized trade-routes and posting officers on duty up to night and with power to examine every article of merchandise as to number, quantity, and quality, to verify statements made about them. False statement was penalized, as also smuggling of goods in hours or by routes which were unauthorized [viii, 400]. Ferries were maintained by the State by charges varying according to load, with exemptions to students, anchorites (*pravrajita*), hermits (*muni*), and pregnant women [viii, 407].

Banking.—Money was lent out on interest (*vṛiddhi-prayoga*) [ix, 333; x, 115] on promissory notes (*karaṇam*) [viii, 154] to be renewed every year [viii, 155]. Debtors were protected by law which disallowed (1) compound interest (*chakra-vṛiddhi*), (2) interest above customary rate, (3) interest equal to the amount of the principal, (4) personal service in lieu of interest, and (5) exorbitant interest agreed to under coercion [viii, 153]. The usual rate of interest was 15 per cent [viii, 140]. Higher rates pointed to unsecured loans [viii, 142], as explained by the commentators.

Coins.—There was gold, silver, and copper currency [viii, 131]. The gold coin was called *Suvarṇa* = 80 *krishṇalas* = 150 grains. The silver currency included the following varieties]:

2 Krishṇala = 1 Raupya-Māsha.
1 Māshaka = 1 Dharaṇa.
10 Dharaṇas = 1 Śatamāna.

The copper coin was called Kārshāpaṇa = 80 krishṇalas = 150 grains [viii, 135–6]. It was usually called simply *paṇa*. The smallest coin was $\frac{1}{8}$th *paṇa*. A paṇa was in fact subdivided into half, one-fourth, and one-eighth, for which the corresponding coins were called ardha-paṇa, pāda-paṇa, and pādārdha-paṇa [viii, 404].

Servants were paid daily wages ranging from 1-6 paṇas [vii, 126].

The relative values of gold, silver and copper coins are not clearly indicated. In one passage [viii, 284], 6 nishkas of gold represent higher value than 100 paṇas.

There were special officers to guarantee the standard of weights and measures and examine it every six months [viii, 403].

Mining.—The use of the following metals was known, viz. gold, silver, copper, bronze (*kāṁsya*), lead (*saisaka*) [xi, 133], pewter (*raitya*) [v, 114], iron and tin (*trapu*) [v, 114]. Alkalis and acids were used for purifying metals [v, 114]. There is mention of iron derived from ore [ix, 321 (*aśmato lohamutthitam*)]. Slabs of stone were in use [xi, 167 (*upala*)]. There was also mining of precious stones like diamonds [viii, 100 (*aśmamaya-ratna*)]. Mining was subject to State-licence [xi, 64] by which the king was entitled to half the profits [viii, 39] which were collected by special officers called *Artha-Samāhartās* [vii, 60].

The other Law Books.—These are subsidiary to Manu and call for short notice.

Vishṇu-Smṛiti.—The *Vishṇu-Smṛiti* contains some amount of material which is as old as the Dharma-Sūtras of Gautama and Āpastamba (e.g. chapters on Rājadharma and punishments), but the bulk of it is based on Manu-Smṛiti, about 160 verses, and numerous Sūtras, which are merely prose translations of Manu's verses. In its present form, it may be even later than Yājñavalkya-Smṛiti from which it borrows.

Its Geography.—Its geographical horizon shows it to be later than Manu. It defines Aryāvarta in terms of culture, as the region marked by the four castes of Aryan society [84. 4], and locates holy places all over India. Thus Āryāvarta or Aryan India was expanding before the retreating barbarians and was no longer confined to the region of the black antelope, as in Manu. It knows of the five rivers of the south (*Dakshiṇe-pañchanade*) [85. 51], and mentions Śrīparvata, Saptārsha (= Satara ?) and Godāvarī.

Works mentioned.—It knows the four Vedic Saṁhitās,

the Aitareya Brāhmaṇa [15. 45], the Vedāṅgas [30. 3, etc.], Vyākaraṇa [83. 7], Itihāsa [3. 70, etc.], Purāṇa [ib.], and Dharma-Śāstras [ib.].

Points of interest.—Other points of interest are its mention of the seven days of the week and of Thursday as *Jaiva*; of the practice of *Satī* [25. 14]; of *pustakas* [18. 44; 23. 56]; of yellow-robed ascetics (probably Buddhists) and Kāpālikas [63. 36] and Śūdra ascetics [5. 114] as inauspicious sights; of special directions for the worship of Vāsudeva [ch. 49]; and its prohibition of speech with Mlechchhas, Antyajas [71. 59] and of journeys to Mlechchha countries [84. 2].

Polity.—Vishṇu's political system is that of Manu. There is mention of lords of ten and 100 villages under the ruler of the whole country (*deśādhyaksha*) [3. 5]. The conqueror of a country should not uproot its customs and usages (taddeśa-dharmān nochchhindyet) and should place on its throne a scion of the old royal family [3. 26, 30].

There is a reference to king's gift recorded on parchment (*paṭa*), or copper-plate (*tāmra-paṭṭa*), bearing the king's seal (*mudrāṅkita*) [3. 58].

Coins.—Vishṇu's currency is more elaborate than Manu's. He mentions :

3 Yavas = 1 Krishṇala.
5 Krishṇalas = 1 Māsha.
12 Māshas = 1 Akshārdha.
1 Akshārdha + 4 Māshas (i.e. 16 Māshas) = 1 Suvarṇa.
4 Suvarṇas = 1 Nishka.
In weight 2 Krishṇalas = 1 Rupya-māshaka; 16 Krishṇalas = 1 Dharaṇa.

Yājñavalkya-Smṛiti.—Yājñavalkya is a famous name in the Brāhmaṇas and Upanishads. He is the promulgator of White Yajurveda. But he cannot be the author of the *Smṛiti* which is so modern in its style and doctrines, though it is closely connected with the White Yajurveda. According to *Mitāksharā*, a pupil of Yājñavalkya abridged the Dharma-Śāstra in the form of a dialogue.

Comparison with Manu.—The work of Yājñavalkya is more systematic and abridged than that of Manu. It compresses the material of 2,700 verses of Manu into a little over 1,000 verses and yet includes in them some new subjects. These are: (1) worship of Vināyaka and the Grahas for propitiation [i, 271–308]; (2) detailed treatment of five kinds of ordeal [ii, 95–113] as against Manu's general reference to two [viii, 114]; (3) considerable anatomical and medical matter [iii, 75–108]. There are also points of difference between Manu and Yājñavalkya, showing that the latter represents more advanced and recent conditions. This may be illustrated as follows:

Manu allows a Brāhmaṇa to marry a Śūdra girl [iii, 13], which Yājñavalkya condemns emphatically [i, 59]. Manu condemns *Niyoga* [ix, 59–68], but not Yājñavalkya [i, 68–9]. Manu is not explicit about the rights of inheritance of a widow, but Yājñavalkya places the widow at the head of all heirs and classifies heirs in a regular order. Manu cannot tolerate gambling [ix, 224–6]. Yājñavalkya brings it under State control and utilizes it as a source of revenue to the king [ii, 200–3]. Yājñavalkya is also more systematic and modern in his treatment of topics like (*a*) ordeals, (*b*) proofs in courts [Manu completely ignoring documentary evidence, though he knew documents (viii, 51–2)], (*c*) rules of procedure in courts [*Manu*, viii, 53–6, and *Yāj.*, ii. 5–11 and 16–21], and (*d*) the doctrine of possession and prescription [*Manu*, ix, 44, 54, and *Yāj.*, ii, 24–9].

Some references.—Yājñavalkya speaks of yellow-robed people as evil sights [i, 273], meaning the Buddhists, because he himself prescribes yellow robes (*kāshāya*) for his seeker after salvation [iii, 157]. He also refers to the monasteries of Brāhmaṇas learned in the Vedas [ii, 185].

Literature known.—As regards learning, Yājñavalkya refers to the four Vedas, six Vedāṅgas and fourteen Vidyās, including Purāṇa, Nyāya, Mīmāṁsā, and Dharma-Śāstra; to Āraṇyakas [i, 145] and Upanishads [iii, 189]; to Itihāsas, Purāṇa, Vākovākya and Nārāśaṁsīgāthās [i, 45]. But all these subjects of study are as old as the Upanishads. He also mentions Ānvīkshikī (Metaphysics) and Daṇḍanīti [i, 311], Smṛitis in general [ii, 5, and i, 154], and Sūtras and Bhāshyas [iii, 189]. He lays down the dictum that where

Dharma-śāstra and Arthaśāstra conflict, the former is to be followed [ii, 21].

Corporations.—Lastly, though Yājñavalkya is silent about polity and administration, he mentions a crop of corporations standing for popular government in different spheres of national interests. The village community is called a *Samūha*, of which the executive officers are called *Kārya-chintakāḥ*, men who are learned in law, pure in character, and free from greed [ii, 191]. Embezzlement of the profits earned by an executive officer for the *Samūha* is punished by a fine eleven times the amount embezzled [ii, 190]. The term for a republic is *Gaṇa* [ii, 187]. Its constitution is called *Saṁvit*, the violation of which is punished with deportation [ii, 187]. The self-governing groups in an ascending order are called *Kula* (clan), *Jāti* (caste), *Śreṇī* (guild), *Gaṇa* (village community as a whole), and *Janapada* (province), each of which laid down its own laws which the king was to respect, uphold, and enforce [i, 361]. The *Kula* and *Śreṇī* also functioned as courts of justice, the former lower than the latter, while the yet higher court was the *Pūga*. The *Śreṇī* was the assembly composed of men of different castes but following a common craft, but the *Pūga* represented all castes and crafts of the locality, and, therefore, carried the highest authority [ii, 30]. Appeals lay from the lower to the higher court.

Mithilā.—It is also to be noted that while Manu legislated primarily for Brahmarṣhideśa, Yājñavalkya is associated with Mithilā [i, 2], the Vedic Videha of Janaka-Yājñavalkya fame.

Nārada-Smṛiti: *Comparison with Manu and Yājñavalkya*—It follows Manu-Smṛiti in the nomenclature and arrangement of the eighteen titles of law. There are about fifty verses common to both, and others containing the same matter. But Nārada has several new points showing his differences from Manu, as well as Yājñavalkya; e.g. his mention and description of five different ordeals as against two of Manu [viii, 114], to which he adds two more [ch. on Ṛiṇādāna, verses 259–348] not known to Yājñavalkya. Against Manu he allows Niyoga (marital relation, 80–8) and re-marriage of women [ib. 97]. He mentions fifteen kinds of slaves against seven known to Manu. Like Yājña-valkya, he allows gambling under State control, and as a source of revenue, and does not interdict it like Manu. He has in fact more of system, of divisions, and subdivisions, than Manu; e.g. his division of law of gift into four sections subdivided into 32, and of 18 titles into 132. He is also later than Yājñavalkya, as shown in his rules of judicial procedure which are more systematic and exhaustive, or in his giving more definitions, or new matter like the seven kinds of ordeals. But in some respects he is more conservative than Yājñavalkya. Unlike Yājñavalkya, he does not recognize the right of widow to succeed to her deceased husband, nor does he mention any rules of succession for *gotrajas* and *bandhus*, as Yājñavalkya does.

Some new positions.—Nārada also lays down certain new principles of law and ethics, e.g. that every man's house is his castle (Riṇādāna, 32) or that the king, however devoid of virtue, must be worshipped by the people, as the husband by his wife (*prakīrṇaka*, 20–2).

Coins.—Nārada mentions the word *Dīnāra* twice, first as a golden ornament, and, secondly, as a coin, also known as *Suvarṇa*. This helps to fix his date. Golden *Dīnāras* were first coined in Rome in 207 B.C. and the oldest pieces corresponding in weight to the Roman *denarius* were struck by the Indo-Scythian or Kushan kings reigning from first century B.C. This should place Nārada somewhere between, say, A.D. 100–300.

Home of Nārada.—It is difficult to locate the home of Nārada. In one place he says that the silver Kārshāpaṇa was current in the south, that it is equivalent to 20 *paṇas* in the east, and that he does not follow the standard of Kārshāpaṇa obtaining in the land of five rivers [Chaurya pratishedha-prakaraṇa, 57 and 59].

Apprenticeship.—To Nārada we owe the rules relating to Apprenticeship and Partnership. The young industrial apprentice must first get the consent of his guardians and period of pupilage settled before admission by his master. He must live with his master whose home is his workshop and is to be treated and instructed as his son. He is not to be exploited and employed on work not connected with the craft of his choice. He cannot leave his master before his term, even if he has completed his training, the profits of which will go to the master. Desertion of a master not failing in character, or as a teacher, is severely punished by confinement or corporal punishment. At the end of pupilage, the apprentice must reward his master as best he can or may accept his service under terms settled [v, 16–21]. It was this industrial training that was so successful in giving to ancient India the palm in handicrafts, feeding her rich export trade for centuries from Pliny to Tavernier.

Partnership.—Industry was carried on by partnerships. The loss, expense, and profits of business were in proportion to the share taken in it. A partner was liable for his individual action and could appropriate its special profits [iii, 1–6].

Corporations.—Nārada also mentions self-governing corporations such as Kula, Śreṇī, Gaṇa [i, 7], Pūga, Vrāta, and guilds of Pāshaṇḍas (heretical merchants) and Naigamas (followers of Vedas) [x, 2]. Each of these corporations rests on a convention or constitution called *Sthiti* or *Samaya* which must be obeyed by its members and upheld by the king [x, 1–2]. According to the *Vyavahāra-Mayūkha*, the term *Vrāta* stands for an association (*Samūha*) of kinsmen, connections, or cognates, i.e. a *Kula*; the *Pūga*, for an association of persons of different castes and crafts; and the *Gaṇa*, for a federation of all these associations, which is thus the largest aggregate in the series and comprised the whole village republic. The *Kula*, *Śreṇī*, and *Gaṇa* also functioned as courts of law subordinate to the king's Court, and to the king himself as the final Court of Appeal [i, 7]. Thus quite a large field of government was left to the people in the villages in these different associations of group-life.

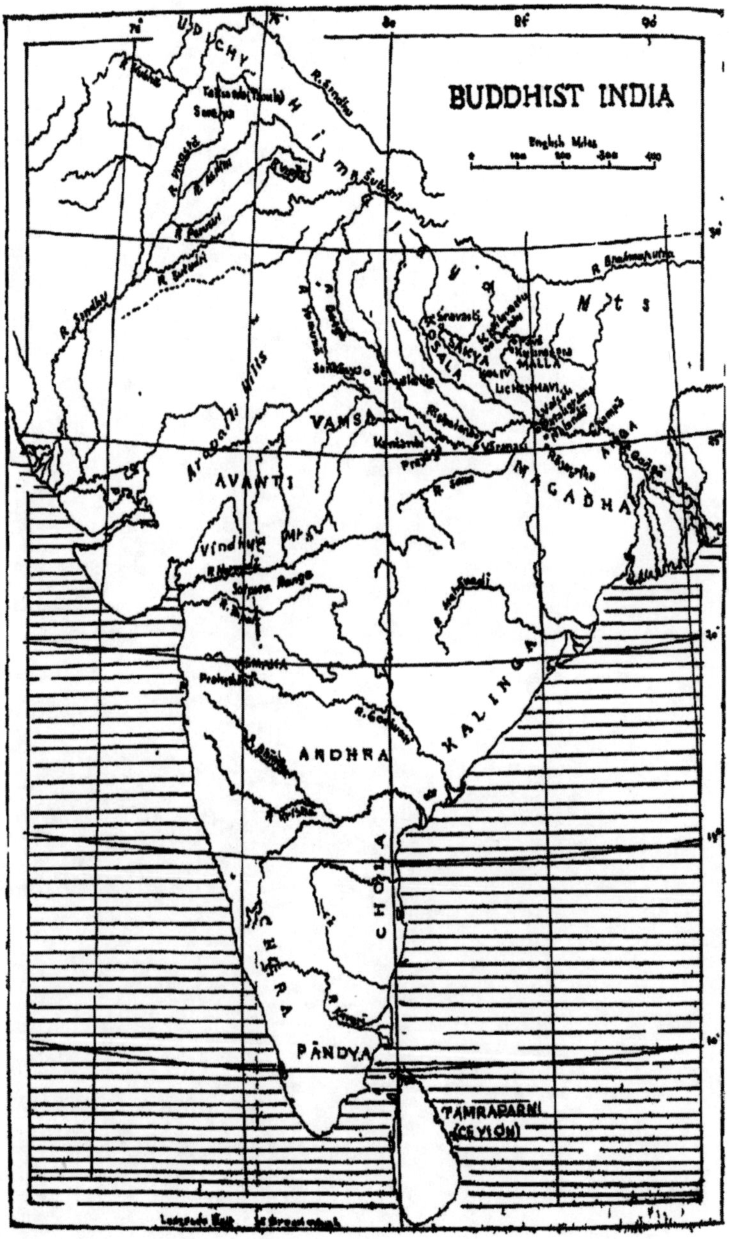
BUDDHIST INDIA
English Miles
0
100
200
300
400
AVANTI
VAMSA
MAGADHA
KALINGA
ANDHRA
CHOLA
CHERA
PĀNDYA
TAMRAPARNI
(CEYLON)
MALLA
LICHHAVI
R. Brahmaputra
R. Godavari
R. Krishna
R. Sona
Satpura Range
Vindhya Hills
Aravalli Hills
Kosambi
Prayāga
Vārānasi
Rājagrha
Campā
Srāvasti

To face p. 179.]

CHAPTER VII

NORTHERN INDIA DURING THE PERIOD c. 650–325 B.C.

Political History.—We have had now a picture of Indian culture and civilization from their origins as reflected in Vedic literature, the Saṁhitās, Brāhmaṇas, and Upanishads, to their complete development and final forms as reflected in the Epics, the Sūtras, and the Smṛitis. We shall now trace the threads of political history as distinguished from cultural history. Political history proper hangs on a framework of chronology. The cultural history of India had, as we have seen, its origins in a remote antiquity, but the beginnings of her chronological history do not appear earlier than about 650 B.C. The threads of political history are, again, isolated and are not woven into the fabric of a unified national history even for Northern India until much later times.

Different States in different epochs.—We have already seen that in the times depicted in Vedic works, there had emerged nine different States representing Aryan civilization as it was extending through the country. These were: (1) Gandhāra, extending on both sides of the Indus, with its two great cities of Takshaśilā and Pushkalāvātī of later times, as mentioned in the *Rāmāyaṇa* [viii, 114, 11]. The *Chhāndogya Upanishad* [vi, 14] shows the acquaintance of its philosopher, Uddālaka Āruṇi, with Gandhāra, while the *Jātakas*, numbered 487 and 377, refer to the association of the Āruṇis, father and son, with Takshaśilā as students (2) Kekaya, famous for its philosopher-king Aśvapati (3) Madra, famous for its teacher, Patañchala Kāpya (4) Vaśa-Usīnara, the northern part of Madhyadeśa, beyond which lay the Udīchyas or northerners, according to the *Gopatha Brāhmaṇa* [ii, 9]; (5) Matsya, a noted place of learning in the *Upanishads* [e.g. *Bṛi. Up.*, ii, 1]; (6) Kuru

(7) Pañchāla; (8) Kāśī, famous for its philosopher-king, Ajātaśatru; (9) Kośala. Beyond these States, comprising the then Aryan India, there were States such as Magadha and Aṅga imperfectly Brahmanized, as we have already seen, and the non-Aryan peoples such as the Andhras, the Pulindas, the Mūtibas, the Śabaras, the Puṇḍras, and the Naishadhas, as mentioned in the *Aitareya Brāhmaṇa* already cited, and making up the Dakshiṇāpatha (*cf.* Dakshiṇāpadā of *Rv.*, x, 61, 8) or the Deccan of those days.

The next landmark in the evolution of Indian States is found in the grammar of Pāṇini of about 700 B.C., which, as we have seen, mentions as many as twenty-two different *Janapadas* or States including several new ones, viz. Sindhu, Cutch, Aśmaka, Swat Valley, Kāmboja, Avanti, Śālva, Bhārata, Yaudheya, Vṛiji, Kaliṅga, besides States generally described as *Prāchya-Janapadas.*

The *Dharma-Sūtra* of Baudhāyana (*c.* 600 B.C.) applies the Aryan ban against the following States, viz. Sauvīra (Multan), Āraṭṭa (in the Panjab), Surāshṭra (Kathiawad), Avanti, Magadha, Aṅga, (Western Bengal), Puṇḍra and Vaṅga (North and East Bengal).

A fuller political map of India is presented in the literature of early Buddhism in which are preserved traditions of older pre-Buddhist times. A list of sixteen principal States (*Mahā-Janapadas*) is given in several places in the oldest Pāli works like the *Aṅguttara-Nikāya* [i, 213; iv, 252, 256, 260], and repeated partially in the Sanskrit work *Mahāvastu* [ii, 2]. The sixteen States are:—

(1) Aṅga, (2) Magadha, (3) Kāsī, (4) Kosala, (5) Vajji, (6) Malla, (7) Cheṭi (Chedi), (8) Vaṁsa [1] (Vatsa), (9) Kuru, (10) Pañchāla, (11) Machcha (Matsya), (12) Sūrasena, (13) Assaka, (14) Avanti, (15) Gandhāra, (16) Kamboja.

Of these, the first twelve are given in the Janavasabha-Sutta [*Dīgha*, ii, 200, ff.]. Another passage in the *Dīgha-Nikāya* [ii, 235], which is reproduced in the *Mahāvastu*

[1] The *Mahāvastu* mentions Śivi and Daśārṇa in place of Nos. 15 and 16. The *Aṅguttara* Text [*PTS.*] however, has the word Vaṅga instead of the form Vaṁsa.

[iii, 208, 209], mentions seven States with their cities as follows :—

(1) Kaliṅga with its capital called Dantapura.
(2) Assaka with Potana as its capital.
(3) Avanti with its capital called Māhissati.
(4) Sovīra with its city of Roruka.
(5) Videha with its capital named Mithilā.
(6) Aṅga with its capital called Champā.
(7) Kāsī with its capital known as Benares.

The later work *Niddesa* (c. 253 B.C.) mentions the Sāgaras and Kāliṅgas of south-eastern India, and the Yonas in place of the Gāndhāras.

The Jain text *Bhagavatī* also mentions sixteen States called : " Aṅga, Baṅga, Magaha, Malaya, Mālava, Achchha, Vachchha (Vatsa), Kochchha, Pāḍha (?Punḍra), Lāḍha (Rāḍha), Bajjī, Moli (Malla), Kāsī, Kosala, Avāha, and Sambhuttara." It must be a later text than the Buddhist for its wider geographical horizon [Hoernle, *Uvāsagadasāo*, ii, Appendix]. Similarly, the *Uttarādhyayana Sūtra* [Lecture xviii] mentions the States of " Dasārṇa, Kaliṅga, Pañchāla, Videha, Gāndhāra, Sauvīra, Kāśi ", and the *Sūtrakṛitāṅga* [ii, 2] mentions in addition " the Draviḍas and Gauḍas ". There is also mention of Mlechchhas not understanding Ārya language [ib., i. 1, 2, 15–16].

Along with the list of countries, there is also given a list of cities which were famous in the Buddha's time, viz. Champā, Rājagṛiha, Śrāvastī, Sāketa, Kauśāmbī, and Kāśī [*Dīgha*, ii, 146, 169].

These States had existed before the rise of Buddhism, because in the time of the Buddha, at least two of them ceased to be independent ; Kāsī being annexed by the Kosala highlanders, and Aṅga absorbed in Magadha.

In the time of the Buddha, the Pali texts bring to light the four great kingdoms of Kosala, Magadha, Avanti, and Vaṁsa and, what is more interesting, numerous republics.

Four Great Kingdoms in the Buddha's time : Kosala.— The texts mention disputes between Kāsī and Kosala. Before Buddha, Kāsī was the more powerful kingdom [*Jāt.*, i, 262 f. ; iii, 115 f. ; *Vinaya*, ii, 13 f.]. There was first an invasion of Kosala under King Dīghīti reigning at Sāvatthī (Śrāvastī) by Brahmadatta, King of Kāsī, who annexed it and returned it to Dīghīti's son [*Vinaya Texts*, ii, 293–305]. Then followed retaliatory invasions of Kāsī by the then Kosalan kings named Vaṅka, Dabbasena and Kaṁsa [*Jāt*., i, 262; ii, 403; iii, 13, 168, 211; v, 112]. Kāsī was finally conquered by Kaṁsa. In the time of the Buddha, the King of Kosala was Pasenadi (Prasenajit). He was educated at Taxila with the Lichchhavi prince Mahāli and a Malla prince of Kusinārā [*Dhp. Com.*, i, 337–8]. He was known for his charity. He gave to two Brahmins the two towns Ukkaṭṭha and Sālavatikā [*Dīgha*, i, 87, 224]. His ministers are named Mṛigadhara [Uvāsagadasāo, ii, App., p. 56], Siri-Vaḍḍha, and Dīgha-Chārāyaṇa [*Saṁ*., ii, p. 118]. He was one of the Buddha's admirers [*Saṁyutta Nikāya*, i, 68, 102] and of the same age ["Bhagavāpi āsītiko aham pi āsītiko" in *Majjhima Nikāya*, ii, 124—"The Buddha is 80 years old; I, too, am 80 years old"].

The relations between Prasenajit and the Buddha are commemorated in stone in one of the Bharhut sculptures. The sculpture bears two inscribed labels: (1) 'Rājā Pasenaji Kosalo,' and (2) 'Bhagavato Dhama-chakaṁ.' This indicates that Prasenajit was an adherent of the Buddha symbolized as *dharma-chakra*. The sculpture depicts the king going out of the gateway of his palace in a chariot drawn by four horses in a procession of footmen and riders of horses and elephants. It also shows in its upper part a two-storeyed building. The ground floor consists of an open-pillared room in which the *dharma-chakra* is placed with a worshipper on each side. The first floor evidently represents the Puṇyaśālā of the story where the king had his last interview with the Buddha.

Kosala had then three chief cities, Ayodhyā, Sāketa, and Sāvatthī, and several minor towns such as Setavyā [Pāyāsi Suttanta] and Ukkaṭṭha [Ambaṭṭha Sutta]. We read of five Rajas under him, the leader of five independent clans now merged in Kosala, and also of wars between him and Ajātasattu, King of Magadha, ending in the latter marrying the daughter of Pasenadi, named Vajirā, after

Prasenajit visiting the Buddha (Bharhut Sculpture).

[*To face p. 182*

his capture. The conflict between them arose out of Pasenadi's resumption of a village in Kāśī which he had given as bath-money to his sister on her marriage with Bimbisāra. The gift was revoked at his sister dying of grief at her husband's assassination by Ajātasattu, who thus went into war over it [*Saṁ.* i, 68 ff.; *Jāt.* ii, 403]. When Pasenadi was away in his old age to meet the Buddha in the Sākiya country in the town called Medalumpa [*Saṁ.*, ii, 89, p. 118], there was a revolution engineered by his minister, Dīgha, who placed his son Viḍūḍabha on the throne. Pasenadi went to seek shelter with his son-in-law, Ajātasattu, at Rājagṛiha, but died outside its gates.[1]

Viḍūḍabha made himself infamous by his slaughter of the innocents in the Śākya country by way of vengeance for the fraud of the Śākyas on his father who asked for a genuine Śākya girl for marriage but was sent instead a slave woman named Vasabha-Khattiyā, who was his mother. Viḍūḍhabha met the Śākyas in battle on the Achiravatī river at Sāvatthī and routed them, but he and his army were soon swept away by the river itself in flood [*Dhammapada Aṭṭhakathā*, i, 359].

These were times of insecurity in Kosala. The *Vinaya* texts [i, 220] inform us that the road between Sāketa and Sāvatthī was infested by robbers.

Kosala was finally absorbed in Magadha.

Avanti.—This was an old kingdom which in the Buddha's time was ruled by Pajjota (Pradyota) who had matrimonial alliance with King Udena (Udayana) of Kosambī, and also with the king of the Sūrasenas at Madhurā (Mathurā), described as Avantiputto. Even Ajātasattu feared his contemplated attack upon Rājagṛiha [*Majjhima Nikāya*, iii, 7]. Although he was nicknamed 'Chaṇḍa' for his ferocity,

[1] The story of the end of Prasenajit is given fully in the commentary on *Dhammapada*, iv, 3: The King appointed Bandhula, a Malla of Kusinārā, first as his Commander-in-Chief, and next as his Chief Justice His popularity caused a conspiracy of officials against him. They won over the King, who contrived his murder at the frontiers where he was deputed to put down an improvised rebellion. The King later repented his folly and appointed to his place Bandhula's nephew, Dīrgha Kārāyana [mentioned as a teacher by Kauṭilya in *Arthaśāstra*, v. 5]. He avenged his uncle's murder by crowning Viḍūḍabha when Prasenajit left his crown and sword to him to see the Buddha.

he later became inclined towards Buddhism under the influence of his Buddhist chaplain, Mahākachchāyana, whom he desired to bring the Buddha to him. Mahākachchāyana, approaching the Buddha, said: "Lord! King Pajjota desires to worship at your feet and hear Dhamma." The Buddha sent him back with seven attendants to teach the king who then became a Buddhist [*Theragāthā Commentary*].

Avanti then became a noted centre of Buddhism, the home of its zealous adherents such as Abhaya Kumāra, Isidāsī, Isidatta, Dhammapāla, Soṇa, and Mahā-Kachchāna, the last two of whom were singled out by the Buddha himself [see *Cambridge History of India*, I, 186, for references]. The language in which these early teachers preached was the popular speech (*laukika-bhāshā*, as Pāṇini calls it) of Avanti, and not the sacred language of Brahmanism (called *chhāndasa-bhāshā*). The Buddha also wanted his teachings to reach the masses in their own vernaculars. Thus though Buddhism was born in Magadha, it was left to Avanti to give it the garb in which we now know it. Its original tongue was not Māgadhī, as usually assumed [ib., p. 187].

Vaṁsa.—It had its capital at Kosambī, connected with Ujjenī by an important trade-route passing through Vedisa. It was ruled in the Buddha's time by King Udena [*Saṁyutta*, iv, 110–13], son of Parantapa. The drama, *Svapna-Vāsavadattā*, ascribed to Bhāsa, mentions as his queen Padmāvatī, sister of King Darśaka of Magadha. The drama, *Priyadarśikā*, ascribed to King Harsha, refers to his marriage with the daughter of Dṛiḍhavarman, King of Aṅga, while his other drama, *Ratnāvalī*, tells of his love for Sāgarikā, an attendant of one of his wives, Vāsavadattā, mentioned in the *Dhammapada Commentary*. This last work gives to him three wives: (1) Vāsuladattā, daughter of the Avanti king, Pajjota, who, by a skilful plot, had Udena captured at hunting and then employed by him to teach elephant training to his daughter at the palace, where they secretly fell in love and escaped to Kosambī for marriage; (2) Sāmāvatī, daughter of the banker, Bhaddavatiya, who became a Buddhist devotee and was killed in a conflagration of the palace engineered for vengeance by (3) Māgandiyā for the Buddha's refusal to marry her. Udena became a supporter of Buddhism under the influence of the monk, Piṇḍola Bhāradvāja, of Ghositārāma [*Saṁ.*, iv, 110–12]. Kosambī was noted for four Buddhist establishments including the famous Ghositārāmā and Pāvāriya's Mango Grove, where the Buddha often came to live and deliver his discourses which have been handed down in the canon. The *Kathāsaritsāgara* describes his *digvijaya* and the *Priyadarśikā* his conquest of Kaliṅga and restoration of his father-in-law, Dṛiḍhavarman, to the throne of Aṅga. Thus tradition marks him out as an important political figure whose influence, both by alliances and conquests, was felt over an extensive area from Avanti to Aṅga and Kaliṅga. *Jātaka* No. 353 describes the Bhagga State of Suṁsumāragiri as a dependency of Vaṁsa.

Magadha : Bimbisāra, *c.* 603–515 B.C.; *his wives and sons.*—Magadha in the Buddha's time forged ahead as the premier state under Bimbisāra and his son Ajātaśatru. Bimbisāra ascended the throne at fifteen [*Mahāv.*, ii, 29, 30]. He started with matrimonial alliances, which counted as powerful factors in his political predominance. One of his queens, as we have seen, hailed from Kosala, the sister of its king, Prasenajit, who brought to her husband the dowry of a village in Kāśī with a revenue of hundred thousand (*Jāt.*, ii, 403]. The *second* is named Chellanā, the youngest of the seven daughters of the Lichchhavi chief, Cheṭaka, of Vaiśālī [Jacobi, *Jaina Sūtras*, i, xli–xv, *SBE.*]. The *Amitāyurdhyāna Sūtra* knows of another wife of his, whom it calls Vaidehī Vāsavī, and states how she served and saved her husband, when imprisoned by Ajātaśatru, by carrying food to him [*SBE.*, xxii, 193, 256]. She may be identified with Chellanā about whom a similar story is related, as will be seen below. The *third* wife was probably from the Punjab, Khemā, daughter of the King of Madda (Madra ?) [*Therīgathā Comm.*, on 139–143].

He had a number of sons causing him worry by their conflicting political ambitions derived from their different mothers. The Jaina and Buddhist texts sometimes differ in their accounts of these. The Jaina texts mention the following sons: Kūṇika (Ajātaśatru), Halla and Vehalla (sons of Chellanā), Abhaya (son of the Lichchhavi courtesan, Ambapālī), Nandisena, Megha Kumāra and others (*Āvaśyaka Sūtra*, p. 697, etc.). Buddhist tradition describes Ajātasattu as *Vedehi-putto* [*Sum.*, i, 139; *Dialogues*, ii, 78] but, later, as the son of the Kosala princess, and mentions other sons, Vimala Koṇḍañña, son of Ambapālī, Vehalla, and Sīlava [*Psalms of the Brethren*, pp. 65, 269 (and *Commentary*, p. 536); *Psalms of the Sisters*, p. 120].

Capital.—Bimbisāra had his capital at Girivraja which the *Mahābhārata* mentions as the capital of King Jarāsandha of Magadha. It also names the five hills protecting the city as Vaihāra, Varāha, Vṛishabha, Ṛishigiri, and Chaityaka. The famous Sattapaṇṇi Cave, where was held the first Buddhist council in 543 B.C., was situated on the "Vebhāra" hill. Ajātaśatru helped in the meeting of the Synod (Dhammasaṁgīti) by building with all speed a splendid hall at the entrance of the cave, two platforms for the president and speakers, and spreading precious mats for seating of members on the floor [*Mahāvaṁsa*, ch. iii]. Later, Bimbisāra changed the capital to Rājagṛiha which is described by Buddhaghosa as Bimbisārapurī [B. C. Law's *Buddhaghosa*, p. 87]. The town-planning engineer and palace architect was Mahāgovinda [*Vimānavatthu Commentary*, p. 82]. The gate of Rājagṛiha was closed to all, including the king, in the evening [*Vinaya*, iv., 116 f.].

Conquest and Territory.—The Jain texts tell of the conquest of Aṅga, with its capital Champā, by Śatānīka, king of Kauśāmbī. But it soon changed hands and was conquered by Bimbisāra who made it a separate province and appointed, as its governor, his son, Kūṇika, with his headquarters at Champā [*Bhagavatī Sūtra*, 300 (Champāyāṁ Kūṇiko rājā babhūva)]. There is mention of a land-grant (i.e. grant of revenues due to government) in Aṅga made by Bimbisāra [*Dīgha*, i, 111]. According to a *Jātaka* (No. 545), Rājagṛiha was once a city of Aṅga. Its chief city, Champā, was one of the six chief cities of the Buddhist world, as already stated. A *Jātaka* (No. 539) refers to its gate, watch-tower, and walls, and its traders sailing as far as Suvaṇṇabhūmi. There was another town in Aṅga, called Āpana [*Saṁ.*, v, 225], and another called Assapina where the Buddha had preached [*Majjhi.*, i, 271 f.]. Thus the conquest of such a prosperous country like Aṅga was a valuable addition to Bimbisāra's kingdom.

His territories now comprised 80,000 villages covering an area of 300 leagues increased to 500 leagues by Ajātaśatru [*Vinaya*, i, 179 ; *Sumaṅgala*, i, 148]. The texts also mention some of the more important villages such as Senānigāma [*Majjhi.*, i, 166], Ekanālā, abode of Brahman Bharadvāja converted by the Buddha [*Saṁ.*, i, 172], Khānumata, another Brahman village [*Dīgha*, i, 127], or Nālakagāma where Sāriputta gave a discourse [*Saṁ.*, iv, 251 f.]. The kingdom of Bimbisāra also included a number of republican communities, each under its leader called *Rāja-kumāra* [*Sumaṅgala*, i, 279, 294].

Administration.—Bimbisāra's government was well-organized and efficient. The chief officers were known as *Mahāmātras* ; the executive as *Sabbātthaka* (in charge of all affairs and interests) ; the judicial as *Vohārika* ; and the military, *Senā-nāyaka*. His penal code was pitiless in its punishments such as imprisonment in jails (*kārā*), mutilation of limbs, and the like [*Vinaya*, vii, 3, 5]. The heads of 80,000 villages (*Grāmikas*) are stated to be meeting in assembly of their own [*Vinaya* cited above].

Religion.—Both Jains and Buddhists vie with one another in claiming him as the follower of their respective faiths. The *Uttarādhyayana-Sūtra* [xx, 58], for instance, describes how Bimbisāra, " the lion of kings," visited, " with the greatest devotion," Mahāvīra, " the lion of homeless monks " (*aṇagāra-sīhaṁ*) at Maṇḍikukshi Chaitya and " together with his wives, servants, and relations, became a staunch believer in his Law ". His Jain leanings are traced to the influence of his Lichchhavi wife, Chellanā. Hemachandra [*Trishashṭi-Śalākā*, x, 6, 10, 11] tells the story that " when the country was under a blight of cold, the king, accompanied by Devī Chellanā, went to worship Mahāvīra ". The Buddhist texts tell their own tale. There is first a reference to the meeting of Bimbisāra and Gotama. The title Gotama shows that he was not then the Buddha. It was seven years earlier, just after his renunciation. Bimbisāra was then at Girivraja [*Sutta Nipāta*, verse 408; *Dialogues*, ii, 2]. Their next meeting took place later when Bimbisara had moved to his new "palace" or city, Rājagṛiha. Even at the first meeting, before Gotama was a Buddha, the king was so much impressed by him that he offered to settle him as a chief with necessary gifts of wealth. The Buddha visited Rājagṛiha with his new and unexpected disciples, the famous Kassapas, and their thousand Jaṭila pupils, who proclaimed him as their "Lord", whereupon Seniya Bimbisāra comes to him with a host of citizens and Brahmans, and receives and understands his doctrine. Next day, the Buddha and his disciples are entertained at the palace, where the king served food with his own hands, and then declared his donation to the Buddha and his Order of the park called Veḷuvana [*Vinaya*, i, 39]. Even his wife, Khemā, is stated to have given instruction in Buddhism to King Pasenadi [*Saṁ.*, iv, 374]. Among other proofs given of Bimbisāra's devotion to Buddhism may be mentioned his appointment of his personal physician, Jīvaka, as the physician in attendance on the Buddha and his Order, or his remission of ferry charges for ascetics out of regard for the Buddha who once had with him no money to pay to the ferryman for crossing the Ganges [*Lalita*, v, 526]. Besides Jainism and Buddhism, Brahmanism also claims to have his support [*Dīgha*, i, 111, 127].

Death.—According to the Buddhist legend of the *Vinaya*, Ajātaśatru, at the instigation of Devadatta, was about to kill his father with a sword when he was apprehended by the ministers to whom he confessed his design. The ministers advised the king to have all the conspirators killed, but Bimbisāra pardoned his son and even resigned to him his kingdom for which he was so impatient [*Vinaya*, ii, 190]. But still Ajātaśatru *did* kill his father and confessed to the Buddha that "for the sake of kingdom he deprived his righteous father of his life". Devadatta incited him to this murder by reminding him that life was short and the throne might be long in coming to him. "So do you, prince, kill your father and become the rājā" [*Vinaya*, ii, 190; *Dīgha*, i, 86; *Sum.*, i, 133–6; *Petav. Comm.*, 105]. According to the *Mahāvaṁsa*, Ajātaśatru killed his father eight years before the Buddha's death, i.e. in 551 B.C., and when he had reigned fifty-two years, i.e. from 603 B.C. Jain records, however, are more charitable to Ajātaśatru. We are told that though Śreṇika made up his mind to choose Kūṇika as his successor in preference to his other sons, Kūṇika, impatient and suspicious, put his father in prison, where he was loyally looked after by his mother Chellanā. Ajātaśatru, however, soon completely changed on learning from his mother how dearly his father loved him (so as to suck once even his swollen finger, streaming with matter, to relieve his pain). "A sorry return have I made to my father," said he, and immediately dashed off to break his fetters with an iron club. But Śreṇika, fearing mischief from his son's advance, took poison and killed himself [*Āvaśyaka-Sūtra*, pp. 682–3, etc.]. Thus Ajātaśatru does not figure as a parricide in the Jain legends.

Ajātaśatru, *c.* 551–519 B.C.: *Conquests.*—The growth of Magadha as an imperial power received great impetus under Ajātaśatru. His murder of his father and the consequent widowhood of the Kosalan princess who could not survive it in grief [*Jāt.*, ii, 403] made King Prasenajit of Kosala retaliate by cancelling the gift of the Kāśī village as her dowry. This led to a war between Magadha and Kosala. At first, it was in favour of Ajātaśatru who drove back his aged uncle to Śrāvastī. But very soon, the uncle got the better of him, entrapped him in an ambush and made him surrender to him with his whole army. In the last stage, peace was restored by Prasenajit giving him back his liberty, army, kingdom, and a daughter named Vajirā in marriage [*Saṁ.*, i, 84–6; *Jāt.*, iv, 342; *Dhammap. comm.*, iii, 259]. In the Jain texts, Ajātaśatru figures as the conqueror of the entire confederacy which had grown up in eastern India, the confederacy comprising Kāśī, Kosala, with their eighteen Gaṇarājyas or republican States, the nine Mallaki States, and the nine Lichchhavi States [Vajjī Videhaputre jaitthā, nava Mallai, nava Lechchhai, Kāsī-Kosalagā aṭṭhārasavi Gaṇarāyāṇo parājaitthā (*Bhagavatī*, sūtra 300)]. The war with this powerful confederation began with Ajātaśatru's attack on the Lichchhavi capital, Vaiśālī. The cause of this conflict is differently told in different texts. According to the *Sumaṅgalavilāsinī* [B. C. Law's *Buddhaghosa*, p. 111], it was a mine of gems at the foot of a hill near a port on the Ganges, about which there was an agreement between Ajātaśatru and the Lichchhavis that the gems should be divided equally between them. The Lichchhavis broke this agreement and brought on the conflict. According to Jain version [Hoernle, *Uvāsagadasāo*, ii, App., p. 7], the cause of the conflict was the state elephant, Seyaṇāga (Sechanaka, " Sprinkler "), with its necklace of eighteen strings of pearls given by Bimbisāra to his son, Vehalla, who escaped with the elephant and the pearls to his grandfather, Cheḍaga, at Vaiśālī, for protection against usurper Ajātaśatru who claimed them. " Kūṇiya, having failed peacefully to obtain the extradition of the fugitive, commenced war with Cheḍaga " [Hoernle, *ib.*; *Āvaśyaka-Sūtra*, p. 684 (. . . na dadyāstadā yuddhasajjo bhavāmīti)]. It is also stated that Ajātaśatru was instigated in this conflict by his wife Paumāvaī (Padmāvatī).

But the subjugation of the Lichchhavis was not an easy job in those days. They were the leaders of a vast confederation of thirty-six States, as already stated, and could count upon their allied strength. King Cheṭaka actually assembled this confederation to ask whether they should yield to or fight Ajātaśatru [*Nirayāvalī-Sūtra*]. The Lichchhavis were also strong in their own internal, republican unity. They were then at the zenith of their power and prosperity which were matters of public comment and commendation. In the Buddha's authoritative opinion based on his supreme insight into men and things, the Lichchhavis were invulnerable and invincible, because they were keeping up all conditions making for the strength and success of a republic, such as holding full and frequent assemblies, unity of counsel and policy, maintaining old traditions, institutions, and worship, reverence to elders, honouring women and ascetics, and so forth (see below). The first information about Ajātaśatru's intentions was given to the Buddha at Rājagṛiha by his minister who agreed and admitted that the king could not succeed except by destroying the unity of the Lichchhavis and creating dissensions among them. Seeds of dissension were then actually sown among the Lichchhavis by Ajātaśatru deputing for the purpose his minister, Vassakāra, who lived at Vaiśālī for three years skilfully plying his nefarious job. Very soon, a new spirit infected the Lichchhavis, jealousy between different classes, between the rich and poor, strong and weak [*Dialogues*, ii, 78 ; B. C. Law, *ib.*, p. 112].

Ajātaśatru, in fact, proved himself fully equal to his difficult task and took recourse freely to the three means prescribed in political treatises for the subjugation of a hostile State, viz. machinations (*chhala*), military strength (*bala*), and strategy (*kauśala*). He was fully seized with the war-fever, declaring, " I will root out and destroy these Vajjians, mighty and powerful though they be, and bring them to utter ruin " [*Mahāparinibbāna-Sutta*].

But his task was stupendous. As a first step, he had to construct a new city and fort before commencing the war. Rājagṛiha was too far inland to serve as a base of operations against the distant Lichchhavis on the other side of the Ganges. Therefore, he selected a convenient site directly on the Ganges for the construction of a fort and laid the foundation of Pāṭaliputra, his new capital. It was constructed under the supervision of his chief ministers named Sunīdha and Vassakāra (" rain-maker ") who gave themselves the honour of inviting the Buddha to dinner at their house and instituted the Gotama gate and the Gotama ferry at the place of his exit from the city and of his crossing the Ganges. It was on this occasion that the Buddha made his prophecy about the future greatness of Pāṭaliputra to be the chief city of Aryan India and a centre of business and trade [ib.]. The completion of the fort of Pāṭaliputra was followed by actual military operations against the Lichchhavis, now considerably weakened by internal dissensions and inviting invasion. As soon as Ajātaśatru invaded their territory, the Lichchhavis argued among themselves as to who should make the first advance, the more cowardly ones saying, "Let the strong Lichchhavis go forward and crush the enemy." Ajātaśatru could thus easily conquer a people who were busy in a wordy warfare among themselves and not able to present a united front against his attack. The Jain texts give some details of his operations. He brought into use certain new and powerful engines of war, the Mahāśilākaṇṭaka, which was a kind of catapult hurling big pieces of stone, and the Rathamusala,[1] a chariot which created havoc by wheeling about and hurling destruction by its attached rods [Hoernle, *Uvāsagadasāo*, ii, App., p. 59, quoting *Bhagavatī*].

It is apparent from even these meagre details of this war between Magadha and the Lichchhavis that it must have been a long and arduous struggle. We have already seen that it was for Ajātaśatru not a war against a single State but an entire federation of three dozens of powerful republics of eastern India on the other side of the Ganges under the leadership of King Cheḍaga of Vaiśalī of unrivalled political influence, strengthened by several matrimonial alliances with the principal monarchies of the period (related below). A long interval was needed for the elaboration of Ajātaśatru's manifold and well-designed preparations for such a war, involving, as we have seen, the construction of a new city, and the three years' plan of secret work at the city of his enemy by his spies, to loosen its internal cohesion and social bonds. The Jain texts are, therefore, right in indicating a period of at least sixteen years for this protracted war. We are told that the sage, Gośāla, who died in 562 B.C. (as will be shown below) saw this war in progress, while the confederacy of thirty-six republics against whom the war was launched was not broken up but fully functioning as late as 546 B.C., when they had organized a common illumination to mark the passing

[1] "It seems to have been provided with some kind of self-acting machinery to propel it, as it is described to have moved without horses and driver; though, possibly, as in similar contrivances in the Middle Ages, it was moved by a person concealed inside, who turned the wheels." [Hoernle, ibid., p. 60.]

away of the light that was in their Lord, Mahāvīra [*Nirayāvalī Sutta* cited by Hoernle, *ib.*, p. 7; *Kalpa Sūtra* in *SBE.*, xxii, 266]. Thus the war must have lasted for at least (562–546 B.C.) sixteen years. Thus was Vaiśālī reduced by one of her own sons, " Vedehi-putto " Ajātasattu.

These conquests of Ajātaśatru, by which he became the paramount power of eastern India, provoked feelings of hostility in his equally ambitious rival of central India, King Chaṇḍa Pradyota of Avanti. This made Ajātaśatru alternate between his two capitals of Pāṭaliputra and Rājagṛiha from which he could meet the menace of the Lichchhavis on one side and of Pradyota on the other. Ajātaśatru was actually fearing an attack of Pradyota upon Rājagṛiha, of which he strengthened the fortifications [*Majjhima Nikāya*, iii, 7]. Bimbisāra, however, was on good terms with Pradyota. When he was suffering from jaundice, Bimbisāra spared his own physician, Jīvaka, for his treatment (see below).

Religion.—As usual, both Jaina and Buddhist texts try to treat Ajātaśatru as the follower of the religion in which they are interested. Perhaps he started as a follower of Jainism. The Jaina texts are full of his devotion to their faith. We have already referred to the Jaina tradition which absolves him from the heinous crime which the Buddhist texts fasten upon him as the murderer of his father. We are told how Kūṇika used to pay frequent visits to Nātaputta with his queens and his large retinue. Both at Vesālī and Champā, he came into contact with Mahāvīra and expressed his appreciation of Jaina monks in general [*Aupapātika*, Sūtras 12, 27, 30; Hemachandra, *Pariśishṭaparvan*, Canto iv; *Āvaśyaka-Sūtra*, pp. 684, 687]. In the *Aupapātika-Sūtra* (30), he openly declares before Mahāvīra and his followers how the Lord has said the right thing and made clear the path of true religion, with his message of renunciation and non-violence. According to the Buddhist texts, however, he transferred his loyalty from Jainism to Buddhism later in life. He began as its enemy through the influence of the Buddha's only and bitterest enemy, his cousin, Devadatta. The texts relate:

"Then Devadatta went to prince Ajātasattu and said: 'Give such order, O King, to our men that I may deprive the Samaṇa Gotama of life'; and Ajātasattu, the prince, gave orders to his men: 'Whatsoever the worthy Devadatta tells you, that do'" [*Vinaya Texts*, pt. iii, p. 243]. The Buddha also reciprocated this attitude by his statement: "Monks, the King of Magadha, Ajātasattu, is a friend to, an intimate of, mixed with, whatever is evil." Their relations, however, soon changed. We have already seen how, after killing his father, he sought the Buddha for consolation and prayed to him: "May the Lord accept my transgression as transgression that I may be restrained in the future." The Buddha accepts his confession, but it did not mean that he was converted. That came much later, perhaps after the Buddha's death [*Dīgha* already cited]. We are further told how the king was once induced by his court-physician, Jīvaka, to see the Buddha in his mango-grove on a full-moon night. The deep silence of the assembly made him suspect an ambush and ask Jīvaka: "You are playing me no tricks, Jīvaka? You are not betraying me to my foes? How can it be that there should be no sound at all, not a sneeze, nor a cough, in so large an assembly, among 1,250 of the bretheren?" Jīvaka assured him that there was no foul play planned, saying: "Go on, O King, go straight on." Then the king came to the assembly, calm as a clear lake, and exclaimed: "Would that my son, Udāyi Bhadda, might have such calm as this assembly of the bretheren has!" [*Dīgha*, i, p. 50].

It is interesting to note that this legend of Ajātaśatru's interview with the Buddha has been translated into stone in one of the Bharhut Sculptures of about the second century B.C., and this itself testifies to the popularity, if not the truth, of the tradition of the texts. The sculpture even bears the significant inscribed label: "*Ajātasatu Bhagavato vaṁdate*," "Ajātaśatru bows down to the Lord." This corresponds to the canonical passage: "Māgadho Ajātasattu Vedehiputto Bhagavato pāde sirasāvandatī," ("bows down at the feet of the Lord) [*ib. Mahāparinibbāna-Suttanta*]. The sculpture shows (*a*) the king on an elephant

Ajatasatru worshipping the Buddha [ditto].

followed by ladies on elephants in a procession; (*b*) his dismounting from the elephant near the abode of the Buddha, and standing with his right hand raised, as if to speak (as related in the legend); and (*c*) his obeisance at the Bodhimaṇḍa, the throne of the Buddha, in front of which are figured the footprints of the Buddha.

This historic visit paid by Ajātaśatru to the Buddha was really a turning point in the king's religious life. He saw the Buddha after seeing in succession the six principal religious leaders or Tīrthikas of the times, including such famous teachers as Makkhali Gosāla and Nigaṇṭha Nātaputta (Mahāvīra), whom he was advised to see by his six ministers but whom he had to leave without the solace he sought [*Sabhiya-Sutta*; *Sāmaññaphala Sutta*; see below]. Next, we find him figuring as an ardent Buddhist, hurrying to Kusinārā, on hearing of the Buddha's death, to assert his claim to a share of his relics, sending a messenger to say, "The Lord was a Kshatṛiya: I too am a Kshatṛiya; I am worthy of a share of the relics of the Lord. I will erect a stūpa over the relics of the Lord and make a feast." [*Dīgha*, ii, 166]. Then the story goes that Mahākassapa, who was in charge of the Buddha's body and its relics, fearing risk to the relics enshrined in eight different stūpas by their different participants, persuaded Ajātaśatru to have one shrine made for them at Rājagṛiha, leaving portions at the other stūpas. [*Mahāpari*. *Sutta* Commentary; cf. *Div.* 380.] According to the *Mahāvaṁsa*, he also built *Dhātu-chaityas* all round his capital, Rājagṛiha, repaired eighteen Mahāvihāras there, which were deserted by the Buddhists after the Buddha's death, and further supported Buddhism, as we have already seen, by permitting the first Buddhist council to be held under his patronage in a pandal especially erected by him at the entrance to the Sattapaṇṇi Cave on one of the five hills of Rājagṛiha.[1]

[1] It may be noted in this connection that the name *Kunika* occurring in two inscriptions on statues found at Parkham and Jhing-ka-nagra, Muttra Dt., suggested its identification with Ajātaśatru. But this identification is unlikely. The Parkham image has the following inscription: "(Ma) (ṇi) bhada (= Maṇibhadra Yaksha) pūge rāmā . . . (ga) aṭha (= gausṭhi) (paṭithā) pi (to) Kuni (ka) tevāsinā (Gomitakena) katā." Here there is a reference to the image being installed in the *Pūga* of

The Republics.—The following Republics are mentioned in some of the oldest Pāli and Jain records :—

1. The Sākiyas of Kapilavatthu.
2. The Bulis of Allakappa.
3. The Kālāmas of Kesaputta.
4. The Bhaggas of Suṁsumāra Hill.
5. The Koliyas of Rāmagāma.
6. The Mallas of Pāvā.
7. The Mallas of Kusinārā.
8. The Moriyas of Pipphalivana.
9. The Videhas of Mithilā.
10. The Lichchhavis of Vesālī.
11. The Nāyas (Jñātrikas) of Vesālī.

1. **The Sākiyas.**—The Buddha was born of these Sākiyas (*Śākyas*) and is described as the foremost of his clan [*ñāti-seṭṭho* in the *Dīgha, PTS.*, ii, 165].

Sākiya Towns and Population.—The capital of the republic was Kapilavatthu. It had several other townships, viz. Chātumā, Sāmagāma, Khomadussa, Silāvatī, Medalumpa, Nagaraka, Ulumpa, Devadaha, and Sakkara. The Buddha's mother hailed from Devadaha and it was on her way to Devadaha that the Buddha was born. Khomadussa was a Brahmin settlement (Rhys Davids, *Buddhist India*, p. 21]. It was so called because it was a centre of manufacture of linen cloth [*Book of the Kindred Sayings*, i, 233]. The republic counted 80,000 families, or about half a million population [Rhys Davids, *Dialogues of the Buddha*, i, 147]. Virudhaka alone is said to have massacred 77,000 Śākyas [Rockhill, *Life of the Buddha*, p. 120].

Its Parliament.—The republic had its parliament which met in a mote-hall (*santhāgāra*) resting on pillars, and transacted both administrative and judicial business. The

Maṇibhadra and constructed by Gomitaka, disciple of Kunika. The second image worshipped as that of Manasā Devī has the following inscription : " (1) Sā putehi kārito ; (2) Yakhilā āvā Kunikāte ; (3) (Vāsinā Nāke) na katā." This also refers to Nāka, disciple of the same Kuṇika, as the sculptor who had fashioned (kṛita) the image of Yakshī Lāyāvā. There is also a third statue found at Pawāya (Padmāvatī) in Gwalior with an inscription which describes it as that of Maṇibhadra installed in the *goshṭhī* by his devotees. [V. S. Agrawala in *UPHSJ.*, May, 1933.]

president of the republic who presided over the assembly was called a *rājā*. The Buddha's father, Suddhodana, was such a *rājā*, and so also was his cousin, Bhaddiya [*Dīgha*, ii, 52; *Vinaya*, ii, 181]. The Śākya parliament consisted of 500 members [*Dialogues*, i, 113]. The *Mahāvastu* calls it *Śākyaparishad*. A new building was constructed in the time of the Buddha who inaugurated it by a series of lectures [*Majjhima*, i, 353 f.; *Saṁ.*, iv, 182 f.]. It was left to the Śākya Parliament to decide the vital question whether they should open the gates of their capital, Kapilavastu, to the invader Virudhaka. " Some said, ' Open them '; others advised not doing so. Some said, ' As there are various opinions, we will find out the opinion of the majority.' So they set about voting on the subject." Eventually the treacherous " headman of the Śākyas advocated opening the gates, and they all voted in the same way " [Rockhill, *Life of the Buddha*, p. 119].

Education and Culture.—The Śākya republic was also a centre of education and social progress. The Buddha as a boy had his education in the various sciences and arts of the time at Kapilavastu, as described in the *Lalitavistara*. There was also a technical school, " a large terraced mansion for the learning of crafts " [*Dialogues*, iv, Part iii, p. 111, n.]. No father would marry his daughter except to an educated bridegroom. To the proposal of marriage of the girl Gopā with young Gautama, her father replied that he could not " make over the girl to a prince reared at home among luxuries and ignorant of the Śilpas and the military arts " [*Lalitavistara*]. And according to *Mahāvastu* [ii, 73], Gautama had to compete in a tournament with 500 Śākya youths for the hand of Yaśodharā. That is why the Śākyas did not marry outside their clan and did not even condescend to give away a true-born Śākya girl in marriage to King Prasenajit of Kosala to whose authority they were politically subject, although this proved their destruction at the hands of revengeful Viḍūḍabha [*Jāt.*, iv, 145]. The Śākyas, both men and women, gave to Buddhism some of its noted figures like Upāli, Nandupananda, Kuṇḍadana, sons of noblemen. Many princes and the sons of the chief minister renounced the world and embraced asceticism as Buddhists [*SBE.*, xix, 226–7].

Women Saints.—The Śākya women had the honour of founding the order of Buddhist nuns. Some of them composed poems preserved in the Therīgāthā. The most famous was Mahāpajāpatī Gotamī, the Buddha's aunt, Tissā, Abhirūpanandā, Mittā, Sundarī Nandā, all of whom attained Arhatship [*Psalms of the Sisters*, pp. 12–13, 22–3, 29, 55–7].

2–5, 8.—These five are minor republics about whom not much is known. The Bulis, the Koliyas, and the Moriyas figure as claimants for shares of the bodily remains of the Buddha as Kshatriyas [*Mahāparinibbāna-Sutta*].

2. **The Bulis.**—The Bulis, from their close relations with the kingdom of Veṭhadīpa, the native place of Brāhmaṇa Droṇa (a co-sharer of the Buddha's relics), should be located near it, i.e. between modern Shahabad and Muzaffarpur (Vaiśālī) [*Dhammapada Commentary*, Harvard Oriental Series, 28, 247].

3. **The Kālāmas.**—The Kālāmas were the community to whom belonged the sage, Āḷāra Kālāma, the teacher of Gautama. The name of their city, Kesaputta, may show their connection with the Vedic people called Keśins who were Pāñchālas.

4. **The Bhaggas.**—The Bhaggas (Bhargas) were connected with the Vatsas, whose prince, named Bodhi, son of King Udena (Udayana), lived in a place called Kokanada built on the Suṁsumāra Hill situated in the deer-park of Bhesakaḷāvana [*Jāt.* No. 353; *Majjhima*, i, 332–8; ii, 91–7; *Saṁ.* iii, 1–5; iv, 116]. One day he had the whole row of steps to the palace covered over with white cloth in honour of the Buddha who, however, had it removed, as he could not tread on it as a monk.

5. **The Koliyas.**—The Koliyas were separated from the Sākiya territory by the River Rohiṇī [*Theragāthā*, v, 529] upon whose waters, stored up by a dam, both the peoples depended for irrigation, and came into conflict. A dispute was once settled by the Buddha himself [*Jāt.*, Cowell, v, 219].

Their Towns.—Their capital, Rāmagāma, is also called

Kola-nagara or Vyagghapajja [*Sum.*, i, 262]. They had a few other towns called Haliddavasana [*Majjhima*, i, 387], Sajjanela [*Aṅgu.*, ii, 62], Sāpūga [ib., ii, 194], Uttara [*Saṁ.*, iv, 340], and Kakkara-patta [*Aṅgu.*, iv, 281].

Police.—The Koliyans were known for their police force marked by a special head-dress as a kind of uniform and notorious for their practice of violence and extortion [*Saṁ.*, iv, 341]. A Koliyan was a Vyagghapajja by surname, as a Sākiyan was a Gotama.

6. **The Moriyas.**—According to the Mahāvaṁsa Ṭīkā (p. 180, PTS ed.), the Moriyas, who were of the Sākiyas, fled from the atrocities of Viḍūḍabha to a Himalayan region where they founded the city of Pipphalivana in a place resounding with the voices of peacocks (*mora*). They were thus Kshatriyas, of whom was born Chandagutta (Chandragupta), the founder of the famous Maurya dynasty of Magadha.

7. **The Mallas** : *Two Branches, at Pāvā and Kusinārā.*—The Malla confederacy had two branches, one at Pāvā, and the other at Kusinārā [*Dīgha*, ii, 165]. Pāvā (from Pāpā, a corruption of Apāpapuri) was the city where Mahāvīra died while dwelling in the house of the scribe of King Hastipālā or at the palace of Shashṭipāla, King of Pāpā, as shown below. Kusinārā, also famous as the place of the Buddha's *nirvāṇa*, was then a mere " wattle-and-daub town, a branch township ". The Buddha came here walking in illness from Pāvā, which was thus not far from it. Other Malla towns named are Anupīya [*Chullavagga*, vii, i, 1] on the Anomā, Bhoganagara, and Uruvela Kappa [*Saṁ.*, v, 228 ; *Aṅgu.*, iv, 438]. Both the Mallas were Kshatriyas [*Dialogues*, ii, 162 f.], and Vāseṭṭhas, i.e. of the Vasishṭha gotra [*Dīgha, PTS.*, iii, 209].

Parliament and Executive.—The Malla State is called a *Saṁgha-rājya* [*Majjhima*, i, 231], i.e. a republic. The Pāvā Mallas built a new parliament house called Ubbhaṭaka, which was formally inaugurated by the Buddha [*Saṅgīti-Sutta* (of *Dīgha* N.]. The news of the Buddha's impending death was first sent by Ānanda to the Mallas of Pāvā who were then holding a session of their parliament in their mote-hall.

Later, after his death, they again assembled there to discuss the disposal of his sacred remains [*Dialogues*, ii, 162–4]. Their executive officers were called *Purisas*, who were like the police [*Dīgha*, ii, 159, 161]. They were a martial race and known as wrestlers [*Jātakas*, Cowell, vol. ii, 65]. The Buddha refers to the complete sovereignty of the Malla Republic in exercising " powers of life and death, outlawry, and banishment " over its citizens.

Learning.—They were also keen on learning. A Malla chief of Kusinārā sent his son, Bandhula, for education to distant Taxila where he found as his fellow students, Mahāli, a Lichchhavi prince, and King Prasenajit of Kośala. Even their mufassil town of Uruvelakappa figures as a centre of philosophical discussion at which householders and lay-disciples like Tapussa [*Aṅgu*, iv, 438–488] and Bhadragako Gāmaṇī took the initiative [*Saṁ.*, iv, 327 f.].

Some famous Mallas.—Buddhism owes to the Mallas some of its greatest characters, such as (1) Ānanda, (2) Upāli, (3) Anuruddha, (4) Devadatta, the Buddha's obstinate opponent, (5) Dabba who was elected to a high position by the Saṁgha [*Vinaya* iii, 4], (6) Khaṇḍasumana who attained six-fold *abhijñā* [*Psalms of the Bretheren*, p. 90], and (7) Sīha [ib., p. 80].

Nine " Mallakis ".—The Mallas, though ardent followers of the Buddha, were catholic enough to show honour to his opponent, Jīna Mahāvīra, at whose death at Pāvā, they had an illumination in place of " the Light of Intelligence that was gone " [*Jaina Sūtras, SBE.*, xxii, 266].

A Republican League.—This illumination was, as we have already seen, the work of a league of nine Mallakis, which had a separate political existence. For the Jaina Kalpa Sūtras refer to a coalition constituted by nine Mallakis, nine Lichchhavis, and eighteen confederate kings (aṭṭhārasa vi gaṇarāyaṇo) of Kāsī and Kosala. This combination was (as already related) due to the menace of Kūṇika-Ajātaśatru.

Relations with Lichchhavis.—But sometimes the Mallas and Lichchhavis themselves quarrelled. An innocent drive of the Mallian general, Bandhula, with his wife Mallikā, to Vaiśālī, and their forced bath in an enclosed tank belonging to Mahāli, the Lichchhavi, led to a regular fight, in which 500 Lichchhavi chiefs pursuing the Mallian general were cut to pieces [*Dhammapada Commentary*, *PTS*., i, p. 349 f.

9, 10, 11. Vajji Confederation.—Among the older sixteen big States figured the Vajjis who, before the time of the Buddha, constituted themselves into a confederacy of eight republics (*aṭṭhakula*) of which the most important were the Videhas, the Jñātrikas, and the Lichchhavis, along with the Vajjis proper. Perhaps the other four were the Ugras, the Bhogas, Aikshākus, and Kauravas who are mentioned, along with the Jñātrikas and Lichchhavis, as being subjects of the same State, and members of the same assembly, in a Jain text [*SBE*., xlv, 339]. The Ugras and Bhogas were Kshatriyas and were honoured by the first Jain Tīrthakara who appointed the former as prefects of towns [*ib*., 71, n.]. Later, the Buddha saw the Lichchhavis leading, and giving their name to the confederacy.

7. **The Videhas.**—Videha, as we have already seen, originally started as a kingdom, and a stronghold of Vedic culture as represented in its exponents, King Janaka, and Ṛishi Yājñavalkya. It is interesting to find that tradition which represents Videha as a monarchy, with its many distinguished kings, describes it as a republic in the Buddha's time.

Mithilā.—Its capital was Mithilā with its four market towns (*yavamajjhaka*) at its four gates [*Jāt*., vi, pp. 330–1], a centre of trade in the Buddha's time, to which merchants came even from Śrāvastī to sell their wares [Dhammapāla's *Paramatthadīpanī* on *Theragāthā*, iii, 277–8]. According to the Jātakas, the city of Mithilā was seven leagues in extent and Videha 300 leagues [Cowell's *Jātakas*, iii, 222], comprising 16,000 villages [*ib*.], and spending 600,000 pieces daily in charity [*ib*., iv, 224]. This was in keeping with the tradition for sacrifice and spirituality of its old kings like Nimi who renounced the world and became a Pachchekabuddha [*ib*., iii, 230] or King Videha who became a hermit and lived in the Himalayas with the King of Gandhāra of the same disposition [*ib.*, 222–3], or King Makhādeva [*ib.*, i, 31–2], or Sādhina, who excelled the gods in virtue [*ib.*, iv, 224–7].

Videha Princesses.—The alliance of Videha was sought after by distant kings for the virtues of its girls. One of the wives of Bimbisāra, according to the *Amitāyurdhyāna Sūtra*, was Vaidehi Vāsavī who saved his life by carrying food to him when imprisoned by Ajātaśatru [*SBE.*, xlix, 161–201]. King Udayana is described in the plays of Bhāsha as a Vaidehīputra. The mother of Vardhamāna Mahāvīra, founder of Jainism, was a Videhan named Videhadattā, also called Triśalā, and Priyakāriṇī [Jaina Sūtras, *SBE.*, xxii, 193–256].

The Jñātṛikas: *Their Association with Jainism.*—The Jñātṛikas were Kshatriyas of Kāśyapa gotra [*SBE.*, xxii, 266], of whom was born Mahāvīra who is called in the Sūtrakṛitāṅga [i, 1, 1, 27] as " the highest Jina, Mahāvīra, the Jñātṛiputra ". His father was Siddhārtha who was the chief of his clan, and married Triśalā, the sister of the most eminent Lichchhavi prince named Cheṭaka. Since she is described as a Vaidehī, Cheṭaka may be taken to have been a native of Videha domiciled at Vaiśālī. By this marriage, he became connected with King Bimbisāra who had married the daughter of Cheṭaka, named Chellanā.

This particular republic of the Jñātṛikas was associated with the towns called Vaiśālī, Kuṇḍaggāma, and Vaṇiyagāma, but it had its headquarters in the place called Kollāga, a suburb (*sannivesha*) of Kuṇḍaggāma. This Kollāga has been described as *Nāya-Kula*, i.e. the residence of Jñātṛikas, and as " Uttara-Khattiya-Kuṇḍapura-sannivesha " or as " Khattiyakuṇḍagāme nayare ", i.e. the Kshatriya part of Kuṇḍapura, as distinguished from its *Māhaṇa* or Brāhmaṇa division [Hoernle, *Uvāsagadasāo*, ii, 1–7]. A Buddhist text states that the Buddha visited Koṭiggāma, the place where the Ñātikas lived, lodging there in the Ñātika brick-hall, on his way to Vesālī, where he converted the Lichchhavi general Sīha the Nigaṇṭha [*Mahāvagga*, *SBE.*, xvii, 104 f.]. Koṭiggāma is probably the same as Kuṇḍaggāma.

Outside Kollāga, the Jñātṛikas built a religious establishment, a park (*ujjāna*) enclosing a shrine (*Cheie*), known by the name of Duipālasa. They were already known for their piety and doctrine of non-violence, abstention from sin, and meat-eating [*SBE.*, xlv, 416], as followers of Pārśvanātha.

Assembly of Elders.—The republic was governed by an assembly of elders one of whom was president who was assisted by a Viceroy and a Commander-in-chief [Hoernle, *Uvāsagadasāo*, ii, 4–5].

The Lichchhavis.—They are represented as Kshatriyas in both Buddhist and Jain texts. As Kshatriyas their claim was admitted to a share of the Buddha's relics [*Mahāparinibbāna-Suttanta*]. As a Kshatriya princess, Triśalā was married to Jñātṛi-kshatriya Siddhārtha, father of Mahāvīra. They were also Vāsishṭhas [Senart, *Le Mahāvastu*, i, 283, 286, 289, etc.]. Triśalā is also described as belonging to the Vāsishṭha gotra in the Jain texts [*SBE.*, xxii, 193].

As Vāsishṭhas, the Lichchhavis become related to the Mallas of Pāvā [*Dialogues*, iii, 202]. A Tibetan tradition represents even Māyā and Mahāmāyā, the wives of Suddhodana, father of the Buddha, as Vṛiji (Lichchhavi) princesses [Law, *Kshatriya Tribes*, p. 15].

Vaiśālī.—The Lichchhavis had their capital at Vaiśālī. It was at the zenith of its prosperity at the time of the Buddha. According to Tibetan tradition [Rockhill, *Life of the Buddha*, p. 62], it had three districts containing 7,000, 14,000, and 21,000 houses respectively. These were probably Vaiśālī proper, Kuṇḍapura, and Vāṇiyagāma. We also read of another town called Ukkāchelā [*Saṁ.*, iv, 261–2; v, 163–5]. A *Jātaka* tells of Vaiśālī itself being encompassed by three walls with gates and watch-towers [Fausboll, i, 504]. The *Mahāvastu* account refers to the Abhyantara-Vaiśālakas and Bāhira-Vaiśālakas, the cockneys, and citizens of Greater Vaiśāli, numbering "twice 84,000", giving to the Buddha a rousing reception by a procession of elephants and chariots decked with gold, and decorating the whole road from the Ganges to their city with flags, garlands, embroidered cloth, besides watering it, throwing flowers and burning incense along its whole length, while the Buddha passed by. The *Mahāvagga* describes Vaiśālī as " an opulent, prosperous, and populous town with 7,707 storeyed buildings, 7,707 pinnacled buildings, 7,707 *ārāmas*, and 7,707 lotus-ponds " [*Vinaya, SBE.*, p. 171]. The city was also rich in a variety of buildings, Chaityas, Vihāras, and Palaces of its 7,707 chiefs. The eight famous Chaityas were: (1) Udena to the east of Vaiśālī; (2) Gotamaka to the south; (3) Saptāmraka (sattaṁba) to the west; (4) Bahuputra on the north; (5) Chāpāla; (6) Kapinahya; (7) Sārandada, and (8) Mārkaṭahrada [*Mahāvastu; Mahāpari. Suttanta*; and *Pāṭika Suttanta* in *Dialogues*, iii, 14]. These Chaityas were originally shrines for the worship of Yakkhas as explained by Buddhaghosa, or shrines of pre-Buddhist worship [*Dialogues*, ii, 80, 110]. But in the Jain texts the word *Chaitya* (*Cheie*) seems to be used in the sense of a park [*SBE.*, xlv, pp. 36, 100], or for a temple or sacred shrine including its whole sacred enclosure containing a garden, grove, or park [*Ujjaana, Vana-saṇḍa* or *Vana-khaṇḍa*), a shrine and attendants' houses [Hoernle, *Uvāsaga-dasāo*, ii, 2, n. 4].

The Lichchhavis made a gift of all these to the Buddha. In addition, he received from the courtesan Āmrapālī her big mango-grove, and from Bālikā, the Bālikārāma [*Le Mahāvastu*, i, 295–9; 300; *Vinaya, SBE.*, p. 408]. The Lichchhavis also built him the famous Kūṭāgārasālā in the Mahāvana, the scene of many of his teachings. Some of its constructions were supervised by the Bhikkhus themselves as architects. Failing such supervision, a poor tailor of Vaiśālī, who was also building a house for the Saṁgha, found that " the laying was out of line and the wall fell down " [*Chullavagga*, vi; *SBE.*, xx, 189–90].

Constitution and Administration.—The Lichchhavis had been republicans long before the time of the Buddha. Their foreign relations were dealt with by a body of " nine Lichchhavis " who joined a coalition of nine Mallakis and eighteen Gaṇarājās of Kāsi-Kosala, as we have already seen, under the leadership of Cheṭaka, the maternal uncle of Mahāvīra. Cheṭaka was driven to form this coalition against a contemplated attack of Kūṇika Ajātaśatru, King of Champā, with a strong army. [*Jaina Kalpa Sūtra*, § 128, and *Nirayāvalī Sūtra*, p. 27, ed. Warren]. Another such leader was Tomara who was elected by the Lichchhavis as their representative to arrange for the Buddha's first visit to their city. Such a leader was called *Nāyaka* [Rockhill, *Life of the Buddha*, pp. 63–4]. Internally, the governing body of the republic comprised 7,707 Rājās, citizens of Vaiśalī, chosen out of a total population of " twice 84,000 ", i.e. 168,000, with as many *Uparājās*, deputy leaders, *Senāpatis*, generals, and *Bhāṇḍāgārikas*, treasurers. As members of a democratic body, all of them were notorious for their arguments and disputations (*Te sabbe pi paṭipuchchhāvitakkā ahesuṁ*) [*Nidānakathā*, preambles, to the *Jātakas*, Ekapaṇṇa (No. 149) and Chulla Kāliṅga (No. 301)]. This assembly of Rājās is in keeping with the old tradition referred to by Pāṇini [vi, 2, 34], according to which the governing body of a *Gaṇa* was to be composed of such Kshatriyas as were specially consecrated for rulership and were designated *Rājanyas* [*abhishikta-rājanya*]. Kauṭilya also refers to *Saṁghas* based on the institution of Rājās (*rājaśabdopajīvinaḥ*). Referring to the numerous Rājās of the Lichchhavi *Gaṇa*, the *Lalitavistara* remarks that the Lichchhavis recognized no distinctions, everyone thinking that he was the Rājā (" ekaika eva manyate ahaṁ rājā ahaṁ rājeti " [iii, 23]).

Each of these Rājās was probably a ruling prince in his own domain with his own staff of officers and treasury and the Assembly of 7,707 such Rājās was thus a federal assembly representative of as many constituent clans making up the total population of the Vajjian confederacy. Probably the executive functions vested in the smaller body of eight (cf. " *ashṭakula* ") or nine mentioned above, and these adopted uniforms of different colours, blue (*nīla*), yellow (*pīta*), green (*harit*), light red (*manjishṭhā*), red (*lohita*), white (*śveta, odātā*), variegated or mixed (*vyāyukta*), marking everything about them, dress, horses, chariots, turbans, umbrellas, down to shoes, whips, and sticks [*Mahāpari. Suttanta, SBE.*, xi, 31; *Aṅgu. PTS.*, ii, 239; *Mahāvastu*, i, 259; *Dīgha*, ii, 96]. The Council of Nine was in charge of foreign affairs, and the Council of Eight, of justice. The *Aṭṭhakulakā* formed the superior Court of Justice before whom criminals were sent up after preliminary investigations by experts had established their guilt. These experts were (1) *Viniśchaya Mahāmātras*, to make sure or ascertain the facts of the case; (2) *Vyavahārikas*, lawyers, and (3) *Sūtradharas* who kept up the "thread" of law and custom and could explain their spirit behind their changing forms. The accused found guilty by the *Aṭṭha-Kulakā* were sent up to receive their due punishments to the *Senāpati*, and from him to the *Upa-rājā*, and, finally, to the *Rājā* who had the punishment measured in accordance with the prevailing penal code called *Paveṇi-potthaka* [Buddhaghosa's *Commentary on Mahāparinibbāna Suttanta*. The Lichchhavi *Gaṇa* governed the social life of its citizens in certain matters such as marriage. The general rule was that no marriage should be contracted outside Vaiśālī and even outside its districts [*ib.*]. The *Gaṇa* is also mentioned as selecting a bride [*Vinaya Texts*, iv, 225].

Strong Points.—The Buddha himself was so convinced of the strong points of the Lichchhavi Republic that he expressed his deliberate opinion that it was invincible against the attack of a mighty king like Ajātaśatru. These strong points he enumerated as follows: (1) "To hold full and frequent public assemblies; (2) to meet together in concord and rise in concord and carry out their undertakings in concord; (3) to enact nothing not already established, abrogate nothing that has been already enacted, and act in accordance with the ancient institutions of the Vajjians as established in former days; (4) to honour, esteem, revere, and support the Vajjian elders and hold it a point of duty to hearken to their words; (5) supporting the old shrines in town or country with continuance of the proper offering and rites as formerly given and performed; (6) honouring the Arhants among them, and (7) honouring women and not detaining them by force or abduction"

[*Mahāpari. Suttanta*]. This passage thus points out the requisites for the success of a republic in those days to be respect of its members (*a*) for their parliament, which should often meet and be fully attended ; (*b*) for their ancient laws, customs, and institutions ; (*c*) for seniority and experience ; and its internal harmony in policy and administration.

National Character.—But the real strength of the republic lay not so much in its government as in the character of its people. The Buddha himself tells how they were free from luxury and sloth, " sleeping with logs of wood as pillows and not on cushions of the finest cotton, active in archery, and not delicate, tender, and soft in their arms and legs " [*Saṁ.*, ii, 267–8]. They were fond of sport, training elephants and hunting with dogs [*Psalms of the Brethren*, p. 106 ; *Aṅgu.*, iii, 76]. The youths were rowdy, seizing on the road sugar cane, plums, cakes, or sweetmeats going as presents to families, but leaving their wildness before the Buddha [*ib.*]. They did not lack moral courage. Vaḍḍha, a Lichchhavi, brought a false charge against Dabba, a Mallian, and frankly admitted his wrong [*Vinaya*, *SBE.*, pp. 118–25]. Their respect for elders and women, their national institutions, has been already noticed, as also their strong conservatism. They were also keen on education. We read of Mahāli going to Taxila for study and, on returning, educating 500 Lichchhavi youths who again became teachers and spread education through the country [*Dhammapada Commentary, PTS.*, i, p. 338]. The psalm of a Vajjiputta even figures in the *Theragāthā* [*Psalms*, p. 106].

Influence of the Buddha and Mahāvira.—The Lichchhavis further improved by contact with the great religious leaders, Mahāvīra, himself " a Vesālie ", or " a Vaiśālika " [Jacobi, *Jaina Sūtras, SBE.*, p. 261], and the Buddha. We have already seen how, decked in their best, and in all their pomp and magnificence, they went out in their thousands to welcome the Buddha to their city. We read of frequent assemblies of 500 Lichchhavi youths listening to the Buddha's discourse, leaving aside their gaiety, so that Mahānāma, the grand old man of the Lichchhavis, expressed his surprise " that these arrogant youths who were rowdy in their daily life had become so mild and gentle before the Exalted One" [*Aṅgu.*, iii, 75–8]. Sometimes, the tumult of their reception of the Buddha disturbed the monks and their meditation [ib., pp. 167–8]. Once, moved by a gāthā sung by a monk named Piṅgiyāni in honour of the Buddha the 500 Lichchhavis presented the monk with 500 garments which the monk gave away to the Buddha [ib., p. 239]. A wicked Lichchhavi prince, the despair of his parents, was transformed by a single discourse by the Buddha who was hailed as "the chief of trainers of men, supreme in bowing men to the yoke of truth" [*Ekapaṇṇa Jātaka*]. Among other famous Lichchhavi Buddhists may be mentioned Bhaddiya [*Aṅgu.*, ii, 190–4], Sāḷho, and Abhaya [ib., 200–2], Nandaka, the Mahāmātra, [*Saṁ.*, v, 389–390], Añjana-Vaniya, a prince, who became an Arhat [*Psalms*, p. 56], Vajjiputta [ib., p. 106], Sīha, the Lichchhavi commander-in-chief, a follower of Nigaṇṭha Nātaputta, i.e. Mahāvīra, who was converted by the Buddha [*SBE.*, xvii, 108 f.], Sachchaka, similarly converted [*Majjhima*, i, 227–237]; and, among women, Sīhā, daughter of the sister of Sīha, who became an Arhat [*Psalms of the Sisters*, pp. 53–4], Jentā [ib., 23–4], Vāseṭṭhī who was converted at Mithilā and became an Arhat [ib., 79–80], and Ambapālī, the courtesan [ib., 120–5]. Jainism had also numerous followers at Vaiśālī. When Sīha, in his new zeal for Buddhism, arranged for a dinner to the Buddha and his disciples, and included meat in the menu, the Nigaṇṭhas running through Vaiśālī from road to road spread the false news that the Buddhists were to eat beef at Sīha's [*Vinaya*, *SBE.*, xvii, 116]. Sachchaka was another famous Jain who with 500 Lichchhavis went to Mahāvana to hear the Buddha's discourse [*Majjhima*, i, 227–237]. So also were Abhaya and Paṇḍita-Kumāra [*Aṅgu.*, i, 220–1]. The religious leader, Purāṇa Kassapa, had also his followers at Vaiśāli, such as Mahāli [*Saṁ.*, iii, 68–70].[1]

[1] The chief authorities on this topic are Rhys Davids' *Buddhist India*, and Dr. B. C. Law's erudite and exhaustive monograph on "Kshatriya Tribes", upon which I have freely drawn for many references. Dr. Law's latest work on "The Geography of Early Buddhism" is also a mine of information.

Democratic Procedure.—The growth of republics as a feature of Indian political evolution implied that of the necessary democratic procedure by which their working was regulated and governed. It is a remarkable testimony to the popular republican instincts and traditions of the times that democratic procedure was applied in every sphere of life, political, economic, and even religious.

Meetings of Saṁghas.—The Pāli texts furnish interesting information on the working of the Buddhist Saṁghas in strict and minute conformity with genuine democratic principles. The essence of democracy is government by decision based on discussion in public meetings or assemblies. The Pāli texts describe the meetings of religious assemblies or Saṁghas in all their stages.[1]

Seating Arrangement.—First there was the hall (*santhāgāra*) or a grove (*ārāma*) for the meeting where seats were arranged in the order of seniority by a special officer called the *Āsanapaññāpaka* who must himself be of 10 years' standing as a monk [*Chullavagga*, xii, 2, 7]. The seats were mats or rugs without fringes (*adasakam nisīdanaṁ*) [ib., xii, 1, 1].

Quorum.—Next, there was the conception of the Quorum. The Buddha declared as invalid a Chapter of two or three Bhikshus performing the second ordination or *Upasampadā* service. For this he fixed a quorum of not less than ten Bhikshus [*Mahāvagga*, i, 31, 2]. In "border countries", however, where "there were but few Bhikshus", and hence "difficulty and trouble in getting together a meeting of the Order in which ten Bhikshus were present" [ib., v, 13, 4], the quorum was reduced by the Buddha to five members including the chairman [ib., v, 13, 11]. The texts, indeed, allow of different numbers for the quorum for different purposes of the Saṁgha. *Mahāvagga*, ix, 4, 1, mentions five kinds of Saṁghas according as the quorum consisted of four (chaturvarga), five, ten, twenty, and more than twenty persons. Thus "the lowest number which can

[1] See on this subject Dr. Sukumar Dutt's *Early Buddhist Monachism* (Kegan Paul, London), Jayaswal's *Hindu Polity* and B. K. Sarkar's *Political Theories and Institutions of Ancient Hindus*.

constitute a Saṁgha is four [ib., viii, 24, 1]," but such a Saṁgha was not entitled to perform important official Acts like the *Upasampadā* Ordination, except in "border countries".

Chairman.—The chairman of the Saṁgha was not counted for the quorum and was called the *Vinayadhara* [ib., v, 13, 12].

Exclusions from Quorum.—The quorum must also exclude *Bhikkhunīs* or nuns, *Sikkhamānās* (female novices), *Sāmaṇeras* (male novices), persons belonging to other Communions or to a different district, or persons against whom the Saṁgha institutes proceedings [ib., ix, 4, 2].

Validity of Proceedings.—A Saṁgha lacking quorum is described as being incomplete (*vagga*, i.e. *vyagra*, as opposed to *samagga*, *samagra*, complete) [ib., ix, 2, 4]. The Act of an incomplete Chapter of *Bhikshus*, *Vagga-Kammam*, is invalid and should not be transacted (akammam na cha karaṇīyam) [ix, 3, 2]. Such an Act could not be validated by the ratification (*anumati*) of absentees [*Chullavagga*, xi, 1, 10]. A full assembly of qualified members is sometimes called *Sammukhā* [ib., i, 3]. An invalid Act could be impugned by another assembly in the form of a *Kichchā* (Kṛityā)-*dhikaraṇa* (lit., settlement of the agenda at formal meetings of a Chapter) [*Chullavagga*, iv, 14, 2]. It is thus defined: "Whatsoever is to the Saṁgha a matter which ought to be done (Kichchayatā = Kartavyatā), an obligation (Karaṇīyatā), a matter for which leave ought to be formally asked (avalokana-karma), the proposal of a Resolution (jñapti-karma), its announcement for once or three times, that is called a legal question of business. Here *avalokana-karma* is explained by Buddhaghosa in his *Samanta-pāsādikā* as "Sīmatthakaṁ (sīmāsthakam) Saṁghaṁ sodhetvā chhandarahānaṁ chhandaṁ āharitvā samaggasa anumatiyā tikkhatuṁ (= trikṛitvaḥ) sāvetvā kātabba-kammaṁ" [quoted in *SBE.*, xx, 37]. This enumerates all the conditions for the validity of Saṁgha proceedings such as (1) its fullness of quorum (samaggasa), (2) its composition including only members who were qualified, (3) collection of votes of all qualified members, present or absent, (4) consent of the Saṁgha to the agenda, and (5) the announcement of the business or motion for three times (trikṛitvaḥ).

Whip.—To secure quorum for a meeting of the Saṁgha, members from other Communions or parishes were brought up to attend it by persons specially deputed for the purpose. A member completing a quorum was called a *Gaṇapūraka* [*Mahāvagga*, iii, 6, 6].

Rules of Business.—The Saṁgha framed sound rules for the conduct of its meetings. No business could be introduced at a meeting except in the form of a Motion or Resolution. There must be a formal presentation (*sthāpanam*) of the motion (*Jñapti*) followed by its regular proclamation (*anussāvanaṁ*) [*Mahāvagga*, ix, 3, 1–2], so that no one could possibly miss it. Discussion was thus strictly limited to the Motion before the House. There was no scope for "pointless" (*anagra*) and irrevelant talks. A Motion, if non-contentious, received one, or, otherwise, three readings called *Jñapti-dvitīya* and *Jñapti-chaturtha-karma* [*Chulla-vagga*, iv, 14, 2, 11] respectively.

Silence as Assent.—Silence on a Resolution put was taken as consent thereto. Members "in favour of it" were asked "to be silent" and "anyone against it, to speak" [*Mahā-vagga*, i, 28, 5].

Acts.—The Resolution passed by the Saṁgha was technically called a *Saṁgha-karma* an Act of the Saṁgha. The text or wording of such an official Act of the Saṁgha was technically called a *Karma-vāchā* [ib., ix, 3, 1].

An Illustration.—The whole of this procedure may be explained by an example taken from *Mahāvagga* [i, 28, 3–6].

The mover first announces to the assembly what Resolution he proposes to move. This announcement or notice is called *Jñapti*. The notice or *Jñapti* is to be followed by a question whether the assembly approves of the Resolution. This question is put either once oı three times as a *Jñapti-dvitīya*- or *Chaturtha-karma*, as will appear from the following description :—

"Let a learned, competent Bhikkhu notify (*jñāpetavyaḥ*) the Saṁgha thus :—

"Let the Saṁgha, reverend sirs, hear me. This person, X, desires to receive . . . ordination . . . If the Saṁgha is ready (*prāptakālaḥ*), let the Saṁgha confer on X . . . the ordination. This is the Jñapti (*eshā jñapti*).

"Let the Saṁgha, reverend sirs, hear me. This person, X, desires to receive . . . ordination . . . The Saṁgha confers on X the . . . ordination. Let any one of the venerable brethren who is in favour of the . . . ordination . . . be silent, and anyone who is not in favour of it, speak (*bhāshet*).

"And for the *second* time I repeat this proposal (*etad artham*): Let the Saṁgha (etc. as before).

"And for the *third* time I repeat this proposal (*tṛitīyamapi etad artham vadāmi*): Let the Saṁgha (etc. as before).

"X has received the . . . ordination . . . The Saṁgha is in favour of it, therefore it is silent. Thus do I understand (*Kshamati Saṁghasya, tasmāt tushṇīm, evam etaṁ dhārayāmīti*)."

Debate.—A Resolution, however, was not always received in silence. It often gave rise to debate. There might "break out among members violence (*bhaṇḍana*), quarrel (*kalaha*), and dispute (*vivāda*)" [*Chullavagga*, iv, 8, 9]; "pointless speeches are brought forth, and the sense of any single utterance is not clear" [ib., 14, 19; xii, 2, 7].

Devices for Agreement.—The ancient Indian democratic method aimed at achieving unanimity of decisions at these meetings at all costs. All possible avenues were explored for this purpose.

One of such avenues to agreement is technically called *Tinavatthāraka* (literally, "covering over as if with grass"). This method was applied in case where the Bhikshus of a Saṁgha were "continuing in quarrels, strifes, and disputes", and were accusing one another of many offences. It was then felt that if the Saṁgha permitted them "to deal with one another for those offences, it might result in further bad blood and divisions among them". Therefore, a very ingenious device was invented to restore unity. The members were "to meet together at one spot". Then they would call upon the leader of each party to bring the matter in dispute before his own party for a settlement. The settlement that may be reached at these party meetings would then be endorsed by the general Saṁgha [ib., iv, 13].

Sometimes, again, the Saṁgha of a particular locality (*āvāsa*) were not able to settle a question among themselves. In such a case they might go to another locality with a larger Saṁgha and refer to them the matter of dispute for a settlement. The incoming Bhikshus would also fix a time-limit for the other Saṁgha to settle the disputed point [ib., iv, 14, 18].

Committee of Reference.—The third means of approach towards a settlement was by the appointment of a sub-committee to negotiate it. It was "by means of a Referendum", technically called *Ubbāhikāya*, literally, "the *turning-over* of the disputed point from the general Saṁgha to a committee" (*Udvāhikā Sabhā*, which may also mean "the committee that can *carry* members over to a decision"). Such a committee was constituted of chosen members, members chosen for their ten virtues, such as *śīla*, *āchāra*, *bahuśruta*, *sūtradhara*, *sūtrasannichaya*, proficiency in the *Vinaya*, and the like [ib., iv, 14, 19].

A committee did not require a quorum. We read of a committee of eight members, one of whom acted as president and another as secretary. The latter puts to the former successively the different points of reference to the committee and announces his decision on each to the other members by casting the corresponding ballot (*idaṁ paṭhamaṁ salākaṁ nikhipāmi*) [ib., xii, 2, 8].

For purposes of undisturbed deliberation, this committee adjourned to a different place, "pleasant, quiet, and solitary," called *Vālika-ārāma*.

Such a committee was of the nature of a body of arbitrators whose award was binding. They were "delegates" deputed (*sammatā*) by the parent body to settle the point at issue (*vūpasametum*) [ib.].

Principle of Representation.—It will be seen that the principle of representation was implied in the manner of appointment of members to this jury or commission.

Res Judicata.—This principle is also implied in the *Chullavagga* [iv, 14, 16] penalizing a person who reopens (*ukkoṭeti* = *utkoṭayati*) a legal question that is settled (*vūpasantam*) or complains (*khīyati*) about a decision to which he has conveyed his consent (*chhandadāyako*).

Proceeding in Presence.—The term *Sammukhavinaya*, " Proceeding in Presence," is applied to cases where decision was reached by agreement among members. The " Proceeding in Presence " implies the presence of the Saṁgha, Dhamma, Vinaya, and the person concerned in the dispute. The presence of the Saṁgha means (1) the presence of all qualified members (*kammāppattā* = *karmāpannāḥ*), (2) production of consent of those who were able to convey it, and (3) absence of objection from members present to the proceedings. This shows that the opinion of absentees counted for decisions at meetings of the Saṁgha. The presence of the Dharma and Vinaya was that of the legal expert. Thus the Saṁgha reached its decisions by giving due representation to the different parties and interests affected by them [ib].

Vote of the Majority.—When all the resources and avenues of amicable agreement failed, or when the committee of reference aforesaid were unable themselves to come to a settlement, the case was handed over to the whole Saṁgha who would then proceed to settle it by vote of the majority, technically called *yebbhuyyasikena* (i.e. by the operation of the process called *yad bhūyasikā kriyā*, " giving effect to the opinion of the majority ") [ib., iv, 8, 9].

As has been already mentioned, the Śākya Parliament had to decide by the vote of the majority the very vital question whether they should open the gates of their city and offer surrender to the invader, the Kosala king, revengeful Virudhaka. This shows how this essential characteristic of democracy marked the working of both political and religious organizations and was not confined to either.

Polling Officer.—A member who was free from partiality (*chhanda*), malice (*dosa*), folly (*moha*), and fear (*bhaya*) was appointed as the polling officer by a special Resolution of the Saṁgha [ib., 14, 26].

Voting.—A vote was called by the significant term *chhanda* which literally means " freedom ". Thus voting was free [*Mahāvagga*, ii, 23; 3, 5; ix, 3, 5, etc.; *Chullavagga*, iv, 14; etc.]. Voting was by tickets (*śalākā*) consisting of slips of wood distributed among the members. They were of different colours to represent different opinions. Each member was asked to choose a ticket of the colour corresponding to his views, with the warning that he should not show it to anybody.

The polling officer collecting these voting tickets was called *Śalākāgrāhāpaka*. They were collected by him in a "secret" manner (*guhyaka*), or by "whispering" (*svakarṇajalpakaṁ*), or "openly" *vivṛitakaṁ*), and "undisguisedly" (*viśvasta*). In the "whispering" method, the teller of votes was to whisper to each voter what the different voting tickets signified and which ticket he should choose [ib.].

According to Buddhaghosa [quoted by Oldenberg, *Vinayapiṭaka*, ii, 315], the polling officer used the "whispering" method to influence voting, but for the right cause. He could also cancel the voting if it was against "Dharma".

Vote of Majority not always applicable.—It has already been noted that the vote of the majority was taken as the last resource, as it amounted to coercion. The texts mention cases in which it should not be applied, namely, where the matter in dispute is trivial (*avaramātraka*), or where the case has not run its prescribed course (including reference to a jury, as explained above), or where the matter in dispute is not clear to members, or when the voting may result in the dissolution of the Saṁgha or overthrow of Dharma. It will appear that the polling officer was invested with plenary powers, so that in some cases he could suspend or suppress the results of voting [*Chullavagga*, iv, 10, 1].

Invalidity of Voting.—Voting was invalid where votes were given irregularly (*adharmeṇa*), or inequally, by sections (*varga*), or against the voter's views (*yathādṛishṭi*) [ib.].

Summary.—Applying the aforesaid regulations, the texts define what constitutes a valid Act of a properly constituted assembly (*dhammena samaggakamma*). A valid Act depends on the following conditions: (1) The assembly is made up only of members who are entitled to vote (*karmāpannāḥ*);

(2) presentation (*sthāpanam*) of the motion (*Jñapti*) by announcing (*anussāvanam*) it once or three times, as already stated ; (3) counting of votes of all those who are entitled to vote (*chhandārahānaṁ chhando āhaṭo hoti*) ; (4) absence of protest from members present (*sammukhībhūtā na paṭikkosanti*), and (5) declaring the Resolution as passed, once or thrice, as may be required (*ekayā kammavāchayā . . . tīhi kammavāchāhi kammaṁ karoti*) [*Mahāvagga*, ix, 3, 9].

It will also appear that each Buddhist Saṁgha was functioning as a direct democracy on the basis of universal suffrage within its field of jurisdiction (*āvāsa*), however small, like the City States of ancient Greece. We have already seen how one of the conditions pointed out by the Buddha for the prosperity of a Saṁgha was participation of all its members in its assemblies which should be " full (*samaggā*) and frequent ".

Assembly Clerks.—A passage in the Mahāgovinda Suttanta of *Dīgha Nikāya* [xix, 14] shows that the Saṁgha had secretaries or clerks to record its minutes. Four officers are said to have been appointed for the purpose of recording the words used (*vuttavachana*) and the business transacted (*pachchanusiṭṭha vachana*) at the assembly of the gods called Tāvatiṁśa Suddhammā Sabhā [Jayaswal, *Hindu Polity*, p. 112].

Referendum.—Lastly, there seems to have been Referendum in use as a constitutional procedure. In Jātaka No. 1, there is a reference to the election of a king by votes of the entire city (*sakala nagara*). The citizens are described to be " of one mind or vote (*ekachchhandāḥ bhutvā*) " [ib., 115].

Religious Movements : *Growth of Ascetic Orders.*—The foregoing account of kingdoms and republics shows how much the politics of the period was influenced by religious leaders of the eminence of Vardhamāna Mahāvīra and Gautama Buddha, the founders, respectively, of the important religions known as Jainism and Buddhism. And yet fundamentally these two religions are to be viewed not as independent and isolated growths but as the offshoots of indigenous culture, of Brahmanism or Vedism. They take their stand on certain aspects of the pre-existing system, which they select and emphasize to the exclusion of other aspects. Both are organized as ascetic orders and brotherhoods, and are thus only additions, though the most important additions, to the existing list of ascetic sects of which the number was nearly a legion.

Vedic Origin of Asceticism.—Asceticism, in fact, has its roots in the Veda and has been directly encouraged by the highest Vedic Thought, the Upanishads. As we have already seen, the centre of Vedic religion is the Ṛishi, or "Seer" who is capable of a direct realization of Truth by practice of *Tapas* or ascetism [*Rv.* x, 109, 4; etc.] whereby he becomes a *Muni* of divine afflatus (*deveshita*) or *Vipra* or *Manīshi* (see references already given). The *Āraṇyakas* are themselves the products of hermitages of the forests whither the Upanishads recommend retirement as essential for those who seek the highest knowledge, *parā-vidyā, vedānta,* the knowledge of the Ātman [*Muṇḍaka Up.*]. "He who knows Brahman becomes a *Muni.* Wishing for that world (of Brahman) only, mendicants leave their homes. Knowing this, the people of old did not wish for offspring and they, having risen above the desire for sons, wealth, and new worlds, wander about as mendicants (*bhikshācharyaṁ charanti*)" [*Br. Up.* cited above]. This *Śruti* practice of asceticism, mendicancy, and renunciation of the world is regularized into a system in the *Smṛitis* which make it obligatory on every Hindu (barring the Śūdra), i.e. a follower of the Varṇāśrama-dharma, to devote the latter half of his life to the two *āśramas* of the *Vānaprastha, Vanī,* or *Vaikhānasa,* Hermit, and the *Parivrājaka* or *Bhikshu,* or *Yati* (*Manu,* v, 137), or *Maunī* (*Āpastamba,* ii, 9, 21, 1), or *Sannyāsī,* wandering Mendicant. Nay, more: the Brahmanical system did not confine asceticism only to elderly people or advanced householders. It was also open for youths who wanted to shun the world in their quest of the Ideal and would then be known as *Naishṭhika Brahmachāris* as we have already seen.

Its Place in Brahmanical Social System.—Thus in the normal Brahmanical system, more than half of society would leave it and wander about as mendicants and ascetics in pursuit of Truth under the guidance of chosen teachers. This floating mass of homeless population was organized into different Orders or Sects in accordance with the different systems of doctrine and discipline they followed under their teachers. These systems were early codified into regular treatises. As early as the time of Pāṇini, we know of what were then called the *Bhikshu Sūtras*, the codes of discipline governing the life of the *Bhikshus* or *Parivrājakas*, wanderers, and of two orders of *Bhikshus* instanced, viz. the Kārmandinas and the Pārāśāriṇas. The Pārāśāriṇas were probably an important sect because we find the Buddha discussing the doctrines of a Brahmin teacher of the name of Pārāsariya [*Majjhima*, iii, 298]. We have also seen how the oldest Dharma-Sūtras, those of Gautama and Baudhāyana, mention the Śāstra or Code promulgated by Vikhanas and followed by the Hermit called Vaikhānasa or Vānaprastha. A Vaikhānasa Śāstra was even known as Śrāmaṇaka because it was meant for the *Śramaṇas*. Among other anticipations of Buddhism which have been already noticed and may be repeated here for convenience are (1) Gautama's injunction that the *Bhikshu* must station himself in a fixed retreat during the rains (*dhruvaśīlo varshāshu*); (2) his other injunctions that the *Bhikshu* must not store up articles of consumption, nor kill life or even seeds; (3) his rules for the regulation of begging, or (4) Baudhāyana's references to the use of cloth for straining water. Jacobi has shown by an elaborate consideration of the rules of the Jaina and Buddhist orders how they are really based on those of the Brahmin ascetic as their model [*SBE.*, xxii, pp. xxii-xxx].

Intellectual Life of Ascetics.—Asceticism was thus represented by the Hermit and the Wanderer, each with his own set of rules. The difference between the two is that while the Hermit is fixed to one place which must be outside the village in its adjoining forests, the Wanderer must be always on the move, " not dwelling a second night in the same place except in rains " [Gautama cited above]. But the two agreed fundamentally in the fact of renouncing the world. In the Pāli texts, it is called " going out of home into homelessness ", " *agārasmā anagāriyam pabbajati* [*Dīgha* i, 60, etc.]. A characteristic of the Wanderer is his love of philosophical discussion and disputation. We have already seen how the Upanishads tell of individual, or circles of, scholars wandering through the country, holding discussions at noted centres of learning, and spreading education. While the Śrutis call them Charakas, literally Wanderers, the Smṛitis call them Parivrājakas. The philosophical discussions were held in Conferences at the courts of kings like Janaka, or in Academies like the Pāñchāla Parishad, or in *Santhāgāras*, or *Samayappavādaka-śālā* as the Pāli Texts calls them, or *Sabhās*, Assembly-Halls, as the Smṛitis call them. Evidence of actual places where such public philosophical discussions were held is ample in Pāli Texts. We have mention, for instance, of the hall in Queen Mallikā's park at Śrāvastī [*Dialogues*, i, 244] " for discussion of different systems of opinion ", or the Gabled Pavilion erected by the Lichchhavis in the Mahāvana outside Vaiśālī, the sweet-smelling Champaka Grove on the lake of Queen Gaggarā at Champā [ib., 144], or the *Mora-nivāpa* (the place where peacocks were fed) at Rājagṛiha [*Majjhima*, ii, 1, 29].

These discussions were due to the proselytizing tendencies of the Parivājakas and often resulted in conversions and borrowings as between their different sects and schools. The story of the Buddha's life is largely the story of the numerous conversions of leaders of non-Buddhist systems effected by his ministry of forty-five years. Jainism is also supposed to have borrowed largely of the *Achelakas* and *Ājīvikas* as shown by Jacobi [*Jaina Sūtras*, Introduction] and Hoernle [*Uvāsagadasāo*, pp. 108–111].

In the picture drawn up by the texts we find that in a hermitage situated in the silence and solitude of the forests, a renowned sage would gather round him a band of disciples who would live with him on a simple fare of raw roots and fruits gathered in the forest, engaging themselves in meditation, in sacrificial rites (the five Mahāyajñas), in practice of penance (*tapaḥ śīlāḥ*), or learning from their teacher the tenets and texts of their particular Sūtras or

Śāstras. The ascetics of the other class, the Wanderers, would live by begging and on cooked food and come into contact with hermits and fellow-wanderers, initiating discourses that would draw lay audiences. "So Dīghanakha calls on the Buddha, the Buddha visits Sakuludāyi Vekhanassa (was he Vaikhānasa of the Dharma-sūtras?), calls on the Buddha, Keniya does the same, and Potaliputta calls on Samiddhi" [Rhys Davids, *Buddhist India*, p. 142].

Non-Buddhist Ascetic Orders.—There were, no doubt, many individual Parivrājakas wandering through the country, but it is doubtful if there were many distinct Saṁghas, Orders, or organizations of these ascetics on the lines of the later Jain and Buddhist organizations. Both Jain and Buddhist texts name many older Brahminical orders of ascetics, but the names generally denote subtle differences of doctrine and are not the corporate names of schools called after their founders, like the Sākiyaputta-Samaṇas or the Nigaṇṭha-Nātaputtas. Thus the *Brahmajāla Sūtra* discusses as many as sixty-two systems of doctrine held by the Śramaṇas and Brāhmaṇas before Buddhism arose, while in some Jain works [e.g. Sūtrakṛitāṅga, ii, 2, 79], their number is 363.[1] As regards their names, a list is found in the *Aṅguttara* as follows:—

1. *Ājīvika*. The followers of this sect went about naked and claimed special strictness in their rules as to means of livelihood.

2. *Nigaṇṭha* (= Nirgrantha, "unfettered"). This was the name of the Jains who wore only loincloth.

3. *Muṇḍa-sāvaka*, "disciple of the Shaveling," stated by Buddhaghosa to be the same as No. 2.

4. *Jaṭilaka*, "he who wears his hair in braids." As seen above, the name *Jaṭila* is given to the Vaikhānasa or hermit by Gautama. The Jaṭilas were Brāhmaṇas and had their headquarters at Uruvelā, "an army township" (*Senāgrāma*) near Rājagṛiha, where they were 1,000 strong

[1] The commentators make up these 363 sects as comprising 180 schools of Kriyāvādins, 84 Akriyāvādins, 67 Ajñānikavādins, and 32 Vainayikavādins.

with their three leaders, Uruvelā, Nadī, and Gayā of the Kassapa gotra. They were fire-worshippers and were granted by the Buddha exemption from the usual probation (*parivāsa*) as members of another monastic order [*Mahāvagga*, i, 38, 3], and also on the ground of their advanced doctrines [ib.].

5. *Parivrājaka*. A generic name for Wanderers in the Brahmanical system.

6. *Magaṇḍika*. Not intelligible.

7. *Tedaṇḍika*, "bearer of triple staff," referred to by Manu [xii, 10]. A name given to Brāhmaṇa Bhikshus by the Buddhists.

8. *Aviruddhaka*, "the not opposing ones, the friends."

9. *Gotamaka*, "the followers of Gotama," distinct from the Gotama, the founder of Buddhism. It was either Devadatta, the cousin of the Buddha, who had founded an Order, or some Brāhmaṇa of the Gautama gotra, who had a following of Bhikshus named after him.

10. *Devadhammikā*, "those who follow the religion of the gods." A sect not mentioned in any other text.

It is apparent that the names appropriated by some of the sects in this list might apply to some others, too, if we take the meanings of the names.

The ascetics of different Orders were described by the general term, *Samaṇa-Brāhmaṇā*, "leaders in religious life" [*Dialogues*, ii, 165]. The *Aṅguttara* [iv, 35] mentions two classes of *Parivrājakas*: (1) *Brāhmaṇa*, and (2) *Aññatitthiya*, i.e. other non-Buddhist ascetics. The Brāhmaṇa Parivrājakas are characterized as *Vādaśīla* or disputatious [*Sutta Nipāta*, 382], *Vitaṇḍas* and *Lokāyatas*, sophists, casuists, and materialists [*Chullavagga*, v, 3, 2], *Tevijjas*, versed in the three Vedas [*Sutta N.*, 594]. *Padakas*, versed in metre, *Veyyākaraṇas*, versed in grammar, and proficient in *Jappa*, recitation or *Jalpa*, *Nighaṇṭu*, vocabulary, *Keṭubha*, etymology (?), *Itihāsa* and the like [ib., 1020].

Their Six Prominent Leaders.—Of all non-Buddhist orders, the Buddhist texts refer to six as the most important, and describe the founders of these systems (*titthakaras*) as "*samaṇa brāhmaṇā saṁghino gaṇino gaṇāchariyā ñatā yasassino titthakarā sādhusammatā bahujanassa* ", " leaders in religious life, heads of Saṁghas (orders), of schools, teachers of schools, well-known and of repute as founders of systems and highly honoured by many people " [*Sabhiyasutta* ; *Sāmaññaphala Sutta*]. All of them were much senior to the Buddha, " for, as compared with them, master Gotama is young in years and is novice in the life of religion [*Saṁ*., i, 69]. They were :—

1. Pūraṇo Kassapo : who taught the doctrine of Akiriyāvāda, Non-action, i.e. the absence of merit in any virtuous action and of demerit in the worst of crimes. He was called Pūraṇo for his fullness of knowledge, and Kassapa, for his being a Brahmin. He went about without any clothing and had as many as 80,000 followers.

2. Makkhali-Gosāla : so called because he was born of a slave confined to a cow-pen by his master. His doctrine was the denial of both Karma and its effect. He admitted the fact of depravity but held that it could be worked out by transmigration and not by any action of the individual concerned.

3. Ajita Kesakambalin : his doctrine was that there was annihilation at death, which shut out the possibility of any effect to be achieved by Karma.

4. Pakuddha Kachchāyana : so-called because he was born at the foot of a Kakudha tree. His doctrine is stated to be : " What *is* cannot be destroyed : out of Nothing emerges Nothing " (*sato nachchi vināso asato nachchi sambhavo*). His theory thus excludes Responsibility. He also assumed the existence of seven permanent, uncreated substances, such as Earth, Water, Fire, Air, Pleasure, Pain, and Soul.

5. Nigaṇṭha Nātaputta : he was the son of a husbandman named Nāta and was called Nigaṇṭha as being free from all bonds.

6. Sañjaya Belaṭṭhaputta, who is not credited with any doctrine in reply to the problems raised.

The standing of these six teachers will be evident from the fact, already mentioned, that even an imperious and imperial king like Ajātaśatru approached everyone of them for instruction. Of these, again, the most famous were Gosāla and Nātaputta. Gosāla figures in the Jaina Texts as the founder of the sect of Ājīvikas made famous by the inscriptions of Asoka recording his gift to them of cave-dwellings. At first he was a disciple of Mahāvīra, but they later quarrelled and separated [Hoernle, *Uvāsagadasāo*]. The Jains nicknamed him Ājīvika, as one who turned an ascetic for earning a living (*ājīva*). The Buddha also could not stand an Ājīvika [*Majjhima*, i, 483]. Nigaṇtha Nātaputta is the name of Vardhamāna Mahāvīra, the founder of Jainism.

Other Leaders named in Buddhist Texts.—Besides these six heretical or non-Buddhist teachers, the Pāli Texts refer to several other teachers with a following of their own and distinguished for their learning and saintliness. There was, for instance, the Brahmin, Bāvarī, living on the banks of the Godāvarī in Assaka territory, who had sixteen other disciples, each of whom had again a " host of pupils " and was " widely renowned throughout the world ". They are represented as itinerant scholars visiting by turns the chief centres of culture in those days, viz. Patiṭṭhāna, Māhissati, Ujjeni, Gonaddha, Vedisā, Vanasabhaya, Kosambī, Sāketa, Sāvatthī, Setavya, Kapilavatthu, Kusinārā, Pāvā, Vesālī, and the city of Magadha. All of them wore matted hair and hides [*Pārāyanavagga*]. We also read of the Brahmin, Sela, with his 300 pupils ; of Chaṁkī, Tārukkha, with his pupil Bhāradvāja, Pokkharasāti with his pupil Vāseṭṭha, Jāṇussoni, Todeyya, all " acknowledged masters of the three Vedas ", and other allied subjects [*Sutta N.*, 594]. In the *Tevijja-sutta* [*Dīgha*, i, 235], Vāseṭṭha refers to several Brahmin schools, the two schools of Yajur-Veda, the Adhvaryus, and Taittirīyas, a Sāmaveda school, the Chhāndogyas, and a Rigveda school, the Bahvṛichas. The texts also mention many *Parivrājakas* with whom the Buddha came into contact. Poṭṭhapāda with 300 pupils lived at Mallikārāma, where he was visited by the Buddha [*Dīgha*, i, 187]. Bhaggavagotta lived at Anupiya and was visited by the Buddha, who was informed of the desertion of Lichchhaviputta, Sunakkhatta, due to his not showing him any miracles [ib., iii, 1]. Nigrodha lived with his pupils in a hermitage close to Gijjhakūṭa at Rājagaha, where the Buddha lived, and was visited by him [ib., 36]. The *Majjhima Nikāya* refers to Jāṇussoṇi and Pilotika [i, 175–7]; Vachchhagotta, living in a Paribbājakārāma at Ekapuṇḍarikā near Vaiśāli [ib., 481–3]; Aggivachchhagotta and Mahāvachchhagotta [ib., 483–497]; Dīghanaka [ib., 497–501]; Māgandiya in the Kuru country [ib. 501–513]; Sandaka living with his pupils at Kosambī and refusing to follow Gotama for the gain and fame he was receiving [ib., 513–524]; Potaliputto, who did not approve of a discourse of Samiddhi, a Buddhist, and left him [ib., iii, 207]; Annabhāra, Sakuladāyī and others dwelling at a great Parivrājaka centre on the river Sappinī [*Aṅgu.*, ii, 29–39]; Anugāra, Sākuladāyī residing at another Parivrājaka centre at Moranivāpa in Veluvana near Rājagṛiha, and seen by the Buddha who was frankly told that he was the most respected of all teachers (including the six famous heretical teachers) because he was content with little food, poor dress, little alms, ordinary shelter, and solitary life [*Majjhima*, ii, 1–22]; Uggāhamāno, son of Samaṇa-Maṇḍika, at Mallikārāma, who was seen by the Śrāvastī engineer, Pañchakaṅga, on his way to the Buddha, who refuted his teaching [ib., ii, 22–5]; Vekhanasa, who first spoke ill of the Samaṇas and was later converted by the Buddha [ib., 40–4]; Sarabha, who was at first a Buddhist Bikkhu and became a Parivrājaka, denouncing Buddhism in an assembly at Rājagṛiha till the Buddha addressed the assembly (Parishad) and won them over [*Aṅgu.*, i, 185–8]; Moliyasīvako converted by the Buddha [ib., iii, 356]; Sutavā and Sajjho [ib., iv, 369–371]; Susīma, with a large following at Rājagaha [*Saṁ.*, ii, 119–128]; Kuṇḍaliya who, living among, and listening frequently to, Samaṇas and Brāhmaṇas discoursing at the Parishad on old religious tenets, visited the Buddha and was satisfied by his teaching [ib., v, 73–5]; Sañjaya, who had 1,000 followers, including the famous Sāriputta and Moggallāna, the Brahmin *Grāmaṇīs* of the two villages, Kolita and Upatissa, and Supiya, and became converted by the Buddha, followed by numerous other conversions which created a stir among the people of Magadha, who murmured that "the ascetic Gotama is come to bring childlessness, widowhood, and subversion of families" [*Dhammapada Commentary*, i, 88–90]; Sabhiya, son of a Kshatriyā Parivrājikā, and born in a *sabhā*, who grew up to be a learned Parivrājaka and invincible disputant, building his hermitage at the city gate and teaching *sippa* to the princes, and became a Buddhist Bhikkhu [*Sutta N. Commentary*, ii, 421–2]. We may also refer in this connection to the Sages, Alāra Kālāma, and Uddaka Rāmaputta, the two first teachers of the Buddha himself [*Majjhima*, i, 240]; to the Ājīvika ascetic, Upaka, whom the Buddha failed to convert, along with a few other sages such as Sandaka, Potaliputta, or Sunakkhatta, mentioned above [ib., p. 64 f.; *Dīgha*, iii, 1, 5]; or to the five Brahmins, Vappa, Bhaddiya, Mahānāman, Assaji, and their leader Koṇḍañña, who were the Buddha's associates in the ascetic life under their common guru, Uddaka, and became his first disciples.

Universal respect for Ascetics of all Schools.—It will thus be clear that a characteristic feature of the religious life of India in the period under review was the number and variety of ascetic groups aptly described thus in the Jachchandhavaggó (4, 5, 6) of the *Udāna*: "*sambahulā nānātitthiyā samaṇabrāhmaṇā paribbājakā . . . nānā-diṭṭhikā nānākhantikā nānā-ruchikā nānādiṭṭhinissaya-nissitā*" [*Udānam*, pp. 66–7, *PTS.*]: "there were very many, and various, sectaries of Śramaṇas and Brāhmaṇas, all Parivrājakas, followers of different *Diṭṭhis*, *Darśanas* or Systems, *Khantis* (*kshānti*), Beliefs, *Ruchis*, aims, and organizations (*Nissaya* = āśraya"). They are described as going through the city of Śrāvastī in a miscellaneous crowd for alms, "uttering their different doctrines, and fighting one another with words, weapons of mouth (*mukha-sattihi*"). In the Kassapa-Sīhanāda Sutta, the Śramaṇas and Brāhmaṇas are described as being "clever, subtle, experienced in controversy, hair-splitters, breaking into pieces by their wisdom, as they go about, the speculations of their adversaries"; as following practices of penance (*Tapas*) as to food and clothing (on the lines laid down in the Dharma-Sūtras), e.g. feeding on wild rice, fruits, and roots, going about naked or wearing cast-off clothes, rags, barks, or skins of black antelopes ; as laying emphasis, besides these merely physical austerities, on *Śīla* (conduct), *Chitta* (heart), *Pañña* (prajñā, mind or intelligence), *Tapojigukkhā* (i.e. ahiṁsā, non-violence) and *Vimukti* (emancipation). In the *Sāmaññaphala Sutta* we are told how the Śramaṇas and Brāhmaṇas were treated to gifts by householders for happiness both in this world and the next [*Dialogues*, i, 69] ; how an emperor, enjoying a full-moon night with his ministers, feels a want and asks, " Who is the Śramaṇa or Brāhmaṇa whom we may call upon to-night to satisfy our hearts ? " [ib., 66] ; how even the slave of an emperor, if he turns a monk, " donning yellow robes and content with mere food and shelter and with solitary life ", would be " greeted by him with reverence and provided with robes and bowl, shelter and medicine, and even watch and ward and guard to protect him " [ib., 77]. These passages are typical expressions of the universal respect for the anchorites and wandering ascetics, which continued to the time of Asoka who, in many of his edicts defining the Dharma, invariably includes as part of that Dharma reverence and liberality towards the Śramaṇas and Brāhmaṇas. This feeling even continues to this day.

Germs of Heresy in Brahminical Ascetic Orders.—It is also evident from the passage quoted above that the non-Buddhist Orders of Brāhmaṇas and Śramaṇas used to admit slaves to their ranks, though the Buddhist Order made a rule that no runaway slave could be admitted, i.e. only a slave who had obtained the consent of his master or emancipation could be admitted [*Vinaya*, *SBE*., i, 199]. Śūdras also were admitted to the Orders, as indicated in the Aggañña Sutta of the *Dīgha* and Madhura Sutta of the *Majjhima*. *Jātaka*, iii, 381, mentions a potter, and iv, 392, a Chaṇḍāla becoming Samaṇas, not Buddhist Samaṇas. Among these non-Buddhist or Brahminical Orders there were, again, already signs of dissent and heresy or heterodoxy in which are to be traced the genuine germs of both Jainism and Buddhism. The Parivrājaka in the Brahminical system was free from the obligations of performing religious ceremonies on account of their peripatetic life but, lest this laxity be carried too far, Vasishṭha [x, 4] gives the warning: "Let him discontinue the performance of all religious ceremonies, but let him never discontinue the recitation of the Veda. By neglecting the Veda, he becomes a Śūdra; therefore he shall not neglect it." A prohibition so pronounced presupposes the prevalence of the practices prohibited, and these practices must have been common among the non-Brahmin ascetics and dissenters, the forerunners of the Jains and Buddhists.[1]

Rise of Jainism: *Life of Pārśva.*—Jain tradition traces Jainism to a remote antiquity represented by a succession of twenty-three *Tīrthakaras* or prophets of whom the first was Ṛishabha, a king who renounced his kingdom in favour of his son, Bharata, and became an ascetic, and the last was Pārśva, an historical personage. According to the *Kalpa Sūtra* [*SBE.*, xxii] written by Bhadrabāhu before 300 B.C.), Pārśva was a Kshatriya, the son of Ikshāku King Aśvasena of Benares and his queen Vāmā, and was married to Prabhāvatī, daughter of Naravarman, King of Kuśasthala,[2] whose son was Prasenajit [Hemachandra, *Trishashṭi-śalākā*, Parva ix]. As a prince, Pārśva was called Purisādāṇīya, "the people's favourite" and "lived thirty years as a householder". Then in his palankin called Viśālā he rode through the town of Benares with a large following to the park called Āśramapada where after three and a half days complete fasting he became an ascetic. After eighty-three days "deep meditation", he attained highest knowledge called *Kevala*. He had eight *Gaṇas* and

[1] The principal authorities on this subject are the writings of Rhys Davids, especially his *Buddhist India*, and Introduction to the Sūtras in the *Dialogues*, and of Dr. B. C. Law, especially his articles in his *Buddhist Studies*, to which I am deeply indebted.

[2] In his *Hemakosha*, Hemachandra identifies Kuśasthala with Kānyakubja, the capital of southern Pañchāla, of which the Purāṇas also mention a ruler called *Senajit* (= Prasenajit ?) [Pargiter, *Ancient Indian Historical Tradition*, p. 146]. The *Uttarādhyayana-sūtra*, again, knows of a famous king named Brahmadatta of south Pāñchāla at Kāmpilya, while the Purāṇas also refer to him [ib. p. 282]. This shows that Jain tradition may be historical. We have also seen how in that age Kāśī, Kosala, and Pañchāla counted among the sixteen great States in both Buddhist and Jain texts.

eight *Gaṇadharas* known as Subha, Āryaghosha, Vasishṭha, Brahmachārin, Saumya, Śrīdhara, Vīrabhadra, and Yaśas. He is also stated to have a following of 16,000 Śramaṇas under Āryadatta as head, 38,000 nuns under the chief Pushpakulā, 164,000 lay votaries under Suvrata, 327,000 female lay votaries under Sunandā. He lived for 100 years and died "on the summit of Mount Sammeta" (thence known as Parsanath Hill near Gomoh on EIR), in the company of eighty-three followers about 250 years before the death of Mahāvīra. He thus lived in the eighth century B.C.

Relations between Pārśva and Mahāvīra.—The next important figure in the history of Jainism was Mahāvīra. The relations between him and Pārśva are indicated in an old canonical text giving an account of a meeting between Keśi and Gautama [*SBE.*, xlv, p. 119]. Keśi was a young Śramaṇa of the school of Pārśva, living in the park called Tinduka in the town of Śrāvastī. In the same town, in another park called Koshṭhaka, lived Gautama, a disciple of the Jina Vardhamāna who was then living. Both Keśi and Gautama had each a crowd of disciples of his own. The disciples of both were troubled by the following questionings:

"Is our Law the right one, or is the other Law the right one? Are our conduct and doctrines right, or the other?

"The Law as taught by the great sage, Pārśva, which recognizes but four Vows, or the Law taught by Vardhamāna, which enjoins five vows?

"The Law which forbids clothes (for a monk), or that which allows an under and upper garment?"

Knowing the thoughts and doubts of their disciples, the two teachers decided to meet for a settlement, Gautama calling on Keśi by way of courtesy due to a follower of "the older section" (of the church). Their meeting became a big one, as "there assembled many heretics out of curiosity and many thousands of laymen".

Pārśva's four prohibitions were not to (1) injure life (2) lie (3) steal and (4) possess any property. Vardhamāna added the fifth vow of Chastity. Gautama solved the doubt raised by explaining that the fifth vow was implied in the fourth of Pārśva, but the implication was not understood and had to be made explicit in later times. This shows that there was a decline in monastic morals during the interval between Pārśva and Mahāvīra and that the interval must have been sufficiently long for that, thus confirming the tradition stating it to be 250 years. Regarding the second point raised, it was explained away by stating that " the various outward marks of religious men introduced to distinguish them do not count towards final liberation, but only knowledge, faith, and right conduct ". From the text cited we can conclude (1) that there were two sections of the Jain church, the older following Pārśva, and the younger following Mahāvīra, in the life-time of the latter ; it may be noted that " the parents of Mahāvīra were themselves worshippers of Pārśva and followers of the Śramaṇas " [*Āchārāṅga Sūtra*, ii, 15, 16] ; (2) that the followers of Pārśva must have been the ancestors of the Śvetāmbaras, " monks in white clothes," and those of Mahāvīra, of the Digambaras, " sky-clad or naked ascetics " ; and (3) that a sort of union between the two sections was effected in the time of Mahāvīra. We are told that " in that meeting of Keśi and Gautama, knowledge and virtuous conduct were for ever brought to eminence, and subjects of the greatest importance were settled ". The *Majjhima Nikāya* (35) also mentions how Sachchaka, the *son* of a Nigaṇṭha, boasts of his having vanquished in disputation Nātaputta. Thus the followers of Pārśva and Mahāvīra continued as distinct Orders in the time of both Mahāvīra and the Buddha.

In fact, the Buddhist references to the Nigaṇṭhas show them to be quite an old and well-established Order. In the *Sāmaññaphala Sutta*, for instance, Makkhali Gośāla divides mankind into six classes of whom the third class comprised the Nigaṇṭhas who could not have been then a newly-created sect. The same text also makes the mistake of ascribing to Mahāvīra called Nigaṇṭha Nātaputta the well-known four vows of Pārśva. The mistake was due to the fact that the doctrines of Pārśva still held the field and that the reform introduced by Mahāvīra was not yet widely accepted by the Nigaṇṭhas.

Time of Mahāvīra.—The time of Mahāvīra is to be inferred from the traditional date of his death which took place 470 years before the birth of Vikrama whose era began eighteen years later in 58 B.C. It, therefore, took place in (470 + 58 + 18) 546 B.C. The Jain author, Hemachandra (A.D. 1172), follows another tradition dating Chandragupta's reign in 313 B.C. and 155 years after the death of Mahāvīra, which thus took place in 468 B.C. The traditional date of the death of the Buddha is 543 B.C., while the Buddhist texts make the Buddha, Mahāvīra, and King Kūṇika Ajātaśatru contemporaries. The date, 543 B.C., for the Buddha's death is also confirmed by certain suggested readings of the inscription of Khāravela [see p. 31 of my *Men and Thought in Ancient India*, London, 1924]. Therefore, the first date, 546 B.C., for Mahāvīra's death is nearer the truth than the other suggested date.

Besides, Buddhist tradition itself makes Mahāvīra predecease the Buddha. In the *Saṁgīti-Suttanta*, Sāriputta reports: "The Nigaṇṭha Nātaputta, friends, has *just* (*adhunā*) died at Pāvā." It is also known that Sāriputta himself had pre-deceased the Buddha. In the *Pāsādika Suttanta*, Chuṇḍa delivers the news of Mahāvīra s death to Ānanda at Sāmagāma in the Malla country. We also read of Prasenajit telling the Buddha that Mahāvīra was senior to him in age and ascetic life [*Majjhi*, ii, 143 ; *Saṁ.*, *Jaṭila Sutta*].

His birth-place.—The place and circumstances of his birth have been already referred to. He was born in the northern Kshatriya district of the town called Kuṇḍapura, Kuṇḍapurī, or Kuṇḍagrāma, described as a Sannivesha in the Āchārāṅga Sūtra, i.e. a halting-place of caravans or processions. It is called Kollāga in the *Uvāsagadasāo* [i, 7]. It was one of the suburbs of Vaiśālī, then the capital of Videha. Therefore, Mahāvīra is called a Vesālie, i.e. a Vaiśālika, in the *Sūtra-kṛitāṅga* [i, 3] and "a Videha, a native of Videha, a prince of Videha", in the *Āchārāṅga Sūtra* [ii, 15, 17].

His father.—His father was named Siddhārtha. He had two other names, Śreyāṁsa and Yaśāṁsa. He belonged to the Kaśyapa gotra. He is always described as a Kshatriya and not a rājā. The chief of a petty village like Kuṇḍagrāma could not be counted as a king, as tradition would have it. His wife is also never styled as a *Devī* but only as a Kshatriyāṇī. He was the chief of his clan, the Jñātṛikas, and must have been more influential than his fellow-chiefs of that region. For he was highly connected by marriage.

His mother.—He married the sister of that powerful Lichchhavi king, Cheṭaka, whose daughter was married to the emperor of Magadha.

Like his father, Mahāvīra's mother is also given three names, Triśalā, Videhadattā, and Priyakāriṇī. She was of Vāsishṭha gotra.

His different names.—He himself was also given three names: (1) Varddhamāna, given by his parents, "because he was devoid of love and hate"; (2) Śramaṇa, "because he stands fast in dangers and fears and is indifferent to pleasure and pain"; (3) Venerable Ascetic Mahāvīra, a name given him "by the gods".

Celebrations at his Birth.—Siddhārtha celebrated the birth of his son on a lavish scale. "The customs, taxes, and confiscations were released, buying and selling prohibited, no policemen were allowed to enter houses, great and small fines were remitted, debts cancelled, measures and weights increased, and all prisoners set free in the town of Kuṇḍapura" [*Kalpa Sūtra*, §§ 100, 102].

His family.—Mahāvīra married Yaśodā of Kuṇḍinya gotra. A daughter was born to them and given two names Aṇojjā and Priyadarśanā [*Āchārāṅga*, ii, 15, 15].

His life as an ascetic.—"He lived thirty years amongst the householders under the name of 'Videha'" [ib., 17] or "in Videha" [*Kalpa*, § 110]. Then his parents died and "he with the permission of his elder brother (named Nandivardhana) and the authorities of the kingdom" [ib.] renounced the world, riding away in his palankin in full state with all his army and retinue, passing along a row of thousands of palaces, right through Kuṇḍapura, up to a park called Shaṇḍavana of the Jñātṛis and proceeded to an Asoka tree under which he stopped and leaving aside his finery he fasted for two days and a half, and, clean-shaven, formally turned an ascetic [ib., 116].

He then arrived at the village called Kummāra [*Āchārānga*, ii, 15, 24] where "neglecting his body" he gave himself to meditation. For the first year and a month "he wore clothes. After that time he cast off clothes in the Suvarṇabālukā river [*Āchārānga*, i, 8, 2] and walked about naked and accepted alms in the hollow of his hand". Thus he went on for twelve years in extreme self-mortification, allowing even all sorts of living beings to gather and crawl about on his body [ib.]. In the thirteenth year, "he reached Nirvāṇa under a Sāl tree near an old temple in the field belonging to a householder named Sāmāga on the River Ṛijupālikā outside of the town called Jṛimbhikagrāma, becoming an *Arhat*, a *Jina*, and a *Kevalin*, an omniscient."

His Wanderings.—He stayed the first rainy season in Asthikagrāma, three rainy seasons in Champā and Pṛishṭi Champā, twelve in Vaiśālī and Vāṇigrāma, fourteen in Rājagṛiha and the suburb (bāhirikā) of Nālandā, six in Mithilā, two in Bhadrikā, one in Ālabhikā, one in Paṇitabhūmi (in Vajrabhūmi), one in Śrāvastī and one in the town of Pāpā, where he died "in King Hastipāla's office of the writers" [*Kalpa*, § 122].

His sufferings.—In all these wanderings, lodging in workshops, assembling places, wells, or shops, in manufactories, or under a shed of straw, in travellers' halls, garden-houses, or towns, on a burying-ground, in relinquished houses, or at the foot of a tree, in all these resting-places, he meekly submitted to extreme suffering from crawling insects, from bad people, the village guards and lance-bearers attacking him, from domestic temptations, single women or men, from wanderers treating him badly for his silence, or from cold [*Āchārānga*, i, 8, 2].

He had special suffering in travelling in the pathless country of Lādha (= Rāḍha, or western Bengal), in Vajjabhūmi (a division of Rāḍha), and Subbhabhūmi (the country of the Suhmas or Rāḍhas), where the people attacked him, had dogs set on him, abused him in the filthy language of peasants, and even beat him. Rāḍha was then the home of wild tribes (*lukkhadesa*) who used clothes of grass instead of cotton, and of wild dogs which made travelling difficult [ib., 3].

Ministry.—He went about preaching and converting people to his faith. " At first he wandered about as a single monk ; but now he has surrounded himself by many monks, and teaches every one of them the Law at length," said Gośāla [*Sūtrakṛitāṅga*, ii, 6 (1)].

Relations with Gośāla.—Not many facts and details are known about his wanderings and preaching. The most important event in his ministry was his association with Gośāla and its consequences to Jainism. They first met at Nālandā and lived together for six years in austere asceticism at a place near Kollāga, called Paṇiyabhūmi [Hoernle, *Uvāsagadasāo*, ii, Appendix]. Then they differed and separated and became critics of each other's doctrines. Gośāla settled down at Śrāvastī, taking up his abode in a potter's shop, the property of a woman named Hālāhalā and became known as the founder of the Ājīvika sect, as already stated [ib.]. In its insistence on nakedness, its denial of all comforts, and in the general mode of life it prescribes, the system of Gośāla is hardly different from that of Mahāvīra. And yet the two became irreconcilable opponents of each other and fought out their differences generally through their followers. The *Sūtrakṛitāṅga* [ii, 6] represents Gośāla criticizing the tenets of Mahāvīra and their defence by his disciple Ārdraka. One of his criticisms is : " As a merchant desirous of gain shows his wares and attracts a crowd to do business, in a similar way acts the Śramaṇa Jñātṛiputra." In another, he says that Mahāvīra avoids public places for fear of questions from more learned monks whom he may meet there. The Jain text on its part ascribes to Gośāla the strange laxity of permitting to the monks of his Order intercourse with women.

Controversy with Rival Sects.—The *Sūtrakṛitāṅga* opens with references to prevailing systems which the commentator identifies with (1) Bauddhas ; (2) Bārhaspatyas ; (3) Nāstikas or Chārvākas ; (4) Vedāntins ; (5) Sāṅkhyas

(6) Adṛishṭavādins (fatalists); (7) Ājīvikas; (8) Trairāśikas (Jain followers of Vaiśeshika philosophy); and (9) Śaivas [*SBE.*, xlv, 235–248 n.].

The same text [ii, 6] refers to Jain controversy with some rival systems, such as Buddhist, Vedic, Vedāntin (Ekadaṇḍin), and Hastitāpasa. It also describes a controversy between Udaka, a Nirgrantha, and follower of Pārśva, and Gautama, a disciple of Mahāvīra, in the park called Hastiyāma, not far from the bathing-hall named Śeshadravyā, belonging to the householder Lepā, at Nālandā, and the conversion of Udaka by Gautama. There is also a reference in the same text [ii, 1, 15. 21] to materialistic doctrines which, in the Buddhist work, *Sāmaññaphala Sutta*, are ascribed to Pūraṇa Kassapa and Ajita Kesakambalī; and to another variety of the materialistic system which is ascribed in the Buddhist records to Pakuddha Kachchāyana and akin to Vaiśeshka philosophy. There is also discussed the heresy of "Fatalism". All these heresies the Jains describe as Kriyāvāda, Akriyāvāda, Ajñānavāda, and Vainayikavāda. Ajñānavāda or Agnosticism is associated in the Sāmaññaphala Sūtra with Sañjaya Belaṭṭhiputta.[1]

Besides opponents, Mahāvīra lost to Buddhism some of his own ardent followers. One such was Sīha, the famous Lichchhavi general, whom the Nātaputta vainly tried to dissuade from seeing the Buddha on the ground that while the Nigaṇṭhas believed in the *Kriyāvāda*, the Buddhists held the opposite doctrine of *Akriyāvāda*. Sīha, ignoring his advice, saw the Buddha and became his disciple (*Mahā-vagga*, vi, 31]. A similar case was that of Upāli [*Majjhima*. 56].

[1] "*Kriyāvāda* is the doctrine which teaches that the soul acts or is affected by acts. Under this head come Jainism, and, of Brahmanical philosophies, Vaiśeshika and Nyāya (which, however, are not expressly quoted in the canonical books of either Buddhists or Jainas) and apparently a great many systems not named but implied in the texts. *Akriyāvāda* is the doctrine which teaches either that a soul does not exist, or that it does not act, or is not affected by acts. Under this subdivision fall the different schools of Materialists; of Brahmanical philosophies, the Vedānta, Sāṅkhya, and Yoga; and the Buddhists. Of the latter, the doctrines of the Kshaṇikavādins and the Śūnyavādins are alluded to in *Sūtrakṛitāṅga*, i, 14, 4, 7." [Jacobi, p. xxv of *SBE.*, xlv.] The *Vainayikas* believe in salvation by *bhakti*, as the *Ajñānavādins* by *tapas*, i.e. Karma-mārga.

His Royal Followers.—Mahāvīra, however, had some powerful supporters to whom was due the spread of his doctrines. Some of these, as we have already seen, were kings and princes, like Bimbisāra and Ajātaśatru of Magadha, or his own uncle, King Cheṭaka of the Lichchhavis. The *Uvāsagadasāo* [i, 9] tells us how Cheṭaka, King of Vāṇiyagāma, under the name of Jiyasattū (= Jitaśatru), which he had assumed by way of rivalry with his enemy, Ajātasattu, was " going out to hear Mahāvīra, just as King Kūṇiya had done on another occasion ". The *Aṅguttara Nikāya* [iii, 74] tells of the great veneration in which Māhavīra was held by the learned Lichchhavi prince named Abhaya. King Bimbisāra had also a son named Abhaya Kumāra who is regarded by the Jains as their patron. But the Majjhima Nikāya (58) relates how he was put up by the Nigaṇṭha Nātaputta to a disputation with the Buddha on the basis of set questions which might confound him, but it had the opposite effect of the Buddha winning and converting Abhaya. As to Bimbisāra and Ajātaśatru, they are claimed both by the Buddhists and Jains as their supporters. The fact is that Hindu kings are always reverential to all ascetics, irrespective of their denominations. As regards Ajātaśatru particularly, a man of his political ambitions and character cared for religion only as means to secular and selfish ends. Bent on the conquest of Videha, Vṛiji, or Lichchhavi territory, as his father was on Aṅga, Ajātaśatru could not consistently carry on with the Jains whose religion was the state-religion of the Lichchhavis. He sided with their rivals, the Buddhists, whom he had previously persecuted as the favoured of his father, so that he could, with a clear conscience, war on the King of the Lichchhavis, who was at once his own grandfather and Mahāvīra s maternal uncle.

The influence of Mahāvīra penetrated into distant kingdoms through matrimonial alliances as recorded in Jaina texts. King Cheṭaka's daughter, Chellanā, was Bimbisāra's queen and was responsible for his Jain leanings. But Cheṭaka had other daughters equally well married. The eldest, Prabhāvatī, was married to King Udāyaṇa of the country of the Sindhu-Sauvīras who ruled over sixteen countries and 363 cities (*Bhagavatī*, Sūtra 49; Meyer, *Hindu Tales*, p. 97).

His second daughter, Padmāvatī, was married to King Dadhivāhaṇa of Champā. Their daughter, Chandanā, was the first Jain nun (*Kalpa-Sūtra*, Sūtra 133; also *Āvaśyaka Sūtra*). Champā early became a centre of Jainism and was frequented by several Tīrthaṅkaras. Sudharman was seen here by Ajātaśatru. His successors, Jambū, Prabhava, Sayambhava, and Vāsupūjya, were all intimately associated with this place [Hemachandra, *Pariśishṭaparvan*, Canto iv]. We are also told that Ajātaśatru made Champā his capital [ib., Canto vi].

The third daughter, Mṛigāvatī, was married to King Śatānīka of Kauśāmbī. Both king and queen were ardent Jains, together with their minister and his wife [*Āvaśyaka-Sūtra*]. The king's sister, Jayantī, was also a Jain [*Bhagavatī*, Sūtras 441–3]. There was a war between him and Pradyota. After his death, Queen Mṛigāvatī was allowed to become a nun by Pradyota through Mahāvīra's intervention. His son, Udāyana, was also recognized as King of Kauśāmbī [Hemachandra, *Trishashṭi-Śalākā*, Parva x, pp. 142–5]. We have already related the story of this Vatsa King Udayana from Sanskrit and Buddhist traditions.

A fourth daughter, Śivā, was married to Chaṇḍa Pradyota, King of Avanti, with whom Udāyaṇa of Sauvīra went to war for the recovery of an image of Jina stolen by him [Meyer, *Hindu Tales*, pp. 109–110].[1]

Thus the five daughters of Cheṭaka were the avenues of Jain influence on their respective husbands, the lords of Sauvīra, Aṅga, Vatsa, Avanti, and Magadha. This also testifies to the proud position and aristocratic rank of the Lichchhavis as a republican people as represented in their chief, Cheṭaka. While Jainism owes so much to him, and its texts are so full of him, the Buddhist texts are correspondingly silent about him.

[1] I owe to Shah's *Outlines of Jainism in Northern India* (Longmans, London) some of these facts and references, and valuable general help in utilizing some Jain texts and sources.

Republican Support.—The federal illumination in honour of Mahāvīra's death by eighteen Gaṇarājās of Kāśī and Kosala, nine Mallakis, and nine Lichchhavis, points to the extent of his influence and to that of his religion over those republican peoples. His greatest influence was with his own people, the Lichchhavis. With him it was not that a prophet is not honoured in his own country. Mahāvīra himself was regarded as its first citizen and is designated in Jain texts as simply *Vesalie* or *Vaiśālika*, while Vaiśālī is correspondingly designated as *Mahāvīra-Jananī*, "the motherland of Mahāvīra" [B. C. Law, *Kshatriya Clans*, pp. 31, 32]. Mahāvīra's own devotion to Vaiśālī is shown by his passing there twelve years out of forty-two rainy seasons of his ascetic life. We have already seen how the Jñātṛikas were devoted to Jainism, as also the Vajjis. The relations between Mahāvīra and the Mallas will be evident from the fact that he died in their country at the palace of its King Śastipāla [Stevenson, *Kalpa-Sūtra*, p. 91]. Their devotion to Jainism survived Mahāvīra. They joined the Ugras, Bhogas, Kshatriyas, and Lichchhavis in giving a reception to the twenty-second Jina [*Antagaḍadasāo*, 8th Aṅga]. The connection of Kāśī with Jainism is as old as Pārśva, as already related. The capital of Kosala, Śrāvastī, was very hospitable to Mahāvīra and was his favourite haunt.

His Chief Disciples.—But Mahāvīra, like the Buddha, was also known for his devoted disciples, some of whom attained to *Kaivalya*. We have in the Kalpa-Sūtra the names of his eleven chief disciples called *Gaṇadharas*, or Apostles of the Jain Church, who between them taught nine *Gaṇas*. In the Jain system, the *Gaṇa* denotes "the school derived from one teacher; *Kula*, the succession of teachers in one line; and the *Śākhā*, the lines which branch off from one teacher" [Jacobi, *SBE.*, xxii, p. 288 n.]. Other notable disciples are also mentioned in the Jain texts, e.g. Gardabhāli, who made a monk of a king called Sañjaya [*Uttarā*, xviii] of Kāmpilya, and the following ten disciples, the subject-matter of *Uvāsagadasāo*, viz. (1) Ānanda, the merchant prince of Vāṇiyagāma, whom even the kings and princes consulted;

(2) Kāmadeva, similarly rich, at Champā under King Jiyasattū, converted at park called Punnabhadda;

(3) Chulānipiyā converted at park Koṭṭhaga near Vārānasī;

(4) Suradeva converted at the above place;

(5) Chullasayaga converted at park Sankhavana in the town of Sāvatthī under King Jiyasattū (Prasenajit? in which case the name *Jiyasattū* should be a title of kings like *Devānāmpiya*);

(6) Kuṇḍakoliya converted in park Sahassambavana in town called Kampillapura, capital of south Pañchāla.

It is interesting to note that he was at first the follower of the Law of Maṁkhaliputta Gośāla "which says that there is no such thing as exertion or labour or vigour or manly strength but all things are unalterably fixed", but it is not so according to Mahāvīra, who held a diametrically opposed view.

(7) Saddālaputta, the potter king of Polāsapura, master of 500 potter shops (turning out "many bowls and jars of various sizes by placing on wheels clay that is first kneaded with water, and then mixed with ashes and dung"), also an Ajīvika, follower of Law of Gośāla. Gośāla tried to reconvert him, but, finding he was not cherished, tried the trick of applauding Mahāvīra as "the great Māhaṇa (= Brāhmaṇa), Guardian (*Gopa*), Guide, Preacher, and Pilot (in the ocean of life)", with whom he could not venture upon a disputation. The potter, pleased, gave him "standing provision of stool, plank, and bedding in his potter shops" for his Order, but he remained a firm Jain.

(8) Mahāsayaga, owning eight krors *kaṃsa* of gold and other properties, converted at the park Guṇasila in the city of Rāyagiha under King Seniya;

(9) Nandiṇīpiyā converted at park Kotthaga in Sāvatthī under King Jiyasattū;

(10) Sālihīpiyā of the same place.

Perhaps the best compliment to Mahāvīra and his teaching is given in the following words which the *Majjhima Nikāya* [ii, 214 ff.] puts into the mouth of the Buddha:

"There are, brethren, certain recluses, Achelakas, Ājīvikas, Nigaṇṭhas, etc., who thus preach and believe: whatsoever an individual experiences, whether it be happy or painful or neutral feeling, all has been caused by previous actions. And thus from the cancelling of old actions by *tapas*, and by abstaining from doing new actions, there is no influx into future life ; by this non-influx, *karma* is destroyed, and so ill is destroyed, and so feeling is destroyed, and so all pain will become worn away. This, brethren, is what the Nigaṇṭhas say . . . Is it true, I asked them, that you believe and declare this? . . . They replied . . . 'Our leader, Nātaputta, is all-wise . . . out of the depth of his knowledge he tells us: Ye have done evil in the past. This ye do wear away by this hard and painful course of action . . . Thus all *karma* will eventually be worn away, and all pain. To this we assent'." We have also seen how in the Buddha's time he was already recognized as Saṁghī, Gaṇī, Gaṇāchārya, Yaśasvī, Tīrthakara, Sādhusammata bahujanasya (revered as a saint by the multitude), senior to the Buddha in age, experience, and in the life of a Parivrājaka.

Some Dates in his Life.—Combining the data furnished by the *Bhagavatī* and the *Kalpa-Sūtra*, we find that Mahāvīra had lived (*a*) for thirty years as a householder, (*b*) for twelve years as an imperfect ascetic, and (*c*) for thirty years as a Kevalin or Jina. In his thirty-second year he met Gośāla, with whom he lived for another six years. He parted from him in his thirty-eighth year. After this, Gośāla spent two years in the preparatory stage before reaching Jinahood and sixteen years as a Jina when Mahāvīra was fifty-six years old. Mahāvīra lived for another sixteen years. These data give to Mahāvīra a life of seventy-two years. If his Nirvāṇa took place in 546 B.C., according to tradition, he was born in 618 B.C.

Jainism as a System of Discipline.—We are not concerned in history with Jainism as a philosophy or religion. But leaving aside its doctrines and its philosophical position on the problems of life and immortality, what it stands for as a system of discipline in its practical aspects may be gathered from a typical passage, the thirtieth lecture of the *Uttarādhyayana Sūtra* on "the Road of Penance". Jainism starts with Karma and its inevitable effects in an endless series of births and deaths, i.e. transmigration. The aim is, therefore, to annihilate karma by austerities, shutting out "the influx of bad karma". There were the five *Vows* to which is added the sixth, viz. "not eating at night"; five *Samitis* (rules regarding walking, begging, speaking, easing nature, and receiving and keeping things necessary for a monk) and three *Guptis* (for restraining body, mind, and speech) by which is to be achieved freedom from *Āśravas*, affections by Karma (*Karmopādāna-hetu*). On this foundation are to be practised the *Austerities*, both external and internal. The external includes (1) *Anaśana* (fasting); (2) *Avamodarikā* (graduated abstention from food from a full meal of thirty-two morsels to one of one morsel); (3) *Bhikshācharyā* (begging); (4) *Rasa-parityāga* (giving up dainty foods such as "milk, curds, ghee, etc."); (5) *Kāya-Kleśa* (mortification of the flesh, including different postures such as Vīrāsana, etc.); and (6) *Saṁlīnatā* (taking care of one's limbs). The *internal* austerities include (1) *Prāyaśchitta* (expiation of sins by confession and other prescribed ways); (2) *Vinaya* (humility); (3) *Vaiyāvṛitya* (service); (4) *Svādhyāya* (study); (5) *Dhyāna* (meditation); and (6) *Vyutsarga* (abandoning the body, i.e. remaining motionless in all positions). Of these, Nos. (3) and (4) are further defined with interesting details. The following persons are entitled to "Service", viz. (1) Āchārya, (2) Upādhyāya, (3) Sthavira, (4) Tapasvin, (5) Glāna (the sick); (6) Śaiksha; (7) Sādharmika. "Service" is also due to the following institutions, viz. (1) Kula, (2) Gaṇa, and (3) Saṁgha. No. (4), Study, is five-fold: (1) saying or learning one's lesson, (2) questioning the teacher about it, (3) repetition, (4) pondering, and (5) religious discourse. A sage performing these *Austerities* will be "completely released from the circle of births".

Jainism is popularly known for its extreme views regarding *ahiṁsā* and mortification of flesh. The former is based on the belief that all nature, even the most inanimate, is endowed with life and capacity for revival and leads to the position that a Jain must treat with sanctity "living beings, mildew, seeds, sprouts, flowers, eggs, lairs or caves, and moisture such as dew, hoarfrost, fog, hailstones, and damps" [Kalpa-Sūtra, §§ 44, 45]. On the other subject of mortification of flesh as a necessity for self-realization, the Jains proceed to extremes of torture, recommending nakedness and even fasting to death, and condemn the Middle Path of the Buddhists as a Path of Pleasure and Luxury. The irony of this extreme position is that there is in practice less care for the life of human beings in conduct towards them than in that of animals, animalculæ, and plants and seeds.

Jainism after Mahāvīra: Schism.—The history of Jainism after Mahāvīra is lacking in facts for a long period. There was no schism in the church in his life-time except for some opposition headed by his own nephew and son-in-law, Jamāli, and, later, by a monk named Tīsagutta. But schism reared its head soon after his death. When Ānanda hears of his death from Chuṇḍa, he exclaims: "Friend Chuṇḍa, this is a worthy subject to bring before the Exalted One" [*Dialogues*, iii, 203 f.]. We are told that after Mahāvīra's death at Pāvā, "the lay-disciples of the white robe who followed Nātaputta showed themselves shocked, repelled, and indignant at the Nigaṇṭhas" (cited at p. 108 of Shah's *Jainism in North India*).

Of his eleven apostles, Gaṇadharas, all pre-deceased him except Sudharman who succeeded Mahāvīra to the headship of the new church. The history of the church is practically a blank for the next 150 years. Jainism was favoured by the Magadhan king, Udāyin, who succeeded Ajātaśatru but was killed by a prince seeing him in the disguise of a Jain monk. The Nanda kings were also favourably inclined towards Jainism, if we may believe in the inscription of the Jain King of Kaliṅga, Khāravela by name, referring to "an idol of the first Jina" in the possession of "King Nanda". In the meanwhile, the first Pontiff Sudharman passed away in 508 B.C. and his successor, Jambu, in 464 B.C., followed by three generations of pontiffs, until about the time of the last Nanda, the church was a diarchy under two high-priests, Sambhūtavijaya, and Bhadrabāhu, the author of Kalpa-Sūtra, as already stated. The former died when Chandragupta Maurya was king, and was succeeded by his disciple, Sthūlabhadra. Soon after, Magadha was in the grip of a twelve years' famine which made Bhadrabāhu, anxious to protect his church against possible evils, lead a migration towards the south, where he settled down in the place known as Sravaṇa-Belgola. It is stated that he was also accompanied in this migration by King Chandragupta Maurya who renounced the throne and the world and embraced monkhood. When the famine ended, the emigrants returned, but the leadership of the church was passed on to Sthūlabhadra by Bhadrabāhu who retired to Nepal. This was a time of revolution for the Jain Church. The returning monks condemned those who stayed behind in Magadha as heretical and lax in discipline, because they violated the rule of nakedness and wore " white clothes ". The cleavage widened for want of the old canon which fell into oblivion. An attempt to recover and fix it was made by convoking a Council at Pāṭaliputra, but the returning monks did not join it, while the old canon comprising eleven *Aṅgas* composed by the Gaṇadharas, and fourteen *Pūrvas* (" earlier " portions composed by Mahāvīra himself) were known only to Bhadrabāhu who permitted Sthūlabhadra, when he saw him in Nepal, to teach only the first ten *Pūrvas*. The Pāṭaliputra Council thus established a fragmentary canon called *Siddhānta* containing some amount of new scriptures from which the present canon of the Śvetāmbaras may be taken to be derived. The returning monks who represented the orthodox section and were the spiritual ancestors of the Digambaras held that the true canon had been lost for ever.

Its Centres outside Magadha : Ujjain and Mathurā.—This internal difference must have considerably weakened the Jains who were losing their hold on eastern India and settling in the west. Asoka refers to the Nirgranthas as one of the principal sects of his times, but his grandson and successor, Daśaratha, favoured their rivals, the Ājīvikas, while the Jains claim as their patron the other grandson of Asoka, namely Samprati, who was ruling at Ujjain, then already a centre of Jainism.

Another Jain centre seems to have grown up at Mathurā where have been found numerous inscriptions testifying to the existence of a prosperous Jain community endowing by benefactions images and shrines dedicated to Mahāvīra and his predecessors. They also show that this community was distinctly *Śvetāmbara*, which was itself subdivided into smaller sects. The oldest of these inscriptions is dated in the ninth year of Kanishka (*c.* A.D. 87) and mentions the erection of a statue by a Jain lay-woman named Vikaṭā at the instance of her preceptor, Nāganandin, who belonged to the Koṭika (Kauṭika) *gaṇa*. This *gaṇa*, according to *Sthavirāvali*, was founded by Sthavira Susthita who died in the year 313 after Mahāvīra, i.e. in 154 B.C. Thus the inscription makes the Svetāmbara sect as old as the middle of the second century B.C. Some of the Mathurā inscriptions also refer to nuns and, therefore, point to the Śvetāmbaras who alone admit women to the Order.

Later Jain history is devoid of records except for lists of teachers and one legend, entitled *Kālakāchārya-Kathānaka* ("the story of the teacher Kālaka"), relating that Kālaka, being insulted by King Gardabhilla of Ujjain, sought the help of Śaka satraps under Sāhāṇusāhi ("king of kings", the title figuring on Kushāṇa coins in the form *Shaonano Shao*), and overthrew him. But his son, Vikramāditya, repelled the Śakas, recovered his kingdom, and established the Vikrama era in 58 B.C. This shows how the Jains settled at Ujjain in that early time and came to be associated with the Vikrama era.

Council of Vallabhī.—The next important event is the Council held in Vallabhī in Gujrāt under the presidency of Devaṛiddhi Gaṇī called the Kshamāśramaṇa. The *Siddhānta*, established long ago by the Council of Pāṭaliputra, gradually fell into disorder and was becoming extinct and so this Council was held to reduce it to order and to fix it in an authorized edition of manuscript "books". The deliberations of this Council resulted in the redaction of the Jain Canon in the form in which it is found in the present day.[1]

Rise of Buddhism: *the Śākyas.*—Buddhist legends

[1] See ch. vi of *Cambridge History*, vol. I.

represent the Buddha as the son of a king, and as one who would have become a universal king had he not renounced the world. His family is described as "a high and an unbroken Kshatriya family" [*Sutta-Nipāta*, 422–3]. This was a family of the Śākyas who, exiled from Sāketa, the capital of Kosala (as stated in the *Mahāvastu*), emigrated to a region on the slopes of the Himalayas and founded there the city of Kapilavastu. The archæological evidence furnished by the Asokan Pillar and Inscription at Lumbinī has helped in the location of the site of Kapilavastu. The Śākya State was a republic, as we have seen, and was governed by an aristocracy of nobles called Rājās. Its city is not one of the six great cities in which Ānanda wished his Master to die. And after His death, the claimants to shares of His relics included King Ajātaśatru, but no *king* of the Śākyas, but only the Śākyas, ranking equally with other republican communities like the Koliyas, Mallas, or Lichchhavis.

The Śākyas by gotra were Gautamas, just as the Mallas were Vāsishṭhas. The Buddha is addressed as an Āṅgīrasa.

They followed some non-Aryan customs, e.g. marrying within the same gotra and prohibited degree of relationship. They were in the outskirts of Vedic civilization. E. J. Thomas [*Life of Buddha*,[1] p. 23], supposes their basic population to be Kol or Muṇḍā.

The Buddha's Parents.—According to the Ceylon Chronicles, the two Śākya chiefs, Jayasena and Devadaha, had each a son and a daughter, and each had his son married to the other's daughter. The issues of each were similarly married. Thus Suddhodana, the son of Sīhahanu, grandson of Jayasena, married Māyā and Prajāpatī, the two daughters of Añjana, the son of Devadaha. The Buddha, then called Siddhārtha (and also Sarvārthasiddha), was the son of Suddhodana and Māyā, while Prajāpatī was the mother of Nanda.

His Birth and Early Life.—The date of the Buddha's birth is inferred from that of his death which, according to Sinhalese tradition took place in 543 B.C. As he lived for

[1] This erudite work I have consulted with great profit on this topic.

eighty years, he was born in 623 B.C. As already stated, this date is taken to be confirmed by certain data and dates found in the inscription of Khāravela. The date, 623 B.C., is, however, at conflict with the ascertained date of Asoka whose consecration, dated in 270 B.C., should, according to the *Ceylon Chronicles*, be dated 218 years after the Nirvāṇa, i.e. in 326 B.C.

"Queen Mahāmāyā, bearing the Bodhisatta for ten months, when her time was come, desired to go to Devadaha, the city of her family. The king approved, caused the road from Kapilavastu to Devadaha to be made smooth and adorned with vessels filled with plantains, flags, and banners, and sent her in a palanquin." On the way, in the Lumbinī grove, she stopped and seized the branch of a sāl tree, when she was "shaken with the throes of birth". Thus the Buddha was born, but seven days afterwards his mother died [*Majjhima*, iii, 118; *Nidānakathā*], and he was nursed by her stepmother and aunt, Mahāpajāpatī Gotamī, who "gave him milk and fed him from her own breast".

The Buddha's exact birth-place has been identified by the discovery of a pillar erected by Asoka in 250 B.C., with the inscription—"*hida Budhe jāte Sakyamunīti,*" "because here was born the Buddha Śākyamuni" at the place called Lumbinī (Luṁmini) in the inscription, now known as Rummindei or Rupan-dehi, in the Bithri district of Nepal, about twelve miles from the nearest railway station, Nautanwa, on B.N.W.R.

On the fifth day took place the name-giving ceremony to which were invited 108 Brahmins.

Luxury.—He grew up in luxury, using sandalwood of Benares and dress of Benares cloth, tunic under-robe and cloak, with three palaces for the three seasons built for him [*Aṅgu.*, i, 145] in his sixteenth year, and also dancing girls provided for his entertainment [*Jātaka Commentary*]. The name of his wife is variously given as Bhaddakachchā [*Buddhavaṁsa*, xxvi, 15], Bimbā [*Commentary on Jātakas* 281 and 485 and on *Mahāpadāna Sutta*], Gopā [*Lalitavistara*], and Yasodharā in the northern texts).

In the midst of luxury and the pleasures of the palace,

he felt profoundly affected by some of the features and facts of life, such as " birth, old age, sickness, death, sorrow, and impurity " [*Majjhima*, i, 163].

Birth of a son: Renunciation.—Then was born to him a son, but he thought " a bond is born ". And so it precipitated his contemplated renunciation. That very night, with a look at his son from the threshold of the chamber where his wife was sleeping, with her hand on the baby's head, he left the palace and the city on his horse Kanthaka, with his charioteer, Chhanna, clinging to its tail. This was when he was twenty-nine.

Riding beyond the territories of the Śākyas, Koliyas, and Mallas, he reaches at daybreak the town Anuvaineya of the Maineyas, six leagues away, crossing the river Anomā. There he gives his ornaments and the horse to Chhandaka, cuts off his hair, and changes his robes for yellow ones [*Lalitavistara*].

The canonical text, *Majjhima Nikāya* [i, 240], puts a simpler version of the Renunciation in the mouth of the Buddha: " Before my enlightenment, while yet a Bodhisatta, I thought, oppressive is life in a house where it is not easy to practise a full, pure, and religious life . . . While yet a boy, a black-haired youth in the prime of life, while my unwilling mother and father wept with tear-stained faces, I cut off my hair and beard and putting on yellow robes went forth from a home to a homeless life."

His First Teachers, Ālāra and Udraka, at Rājagṛiha.—His first task in this new life was to find the teacher. The necessity for a teacher is first emphasized in the Upanishads which consider self-education like the blind man's wandering. He first went to Ālāra Kālāma, seeking " the good and the supreme state of peace ". Ālāra was a sage known for his powers of concentration, because sitting on the road he did not see or hear 500 carts rattling past him [*Mahāparinibbāna Sutta*, iv, 35]. First, Gautama mastered his doctrine in the sense that he could repeat or recite it. But it was not realization of truth. This came later. It was attainment of the state of nothingness. Then the teacher set his pupil as equal to himself. But the pupil thought his attainment was not complete. It was not attainment of Nirvāṇa. So he left his teacher in further quest of Truth.

The same thing happened with his second teacher, Udraka Rāmaputra, who taught the attainment of "neither-consciousness-nor-non-consciousness".

Penances.—Then he made his way to the Magadhas, to the army-township called Uruvelā, where in a grove close to a river and a village where he could seek alms he settled down for further striving after higher knowledge. The striving took the form of a graduated course of austerities associated with Jainism,[1] by which he reduced himself to a mere skeleton, skin and bone. He regulated and restrained breathing as well as food, taking only "juice of beans, vetches, chickpeas, or pulse", such as could be held in his hollowed palm.

But this severe mortification proved equally fruitless. So he gave it up and thought of another way of enlightenment, only keeping free from "sensual desires and evil ideas". He resumed "solid food, rice, and sour milk", whereupon his five Brahmin associates, thinking that "he gave up striving, living in abundance", deserted him in disgust.

Mrs. Rhys Davids reconstructs the history of Gautama's early training thus: He begins his Quest in association with five other Parivrājakas called *Pañchavaggiyā bhikkhū*, "five-set-ter alms-men," and named Aññā Kondañña, Assaji, Vappa, Mahānāma, and Bhaddiya, who were "of great help to him" (*bahūpakarā*) in mental and moral companionship. They first began by penance or *tapas*,

[1] The Jaina author Devasenāchārya of the eighth century A.D. in his *Darśanasāra* [6–10] actually states that the Buddha started as a Jain, being ordained as Muni Buddhakīrti by the Jaina saint, Pihitāshrawa, in the Saṁgha of Śrī Pārśva at the town of Palāsha on the river Sarayu, and that, after a time, he took to eating fish and flesh, wearing red cloth, preaching his own Dharma, and saying there was no harm in taking such food [Kampta Prasad Jain in B. C. Law's *Buddhistic Studies*, p. 118]. The *Majjhima Nikāya* also refers to his "shearing off hair and beard". [ii, 5, in Sīlāchāra's translation], corresponding to the Jain practice called *Keśa-loncha-kiriyā*. The fact seems to be that the Buddha first tried the two prevailing systems of self-realization, Brahmanical (under Ālāra and Udraka) and Jain, and then developed his own. Mrs. Rhys Davids also holds that the Buddha first went to Vesālī to seek his teachers and found there Ālāra Kālāma and Uddaka and later began Jain practices [*Gotama the Man*, 22–5].

then greatly in vogue among the Jains at Vaiśālī. They also discussed the doctrines of the day, "about orderly process in nature (*prakṛiti*), in man's world way (*karma*)—this from the Nigaṇṭhas—about system in musing or Jhāna, from Ālāra and Uddaka, about the academic lay or secular training of thought (non-Brāhman) in naming, numbering, analysis (Sāṅkhya)," first taught by Kapila at Mathurā or Taxilā, and "much besides". Out of all this material Gautama hammered out a new system [*Sākya*, p. 123].

Stages of Progress.—His progress was in stages thus described: (1) First trance of joy combined with reasoning; (2) second trance of joy in which reasoning ceased; (3) third trance marked by equanimity towards joy and aversion; (4) fourth trance, "which is without pain and pleasure"; (5) remembrance of former existence "with mind concentrated, cleansed, spotless, and with defilements gone"; (6) vision of "passing away and rebirth of beings in conditions determined by their Karma"; (7) "knowledge of the destruction of the *āsavas*, viz. sensual desire (*kāma*), desire for existence (*bhava*), and ignorance (*avijjā*)"; "knowing what is pain, the cause of pain, the destruction of pain, and the way that leads to its destruction"; (8) knowledge of emancipation, realizing that "destroyed is rebirth" [*Majjhima*, i, 240 ff.].

Sujātā and Sotthiya.—This is the canonical account of Gautama's striving for Truth. The scriptures make it a six years' striving. But the period is made more eventful by later authorities. The Jātaka makes Gautama first go to Rājagṛiha, where he is received by Bimbisāra with great devotion which he does not accept in his search after Truth and its teachers. According to *Mahāvastu*, he sees Ālāra first, then Bimbisāra, and then Udraka, whose teaching he practised at Rājagṛiha. When Gautama decides to take solid food, it was Sujātā, the daughter of Senānī of Uruvelā, who gives that food according to the Jātaka. He was seen in meditation under the Banyan or Bodhi-tree to which the scriptures make no reference. The grass-cutter, *Sotthiya*, is introduced as giving him handfuls of grass on which he sat till his Enlightenment.

His First Pupils.—After Enlightenment, the Buddha thought of teaching his doctrine first to his two teachers, Ālāra, and Udraka. But they were then not living. He then thought of the five monks who did so much for him and were then in the deer-park of Isipatana near Benares. So from Uruvelā he made his way to Benares, meeting on the road, between Bodhi-tree and Gaya, the Ājīvika ascetic, Upaka, who was sceptical about his Enlightenment and went his own way. At Isipatana, he met the five monks to whom he gave his first sermon called Dharma-chakra-pravartana-sūtra in *Saṁ.*, v, 420, in which are to be found the fundamental principles of Buddhism. These may be stated as follows.

First Sermon.—A monk should avoid the two extremes " conjoined with (1) Self-torture and (2) Passions ".

He should follow the Middle Path by first grasping the four truths: (1) " the truth of pain," as manifest in " birth, old age, sickness, death, sorrow, lamentation, dejection, and despair"; (2) " the truth of the cause of pain," viz. craving for existence, passion, pleasure, leading to rebirth; (3) " the truth of cessation of pain," by ceasing of craving, by renunciation; and (4) " the truth of the way that leads to the cessation of pain," viz. the Middle Path, which is the Eight-fold Path consisting of " right views, intention, speech, action, livelihood, effort, mindfulness, and concentration."

After the sermon, the Buddha had his first disciples in the five Brahmins Koṇḍañña, Vappa, Bhaddiya, Mahānāma, and Assaji.

First Saṁgha.—His next disciples were Yasa, son of a wealthy gildmaster of Benares, his father, who became his first *upāsaka* or lay-disciple, his mother and former wife who became his first women lay-disciples, four friends of Yasa, followed by fifty, bringing a total of sixty monks with whom the Buddhist church began its work.

Bhadravargīya.—After rains the Buddha left Isipatana and returned to Uruvelā, converting on the way thirty wealthy young men with Bhadra as their leader (Bhadravargīya).

1,000 Jaṭilas.—At Uruvelā lived 500 Jaṭila (matted-haired) ascetics, fire-worshippers, under their leader Kassapa, and, down the river, his two brothers, Nadī, with 300, and Gayā, with 200, disciples. This brotherhood of 1,000 Jaṭilas was converted by the Buddha who then went with them to Rājagṛiha where King Bimbisāra and his people were surprised to see a sage of the standing of Kassapa publicly paying homage to the Buddha as his Lord.

Veluvana.—Bimbisāra made a gift of the park called Veluvana to the Buddha and his Order.

Sect of Sañjaya: Sāriputta and Moggallāna.—The next event at Rājagṛiha was the breaking up of the Order of Sañjaya with his 250 disciples and their conversion to Buddhism. The lead in the matter was taken by Sāriputta and Moggallāna who at once became the Buddha's chief disciples. The commentators make the former the son of Sārī or Śāradvatīputra who was born in the village called Upatissa. The latter was born in the village called Kolita, the son of a brahmin woman, Moggalī.

These numerous conversions created a sensation in Magadha where the people complained that " the ascetic Gotama is come to bring childlessness, widowhood, and subversion of families ".

Rāhūla and Nanda at Kapilavastu.—The next important events in his ministry took place at his own native place, Kapilavastu, where he imparted his teaching to his father and the ladies of the palace, including his wife, and made monks of both Rāhūla, his son, and Nanda, his cousin, the son of his step-mother, Gotamī, on the very day fixed for Nanda's installation as Crown Prince and for his marriage with a local beauty, named Janapada-Kalyāṇī. By the monkhood of these two boys, King Suddhodana had no other heir left for his kingdom. In great anguish, he said to the Buddha: " The love for a son, Lord, cuts into the skin, the flesh, the bones, and reaches the marrow." His case made Buddha give the ruling that no one should be admitted as a monk without his parents' consent.

Bhadrika, Anuruddha, Ānanda, Upāli, and Devadatta at Anupiya.—Further important conversions took place at Anupiya where the Buddha was staying on his way back to Rājagṛiha. There he was seen by Bhadrika (Bhaddiya), one of the Śākya kings, accompanied by Anuruddha, Ānanda, Upāli, the barber, and Devadatta, his cousin, all of whom embraced monkhood, and became famous figures in the history of Buddhism, except the last, the Buddhist Judas. The Buddha appointed Ānanda as his personal attendant.

Sudatta Anāthapiṇḍika ; his gift of Jetavana at Śrāvastī.— At Rājagṛiha he was staying at Sitāvana where he converted a merchant of Śrāvastī named Sudatta who came there on business and was much moved by the lavish entertainment given to the Buddha and his Order by his own sister, the wife of the gildmaster of Rājagṛiha. On returning to Śrāvastī, he wanted to acquire the park of Prince Jeta for the Buddha's retreat. But Jeta said it could not be bought except with as many gold pieces as could cover it. The merchant closed with the offer, but Jeta tried to back out till the case was decided against him by the law-court. Sudatta then brought carts of gold to cover the grove, amounting to eighteen koṭis, while Jeta himself contributed the cost of the gateway with a storehouse. Sudatta is known by his title, Anāthapiṇḍika, or Anāthapiṇḍada, "giver of alms to the destitute" [*Chullavagga*, p. 159 ; Fausboll's *Jatakas*, i, 92–3].

This singular gift is commemorated in stone in one of the Bharhut sculptures bearing the inscribed label : Jetavana Anadhapeḍiko deti Koṭisaṁthatena Ketā : " Anāthapiṇḍika gives away Jetavana as its purchaser for a layer of koṭis of coins." This is based on the canonical passage : " Anāthapiṇḍiko Gahapati sakaṭehi hiraññaṁ nibbāhāpetum Jetavaṅam koti-santhāram santharāpesi [ib.] : " Anāthapiṇḍika, banker, carrying gold coins in carts, covers up Jeta park by a layer of *koṭis* (of coins)."

The sculpture, translating into stone this canonical account, depicts (*a*) a cart with its bullocks released and coins (square pieces) unloaded and spread on the ground ; (*b*) the Bodhi-tree surrounded by railing and four other trees to indicate the garden (*vana*) ; and (*c*) the two cottages, the Buddha's private chambers, which are labelled as *Gaṁdha* (fragrant) *kuṭi* and *Kosaṁba* (perfumed, from *Kausumbha*, bearing the scent of *kusumbha* flower)—*kuṭi* (cottage).

Viśākhā : her gift of Pūrvārāma.—The legends [*Dhammapada Commentary*, i, 384 ; *Aṅgu. Commentary*, i, 404] tell of another great benefactress of the church from the same city, viz. Viśākhā, daughter of a gildmaster of Bhaddiya, a town of Aṅga from which he was deputed by King Bimbisāra to King Prasenajit for settlement in Kosala as a banker. On his way to Śravastī, he found a pleasant place where he spent the evening (*sāyam*) for which it was called Sāketa where he was permitted to settle by Prasenajit. Viśākhā was married to Puṇyavardhana, son of Migāra, a gildmaster of Sāketa and a follower of the naked ascetics, at whose instigation he brought charges against Viśākhā to get her out, but she disproved them and wanted to leave him when he was converted by the Buddha after a visit. Once, Viśākhā forgot to take her costly headdress left at a monastery where she was hearing the Buddha's discourse. It was kept safe by Ānanda, but Viśākhā would not take it back but put it up for sale. It was too costly for a buyer, and so it was appropriated for building a monastery at Śrāvastī called Pūrvārāma which the Buddha used as Retreat alternately with Jetavana. She further endowed the permanent supply for the monks of eight kinds of alms, viz. robe for the rains, food for an incoming or departing monk, and for his attendant, as also for a sick monk and his attendant, medicine, and gruel, and bathing-dresses for nuns.

This benefaction illustrates the spirit of humanitarianism and positivist social service inspiring early Buddhism which made for both moral and spiritual uplift of its votaries.

Within two years of the first preaching, there were thus founded three most important monasteries at Rājagṛiha, Kapilavastu, and Śrāvastī.

Order of Nuns.—The fifth year of his ministry was marked by an important event, the establishment of the Order of Nuns. The Buddha was then staying at the Pinnacled Hall (Kūṭāgāraśāla) at Vaiśālī when his father died and he returned home. He had to settle there a feud between the Śākyas

Gift of Jetavana Monastery by Anāthapindika to the Buddha [Ditto]

[To face p 252

and Koliyas regarding irrigation from the Rohiṇī and was then approached by his widowed stepmother, Mahāprajāpatī, for permission to become a nun. The permission was thrice refused by the Buddha who returned to Vaiśālī only to be followed by her "with swollen feet, and covered with dust, and weeping outside the door" till Ānanda intervened and got her the permission on condition of eight strict Rules requiring a nun always to salute a monk irrespective of her standing, and never to rebuke or abuse a monk on any pretext, not to spend Retreat in a place where there is no monk, and so forth. The Buddha, however, was careful to state that these strict Rules were necessary like dykes to check the overflow of a reservoir, but by the admission of women to the church, it would be like a house of more women than men, liable to be broken into by robbers, and where it should have lasted long, for 1,000 years, it would last now for 500 years, and not last long.

Famous Nuns.—In connection with the Order of Nuns it may not be amiss to give here its brief history. Gotamī was followed by her daughter Nandā, and Bhaddā Kachchānā, the Buddha's wife. Over seventy nuns are mentioned in the *Therīgāthā*, of whom twelve appear to be more historical and famous. Khemā, wife of Bimbisāra, was good enough to give instruction to King Prasenajit. Dhammadinnā composed a whole Sutta [*Majjhima*, i, 299]. Kisā (*Kṛiśā*, lean) Gotamī of Śrāvastī became a nun, after losing her only child, and later an Arhat.

Non-Buddhist female Ascetics.—The commentaries bring to light the existence of non-Buddhist female ascetics. The Jain girl Paṭāchara was converted by Sāriputra and became a nun. Some hostile ascetics got hold of the female ascetic (*māṇavikā*), Chiñchā, to assail the character of the Buddha. Another female ascetic (parivrājikā) named Śundarī, was similarly used by conspirators against the Buddha.

To resume now the narrative of his ministry, we have seen that during the first five years the Buddha had visited five important centres, viz. Benares, Rājagṛiha, Kapilavastu, Śrāvastī, and Vaiśālī. It is, however, difficult to determine the exact chronological sequence of the events of his forty-five years' ministry on the basis of the available records, which are not canonical but mostly commentarial. We shall mention only the typical incidents.

Vihāras at Vaiśālī.—We have referred to his visit to Vaiśālī. It has been already related how his first visit to Vaiśālī was prayed for by the whole Lichchhavi nation in order that his sacred presence might purify their city and purge it of the plague then raging there and how he was given a right royal reception by a procession of innumerable elephants and chariots. Vaiśālī provided for the Buddha's residence the Kūṭāgāraśālā, Pinnacled Hall, in Mahāvana and eight other parks, as already related, while, like Viśākhā of Śrāvastī, Vaiśāli also gave to the church benefactresses like the courtesan Ambapālī and Bālikā, whose gifts are already noticed.

Miracles Condemned.—In one of his visits to Rājagṛiha, one of his disciples tried to humiliate the six prominent leaders of non-Buddhist sects already referred to by exhibition of superhuman powers. The Buddha severely castigated him and ruled out such practices by his monks, as it would not be to the advantage of the converts or the unconverted.

Prince Bodhi of Bharga Country.—The Buddha's eighth Retreat was at the Crocodile Hill (Suṁsumāragiri) in the deer-park of the Bheskalā forest in the Bharga country, of which the chief, Prince Bodhi, gave the Buddha and his Order an entertainment in his new palace which the Buddha would not enter till the white cloth, on the steps, on which he could not tread, was removed. There he also saw the pious householder Nakulapitā and his wife whom he ranked as the chief of those that win confidence [*Aṅgu. Commentary*, i, 400].

Ghoshitārāma, gift of Vatsa King Udayana, at Kauśāmbī; Pārileyyaka forest.—The ninth Retreat at Kauśāmbī in the Vihāra called Ghoshitārāma, the gift of one of the three ministers of the Vatsa King Udayana, was marked by two important events. A Brahmin wanted to marry his proud daughter, Māgandiyā, to the Buddha as the only suitable husband for her. She was rejected and became the wife of King Udayana who had another wife, Sāmāvatī, a Buddhist lay-devotee, upon whom she avenged her insult by encompassing her death in a conflagration of the palace [*Sutta Nipāta*, iv, 9; *Dhp. Com.*, i, 199–222; *Udāna*, iv, 10]. The next event was the first schism in the church due to a monk, not confessing guilt, being expelled under rules which were challenged. The Buddha failing to settle the difference retired to keep retreat alone in the Pārileyyaka forest, away from his monks. The monks, forfeiting by their behaviour the sympathy of the city, sought out the Buddha, then at Śrāvastī, his tenth Retreat, and asked pardon [*Vinaya*, i, 337; *Jāt.*, iii, 486; *Dhp. Com.*, i, 53]. According to *Udāna* [iv, 5], the Buddha left Kauśāmbī as it was crowded with monks, nuns, lay people, and heretics.

Famine at Verañjā.—At Verañjā, his twelfth Retreat, the Brahmin Verañja, being converted, invited the Buddha and his monks to spend the rains there. But he was unable to arrange for his promised hospitality, as it was a time of famine, and he had so many other duties in his household. It was left to 500 horse-merchants to feed the monks, whereupon Moggallāna contemplated getting food by exercise of his superhuman powers, which, as usual, the Buddha could not permit [*Vinaya*, iii, 1–11; *Jāt.*, iii, 494; *Dhp. Com.*, ii, 153].

Nursing a Sick Monk.—At his fifteenth Retreat in the Nyagrodha grove at Śrāvastī, the Buddha addressed a discourse to his cousin, Mahānāman, on his succeeding to the headship of the Śākya republic after Bhaddiya becoming a monk. At this time, his father-in-law, angry at his desertion of his daughter, misbehaved towards him, getting drunk and waylaying him, but he immediately died *Dhp. Com.*, iii, 44]. Rāhula, then twenty years old, received his full ordination (*upasampadā*).

A striking story is also told of the Buddha's fellow-feeling and humanity in himself nursing a forsaken sick monk, Tissa of Śrāvastī, suffering from a skin disease and smelling foul. The Buddha with his own hands washed him in hot water and had him clothed in fresh robes and exhorted the monks thus: "You have neither father nor mother, wherefore be father and mother to one another!" [*Dhp. Com.*, i, 319].

Aṅgulimāla.—His twentieth Retreat was at Śrāvastī, where several important events took place. The first was the conversion of the bandit Aṅgulimāla, so called because he wore a "garland of fingers" severed from his victims. The Buddha met him in a forest near Chālikā and tamed his wild nature on the spot. He became a monk and sat with the Buddha when King Prasenajit came in. The king was horrified on learning that the bandit was there till he was reassured by the Buddha. Then the king offered him robes and other requisites, but Aṅgulimāla answered, "Enough, O King, I have my three robes" [*Majjhima*, ii, 98; *Dhp. Com.*, iii, 169].

Ānanda.—The second event was the appointment by the Buddha of Ānanda as his permanent personal attendant. Hitherto the Buddha was served by turns by monks carrying his bowl and robe. Once an attendant, Nāgasamāla by name, at a crossing of roads, went his own way and not the way that the Buddha wished, throwing down his bowl and robe, only to be pounced upon by robbers. At another time, the attendant, Meghiya, similarly disobeyed him to meditate in a mango-grove for which he was not considered fit for his evil thoughts. The Buddha, therefore, declared that he needed a reliable attendant in his advancing age. Sāriputta at once rose and offered his services which the Buddha did not accept, as he had other work to do. Then rose Moggallāna and the eighty chief disciples. But the Buddha chose Ānanda who was waiting in silence to be asked. Ānanda agreed under certain conditions dictated by his devotion to the Buddha. These were that he must refuse the things meant for the Buddha personally, whether fine robes, special alms, scented chamber, or personal invitation, and that he must have the privilege to accompany him going on invitation, to present people to him, to have free access to him, and to repeat to him the teaching given in his presence.

Śrāvastī.—The chronicle of the ministry breaks off at

this point. As stated in the commentary on the *Buddha-vaṁsa* which mentions these Retreats, the Buddha hereafter stayed permanently at Śrāvastī, alternating between the Vihāras of Jetavana and Pūrvārāma.

Devadatta.—Perhaps the only unpleasant phase of his career was that connected with the opposition and jealousy of his cousin Devadatta. The Devadatta legends are variously given in the different sources. Some tell of their youthful rivalries in sport and love. But the Pāli accounts start him as a follower of the Buddha who cherishes him as one of his eleven chief disciples. Only once he hints at his evil wishes [*Saṁ.*, ii, 156]. The story of his defection is given in the *Vinaya* [ii, 196] and later works [*Jāt.*, v, 333; *Dhp. Com.*, i, 133] and in fragment in the *Aṅguttara* [ii, 73; iii, 123, 402; iv, 160].

Devadatta's plan was first to win over Ajātaśatru by show of superhuman powers he had acquired in his early training. Next, he claimed the leadership of the Order which he expected the Buddha to give up in his old age. He was then seventy-two. But the Buddha was not prepared to hand over the Order even to disciples like Sāriputta and Moggallāna, much less to a "vile one" like Devadatta. Devadatta now became his open opponent and the Buddha had an Act of Proclamation issued declaring that neither he nor his Order was responsible in any way for anything done by Devadatta. He now plotted that he should kill the Buddha, and Ajātaśatru, his father, Bimbisāra. The first plot failed in spite of several attempts. The second succeeded. In the *Dīgha* [ii, 72], Ajātaśatru repents, saying: "For the sake of lordship, I deprived my righteous father, the righteous king, of life." But in the *Vinaya*, Bimbisāra himself resigns his kingdom to his son on discovering that he wanted to kill him. Then Devadatta openly promoted schism by pressing for stricter rules requiring monks to dwell only in forests, at the foot of a tree, and not under a roof, to live on alms and not to accept invitations, to wear cast-off rags and not robes given by laymen, and not to eat flesh or fish. The Buddha said these rules were permissible but not obligatory. This led Devadatta to defame the Buddha as one given to luxury, and get together with his associate, Kokālika, a following of 500 new monks from Vaiśālī. He was discoursing to the Congregation which the Buddha asked Sāriputra and Maudgalyāyana to attend. When he was tired, he asked Sāriputra to address the Congregation and himself went to sleep. He woke up to find that all his recruits were won over by Sāriputra.

Ajātaśatru.—As regards the attitude of Ajātaśatru, we have already seen how, repentant as a parricide, he sought consolation from each of the six heretical teachers, including Gośāla and Mahāvīra, and ultimately found it by approaching the Buddha under the advice of his physician Jīvaka.

Jīvaka.—This Jīvaka was an ornament of the Order both for his medical skill and devotion to the Buddha. He specialized in children's diseases and was known as Komārabhachcha. He was sent for study to Taxila by a son of Bimbisāra, Prince Abhaya, who brought him up when he was thrown away on a dust heap by his mother, the courtesan Sālavatī of Rājagṛiha. For seven years he studied medicine at Taxila, cultivating by fieldwork a direct knowledge of medicinal plants within a radius of a *yojana*. The completion of his study was announced by his teacher who said: "You have done your learning, my good Jīvaka; this will do for acquiring your livelihood." He then left for home. On the way, he treated a rich merchant's wife at Sāketa and earned a fee of 16,000 *kāhāpaṇas*. He next cured King Bimbisāra of his fistula by "one anointing", and was appointed by him as state-physician and also physician to the Buddha and his Order. He also cured a commercial magnate of Rājagṛiha by a surgical operation, making him lie down on each side for a week and on his back for another week. He earned a fee of 200,000 *kāhāpaṇas*. He was called to Benares to treat a merchant's son suffering from intestine entanglement which had to be removed by operation. He got a fee of 16,000 *kāhāpaṇas*. He was also called to Ujjenī to treat King Pajjota (Pradyota) "suffering from jaundice". He sent him a present of costly cloth which he gave to the Buddha. At this time the Buddha himself suffered from constipation. He first prescribed a fat with which his body was rubbed for a few days by Ānanda and then three handfuls of three drugged lotuses to be smelt by the patient who was also kept on liquid diet till he was cured [*Vinaya, SBE.*, xvii, pp. 171–195].

Last days and Illness.—Up to the last days of his life the Buddha kept to his full programme of travelling and preaching. In his seventy-ninth year he was at Rājagṛiha whence he proceeded to Ambalaṭṭhikā, Nālandā, and Pāṭaligrāma, where Ajātaśatru was laying the foundations of a fort for his projected conquest of the Lichchhavis on the other side of the Ganges. Here he prophesied: "As far as Āryan people resort, as far as merchants travel, this will become the chief city, Pāṭaliputra" [*Mahāparinibbāna-Sutta*]. He then went out of the city by a gate named Gotama Gate and crossed the river at the point called the Gotama Ferry and arrived at Vaiśālī. There, in the village Beluva, close by, he fell seriously ill and prophesied: "At the end of three months hence the Tathāgata will die." Leaving Vaiśāli, he passed through several villages, Bhaṇḍagāma, Hatthigāma, Ambagāma, Jambugāma, and Bhoganagara till he came to Pāvā, where he stayed in the mango-grove of Chunda, the smith, who treated him to his last meal consisting of hard and soft food and a quantity of *sūkaramaddava*, which the oldest commentators explained as "the flesh of a pig made soft and oily" but which meant "the sprout of a plant trodden by pigs, or a mushroom (*ahichchhattaka*) growing in a place trodden by pigs, or a flavouring substance" [*Udāna Com.*, i, 399]. After the meal, the Buddha had an attack of dysentery, with discharge of blood, and violent deadly pains which he controlled, and then moved on towards Kusinārā.

From Pāvā to Kusinārā.—On the way he asked Ānanda to spread a robe fourfold for a comfortable seat and to bring water to drink from the stream called Kakutthā close by. Just then 500 carts crossing the stream had made its waters muddy and turbid. But Ānanda found them clear and pure. Here he had a visitor, Pukkusa, a Malla, and a pupil of his teacher, Ālāra Kālāma, who became a lay disciple. To him the Buddha related an anecdote. Once he was at a place called Ātumā where it rained with thunder and lightning, killing two farmers and four oxen, and bringing a great crowd without his knowing why, so intense was his concentration.

After bathing in the river, the Buddha took further rest in a mango-grove where he thought that as his end was approaching, Chunda might be blamed for the meal that brought on his illness and so he left with Ānanda a message that the meal that Chunda gave was the last meal of the Tathāgata and would bring him great gain.

Last Words.—The Buddha rose and proceeded farther, crossing the Hiraṇyavatī, and reached Kusinārā where he took his last rest in a grove of sāl trees. He said: " Come, Ānanda, arrange a bed with the head to the north: I am suffering and would lie down." He was fanned by the elder Upavāṇa. He sent Ānanda to tell the Mallas of Kusinārā of his coming end and they came with their whole families and were presented to him by families and not individually, as they were too many. In the meanwhile, a local ascetic Subhadda received his last teaching. Next he asked the assembled monks to question him about any doubts they had, but all remained silent. Then he addressed to them his last words: " Now, monks, I have nothing more to tell you than this: subject to decay are all compounded things: work out your salvation with earnestness."

Last Scenes.—Among the monks was Anuruddha consoling the lamenting lay-public.

Kassapa the Great was coming along from Pāvā with his company of monks and heard of the Master's death from an Ājīvika ascetic on the way.

The Mallas assembled with scents, garlands, music and robes to do honour to the body of the Lord. After cremation they threw scented water on the relics which they protected by a fence of spears.

Then came eight claimants for share of the relics over which each promised to erect a stūpa. Their names are already stated.

Genuine Relics.—Archæological excavation has brought to light some shrines containing the relics and proved the truth of the texts. In 1898 Peppe excavated a stūpa at Piprahwa close to the Nepal border, and found in its interior stone chamber several vessels containing bones among other things. And, what is more interesting, round the rim of the lid of one stone vessel runs an inscription in Asokan characters which is read as follows: "*Sukitibhatinaṁ sabhaginikanaṁ saputadalanaṁ Iyaṁ salilanidhane Budhasa Bhagavate Sakiyanaṁ*"; "This relic treasury of the Lord Buddha—the *sukṛiti*, pious foundation, of the Śākya brethren, with their sisters, children, and wives"; implying that it was the stūpa constructed by the entire Śākya community, males, females, and children, to enshrine the sacred relics.

There is doubt about the meaning of the inscription and about its date, which may be of the time of Asoka from the script used, but the authenticity of the relics need not be doubted.

A stūpa was unearthed near Peshawar at Shah-jī-ki-dherī containing a relic-casket on the bottom of which was found a six-sided crystal reliquary in which were contained three small fragments of bone believed to be the original relics deposited in the stūpa by Kanishka which, as Yuan Chwang tells us, were the relics of the Buddha [*Arch. Sur. Rep.*, 1908–9, p. 49]. The name of Kanishka is inscribed on the casket.

A few more relics were discovered by Sir John Marshall at Taxila in 1913–14 and presented to the Buddhists of Ceylon. The relic chamber was placed six feet below the foundations of the stūpa unearthed. In the chamber were found four coins of Kings Maues and Azes I and a vase of steatite. The vase contained a miniature casket of gold shaped like an ancient dagaba of Taxila. And inside the casket was found the bone relic.

Later, Sir John Marshall discovered some more relics in a group of chapels attached to the Dharmarājikā Stūpa in the Chir Tope Mound at Taxila. In one of these was found a steatite vessel containing a silver vase in which were found an inscribed scroll and a gold casket containing minute bone-relics which, as stated in the inscription (of the year 136 of

Azes I), were the very "relics of the Holy One" (the Buddha).

Another body-relic of the Buddha has been lately recovered from the remains of a stūpa at Nagarjunikonda in Guntur district. The name Nāgārjuna is that of the founder of the Mādhyamikā school and adherent of Mahāyāna Buddhism who had lived about second century A.D. The relic was deposited in a round gold box of ¾ in. diameter. Several structures built round the stūpa bear inscriptions which describe it as the Great Stūpa (*Mahāchetiya*) "protected by the corporeal relics" (*dhātuvara-parigahita*) of the Blessed One, so that it was really erected to enshrine relics of the Lord Buddha [*Ep. Ind.*, xx, 1–37].

This relic was also in the neighbourhood of another relic which was discovered as early as 1892 in a stūpa at Bhattiprolu in the same district.

Indebtedness of Buddhism to previous Systems, Jainism, Sāṅkhya, or Yoga.—It is beyond the scope of history to deal with the doctrines, practices, and principles which distinguish Buddhism as a religion and a philosophy. It may, however, be generally noted that Buddhism is very largely the outcome of the pre-existing Brahminical thought. It was known as a New Word for the emphasis it laid on life as distinct from ritual. But even here it is anticipated by some of the Upanishads which, as we have seen, put the knowledge of the Ātman as the sole and ultimate Reality above Veda and ritual, and especially by the teachings of the Ṛishi Yājñavalkya insisting not merely on the ultimate oneness of the man with the Highest or Brahman but also on the achievement of that Oneness or self-realization as a progressive process figured as a Way (*mārga* or *yāna*) through worlds of rebirth or transmigration [*Bri. Upa.*, iv, 4, 8]. Buddhism was also anticipated in some of its features by Jainism which led it by about a generation, as we have seen. Both Jainism and Buddhism agree in stressing the possibility and need of altering by deliberate deeds (*karma*) the consequences of deeds, and also in the doctrine of *Ahiṁsā*. Buddhism is also supposed to have been very much influenced by that phase of Brahminical thought which goes by the name of Sāṅkhya of which the founder was Kapila of

Mathurā. Jacobi goes so far as to say that Buddhist philosophy is "derived from Sāṅkhya [1]". Another feature of the older conditions influencing Buddhism was the system of *Yoga* or *Dhyāna* (Pāli *jhāna*).

The Śramaṇa in Sanskrit and Pāli Texts.—Buddhism as a System of Release was also anticipated by various other Systems of Release for which India then, as now, offers a special field. The Buddhist had his forerunner in the Achelaka, the Nigaṇṭha, the Ājīvaka and others, all aiming at salvation termed *mukti, moksha, vimutti*. The man achieving it, the man at peace, was called *Śramaṇa* (Pāli *samaṇa*), "the toiler" in the original sense, but later "one who has toiled and reaped the result". The *Śramaṇa* was a social feature existing before Buddhism. The word first occurs in the *Bṛihadāraṇyaka* Upanishad [iv, 3, 22]. It is very usual in the Pāli books, and especially the expression, *Samaṇa-Brāhmaṇa,* making up the religious world of the times. The Buddha is often called Samaṇa Gotama. The term came to mean the ordinary *bhikkhu* or almsman (from *bhikkhā* = broken meats) with the derivative Sāmaṇera denoting the novice. But the original *Śramaṇa* of the Brahmin books was, as we have seen, more thoroughgoing in his renunciation. He was not the alms-fed almsman haunting the doorsteps of villages. He lived on wild roots and fruits in the forest, away from the village which he must not enter. Such a recluse was not of colder climes. He needed a climate where he could maintain himself without taking life, and not perish for want of clothing and shelter.

In the Pāli works, the Piṭakas, the *Samaṇa* had become

[1] This is an exaggerated view. There are both resemblances and differences between the two systems. The chief resemblances are (1) in the dialectic presentation of Reality, e.g. in the doctrine of *Paṭichcha-samuppāda* and the Sāṅkhyan scheme of evolution from *Prakṛiti* to the Tanmātras, Mahābhūtas, etc.; (2) in the doctrine of Evil and Impermanence (cf. "Duḥkha-trayā-bhighātāt jijñāsā-tadavaghātake-hetau" of Sāṅkhya and Buddhist "*Anichcha, Dukkha* and *Anatta*"); (3) in the Way of Release being inner discipline without references to any divine grace or teleological principle. The main differences are that the Sāṅkhya posits the duality of Subject and Object (Purusha and Prakṛiti) and Buddhism their identity and that there is no identity of concepts like the Buddhist *rūpa, vedanā,* etc., which are not known in Sāṅkhya.

less of a recluse of this type but a regular almsman. Yet he won the respect and support of the masses for his self-sacrifice that did not wait for time and age, as was usual with Brahmans. Accordingly, in the Suttas and *Vinaya*, the alms-giving of the laity to the *Samaṇa* has become an institution, but in Brahminical circles these men of the bowl were still disfavoured as having renounced social life and ties prematurely. A Brahman householder of Sāvatthī abused even the Buddha approaching him for alms in the following words: "Stay there, O shaveling, stay there, O Samaṇaka, stay there, O Vasalaka (from *vṛishala*, an outcast) [*Saṁ.*, i, 162].

Progress of Buddhism in eastern India as less Brahminical. The fact was that Buddhism was making greater headway in eastern India for its imperfect Brahmanization, or as the region where the standard and prestige of Brahmanical culture were lower than in the western parts of northern India. And hence we can believe in the strictures passed, for instance, by the Tevijja Suttanta [*Dīgha*, xiii] on the average moral conduct among Brahmans, or by the Sagātha Vagga [*Saṁyutta-Nikāya*] on their muttering (*japanā*) of mantras for fees. Perhaps even in the east there was a minority thus lax and unworthy. The *Saṁyutta-Nikāya* [i, 171] refers to Brahmans tilling their farms and estates without the opprobrium attaching to such conduct which was fit for the Vaiśya. But the ideally good man was still called a Brahman in the Buddhist texts and even in Asoka's edicts, while the term was still holding its own and alternating with the new term, *Arahan*, indicative of the highest saintliness.[1]

The Buddha as a Man.—We may now in conclusion attempt an estimate of the greatness of the Buddha as a man, and not as the founder of a religion followed by more than a fifth of the human race. We can make an estimate of that greatness on the basis of some of the sayings attributed to him, or anecdotes told about him in the texts compiled after his death.

Stages in his Life.—The Buddha was married at sixteen.

[1] See *Sakya or Buddhist Origins* [ch. ii] by Mrs. Rhys Davids.

His only son was born after more than twelve years of married life. He renounced the world when he was enjoying it most, at twenty-nine. He spent six years in a life of uttermost austerities, achieving Buddhahood or Enlightenment at thirty-five. From thirty-five up to his death at eighty, for a period of forty-five years, he gave himself completely to active social service and ministry.

Initial Weaknesses.—The Buddha, like the lotus, blossomed into perfection out of the ordinary conditions of life. He was not initially above the ills which flesh is heir to. He did not, like ordinary men, find renunciation and asceticism at all easy. He himself confessed: "I also, ye monks, before I had attained Enlightenment . . . myself subject to birth, growth and decay, sickness and death, pain and impurity, sought after what also is subject to these, viz. wife and children, slaves male and female, goats and sheep, fowls and swine, elephants, cattle, horses, mares, gold, and silver! . . . How if I seek the birthless, ageless, diseaseless, deathless, and the stainless incomparable surety, the extinction of illusion! And, ye monks, after some time, while still in my first bloom, shining, dark-haired, in the enjoyment of happy youth, in the first years of manhood, against the wish of weeping and wailing parents, with shorn hair and beard, clothed in ragged raiment, I went forth from home to homelessness." And again: "Before my full Awakening, I clearly perceived the wretchedness of desires but not finding happiness or aught better outside of desires and evil things, I knew not to turn away from following after them" [*Majjhima*, i, 91 ff.].

Mendicant's Meal.—His first meal as mendicant he could hardly eat. "His stomach turned and he felt as if his inwards were on the point of coming out by his mouth, for in that existence he had never before so much as seen such fare," till by self-admonition he overcame his feeling of "distress at that repulsive food".

Fear of Solitude.—His next problem in this new life was its solitude and the fear of it. He himself thus describes it: "How hard to live the life of the lonely forest-dweller . . . to rejoice in solitude. Verily, the silent groves must bear heavy upon the monk who has not yet won to fixity of mind! . . . He is seized with mortal fear and terror" to overcome which he would "go forth to the lonely tombs in the woods, out under the trees and abide the night through in those places of horror and affright . . . And, as I tarried there, a deer came by, a bird caused a twig to fall, and the wind set all the leaves whispering; and I thought: 'Now it is coming—that fear and terror . . . but I neither stood still, nor sat, nor lay down until, pacing to and fro, I had mastered that fear and terror.'"

Paul Dahlke well remarks [*Buddhist Essays*, p. 15]: "Never before did founder of religion speak like this. One who thus speaks needs not allure with hopes of heavenly joy. One who speaks like this of himself attracts by that power with which the Truth attracts all who enter her domain."

Daily Routine.—His life of ministry for nearly half a century was a life of strenuous work following a strict time-table of daily duties. Rising early morning, washing and dressing himself, he meditated and then went out for alms, bowl in hand, alone or with his followers. Taking his meal with some hospitable host, he gave a discourse and returned to his retreat, waiting to hear if all his disciples had taken their meals. Then he would suggest to them topics for meditation and retire for "meditation during the noon-day heat" [*Saṁ.*, i, 146–8]. The afternoon was given to public discourse followed by evening bath, meditation, discourse to his monks, and retirement for meditation and sleep [from account of Buddhaghosa as given in Rhys Davids' *American Lectures*].

A Beggar before whom Kings bowed.—He behaved like an ordinary monk all through his life. "In the days when his reputation stood at its highest point, and his name was named throughout India among the foremost names, one might day by day see that man, before whom kings bowed themselves, walking about, alms-bowl in hand, through streets and alleys, from house to house, and without uttering any request, with downcast look, stand silently waiting until a morsel of food was thrown into his bowl"

[Oldenberg]. Once at Ālavī, in the Siṁsapā forest, he was found resting on the cattlepath upon a couch of leaves in deep meditation, while it was bitterly cold winter and frosting: "rough is the ground trodden by the hoofs of the cattle; thin is the couch of leaves; light the monk's yellow robe; sharp the cutting winter wind," and yet the Master said: "I live happily, with sublime uniformity." [From a Sutta of the *Aṅguttara*.]

Superhuman in Humility.—His humility, utter and sincere, was itself superhuman. Once, "at the annual final Assembly of the monks, before the time of wandering began, the Exalted One looked round over the silent company and said to the monks: 'Well, ye disciples, I summon you to say whether you have any fault to find with me, whether in word or in deed' [*Saṁ.*, i, 190]. Again, when a Brahman asked him, 'Does the honoured Gotama permit sleeping in the day time?' the Buddha's frank answer was: 'In the last month of summer, after the meal, when one has returned from the begging round, I confess to lying down upon the right side, upon the cloak, folden in four, and, with collected senses, falling asleep.'" He is always careful to disclaim any superhuman virtues: Once he says to his disciples, 'It is lack of understanding and insight into the Four Holy Truths that is to blame, O Brothers, that we —both you and I—so long have travelled the dreary road of *saṁsāra*.' We irresistibly feel: 'This is the highest; farther can no man go!'" [Dahlke].

Detesting Divination.—Thus, as we have already seen, he did not permit exhibition of superhuman powers by his monks. "It is because," says he, "I perceive danger in the practice of mystic wonders that I loathe, and abhor, and am ashamed thereof" [*Kevaddha Sutta*]. All kinds of "divination, sooth-saying, foretelling, or forecasting", he condemns as "low arts" [*Brahmajāla Sutta*].

More anxious for Truth than Followers.—Therefore he was anxious that the Truth should spread and not that his followers should increase. He was anxious that "the bad things should be put away, things that are corrupting, entailing birth renewal, bringing suffering, resulting in ill, making for birth, decay, and death in the future; that the things that make for purity shall grow, so that full and abounding insight may be attained even here and now"—" and not because I wish to gain pupils." Thus he could say to an intending convert: " Let him who is your teacher be your teacher still." He asked Uruvelā Kassapa, revered by " all the people of Aṅga and Magadha ", and the leader of 500 Jaṭilas at Rājagṛiha, " to go first and inform them of his intentions " before changing to Buddhism [*Mahāvagga*, i, 18, 20]. Before permitting the Lichchhavi general, Sīha, to be his disciple, he desired him not to withdraw his support from his quondam co-religionists, the Nātaputtas or Nirgrantha Jains, lest they should be left helpless [ib., vi, 31, 11].

Impatient of Praise by Pupils.—He could not stand his own praise by his disciples, however devoted and sincere. Once his favourite pupil, Sāriputta, burst out: " Such faith have I, Lord, that methinks there never was nor will be nor is now any other greater or wiser than the Blessed One." The Buddha replied to this emotional outburst in his usual quiet and humorous manner: " Of course, Sāriputta, you have known all the Buddhas of the past? " " No, Lord," said Sāriputta. " Well then, you know those of the future? " " No, Lord." " Then at least you know me and have penetrated my mind thoroughly." " Not even that, Lord." " Then why, Sāriputta, are your words so grand and bold? " [*Mahāpari*. i, 61].

Unmoved by Slander.—He was equally unmoved by blame or slander. The Lichchhavi chief, Sunakkhatta, " unable to live the holy life under the Buddha," deserted the Order and went about Vaiśālī " proclaiming to all and sundry that the Blessed One has no knowledge of the things that lie beyond the ken of ordinary mortals, that his doctrine was a product of mere reasoning, a thing of his own wit's devising," and so forth [*Majjhima*]. Sāriputta reported this to the Buddha who only said that Sunakkhatta " had said this thing only of his anger ". His teaching was: " Who doth not, when reviled, revile again, a two-fold victory wins ": " Abuse that is not answered is like the food rejected by the guest which reverts to the host."

His one thought was how to make people realize the Truth that would end all suffering. He used to say: "Let a man of intelligence come to me, honest, candid, straightforward; I will instruct him . . . and if he practise according as he is taught, then to know for himself and to realize that supreme religion and goal, for the sake of which clansmen go forth from the household life into the homeless state, will take him only seven days" [*Dīgha*, iii, 56].

Control over Assemblies.—The Buddha's greatness is also brought out in the debates and discourses marking every day of his ministry. There was perfect order in his Assemblies. King Ajātaśatru, led by his physician, Jīvaka, to one such Assembly prolonged into a full moon night, fearing its silence, said: "You are playing me no tricks, Jīvaka? You are not betraying me to my foes? How can it be that there should be no sound at all, not a sneeze, nor a cough, in so large an Assembly, among 1,250 of the brethren?" Looking on the Assembly seated in silence, calm as a clear lake, the king sighed: "Would that my son, Udāyi Bhadda, might have such calm!" [*Dīgha*, ii].

Superiority in Debate.—His controversial method was to put his opponent on the defensive. Nigrodha, the leader of 3,000 disciples, tried to outwit him, thinking that for his seclusion "his insight was ruined, he is not at home in conducting an Assembly, nor ready in conversation, but occupied only with the fringes of things", and asked him to expound his doctrine. The Buddha said it was difficult "for one of another view, without practice or teaching, to understand" it, but, "Come now, Nigrodha, ask me a question about your own doctrine." By this question, Nigrodha was dumbfounded. The Buddha himself said: "That in disputation with anyone whatsoever I could be thrown into confusion or embarrassment—there is no possibility of such a thing; and, because I know of no such possibility, on that account it is that I remain quiet and confident." And to Sāriputta he further said: "And, when ye shall carry me hither upon a bed, the intellectual vigour of the Perfect One will remain unabated."

Greatness at Death.—The truth of this remark is amply

borne out by the scenes at his death-bed. To weeping Ānanda he calmly said: "Be of good cheer, Ānanda. Do not weep. Have I not told you oftentimes that this is the regular course of things, that we must part from all that is precious and dear to us?"

Last Words.—Great in life, the Buddha was greater in death. The founder of a System found no place in it for himself. When questioned in his dying moments by Ānanda for instructions for the Order, he answered: "The Tathāgata thinks not that it is he who should lead the brotherhood or that the Order is dependent upon him. Why then should he leave instructions in any matter concerning the Order?" And then came his classical declaration:

"Therefore, O Ānanda, be ye lamps unto yourselves. Be ye a refuge to yourselves. Betake yourselves to no external refuge. Hold fast to the Truth as a lamp. Hold fast as a refuge to the Truth. Look not for refuge to any one besides yourselves."

And then when the question of honouring his memory arose, he said in the same spirit: "The brother or sister who continually fulfils all the greater and lesser duties, who is correct in life, observing the precepts—it is he who rightly honours him with the worthiest homage." And when Ānanda asks the dying Buddha, "What are we to do, Lord, with the remains of the Tathāgata?" he answered: "Hinder not yourselves, Ānanda, by honouring the remains of the Tathāgata. Be zealous, I beseech you, Ānanda, in your behalf! Devote yourselves to your own good! Be earnest, be zealous, be intent on your own good! And after I am gone, let the Truths and Rules of the Order which I have set forth and laid down for you all be the Teacher to you!"

A Contemporary Opinion.—The contemporary opinion about him is thus summed up by the Brahman, Soṇadaṇḍa, in a public speech:—

"Truly, sirs, the venerable Gotama is well-born on both sides, of pure descent, and with no reproach in respect of birth.

"He has gone forth into the religious life, giving up the

great clan of his relations, much money and gold, and treasure.

"He is handsome, pleasant to look upon, inspiring trust, gifted with great beauty of complexion, fair in colour, fine in presence, stately to behold.

"He has a pleasant voice and a pleasing delivery, gifted with a polite address, distinct and not husky, suitable for making clear the matter in hand.

"He is the teacher of the teachers of many, one who puts righteousness in the forefront of his exhortations to the Brāhman race.

"Of him people come right across the country from distant lands to ask questions, and he bids all men welcome, is congenial and conciliatory, not supercilious, accessible to all, not backward in conversation.

"Whereas some Samaṇas and Brahmans have gained a reputation by all sorts of insignificant matters ("such as by wearing the clothes," etc.), his reputation comes from perfection in conduct and righteousness.

"And he is trusted, honoured, and venerated by the King of Magadha, Seniya Bimbisāra, King Pasenadi of Kosala, and even by the leading Brahman teacher Pokkharasādi, with their children and wives, their people and courtiers or intimates" [*Sonadaṇḍa Sutta*].

Magadha after Ajātaśatru.—The names of kings after Ajātaśatru and the years of their reigns are differently given in different sources, Ceylonese (Dīpavaṁsa and Mahāvaṁsa), Burmese, Nepalese (Aśokāvadāna), Jaina (Pariśishṭaparvan of Hemachandra), and Brahmanical (the Purāṇas). We shall deal with the kings as listed in the Buddhist sources, following Geiger [*Mahāvaṁsa*, English translation, Intro., pp. xl-xlvi] who takes them to be more reliable. The following were the successors of Ajātaśatru :—

(1) **Udayabhadra,** who, according to Mahāvaṁsa, reigned for sixteen years, i.e. up to 503 B.C. Jain texts (*Kathā Kosha*, p. 177) describe him as the son of Kūṇika by his wife Padmāvatī. Buddhist tradition represents Udāyibhadda, son of Ajātaśatru, as a parricide like his father, while Jain tradition takes an exactly opposite view and

even goes so far as to state that he was overwhelmed with grief at the death of his father whom he was serving as his Viceroy at Champā [Hemachandra, *Parishishṭaparvan*, VI, vv. 32–180; *Trishashṭi-śalākā*, X, v. 426; Tawney's *Kathākosha*, p. 177; *Āvaśyaka-Sūtra*, p. 687 (*Koṇikaḥ . . . mṛitaḥ . . . tadā rājāna Udāyinaṁ sthāpayanti*)]. He transfers himself from Champā to Pāṭaliputra, to the development of which he made an important contribution. The *Vāyu Purāṇa* even describes Udāyi as the builder of a new Pāṭaliputra called Kusumapura [Pargiter, *Dynasties*, p. 69]. As usual, the Jains give both Ajātaśatru and Udāyibhadda a good character presumably for their faith in Jainism, the reason why their character is blackened by the Buddhists. The *Āvaśyaka-Sūtra* (p. 689) tells us that Udāyi had a Jaina shrine (*chaityagṛiha*) constructed in the heart of the capital (*nagara-nābhau*), and that he was also as an orthodox Jain observing fast (*paushadhaṁ karoti*) on eighth and fourteenth *tithis* (ib., p. 690). On one such day, a teacher came to the palace to give him a discourse, accompanied by a novice who, with his concealed dagger, murdered the king! This was the result of a plot engineered by the king of Avanti on behalf of the son of another king whom Udāyin had defeated and killed in a battle [ib.]. It was thus a hereditary hostility between the Magadha and Avanti kings. This king of Avanti was Pālaka, the son of his father's enemy, Pradyota, who extended his power by annexing Kauśāmbī kingdom [*Kathā-saritsāgara*, Tawney's tr., ii, 484]. The Jain texts tell us that the king of Ujjain was many times defeated by Udāyin [*Āvaśyaka Sūtra*, p. 690].

One of the Patna statues in the Bhārhut Gallery of the Indian Museum in Calcutta has been supposed by Mr. K. P. Jayaswal as a statue of Udāyi from its inscription read by him as "*Bhage Acho chhonidhiśe*", *Acho* being = *Aja*(*ya*), the name given in the *Bhāgavat Purāṇa* for Udāyi. The reading is doubtful. Cunningham read it as "*Yakshe Achusanigika*", and R. P. Chanda, "*Bha*(?)*ge Achachha-nīvika*, i.e. Bhagavān Akshatanīvika, the god possessing inexhaustible treasure, the god of wealth known as Kubera Vaiśravana.

The Purāṇas represent **Darśaka** as the successor of Ajātaśatru and assign to him a reign of twenty-five years.

(2) **Anuruddha** and

(3) **Muṇḍā,** reigning for eight years, i.e. up to 495 B.C. The *Aṅguttara* [iii, 57–63] mentions him as living at Pāṭaliputra with his wife Bhaddā at whose death he would not cremate her body in grief until he was consoled by a *thera* named Nārada who lived in the monastery of Kukkuṭārāma referred to by Yuan Chwang [*Watters*, ii, 98, 99; also *Saṁ.*, v, 171; *Aṅgu.*, v, 342; *Majjhi.*, i, 350].

(4) **Nāgadāsaka,** with a reign of twenty-four years up to 471 B.C. He may be identified with the King Darśaka of the Purāṇas, whose reality is attested by the Sanskrit drama, *Svapna-Vāsavadattā*, attributed to Bhāsa.

(5) **Susunāga,** with a reign of eighteen years ending in 453 B.C.

According to Ceylon Chronicles, he was an *amātya* (minister) and was placed on the throne by the people rebelling against the dynasty of parricides from Ajātaśatru to Nāgadāsaka.

The Purāṇas which call him Śiśunāga mention two important facts about him. He destroyed the fame of the Pradyotas of Avanti and took up his abode at Girivraja, placing his son at Vārāṇasī. As we have seen, the historical hostility between Avanti and Magadha dates from the days of Ajātaśatru [*Majjhi.*, iii, 7], and was not known in the time of Bimbisāra, while Vārāṇasī which, according to the Purāṇas, was a part of Magadha under Śiśunāga, was annexed to Magadha by Ajātaśatru. On these two grounds, the Purāṇas appear to be wrong in making Śiśunāga a predecessor of Bimbisāra and Ajātaśatru. The theory of his priority on the ground of his association with the older capital, Rājagṛiha, may be answered by the fact that he posted himself there to meet the menace to that part of Magadha from Avanti, just as he had posted his son at Benares to secure the other frontier of his kingdom. Probably the kings of Magadha in those days alternated between the two capitals, Rājagṛiha and Pāṭaliputra, to deal with the menace of Avanti and Lichchhavi respectively.

The Purāṇas mention **five Pradyotas:** Pradyotana,

Pālaka (Gopālaka in another text), Viśākhayūpa, Janaka (Ajaka in *Vāyu* ; Sūryaka in *Matsya* ; Rājaka in *Bhāgavata*), and Nandivardhana (also Vartivardhana) who was the adversary of Śiśunāga. A son of Pālaka is called Avantivardhana (= Nandivardhana?) in the *Katha-sarit-sāgara* [Tawney, ii, 485].

(6) **Kālāsoka,** reigning for twenty-eight years up to 425 B.C. He is called Kākavarṇa in the *Purāṇas* and Kākavarṇin in *Aśokāvadāna*.

(7) His ten sons, jointly reigning for twenty-two years, i.e. up to 403 B.C.

There must have been some revolution at the palace at this time, glimpses of which are preserved in two sources, Sanskrit and Greek. Bāṇa's *Harshacharita* states that Kākavarṇī Śaiśunāgi was killed by a dagger thrust into his throat in the neighbourhood of his city. This incident may be referred to in the statement of Curtius that "the father of 'Agrammes' was a barber who became the paramour of the queen and being "by her influence advanced to too near a place in the confidence of the reigning monarch", treacherously murdered him, "and then, under the pretence of acting as guardian to the royal children, usurped the supreme authority and having put the young princes to death begot the present king." [1]

The "young princes" in this account may be taken to correspond to the ten sons of Kālāsoka-Kākavarṇī.

The murderer of Kālāsoka must have been the founder of the next dynasty of kings, that of Nine Nandas. The *Mahābodhivaṁsa* calls him Ugrasena whom Curtius describes as "the father of Agrammes". Agrammes, therefore, was the son of Ugrasena, i.e. an *Augrasainya* corresponding to Greek "Agrammes".[2]

[1] Diodorus gives a somewhat different version of the incident : "The King of the Gandaridai (i.e. King Nanda) was a man of quite worthless character, and held in no respect, as he was thought to be the son of a barber. This man, the king's father, was of a comely person, and of him the Queen had become deeply enamoured. The old king, having been treacherously murdered by his wife, the succession had devolved on him who now reigned" [xvii, 93].

[2] This is the suggestion of Dr. H. C. Ray Chaudhuri in his *Political History of Ancient India* to which the present chapter of the work is

The Greek statement that the first of the Nandas was a barber is also confirmed by both Jaina and Brahminical traditions. The *Pariśishṭaparvan* (p. 46) regards Nanda as the son of a barber by a courtesan, while the Purāṇas describe him as being born of a Śūdra woman.

The ten sons of Kālāsoka are named in the *Mahābodhi-vaṁsa* as (1) Bhadrasena; (2) Koraṇḍavarṇa; (3) Maṅgura; (4) Sarvañjaha; (5) Jālika; (6) Ubhaka; (7) Sañjaya; (8) Koravya; (9) Nandi-vardhana; and (10) Pañchamaka.

Of these, No. (9), **Nandi-vardhana,** has been the subject of some recent controversial speculation.

He is named also in the Purāṇas as a predecessor of the Nandas.

His historicity is sought to be further confirmed by attempted readings of the second line of the inscription found on the headless Patna statue already referred to. Mr. Jayaswal's reading is: "*Sapa* (or *Sava*) *khate Vaṭa Naṁdi.*" He connects *Vaṭa Naṁdi* with the forms Nandi-vardhana, and Vartivardhana (the *Vāyu* Purāṇa name of Nandi-vardhana Pradyota). The late Dr. Haraprasad Śāstrī made the further ingenious suggestion that Vaṭa Naṁdi meant Vrātya Naṁdi and confirmed his suggestion by the fact that the statue showed the particular features of dress prescribed for the Vrātya Kshatriya by Kātyāyana. The Purāṇas again describe the Śiśunāga kings as "Kshatra-bandhus", i.e. Vrātya-Kshatriyas.

Mr. R. P. Chanda gives a different reading of the inscription: "*Yakha sa(?)rvaṭa naṁdi*"; and suggests that the statue is that of a Yaksha called Sarvatra-Nandi.

(8) **Nine Nandas** reigning for twenty-two years, i.e. up to 381 B.C. The Purāṇas, which also agree as to the nine Nandas, assign 100 years to them. If, as has been already shown, the first Nanda had become king at twenty, i.e. in 403 B.C. the nine Nandas should have ruled for eighty years,

indebted. The *Cambridge History of India*, vol. I (p. 469), however, still holds to the old view that Agrammes, or Xandrames, as Diodorus calls him, is to be identified with the last Nanda known as Dhana-Nanda, while the very form Nandrus is found in the text of Justin. But this does not take into account the tradition representing the *father* of Agrammes as an assassin and usurper. Dr. Ray Chaudhuri's supposition is, therefore, more tenable.

i.e. up to 323 B.C., which is curiously enough the very date arrived at for the sovereignty of their successor, Chandragupta Maurya, on the basis of quite different sets of data.

The Nine Nandas are named in the *Mahābodhivaṁsa* as (1) Ugrasena; (2) Paṇḍuka; (3) Paṇḍugati; (4) Bhūtapāla; (5) Rāshṭrapāla; (6) Govishāṇaka; (7) Daśasiddhaka; (8) Kaivarta; and (9) Dhana.

The Purāṇas name the father and only one of his eight sons, viz. Sumālya, or Sumātya. The father is named **Mahāpadma Nanda.** The *Bhāgavata* Purāṇa dubs him Mahāpadma-pati, "the lord of Mahāpadma," which the commentator takes to mean "sovereign of an infinite host or immense wealth", *Mahāpadma* signifying 100,000 millions [Wilson's *Vishnu Purāṇa*, iv, 184].

This is in keeping with the Greek account of his army. Curtius credits the first Nanda king called Agrammes (= Augrasainya) with an army of 20,000 cavalry, 200,000 infantry, 2,000 four-horsed chariots, and 3,000 elephants.

He is described in the Purāṇas as "a second Paraśurāma or Bhārgava, as the exterminator of all Kshatriyas, and as the sole sovereign (*Eka-rāṭ*) who brought the whole earth under the one umbrella of his authority (*eka-chchhatra*)".

The contemporary Kshatriya dynasties of the period mentioned in the Purāṇas were, as we have seen, the Aikshvākus, Pañchālas, Kāśīs, Haihayas, Kaliṅgas, Aśmakas, Kurus, Maithilas, Śūrasenas, and Vītihotras.

The Greeks also heard of powerful peoples beyond the Beas ruled by one sovereign, the king of "the Gangaridae, and the Prasii", with his capital at Pāṭaliputra. The Gangaridae were, according to Megasthenes, the people occupying the delta of the Ganges and the Prasii, *Prāchyas*, or Easterns, were the peoples to the east of the Middle Country such as the Pañchālas, Śūrasenas, Kosalas, and the like.

Jain texts also know of nine Nandas [*Āvaśyaka-Sūtra*, p. 693 (*navame Nande*)]. They also describe Nanda as the son of a courtesan by a barber [ib., p. 690 (*nāpitadāsa . . . rājā jātaḥ*]. But they omit kings between Udāyin and the nine Nandas. Perhaps they omit them as nonentities.

The caste of the Nandas perhaps explains their leanings towards Jainism. Barring the first Nanda, the Jains have nothing to say against the other Nandas. The Nanda kings had Jain ministers. The first of them was Kalpaka upon whom the office was forced. It is stated that it was this minister who was the chief support of King Nanda in the prosecution of his military programme for the extermination of all the Kshatriya dynasties of the times. The ministers of the later Nandas were his descendants [ib., 691–3]. The minister of the ninth Nanda was Śākaṭāla. He had two sons, Sthūlabhadra and Śrīyaka. After his father's death, the king offered Sthūlabhadra the ministership, but he declined it and became a Jain monk under the sixth Jina [ib., 435–6, 693–5]. It was then given to his brother Śrīyaka.

The tradition of the Jains about their influence on the Nandas is recognized in the later Sanskrit drama, *Mudrā-Rākshasa*, in which Chāṇakya selects a Jain as one of his chief agents. Jain influence is a factor in the social background of the drama.

The Hāthigumphā inscription of Khāravela confirms Nanda's sovereignty of Kaliṅga. One passage refers to him as Nanda-rājā associated with an aqueduct which had remained unused for 300 (or 103?) years until it was conducted into the city by Khāravela in the fifth year of his reign. Another passage is to the effect that King Nanda carried away as trophies to Magadha the statue (or footprints) of the first Jina and heirlooms of the Kalinga kings.

The Nandas were also notorious for their riches, avarice, and unpopularity associated with their obnoxious origin, their status as Śūdras. The Buddhist tradition about their riches and exactions is thus given by Turnour [*Mahāvaṁsa*, p. xxxix]: " The youngest brother was called Dhana Nanda, from his being addicted to hoarding treasure . . . He collected riches to the amount of eighty *koṭis* in a rock in the bed of the river (Ganges). Having caused a great excavation to be made, he buried the treasure there . . . Levying taxes, among other articles, even on skins, gums, and stones, he amassed further treasure which he disposed of similarly." This story is hinted at even in a Tamil poem referring to the wealth of the Nandas "which having accumulated first in Pāṭali hid itself in the floods of the Ganges" [Aiyangar's *Beginnings of South Indian History*, p. 89]. The tradition of Nanda's riches is recorded also by Yuan Chwang who refers to five topes at Pāṭaliputra representing "the five treasures of King Nanda's seven precious substances" [Watters, ii, 96]. The *Kathā-sarit-sāgara* refers to King Nanda's possession of 990 millions of gold pieces [Tawney, i, 21].

The report about the military strength and unpopularity of the Nanda King reached Alexander through an Indian chief called Phegeus or Phegelas. It was corroborated by King Poros of the Punjab, who "added that the king of the Gandaridai was a man of quite worthless character and held in no respect, and he was thought to be the son of a barber" [*Diodorus* already cited]. According to Plutarch, Androkottos, i.e. Chandragupta Maurya, also reported that the Nanda king was "hated and despised by his subjects for the wickedness of his disposition and the meanness of his origin."

The Purāṇas dub the Nandas as irreligious (*adhārmikāḥ*).

Thus the conditions were getting ripe for another revolution to rid the country of the abuses of an evil administration.

Foreign Invasions.—India, during this period, witnessed two foreign invasions, Persian, and Macedonian, though they were separated by an interval of about two centuries.

Persian Invasion.—Since the dawn of history, Persia and India have had close relations reflected in their respective sacred works, the Avesta and the Rigveda, as already related. Both works contain references indicative of common borderlands or Indo-Iranian domains. Such are the Rigvedic references to the Rivers Kubhā, Krumu, or Gomatī, or to the district called Gandhāra and to the people called the Mūjavants. References to Persia are read by some scholars in certain Rigvedic terms like Pārthavas [vi, 27, 8], Parśavas [x, 33, 2], or Balhika, found in the Atharvaveda [v, 22, 5. 7. 9]. The Avesta in its turn shows equal familiarity with India which it calls *Hindu*, derived from the Sanskrit word *Sindhu*, denoting both the river, and the country it marks out. It even hints at some kind of hold on the Panjab named *Hapta-Hindu*, the region of *Sapta-Sindhavas* (seven rivers) of the Rigveda [viii, 24, 27], and described as one of the sixteen regions of the Avestan world in the first chapter of the Vendīdād, while in another passage [Yasht, x, 104] the Avestan deity, Mithra, is described as smiting sinners from "Western India" to "Eastern India", and in a third passage [Yasna, lvii, 29] the same extent of authority is attributed to Sraosha, the protecting god of mankind.

These earlier relations were reinforced by commercial relations between the two countries.

By sixth century B.C. we come to definite political relations between them. They were due to the eastern conquests of Cyrus (558–530 B.C.) which included the district called Gandaritis or Gandhāra (Herodotus, i, 153 and 177]. It is even stated that Cyrus died from wounds received in a battle with "the Indians" [*Ctesias*, fragment, 37, ed. Gilmore]. According to Xenophon [*Cyropaedia*, i, 1, 4], Cyrus "brought under his rule Bactrians and Indians", and extended his sway up to the Erythraean Sea, i.e. the Indian Ocean. He further records [ib., vi. 2, 1–11] the despatch to Cyrus by an Indian king of an embassy conveying money, probably in payment of tribute.

No extension of the Persian advance into India is recorded in the time of the next King Cambyses, but for the reign of Darius (522–486 B.C.] we have documents proving the actual extent of his Indian conquests. In his Bahistun Rock inscription (*c.* 520–518 B.C.), India does not figure in the list of his twenty-three provinces given, but in his two later inscriptions at Persepolis (518–515 B.C.), and at Naksh-i-Rustam (515 B.C.), *Hi(n)du* or Panjab *does* figure as a part of his dominion. Therefore, this Indian conquest of Darius must have taken place about 518 B.C.

Herodotus [iii, 94] also states that India counted as the twentieth satrapy of the empire of Darius, to which, however, it contributed a third of its revenue, 360 talents of gold-dust, equivalent to over a million pounds sterling. All this gold must have come from the washings of the

Indus beds which, according to geologists [V. Ball in *IA.*, August, 1884], were distinctly auriferous in those days, and also from what Herodotus calls "the gold-digging ants" supposed to be Tibetan mastiffs digging up gold.

Herodotus [iv, 44] also tells of a naval expedition despatched by Darius in 517 B.C. under Scylax to explore the Indus. This was only possible after Darius had established his hold on the Indus region.

The next emperor, Xerxes (486–465 B.C.), utilized his Indian provinces to secure an Indian contingent to fight his battles in Greece. It comprised "Gandharians" as well as "Indians". The former bore bows of reed, and short spears for fight at close quarters, while the latter, clad in cotton, also bore similar bows and arrows tipped with iron. These Indian troops were thus the first Indians to fight in Europe and must have marched through the bloody defiles of Thermopylae. They rendered such a good account of themselves in this war in a foreign land that they were detained, after the retreat of Xerxes, to take part in the Boestian campaign by the Persian commander, Mardonius [Abbott's *History of Greece*, vol. ii]. Besides infantry, India also supplied Xerxes with cavalry and chariots, riding horses, as also horses, and wild asses, to draw the chariots, together with a very large number of dogs [Herodotus, vii, 65].

The Persian hold on India continued up to 330 B.C. when we find Darius III, the last of the Achaemenian emperors, indenting upon India for a supply of troops to fight his battle at Arbela to resist Alexander's invasion. According to Arrian [*Anabasis*, iii, 8, 3–6], a part of the Indian soldiery was led by the satrap of Bactria, along with the Bactrians and the Sogdians, while another part, the "mountainous Indians", fought under the satrap of Arachosia. India also sent a small force of elephants.

Alexander's Invasion.—Alexander's invasion of India followed his conquest of Persia, the defeat of Darius III, and burning of Persepolis, the Achaemenian capital, in 330 B.C.

Cities to protect his Rear.—Alexander's method was to

mark the course of his conquests by a chain of cities established as so many Greek garrisons to protect his rear. Thus were built the cities of "Alexandria-among-the-Arachosians", i.e. Kandahar, "Alexandria-under-the-Caucasus," i.e. at the foot of Hindu Kush, Cartana (Begrām), Cadrusi (Koratas), and Nicaea between Alexandria and the Kabul River.

Arrival at Nicaea.—Up to the summer of 327 B.C. Alexander was busy conquering Eastern Irān, Bactria, and the region now known as Bukhāra, as far as the Syr Daria (Jaxartes), lying beyond the Hindu Kush, pushing up the Panjshir Valley through the Khawak Pass. He returned through the Kushan Pass and descended on Alexandria. From there he came to Nicaea, whence he despatched a herald to the king of Taxila, and other princes on the west of the Indus, asking them to meet him in the Kabul Valley.

Help from Taxila.—Already at Bukhara, the old King of Taxila and his son, Āmbhi [1] (Omphis), sent envoys to Alexander, offering to help him [2] in his invasion of India in return for their own safety. It appears that he turned a traitor to his country and invited a foreign invader only to crush the growing power of his neighbour, Prince Porus (Paurava), who ruled between the Hydaspes (Jhelum) and the Hydraotes (Rāvi) and was making a bid for an empire, pushing his conquests beyond the Rāvi into the territory of the republican tribes of the east and threatening the frontiers of Taxila on the west. Unlike the King of Taxila, he made a common cause in this imperial endeavour with his neighbour, the King of Abhisāra country (modern Punch and Naoshera districts of Kashmir), and also with many of the republican peoples whom he organized into a powerful army, although he failed to subdue to his system one of these peoples, the Kathaioi (*Kshatriyas*),[3] beyond the Rāvi. He thus stood out as the embodiment of Indian power and patriotism at this national crisis.

[1] Mentioned in the Gaṇapāṭha to Pāṇini, iv, 1, 96.
[2] According to Curtius, he helped Alexander with gifts of "65 elephants, great many sheep of extraordinary size and 3,000 bulls of a valuable breed" [McCrindle, *Invasion of India by Alexander*, p. 202].
[3] Sanskrit *Kaṭhas* according to Weber, *IA.*, ii, 143 ff.

Śaśigupta.—Alexander was also helped at the outset by the treachery of another Indian chief, Śaśigupta (Sisikottus) by name, who was already in Alexander's train. He was probably a ruler of one of the frontier hill-states, who had been to Bactria to help the Irānians against Alexander and now had changed to the side of the European.[1]

Alexander's Army.—Alexander's army is estimated modestly at 30,000 men and was a heterogenous composition made up of Macedonian infantry, heavy-armed, and marked by the long spear, Macedonian cavalry, European mercenaries from Greek cities, highlanders of the Balkans, Agrianes, and Thracians serving as slingers, javelineers, and bowmen, eastern peoples, horsemen from Iran, Pashtu, and Hindu Kush, Central Asiatics good at riding and shooting, and even Phoenicians known for their ship-craft and Egyptians proud of their antiquity [Arrian, iv, 17, 3 ; v, 11, 3 ; iv, 24, 1 ; quoted in *Cambridge History of India*, I, 351].

Astes (Ashṭakarāja) and Sañjaya.—The army was now divided into two parts. One part led by Hephaestion and Perdiccas, two Macedonian nobles, moved along the south bank of the Kabul, through the Khyber Pass [Holdich, *Gates of India*, p. 94], towards the Indus, emerging upon the plains of Peshawar, accompanied by the King of Taxila. But here an Indian chief of a different type, a true patriot, was prepared to fight the foe. He is called by the Greeks Astes, his people, the Astakenoi, and his capital, Peukelaotis. In Indian language, he may be taken to be Ashṭakarāja,[2] king of the people called Ashṭakas, with his capital at Pushkalāvatī. For full thirty days he stood the Greek siege in his walled town till he fell fighting. A hanger-on of the King of Taxila, Sangaya[3] by name, was rewarded by the gift to him of this Ashṭaka kingdom.

Opposition of Aśvakas.—The other division of the army led by Alexander himself moved up the hills on the north

[1] McCrindle, *Invasion of India by Alexander*, p. 76.

[2] He may be connected with what Cunningham calls *Hashtnagar* or eight cities on the eastern bank of the lower Swat river, of which Pushkalāvatī, the capital of Gandhāra, was one [McCrindle, *Invasion*, p. 59, n. 5].

[3] Sanskrit *Sañjaya*. A Shinwari tribe called *Sangu* is still found in these parts [ib., p. 60, n. 1].

side of the Kabul River, the valleys of the Kunār, Panjkora, and Swat, the home of free peoples called *Aspasioi* (from Irānian *aspa* = *aśva*, horse) and Assakenoi, the *Aśvakas*, (= Aśmakas mentioned by Pāṇini, iv, 1, 173), who were ready in their rock citadels to hurl defiance at Alexander. At one place Alexander was himself wounded, together with his companions, Ptolemy and Leonnatos, in trying to scale the outer and inner walls of the city. There was some stubborn resistance at another city called Andaka. That these people fought to a man will be evident from the fact that 40,000 were taken as captives. This small State was economically prosperous when the loot in cattle amounted to 230,000 oxen. The coins known as Vaṭāśvaka coins are believed to be those issued by these Aśvakas [*JRAS.*, 1900, pp. 98–106].

Defence of Massaga under the Aśvaka queen.—The eastern Aśvakas (of modern Kafiristan) gave battle to Alexander with an army of 30,000 cavalry, 38,000 infantry,[1] and thirty elephants, aided by 7,000 mercenaries from the plains, all garrisoned in the fortress called Massaga [Sanskrit Masaka, capital of the district called Maśakāvatī by Pāṇini (iv, 2, 85 ; vi, 3, 119) ; probably same as *Mashanagar* on the Swāt mentioned in Babar's *Memoirs*, cited in McCrindle's *Invasion*, p. 334, N.D.] under the command of the late king's mother, Queen Cleophis. The fortress was built on an eminence and protected by inaccessible sides, treacherous morasses on two sides, a natural rivulet on the third side, and on the fourth side by ramparts of brick, stone, and timber, and further girdled by deep moats along its entire circumference of four miles. Even the women took part in the defence,[2] while the mercenaries, at first vacillating, preferred death to " dishonour ". The defence was further strengthened by an alliance [3] between King Assakenos and the neighbouring king of " the Indians of the hill-country " called Abhisāra who sent contingents for his support. But after several days' resistance, the king fell, his mother and daughter were taken captives, and the city capitulated.

[1] According to Curtius [McCrindle, *Invasion*, p. 194].
[2] Diodorus [ib., p. 270]. [3] McCrindle, *Invasion*, pp. 69, 77, 92.

Friendliness of Nysa.—A little respite came to Alexander in that hostile country from the friendly attitude of a city called Nysa,[1] 300 of whom on horses joined his army.

New Satrapies.—Alexander constituted this hilly country and the lower Kabul Valley into a new satrapy under Nicanor. It was called " India-west-of-the-Indus ". Further west was the earlier satrapy of the Paropanisadae under Tyriespes with his capital at Alexandria-under-the-Caucasus.

Help from Indian Chiefs.—Then he descended to Pushkalāvatī (Chārsadda), where he planted a Greek garrison under Philip. The lower Kabul Valley was further secured by seizing small towns between Pushkalāvatī and the Indus. In this Alexander was aided by two Indian chiefs called " Cophæus ", ruler of the Valley of the Cophen, or Kabul, and " Assagetes ",[2] the King of the Assakenoi who had succeeded the king killed at Massaga.

Siege of Aornos.—Next followed the siege of Aornos, a place not identified. It was probably a rock-citadel where the northern highlanders made their last stand. After reducing it, Alexander planted here a garrison under the Indian chieftain Śaśigupta.

Renewed Aśvaka Opposition.—Alexander had again to move up the hills in pursuit of the flying defenders of Aornos led by the brother of the late Assakenoi chief with a force of 20,000 soldiers and fifteen war-elephants. He pursued them up to the town called Dyrta [3] which he found deserted and made his way back towards the Indus, having two companies of light troops to scour the hills further.

[1] Nysa is described as a republican state governed by a Parliament of 300 members under President Akouphis (= Sanskrit *Akubhi*) who " sent his son and his daughter's son to Alexander to attend him on his expedition " [ib., pp. 79–81]. Jayaswal explains Akouphis = *Ā-kaubhi*, connected with the river Kophen, *Kubhā* or Kabul [*Hindu Polity*, p. 148, pt. i]. McCrindle suggests Nysa = Nagarahāra or Jalalabad [*Invasion*, p. 338, N.G.].

[2] McCrindle suggests *Aśvajit* as the Indian equivalent [*Invasion*, p. 72, n. 4].

[3] According to Arrian [Ib., pp. 69, 70], the storming of Massaga was followed by the siege of the towns called Bazira and Ora which had preceded the siege of Aornos. Cunningham has identified Bazira with Bāzār situated between the Swāt and the Indus, an important centre of trade [ib., p. 335, n. E]. The brother of the deceased Assakenoi chief is called Eryx by Curtius and Aphrikes by Diodorus [ib., pp. 76, 200, 272].

On his way he had an elephant hunt and secured a few elephants for his army with the help of Indian hunters.

Building of Boats.—Alexander arrived at a higher point in the Indus where the timber of forests was very helpful in building boats on which a part of his army floated down the river to the bridge of boats already made ready along with two thirty-oared galleys by Hephæstion, at a place called Ohind, 16 miles above Attock.

Crossing of the Indus, 326 B.C.—It was in the spring of 326 B.C. that the European first set his foot on Indian soil. The entire Greek army with an Indian contingent of 5,000 from Taxila and other chiefs, with squadrons of Indian horse, and thirty elephants crossed over to the other side of the Indus where Āmbhi, the new King of Taxila, was ready for a complete surrender to Alexander as his liege-lord.

Halt at Taxila ; Kalanos.—A move was made from the Indus to the city of Taxila, a noted centre of Indian culture, where Alexander felt greatly interested in Indian ascetics, fifteen of whom were traced in a suburb of the city. Alexander sent for them through Onesicritus, but none came, except one called Kalanos (from the word *Kalyāṇa* used in greeting). They all expressed their contempt for Greek luxury.

Presents from Petty Chiefs.—Alexander held a durbar at Taxila, receiving homage and presents of smaller chiefs of the neighbourhood and returning presents lavishly, in vessels of gold and silver and embroideries secured in Persia. Among these chiefs is mentioned " Doxares, the chief of the province " [McCrindle, *Invasion*, p. 92].

Defiance from Poros.—He also received there a message of defiance from Paurava,[1] one of the heroes of Indian history.

A Resident for Taxila.—Leaving a Macedonian garrison and a satrap, Philip, as " Resident " in the realm of Āmbhi, Alexander moved on to the frontiers of Paurava kingdom on the Hydaspes by a road not traced.

Crossing of the Jhelum.—To cross the Jhelum in that

[1] Greek *Poros*. Jayaswal points to Pāṇini, iv, 1, 151, and the *gaṇapāṭha*, mentioning the word *Pura* with which Greek *Poros* should be connected.

season (May, 326 B.C.) was a difficult job, as the river was rising from the melting of snows at its sources, while the enemy was in full strength to oppose the crossing. The Greeks moved up and down to discover a convenient crossing, and their constant movements kept the Indians in suspense and in the dark about their designs. At last one morning, after a night of torrential storm and rain, the bridge of boats was moved up 17 miles from the original camp, where it lay hidden behind a wooded island and helped in the unseen passage of the Greek army across the river. One boat was big with history, carrying, as it did, Alexander, Perdiccas, his future Regent, Ptolemy, the prospective King of Egypt, and Lysimachus, of Thrace, and would-be conqueror of Roumania, and, lastly, Seleucus, the would-be successor of Alexander's Asiatic empire who would come into conflict with Chandragupta Maurya.

Opposition and death of young Poros.—Alexander crossed with a part of his army, about 11,000 men, who were met by a detachment of Indian army, 2,000 mounted troops, and 120 chariots, sent by Paurava under his son's command.[1] They could not stand the charge of Macedonian cavalry led by Alexander himself, and young Paurava was slain.

Army of Poros.—It was now for Paurava to meet the Greeks in his full strength estimated by Arrian at 30,000 foot, 4,000 horses, 300 chariots, and 200 elephants. He made the following disposition of his forces: elephants in front like bastions in a wall; line of foot projecting at both ends of the line of elephants; cavalry beyond foot to guard the flanks; and chariots in front of cavalry. Paurava planted himself at the centre on the back of his huge state-elephant.

At the sight of the Indian army Alexander exclaimed: "I see at last a danger that matches my courage, it is at once with wild beasts and men of uncommon mettle that the contest now lies" [Curtius, ib., p. 209].

Weather Conditions Unfavourable to Indians.—But the issue of the battle was settled by Fate. Nature created conditions adverse to the operation of the various limbs

[1] According to Curtius, it was "his brother Hages" [McCrindle, *Invasion*, p. 207].

of the Indian army. Already, cloud and storm, rain and thunder had helped the Greeks to cross the river without being seen or heard. And now, on the main battlefield, the rain "had rendered the ground slippery and unfit for horses to ride over, while the chariots kept sticking in the muddy sloughs formed by the rain and proved almost immovable from their great weight. The charioteers were hurled from their seats when the chariots, in rushing into action, jolted over broken and slippery ground. The infantry were unable even to use their arrows. These weapons were so long and heavy that the archers could not readily adjust them on the string unless by first resting their bow upon the ground. Then, as the ground was slippery and hindered their efforts, the enemy had time to charge them before they could deliver their blows ".[1]

Defeat of Poros.—The battle began with the charge of 1,000 mounted archers from Central Asia supported by that of the superior Macedonian cavalry which threw into confusion both the Indian cavalry and infantry whose lines were broken. Horses and elephants in the absence of order and direction created havoc on their side [2] and reduced the army to an undisciplined mob. Those who fled back to the base were mown down by fresh Greek soldiers crossing the river under Craterus. Thousands were slain, including "the two sons of Porus, Spitaces,[3] the monarch of that district, all the great captains of Porus ".

His Last Stand.—Paurava fought "as long as he saw any Indians maintaining the contest in a united body, and did not, after the manner of Darius, abandon the field

[1] Curtius [ib., p. 208].

[2] Alexander's own comment on the military value of elephants and horses of the Indian army is interesting: "As for the elephants, we had an example before our eyes in the late battle (this battle of the Hydaspas) when they charged more furiously upon their own ranks than upon ours and when their vast bodies were cut and mangled by our bills and axes . . . If one or two of them be wounded, the rest swerve aside and take to flight . . . When so many thousands of them are crowded together, they cannot but hamper each other when their huge unwieldy bodies want room either to stand or run" [Curtius, ix, ch. ii].

[3] "Probably the same as Pittacus who is recorded by Polyaenus to have had an encounter with Alexander during the march of the latter from Taxila to the Hydaspes, as Droysen and Thirlwall agree in thinking" [McCrindle, *Invasion*, p. 107, n. 2].

and show his men the first example of flight ",[1] as stated by the Greek writer. When all was lost, he left the field with nine wounds [2] on his body. A man with a message from Alexander galloped after him. Recognizing him to be the traitor-king [3] of Taxila, he made his last exertion by throwing a javelin at him. Head has suggested that this encounter is represented on a well-known coin [*Cambridge History*, i, 367]. Other envoys came up to him, including his friend Meroes. Then he surrendered himself. He was conducted to Alexander who asked him how he should like to be treated. He replied: " Act as a king."

Poros Reinstated.—Alexander gave back to Paurava his kingdom with some additions towards the east comprising the territories of " fifteen republican peoples with their 5,000 considerable cities and villages without number " [Plutarch, *Alexander*, lx]. He now took his place as a king in a new imperial system under Alexander as king of kings.[4]

Conquest of a Free State.—With the brunt of Indian opposition thus broken, Alexander marched farther into the country of the free tribe called Glachukāyanaka [5] [= Glaukanikoi, according to Weber, *IA.*, May, 1873], whose prosperity was represented in thirty-seven towns,[6] each with a population ranging between 5,000 and over 10,000. Alexander annexed this country to the kingdom of Paurava.

Progress Impeded by Revolts.—Farther march of Alexander was impeded by reports of revolts from regions reduced by him. Kandahar revolted with the help of an Indian chief named Samaxus or Damaraxus. The Aśvakas rebelled, killing the Greek Satrap Nicanor. Śaśigupta, then " the satrap of the Assakenians " (eastern Aśvakas) [McCrindle, *Invasion*, p. 112], asked for urgent help. It was sent from

[1] Ibid., p. 108.
[2] Curtius, ib , p. 212.
[3] According to Curtius, he was the brother of the king of Taxila [ib.].
[4] Philostratus in his *Life of Apollonius* states that within the walls of a temple he saw brazen tablets on which were portrayed the deeds of Porus and Alexander. This temple is identified as the one unearthed at Jandial at the Taxila site by Sir John Marshall [see his *Guide to Taxila*].
[5] Mentioned by Kāśikā on Pāṇini, iv, 3, 99.
[6] McCrindle, *Invasion*, p. 112.

the westernmost satrapy of Tyriespes, and from Taxila under Philip. The King of Abhisāra at this time sent to him envoys with presents, but he demanded his personal homage.

Conquest of Kingdom of Poros II.—It was only when Thracian reinforcements came from Irān, the Parthian satrapy, that Alexander thought of crossing the next river, Acesines (Aśiknī, Chenab). Paurava II, the ruler of that region, fled, leaving his kingdom to its fate. He fled for shelter "to the nation of the *Gandaridae*",[1] i.e. to the territories of the Nanda king. The whole territory between the Chenab and the Ravi (Hydraotes) was annexed by Alexander to the Kingdom of Paurava.

Fight of Free Peoples : Adhṛishṭas and Kaṭhas.—Alexander then moved farther on to the Rāvi and beyond, the region of republican peoples noted for their love of freedom. The Adraistai [2] (= *Adhṛishṭas?*) offered submission but the Kathaoi (= *Kaṭha*, according to Weber already cited), who "enjoyed the highest reputation for courage" [Arrian, v, 22, 2], were prepared for fight from their fortified town of Sangala [3] (= Jandiāla), but in vain. We are told that their casualties amounted to 17,000 killed, and 70,000 captives. Even Paurava came to the help of Alexander with elephants and 5,000 troops.

With the fall of their capital, the other towns of the Kshatriyas were deserted. Their country was, as usual, made over to Paurava.

Saubhūti.—Somewhere in this region lay the kingdom of

[1] Ib., p. 279.

[2] Sanskrit *Āraṭṭa*, name of a people of the Pañcha-nada country or the Panjab in the *Mahābhārata*. The *Mbh.* describes them also as *Vāhīkas* who were devoid of religion (nashṭadharmāḥ) and should be shunned (varjanīyāḥ) as *kutsit*, impure, along with the following peoples, viz., Prasthala, Madra, Gāndhāra, Khaśa, Vasāti, Sindhu, and Sauvīra [viii, 44, 2056–2070 ; 45, 2100] Baudhāyana, as we have seen, applies the Aryan ban against the Āraṭṭas. The term, *āraṭṭa*, is also connected by some with *arāshṭraka*, or kingless, republican peoples.

[3] Cunningham suggested its identification with the *Śākala* of Sanskrit writers, described as the chief city of the Madras [in the *Mbh.*, ii, 1196 ; viii, 2033]. But, according to Sylvain Levi, Greek Sangala should correspond to Sanskrit *Sāṁkala* mentioned in the Gaṇapāṭha to Pāṇini, iv, 2, 75, along with the word *Saubhūta* = Greek Sophytes, the name of the king in whose territory probably lay Sangala [McCrindle, *Invasion*, p. 348, N.M.].

Sophytes (= Saubhūti) who made friends with Alexander and entertained him by an exhibition of his remarkable hunting dogs.

Bhagalā.—Alexander next received the submission of the neighbouring king, Phegelas,[1] and now came to the fifth river, Hyphasis (= Beas), where he was brought to a halt by his army declaring: "Thus far and no farther." This was about the end of July, 326 B.C.

Retreat from the Beas.—He now gave the word for retreat, along the road by which he came, back to the Rāvi, the Chenab, and the Jhelum. Here he changed his course and decided on sailing down the Indus to the ocean. For this a fleet of 1,000 boats was required and locally prepared. It included "luggage-boats, horse-transports, and war-galleys" [McCrindle, *Invasion*, p. 135].

Greek Conquests Placed under Indian Kings.—In the meanwhile, necessary administrative arrangements were made for the consolidation of Greek conquests. Paurava was to be the paramount ruler of the territory between the Hyphasis and the Hydaspes, ruler of fifteen republican nations with more than 5,000 cities [McCrindle, *Invasion*, p. 309] as already stated; Āmbhi to the west of the Hydaspes,[2] and the King of Abhisāra to rule in Kashmir with the state of Arsaces (Uraśa, Hazara) added to his kingdom.

Voyage down the Jhelum.—Then Alexander started on his voyage in November, 326 B.C., with troops protecting him on either bank, and Philip, satrap of the province between the Hydaspes and the Hindukush,[3] following three days later to protect his rear. The crew included seafaring peoples like the Phoenicians, the Egyptians, and the Cypriots.

Resistance of Republican Peoples: Mālavas and Kshudrakas.—The armada floated down the Jhelum and reached

[1] Ib., pp. 121, 221, 281. The name corresponds to Sanskrit *Bhagalā*, the name of a royal race of Kshatriyas which the *Gaṇapāṭha* to Pāṇini, iv, 1, 96 classes, along even with the Taxila king, Āmbhi, under the rubric "Bāhu, etc."

[2] According to Curtius [ib., 231], Alexander ended the feud between Paurāva and Āmbhi by uniting them by a marriage alliance.

[3] Arrian describes him as "Satrap of the province lying west of the Indus in the direction of the Bactrians" [McCrindle, *Invasion*, p. 134].

its confluence with the Chenab in ten days. Here opposition was organized by a confederacy of free tribes with an allied strength[1] of 90,000 foot, 10,000 horse, and about 900 chariots. The Malloi (= *Mālavas*) and the Oxydrakai (= *Kshudrakas*) led the confederacy, the former holding the region between the lower Rāvi and the Chenab, and the latter higher up between the Rāvi and the Beas. All the Mālava towns were centres of resistance. At one of these, a town of Brahmans (Greek " Brachmans "), the Brahmans left their pen for the sword and died fighting, about 5,000, " with few taken as prisoners."[2] Of another town, finding the morale of his troops shaken, Alexander himself scaled the walls and fell down with a severe wound on his breast.

Śivis ; Arjunāyanas (*Agalassoi*).—Other tribes also resisted Alexander, though in vain. The *Śivis*[3] (" Sibae " in Greek) offered submission, but the *Agalassoi*[4] fought heroically, with an army of 40,000 foot and 3,000 cavalry. We are told that in one of their towns the citizens numbering about 20,000 cast themselves with their wives and children into the flames, anticipating Rajput heroism.

The collapse of Mālava opposition damped the spirit of the Kshudrakas. In offering submission to Alexander they pointed out that their crime after all was their love of freedom.

Alexander attached the Mālava and Kshudraka territories to the satrapy of Philip.

Ambashṭhas ; Kshatriyas ; Vasātis.—Down the stream, Alexander passed by other tribes called the *Abastanes* (= *Ambashṭhas*,[5] according to Pāṇini, iv, 1, 74), with an

[1] The *gaṇapāṭha* of Pāṇini, iv, 2, 45, refers to the formation *Kshaudraka-Mālavi-senā*, the collective army of the confederate Kshudraka and Mālava clans. Curtius uses the form, *Sudracae*.

[2] McCrindle, *Invasion*, p. 144.

[3] Curtius credits them with 40,000 foot soldiers [ibid., p. 232]. The *Mahābhārata* [iii, 130–1] mentions Śivi-rāshṭra under King Uśīnara. The Śivis may have issued coins known as *Sibi coins* [*JRAS.*, 1900, pp. 98–106].

[4] There are other forms of the name such as *Agesinae*, *Argesinae* from which McCrindle suggests the Indian equivalent, *Arjunāyana*, figuring in Samudragupta Allahabad Pillar Inscription [*Invasion*, p. 367].

[5] The Ambashṭhas are mentioned along with the Śivis, Kshudrakas, Mālavas in the *Mahābhārata* [ii, 52, 14–15].

army of 60,000 foot, 6,000 horse, and 500 chariots, the *Xathri* (*Kshatriyas*), and the *Ossadii* (*Vasāti*) [1] who did not choose to show fight. He reached the last confluence in the winter of 326 B.C.

Sūdras ; Mūshikas.—Farther down, he passed through the country of the *Sogdi* [2] under Brahman ascendancy, of King Musicanus (King of the *Mūshikas*?) who was at feud with the neighbouring King Sambus (Śambhu), and of Oxycanus.[3]

Militant Brahmans.—The whole of this region was remarkable for the supremacy of the Brahmans who were the real power behind the throne and determined its politics. They declared for opposition to the foreign invader as a matter of duty they owed to their *dharma* or national religion, denouncing the submissive princes as traitors and goading the republican peoples into revolt [Plutarch, *Alex.*, 59 ; *Cambridge History*, i, 378]. Musicanus revoked his submission to Alexander. So also did Oxycanus. They were all put to the sword together with the patriotic Brahmans.

Pattala Diarchy.—The next move along the lower Indus was towards Pattala, where the river divided into two branches in those days. Pattala was ruled by two kings and a Council of Elders. It was deserted at the approach of Alexander. Alexander explored the western arm of the river and the region up to the sea, and, on return to Pattala, went up to the eastern stream and saw a lake, probably the Rann of Cutch.

Alexander Leaves India, 325 B.C.—It was in September, 325 B.C., that Alexander left Pattala on his homeward journey, passing through the country of the Arabitae and the Oritae into Gedrosia and out of the field of Indian History.

Results of Invasion : Critical Estimate.—The consequences

[1] Cunningham preferred to identify them with the *Yaudheya* or *Ajudhiya*, now the *Johiyas*. *Assodioi* or *Ossadioi* corresponds to *Ajudhiya* [McCrindle, *Invasion*, p. 156, n. 2].

[2] Called *Sodrai* (= *Sūdra*) by Diodorus [ib., p. 293].

[3] Called by Diodorus [ib.] Portikanos from Sanskrit Pārtha, a prince [ib., p. 158, n. 1].

to India of Alexander's campaigns have been somewhat overstated by the Greek writers. They must be judged by their permanent results. No doubt Alexander had a successful and spectacular march through the Panjab and Sindh. But even then it was not always easy and smooth. The amount of Indian opposition offered to it at different centres, in regions beyond the Indus, or in the land of the five rivers, or in the region of the lower Indus, was not negligible. There was in evidence all over this vast area a general spirit of patriotism instigating resistance to foreign invasion. Perhaps it lacked leadership and resources. It was more in evidence in the lowly than in the high places. Many of the kings with few notable and noble exceptions turned traitors and purchased their position by accommodation with the enemy. But not so were the free peoples of the Panjab, whose love of freedom, and self-sacrifice in its defence, constitute some of the brightest features of Indian history.

Considering the small sizes of these republican states and the large sizes of the armies they could mobilize for defence, it may be assumed that they literally fought to a man. In some cases, even the women fought with the men. It only shows the efficiency of these republican administrations which could produce such a fine and high sense of duty to country in whose defence youths undertook military service and offered their lives without conscription.

Thus the volume and intensity of Indian opposition to Alexander have not been duly assessed and praised by the Greek writers. Nor have they considered how far the Indians took seriously Alexander's campaigns in their midst. From the very nature of the case, in those days of difficult communication, such campaigns in lands so distant and alien could not affect them very much. That this was the popular view was graphically described by one of the Indian "philosophers" or ascetics who represented the better mind of the country and were the preceptors of the people. He pointed out to Alexander the futility of his plans by showing how, as he trod on a piece of dried-up hide, and pressed on one end, the other ends would fly up. By this he hinted that Alexander should not count on conquests so remote from the centre of his kingdom.[1] The practical results of his campaigns corresponded to this description. They were of the nature of raids, of passing shows, and not permanent conquests establishing Greek dominion in India.

The character and degree of the conquest may be understood from the administrative arrangements following it. The Greek governors were posted on the Indian borderland to the west of the Indus ; Peithon in Sindh ; Philip, above Sindh as far as the lower Kabul Valley and Bactria ; and Oxyartes in charge of the Paropanisadae.

To the east of the Indus, in India proper, were created three satrapies, but all under Indian princes, the kings of Taxila and Abhisāra, and Paurava. At Taxila, there seems to have been a kind of dual government under Āmbhi and Philip whose identity is somewhat uncertain. But Paurava was left to rule over the largest territory which included "fifteen republican peoples, 5,000 considerable cities, and villages without number" [Plutarch, McCrindle, *Invasion*, p. 309].

Thus Greek rule which had to depend so much upon Indian co-operation could not take root. It was not accepted by the people. Resistance and rebellion were dogging the steps of Alexander. His satrap, Nicanor, was killed by the Aśvakas. And now, as soon as his retreat from India was known, his most important satrap, Philip, who controlled the whole country between the Hydaspes and the Hindu Kush, was himself murdered. The only step that Alexander could possibly take against this serious blow to his authority was to ask the Indian king of Taxila to take the place of Philip, with his Greek lieutenant, Eudemos, commander of the Thracian contingent attached to that satrapy. Was this Greek authority normal or real?

Like all foreign invasions, Alexander's invasion promoted the political unification of the country. Smaller states which handicapped unity were now merged in the larger ones, such as those of Paurava, Abhisāra, or Taxila. Thus

[1] Plutarch, McCrindle's *Invasion*, p. 315.

A
MEDAL SHOWING POROS ON ELEPHANT ATTACKED BY HORSEMAN.

B
COIN OF SOPHYTES.

To face p. 295.]

conditions were favourable for the rise of an Indian empire to be shortly founded by Chandragupta.

The general Indian position with reference to this Greek invasion is well expressed by the poet :—

> " She let the legions thunder past
> And plunged in Thought again."

Coins.[1]—These foreign invasions introduced foreign coins into India.

The Persian gold *daric,* weighing about 130 grains (8·42 grammes), first minted by Darius, found its way into India where, however, it bore to silver the unfavourable ratio of 1 : 8 as against 1 : 13 in Persia, and could not hold its own. Thus Persian gold coins are rarely found in India.

But the case was different with the Persian silver coins, *sigloi* (shekels), twenty of which were equivalent to one *daric.* A *sigloi* at most weighed 86·45 grains (5·6 grammes). These *sigloi* came freely into India and closely resembled the indigenous silver coins of India, the punch-marked square pieces.

The Persian *sigloi,* however, did not long survive the overthrow of Darius III by Alexander.

Imitation Athenian " owl " coins first appear in the period of Macedonian ascendancy, but the specimens at the British Museum from Rawalpindi were not of Indian but Central Asian origin.

Indeed, the Indian provenance is not established for all imitation Athenian tetradrachms, as well as didrachms and drachms, found in India.

A few smaller silver drachms of Attic weight (58 grains or 3·75 grammes) are, however, traceable definitely to India and the Panjab as the issues of King Saubhūti (Sophytes). They form the only memorial of Alexander's invasion of India.

A group of silver Macedonian tetradrachms, showing Zeus and Eagle, and the significant symbol of a satrapal tiara, though found at Rawalpindi, are really of Central Asian origin. We find the later issues of these coins among

[1] See chapter xiv of *Cambridge History.*

the coins of Antiochos I who had no connection with India after the defeat of his predecessor, Seleucos, by Chandragupta Maurya.

Especially noteworthy in this connection is the extraordinary silver decadrachm of Attic weight preserved in the British Museum for its supposed Indian connection. It commemorates an important incident in Alexander's campaign, as already noticed. Its reverse shows a tall figure, wearing cuirass, cloak, and cap, with a sword by its side, and holding a spear. It is supposed by Head to be the figure of Alexander himself. The obverse represents a retreating elephant bearing two riders, one of whom drives a lance into a pursuing horseman. Head takes this to represent Paurava mounted on his state elephant at the Battle of the Hydaspes and aiming his javelin at Āmbhi, the traitor king of Taxila, galloping after him on horse.

Economic and Social Conditions during the Period: *Buddhist,*[1] *Jain, and Greek Sources.*—Buddhist texts like the Vinaya, Sutta Piṭaka, and the Jātakas, and Jain texts like the Āchārāṅga, Uttarādhyayana and other Sūtras furnish incidental allusions to economic and social conditions, and these may be pieced together into an interesting whole. No doubt all this evidence comes largely from fiction or stories, but even then the stories cannot escape from their local setting or colour, their geographical and social background.

Centres of Settlement: *Kula.*—The unit of settlement was the *griha*, house or homestead, the habitation of the family or *kula*. The *kula* was a fairly comprehensive unit, a joint family including father and mother, children and grandparents, and wives and children of the sons.

Grāma: Houses.—A group of houses and of such large families made the *grāma* or village. It might be of two or three houses [*Prātimoksha*, 65]. But the average *grāma* of the Jātaka tales consisted of families numbering from

[1] The Buddhist sources are completely utilized in the writings of both Dr. T. H. and Mrs. C. A. F. Rhys Davids: *Buddhist India* of the former and articles on the subject by the latter in the *Economic Journal* for September, 1901, and in *JRAS.* for October, 1901, and chapter viii of *Cambridge History.*

30 to 1,000. The cottages of a village were fairly close to one another. A fire starting in one might spread to the whole village [*Milindapañha*, 47].

The village proper was the cluster of dwellings enclosed by a wall or stockade with gates, *grāma-dvāra* [*Jāt.*, i, 239; ii, 76, 135; iii, 9].

Arable Land.—Beyond this enclosure lay the arable land of the village, the *grāma-kshetra*, which was itself protected from pests, beasts, and birds, by fences [*Jāt.*, i, 215], snares, [ib., i, 143, 154], and field-watchmen [ib., ii, 110; iv, 277]. Additions to the *kshetra* came from fresh clearings of forest land [ib., ii, 357].

Holdings.—The village land under cultivation was made up of individual holdings separated from one another by channels dug for co-operative irrigation [ib., i, 336; iv, 167; v, 412; *Dhammapada*, v. 80 = 145 = Theragāthā, 19]. These dividing ditches, rectangular and curvilinear, which the Buddha saw among the cultivated fields of Magadha, suggested to his mind the pattern of his monk's uniform, a patchwork of torn pieces of cast-off clothing [*Vinaya Texts*, ii, 207–9].

A holding was generally small enough to be managed by the family owning it, sometimes with the help of a hired labourer [*Jāt.*, i, 277; iii, 162; iv, 167]. But the ideal was the landlord not divorced from his land but cultivating it himself. A social stigma attached to the "hireling" who is ranked below the slave [*Dīgha.*, i, 51; *Aṅgu.*, i, 145, 206; *Milinda*, 147, 331]. The sorry spectacle of sturdy peasants leaving at home their own empty barns and toiling as hirelings on the estates of the royal capitalist is deplored as a symptom of social decadence in the Jātaka [i, 339].

Large holdings were not unknown. We read of estates of 1,000 *karīsas* (probably acres) and more [ib., iii, 293; iv, 276] farmed by Brahmans, and of one requiring for its cultivation as many as 500 ploughs with hired labourers (*bhatikā*) to ply plough and oxen [ib., iii, 293; ii, 165, 300; *Saṁ.*, i, 171; *Sutta Nipāta*, i, 4].

Pastures.—Beyond the arable land of the village lay its

common grazing grounds or pastures [*Jāt.*, i, 388] for its herds of cattle [ib., iii, 149; iv, 326] and goats [ib., iii, 401], whether belonging to the king [ib., i, 240] or the commoner [ib., i, 194, 388; cf. *Rv.*, x, 19]. The villagers employed a common communal neatherd whose business was to pen the flocks at night or to return them to their owners by counting heads [ib., i, 388; iii, 149]. He was called *Gopālaka* as the protector of the flocks [ib., v, 350]. Dairying was not included in his work. The pasturage was also changed from day to day [*Aṅgu.*, i, 205].

Groves.—Besides pastures, there were suburban groves of the villages like the Veluvana of King Bimbisāra, the Añjanavana of Sāketa or the Jetavana of Śrāvastī, already referred to.

Woodland.—The village ended in the uncleared jungles, the sources of its firewood and litter [*Jāt.*, i, 317; v, 103]. Examples of such jungles were the Andhavana of Kosala, the Sītāvana of Magadha, or the Prāchīnavaṁsa-dāya of the Śākya territory, the haunts of wild beasts and brigands preying on caravan traffic passing through them [ib., i, 99].

Tenure, Rents, and Taxes.—The rural economy of India was marked by village communities of individual peasant proprietors whose rights to land were limited only by the demands of the State. Such demands were of different forms, e.g. (1) Tithe on raw produce, realized in kind at the barn doors [ib., ii, 378] or by survey of the crops [ib., iv, 169] under an official (*Mahāmātra*) or measured out by the village syndic or headman (*Grāmabhojaka* himself. The State's share of produce varied from one-sixth to one-twelfth in the Hindu law-books [e.g. *Manu*, vii, 130], or according to the decisions of the governing authorities [*Jāt.*, iii, 9].

Such tithes or taxes were levied by kings as well as republics. We read of the Mallas of Kusinārā fixing a fine of 500 pieces on anyone who " went not forth to welcome the Blessed One " passing by their town [*Vinaya*, i, 247]. They also agreed to provide food for the Buddha and his Order by turns definitely fixed. The Śākyas levied on Lumbinī the taxes called *Bali* and *Bhāga* (share of the produce), of which the former was remitted completely by Asoka and the latter reduced to one-eighth, as stated in his Lumbinī Pillar Inscription.

The sovereign could remit, reduce, or give away in charity these tithes and taxes. We read of such gifts of a king or his chief queen [*Jāt.*, v, 44] to a daughter at marriage [ib., ii, 237, 403], a minister [ib., i, 354 ; vi, 261], a Brahman [ib., iii, 229 ; *Dīgha*, i, 87], or a merchant [*Jāt.*, vi, 344]. We are also told of a king remitting the tithe to an individual [ib., iv, 169] or a group [ib., i, 200].

(2) Special levy on produce for purposes of provision in State granaries against emergencies like war or famine [*IA.*, 1896, pp. 261 f.].

(3) Forced labour or *corvee*. We read of peasant proprietors providing deer-preserves for their king to escape from his summons to beat up game for him, leaving their own work [*Jāt.*, i, 149 ; iii, 270]. Oppressive *corvees* were also known [ib., i, 339].

(4) Occasional exactions like " milk money " presented by his people to a king at the birth of an heir to him [ib., iv, 323].

(5) Sovereign's right to forest lands [*Dīgha*, i, 87] and " ownerless " estates [*Saṁ.*, i, 89].

There were transfers of land by gift or sale. We read of a Brahman proprietor making a gift of 1,000 *karīsas* out of his estate [*Jāt.*, iv, 281] and a merchant enforcing, on the ground of a stipulation, the sale of a park belonging to a noble against his wishes [*Chulla.*, vi, 4, 9 f.]. The Hindu law-books contemplate non-cultivating landlords letting out land against a share of the produce, as we have already seen [Āpastamba, i, 6, 18 (20) ; ii, 11, 28 (1)].

Town.—Larger than the *kula* and *grāma* was a " townlet " or *nagaraka*, of which the example cited is the famous Kusinārā, the place of the Buddha's death [*Dīgha*, ii, 146]. *Nigama* is also the term for a town, as in the expression *gāma-nigama* frequently found in Pāli literature. There was, of course, no hard and fast line between the *grāma* and the *nigama*, " village " and " town ". A town was also called a *nagara*, e.g. Mithilā, the capital of the king of

Videha, whose realm included 16,000 *gāmas* [*Jāt.*, iii, 365]. There were, lastly, the chief towns or great cities called *mahā-nagarā*, of which six are cited as flourishing in the Buddha's time, as already described.

Centres of Settlement mentioned in Jain texts.—The Jain text, *Uttarādhyayana Sūtra* [xxx, 15–18], specifies a large number and variety of settlements. These may be indicated as follows in an ascending order: *Ghara*, house; *Rathyā*, highways; *Vāṭa*, garden; *Āśrama*, hermitage; *Vihāra*, "abode of Bhikshus, or a temple (deva-gṛiha)"; *Sannivesha*, "a halting-place for processions"; *Samāja*, "a resting-place for travellers"; *Ghosha*, "a station of herdsmen"; *Sthala-senāskandhāra*, "a military camp on high ground"; *Sārtha* (sattha), "a caravan's camp"; *Grāma*, "village"; *Pallī*, "settlement of wild tribes"; *Kheṭa*, "a place fortified by an earthen wall" ("*Kheṭe pāmśuprākāraparikshipte*"); *karvaṭa* or *kharvaṭa*, "a poor town" "surrounded by a low wall" (*kshullaprākāraveshṭitam*) or "the dwelling-place of the Karvaṭa people", or, according to Kauṭilya, "the centre of a circle of 200 villages" (*khārvaṭika*); *Droṇa-mukha*, "a town with a harbour, to which there is access by water and by land like Bhṛigukachchha or Tāmralipti"; the centre, according to Kauṭilya, of a circle of 400 villages; *Pattana*, "a large town" or a centre of trade; *Maṭamba*, "an isolated town," which is more than 3½ yojanas distant from the next village; *Saṁvāha*, "an open town," "the abode of multitudes of men of four castes" (*prabhūtachāturvarṇyanivāsa*), but, according to other commentators, "the fortified place (*durga-bhūmi*) to which are carried for safe custody the crops from the fields" (*saṁvāhāḥ samabhūmau kṛishim kṛitvā yeshu durgabhūmishu dhānyāni kṛishivalāḥ saṁvāhanti rakshārtham*), or "a depot (*sthāpanī*) located in a fort in the interior of hills (*parvatanitambādi durge*); *Nagara*, "a scot free town" which does not pay any of the eighteen taxes levied on a village; *Rājadhānī*, capital of a kingdom; *Nigama*, settlement of merchants; *Ākara*, mines; and *Saṁvaṭṭa-koṭṭa*, "a fortified place of refuge" [*SBE.*, xlv, pp. 176-7; text, ed. Charpentier, pp. 213, 384].

The *Sūtrakṛitāṅga* [ii, 2 (13)], however, defines somewhat differently some of these terms. The *Grāma* is characterized by an enclosure (of thorns, bushes, and trees); *Nagara* by four large *gopuras* or gateways; *Kheṭa* by river and hill surrounding it; *Kharvaṭa* by hills on all sides; *Maṭamba* by its association (as headquarters) with a cluster of 10,000 *grāmas* (*dalitadaśaśataiḥ grāmairyuktam*); *Pattana* as a mart for precious metals (*ratna-yoniḥ*), or a mining centre; *Droṇa* as being encircled by the sea (*sindhuvelāvalayitam*); and *Sambādhana* as being situated on the summit of a hill.

Arts and Crafts.—A considerable degree of economic development seems to have been achieved on the basis of the settled life and physical conditions described above. We have already indicated the agricultural conditions and progress of the times. As regards arts and crafts, eighteen important handicrafts are frequently referred to in the Jātakas which make specific mention of some of these, "the wood workers, the smiths, the leather-dressers, the painters, and the rest, expert in various crafts" [*Jāt.*, i, 267, 314; iii, 281; iv, 411; vi, 22]. The term for smith was *kammāra* which, like its English equivalent, applied to a worker in any metal. The term *vaḍḍhaki* similarly applied to all kinds of woodcraft, whether cart-making or ship-building [*Jāt.*, iv, 207]. Carts were of different kinds, *yāna*, *ratha*, or *śakaṭa* [ib.]. Architecture also involved special modes of woodwork done by the *thapati*, *tachchhaka* (planer) and *bharmakāra* (turner) [ib., i, 201; iv, 323; *Mil.* 330, 345; *Majjhima*, i, 56, 396; iii, 144; *Dhp.*, ver. 80]. A *vaḍḍhaki* settlement is mentioned as turning out furniture as well as seagoing ships [*Jāt.*, iv, 159]. There was also the worker in stone, *pāshāṇa-koṭṭaka*, building houses or hollowing a hole in a crystal as a cage for mouse [ib., i, 479]. Other dignified crafts mentioned are ivory-working, weaving, confectionery, jewellery, and work in precious metals, pottery, making of bow and arrow, of garlands, and the like.

Undignified Labour.—The dignity of labour was not always recognized. Certain arts and crafts were condemned as *hīna-sippas*, despised callings, such as those of hunters and trappers, fishermen, butchers, and tanners, deriving their livelihood from destruction of life; as also snake-charming, acting, dancing, music, rush-weaving, and chariot-making, the peculiar occupations of the aboriginal folks.

Localization of Industries.—Villages grew up by specializing in certain crafts. We have mention of villages of potters [*Jāt.*, iii, 376], of woodwrights [ib., ii, 18, 405; iv, 159, 207], or of ironsmiths [ib., iii, 281] serving the whole countryside with a supply of such articles as razors, axes, ploughshares, goads, and needles. On the Ganges, or farther inland, lay villages of trappers [ib., vi, 71 (*nesādagāma*); *Therīgāthā Comm.*, 220 (*migaluddakagāma*)], supplying game, skins, ivory, and the like.

Within the town, industries located themselves along certain streets or in certain parts. We read of the ivory workers' street (*vīthi*) in Benares [*Jāt.*, i, 320; ii, 197], the dyers' street [ib., iv, 81], the Vessas' (Vaiśyas=merchants) street [ib., vi, 485], or the weavers' "place" (*ṭhāna*) [ib., i, 356].

Trade.—Trade was both foreign and inland, sea-borne and riverine, export and import.

The evidence on the foreign sea-borne trade is comparatively meagre. But it is definite. We read of Prince Mahājanaka sailing from Champā for Suvaṇṇabhūmi [ib., vi, 34 f.], of Mahinda from Pāṭaliputta to Tāmalitti and thence to Ceylon [*Vin.*, iii, 338 (*Samantapāsādikā*)]. A whole village of defaulting woodwrights is described as escaping at night down the Ganges in a "mighty ship" from Benares out to the sea [*Jāt.*, iv, 159]. An accomplished helmsman brings safe by ships "passengers for India from off the sea to Benares by river" [ib., ii, 112]. We read of traders coasting round India from Bharukachchha to Suvaṇṇabhūmi [ib., iii, 188], touching at a port of Ceylon on the way [ib., ii, 127 ff.]. The cargo of a newly arrived ship attracts a hundred merchants to buy it up [ib., i, 122].

The ships of the times were large enough to accommodate "hundreds" of passengers. We read of 500 traders on board ill-fated ships [ib., 128; v, 75], and of 700 under the safe pilotage of Suppāraka [ib., iv, 138 ff.].

Later evidence of about first century A.D. points to a wide range of Indian sea-going trade. The *Milindapañha* [359 ; ii, 269 in *SBE.*, xxxvi], has the following interesting passage :—

" As a shipowner who has become wealthy by constantly levying freight in some seaport town, will be able to traverse the high seas, and go to Vaṅga or Takkola, or China, or Sovīra, or Surat, or Alexandria, or the Koromandel coast, or Further India, or any other place where ships do congregate."

These were the days of brisk sea-trade between India and the Roman empire as testified to in foreign works like the *Periplus* and Pliny's *Natural History* and in indigenous Tamil works speaking of a number of port-towns developed on the coasts of southern India, such as Kāviri-paṭṭinam (Kamara in *Periplus* = Khabari of Ptolemy), capital of Chola Kingdom at the mouth of the Kāveri, where were found many Yavana (Yona = Ionian) merchants [see my *History of Indian Shipping*].

Inland Trade and Trade-routes.—Inland trade was carried on by carts and caravans. We read of Anāthapiṇḍika's caravans travelling south-east from Sāvatthī to Rājagaha and back (about 300 miles) [*Jāt.*, i, 92, 348], and also to the " borders ", probably towards Gandhāra [ib., i, 377 f.]. To ensure easy fording of rivers, this route must have passed along the foot of the mountains up to Kusinārā between which and Rājagaha lay halts at twelve intermediate stations (*gāmas* or *nagaras*) including Vesālī, with a single crossing of the Ganges at Patna according to the recorded itinerary of the Buddha's last ministering journey [*Dīgha*, ii, Suttanta xvi, 81 ff.].

Another important route led south-west from Sāvatthī to Patiṭṭhāna (Paitham) with six intermediate halts [Sutta Nipāta, vv. 1,011–13] and frequent crossings of rivers. We read of boats going up the Ganges to Sahajāti [*Vinaya Texts*, iii, 401] and up the Yamunā to Kosambī [ib., p. 382]. There were no bridges in those days but only fording-places and ferries for crossing rivers [*Jāt.*, iii, 228]. Manu, as we have seen, speaks of cart-ferries [viii, 404 ff.]. *Setu* was not a bridge but only an embankment.

A third route led westwards to Sind, the home of horses and asses [*Jāt.*, i, 124, 178, 181; ii, 31, 287], and to Sovīra [*Vimāna-vatthu* (Comm.), 336] and its ports, with its capital called Roruva [*Jāt.*, iii, 470], or Roruka [*Dīgha*, ii, 235; *Divyāvadāna*, 544]. We read of overland caravans going "east and west" [*Jāt.*, i, 98 f.], and across deserts requiring days to cross (the deserts of Rajputana), steering in the coolness of nights by the stars, under the land-pilot, *Thala-niyyāmaka* [ib., i, 107].

Beyond the western ports, merchants went "out of sight of land" into the ocean and traded with Bāveru (Babylon).

Lastly, there was the great north-west overland trade route linking India with Central and Western Asia by way of Taxila and cities of the Gangetic valley like Sāketa, Sāvatthī, Benares, or Rājagaha [*Vin. Texts*, ii, 174 f.; *Mahāvagga*, viii, 1, 6 ff.]. As a very frequented road, it was free from dangers. We read of students travelling in numbers to Takkasilā, unattended and unarmed [*Jāt.*, ii, 277], for education (see my article on "Ancient Indian Education from the Jātakas" in Law's *Buddhist Studies*].

Bazaars.—Foodstuffs were generally not introduced into towns but sold at their gates. We read of the sale of fish at a gate of Sāvatthī [*Psalms of the Brethren*, 166], of green-grocery at the four gates of Uttara-Pañchāla [*Jāt.*, iv, 445] and of venison at the cross-roads (*siṅghāṭaka*) outside Benares [ib., iii, 49; v, 458; vi, 62], where were located the *sūnā* or slaughter-houses. We are told of people "going for alms to a village just outside the gates of Benares where they had plenty to eat" [ib., i, 361]. The city of Mithilā was served by four *nigamas* in its four suburbs, east, south, west, and north. These are also called *yava-majjhako*, "market-towns" [ib., vi, 330 (Cowell's trans. p. 157)]. On some of the bas-reliefs on the Bharhut Stūpa, the Jātaka is labelled *Yava-majjhakiya*.

Within the towns could be seen workshops [*Psalms of the Brethren*, 24] and bazaars. We read of *āpaṇa*, or shops, where arrows, carriages, and other goods for sale are kept on view [*Jāt.*, ii, 267; iv, 488; vi, 99; *Vin.*, iv, 248 (*Chulla*

Vagga, x, 10, 4], and also of Stores called *antarāpaṇa* [*Jāt.*, i, 55, 350; iii, 406]. The successful shopkeeper (*āpaṇika pāpaṇika*) was noted for his shrewdness, judgment, industry, and business connections [*Aṅgu.*, i, 115 f.]. In the bazaars could be had textile fabrics [*Vin.*, iv, 250 f.], groceries and oils [ib., iv, 248–9], grain [*Jāt.*, ii, 267], greengroceries [ib., i, 411], perfumes and flowers [ib., i, 290 f.; iv, 82; vi, 336; *Vin. Texts*, iii, 343], works of gold and jewellery [*Jāt.*, iv, 223], and other commodities. Strong liquors were sold at the taverns (*pānāgāra* or *āpāna*) [ib., i, 251 f.; 268 f.; vi, 328]. But dealing was disapproved for pious people in strong drinks, poisons, flesh, daggers, and slaves [*Aṅgu.*, iii, 208].

Prices.—These were not regulated by statute but left free to be determined by haggling [*Jāt.*, i, 111 f.; 195; ii, 222, 289, 424 f.], by competition [ib., iii, 282 f.], and even by adulteration [ib., i, 220], and sometimes by custom, as in the case of "a 100-piece slave-girl" [ib., 1, 299].

Speculation or "dealing in futures" was also practised. We read of a local corner in hay [ib., i, 121], and of huge profits of 200 and 400 per cent [ib., i, 109; iv, 2]. In one case, there was a profit of 20,000 per cent, in spite of a heavy drain of 1,000 coins paid for a carriage, a pavilion at the Benares docks, and to the men (*purisā*) and ushers (*patīhārā*) who had to be satisfied [ib., i, 121 f.]. There is also on record the famous fancy price paid by the merchant-prince Anāthapiṇḍika in coins numerous enough to cover the ground of the grove called Jetavana, though the metal of the coin is not stated [ib., i, 92; *Vin.*, ii, 158 f. (*Chulla Vagga*, vi, 4, 9)].

Prices were, however, fixed for royal purchases by the court valuer (*aggha-kāraka*) whose task was difficult in buying at the cheapest rates for the king and refusing bribes offered by tradesmen for higher rates [*Jāt.*, i, 124 f.; ii, 31; *Psalms of Brethren*, 25, 212]. He might still fail to please the king and get from him a niggardly bonus [*Jāt.*, iv, 138].

Taxes and Trade.—These amounted to one-twentieth on each consignment of indigenous goods imported into a town and to one-tenth, *plus* a sample, on each foreign import, according to Baudhāyana [i, x, 18, vv. 14, 15], Gautama [x, 26], and Manu [viii, 398–400] already cited. One Jātaka [vi, 347] tells of a king remitting to a subject these octrois collected at the gates of his capital. The king was also entitled to a discount on sale of one article to him every month by way of commutation of the *rājakārya* due from a merchant (*arghāpachayena*) [*Gautama*, x, 35].

Medium of Exchange: Coins.—Barter was giving place to money economy and was confined to certain contingencies. The use of money was forbidden to a Saṁgha [*Vin.*, iii, 237; ii, 294 f. (*Chulla Vagga*, xii, 1 f.)]. A wanderer gives a woodlander his gold pin for getting a meal [*Jāt.*, vi, 519]. A dog is bought for a cloak and a coin [ib., ii, 247]. But normally coins were used to state prices of all marketable articles, including "fees, pensions, fines, loans, stored treasure, and income" [*JRAS.*, 1901, pp. 882 f.].

The term for coin in Buddhist texts is kahāpaṇa (= kārshāpaṇa). They do not know of the *Purāṇas*. Other varieties of coins were known as *nikkha* and *suvaṇṇa*, both of gold, and bronze or copper tokens as *kaṁsa*, *pāda*, *māsaka* (*māsha*), and *kākaṇikā*.

The values of coins varied with time and place. The *Vinaya* [iii, 45] states: "At that time (of Bimbisāra or Ajātasattu), at Rājagaha, five *māsakas* were equal to one *pāda*."

Credit.—We read of signet rings given as deposit or security [*Jāt.*, i, 121], of wife or children pledged or sold for debt [ib., vi, 521; *Therīgāthā*, 444], of I.O.U.'s or schedules of debts (*iṇa-paṇṇāni*) [*Jāt.*, i, 230; cf. 227, *paṇṇe āropetvā*], and of a bankrupt asking his creditors to produce their schedules of debts only to drown himself before their eyes [ib., iv, 256]. A debtor was disqualified from admission as a *Bhikkhu* to a Saṁgha in the interests of social order [*Vin.*, i, 76 (*Mahāvagga*, i, 46)].

Money-lending and Interest.—The term for interest was *vṛiddhi*, Pāli *vaḍḍhi*. Money-lending, *iṇa-dāna*, is approved as an honest calling, along with tillage, harvesting, and trade [*Jāt.*, iv, 422]. It is also tolerated by Gautama [x, 6; xi, 21]. But usury is universally condemned [*Manu*, iii, 153, 180;

viii, 152, 153; Vasishṭha, ii, 41, 42; Baudhāyana, i, 5, 10, 23–5; already cited].

Money-lending was a profession. The richer folks preferred to hoard their wealth in various ways. It was hidden under the ground [*Jāt.*, i, 225, 375 f., 424; ii, 308; iii, 24, 116], or under the river bank in brazen jars [ib., i, 227, 323], or kept in custody with friends [ib., vi, 521]. In the case of large mansions, a convenient place for securing it was found above the doorway (*dvāra-koṭṭhaka*) [ib., i, 351; ii, 431]. Particulars of the wealth thus hoarded, its nature and amount, were recorded on gold or copper plates [ib., iv, 7, 488; vi, 29; iv, 237].

Organization: Guilds.—There was some amount of economic organization in the form of guilds, partnerships, and varieties of co-operative enterprise. Gautama [xi, 21], as we have already seen, mentions guilds (*vargas*) of "ploughmen, traders, herdsmen, money-lenders, and artisans", and recognizes their right to make their own laws to be respected by the king. The Jātakas tell of eighteen craft-guilds called *Śreṇis* [*Jāt.*, i, 267, 314; iii, 281; etc.]. Each Guild had its President (*Pamukha*) or Alderman (*Jeṭṭhaka*) who counted with the king. Sometimes, different guilds were federated under a common head who was both their president and treasurer (*Bhaṇḍāgārika*) when there were internal quarrels, as there were at Sāvatthī [ib., ii, 12, 52] and Benares. Such a federation among carpenters' guilds is perhaps indicated in the expression *Mahā-vaḍḍhaki* in the Jātaka [vi, 332].

Each industry was organized under an elder, if not a full-fledged guild. We read of *Jeṭṭhakas* for garland-makers [*Jāt.*, iii, 405], robbers or brigands, 500 families of whom lived in a village near Uttara-Pañchāla [ib., i, 296 f.; ii, 388; iv, 430], and for seamen (*niyyāmaka* = pilots) [ib., iv, 137].

Trade had its chief called *Seṭṭhi*. The great Seṭṭhi was the commercial magnate Anāthapiṇḍika of Sāvatthī who was attended by 500 Seṭṭhis at his function of presenting the Buddha with the Jetavana Vihāra [ib., i, 93]. He was the head of a commercial federation, a *Mahāseṭṭhi*, with so many *anuseṭṭhis* under him [ib., v, 384; *Vin.*, i, 19 (*Mahāvagga*, i, 9)]. The jurisdiction of a *Seṭṭhi* is indicated by the expression *seṭṭhi-chhatta* (umbrella of sovereignty) [*Vimāna-vatthu* (Comm.), 66]. The word *seṭṭhi* is itself connected with the word *thāna* or office [*Jāt.*, i, 122; *Vin. Texts.*, i, 102, n. 3].

Caravan traffic called for its special organization and staff to cope with its dangers and difficulties. Different merchants with their carts and caravan followers made up a company under a captain called *Sattha-vāha* to whom they looked for direction as to halts, watering, routes, fording, and danger-spots [*Dīgha*, ii, 342 f.; cf. *Jāt.*, i, 98], though his authority was not always obeyed [*Jāt.*, i, 108, 368; ii, 295; iii, 200]. It was a loose kind of federation or syndicalism. There were also other common officers, the *Thalaniyyāmaka*, "land-pilots, who acted as escorts and guides against dangers to travel from "drought, famine, wild beasts, robbers, and demons" [*Jāt.*, i, 107; i, 99].

Agriculturists also had a chief called *Bhojaka* who represented them in matters municipal and political, and was entitled to certain special dues and fines for his position [ib., i, 199].

Partnerships.—These were permanent [ib., i, 404; ii, 181] as well as temporary or occasional [ib., i, 111; *Dīgha*, ii, 342]. We read of a caravan of many merchants sharing a treasure trove and its profits and making collective gifts to the Buddha [*Jāt.*, ii, 294 ff.]; of Benares traders combining in work and play [ib., ii, 248]; of concerted action in freights between dealers [ib., i, 121]; of merchants chartering a common vessel [ib., iv, 138 ff.; vi, 34].

Caste and Craft.—Craftsmanship rested on hereditary skill. It was usual for the son to follow the calling of his father. "Chunda the smith is called Chunda Smithson" [*Majjhima*, i, 256; *Dīgha*, ii, 127 f. (*Kammāraputto* and *Kammāro*); *Jāt.*, i, 98, 194, 312; ii, 79; iii, 330 f. (*Nesādo* = *Luddaputto* = *Luddo*); v, 356–8].

But the social atmosphere of the Jātakas does not show that caste was completely determining craft. We find instances of princes working as trader with a caravan [ib., iv, 84], as a potter, florist, and cook in succession [ib., v, 290–3], as an archer [ib., ii, 87] on hire, or as a menial servant [ib., iv, 169]. We find Kshatriyas of the Śākya and Koliya clans working in the fields of their "*bhojakas, amachchhas*, and *uparājas*" and quarrelling for priority of right to irrigate [ib., v, 412]. Similarly, we find Brāhmans taking to trade [ib., iv, 15 f.; v, 22, 471], and even working as archers [ib., iii, 219; v, 127 f.; i, 356 f. (servant of a weaver)], trappers [ib., ii, 200; vi, 170 ff.], and carpenters [ib., iv, 207 f.]. The Jātakas give to Brāhmans the following occupations: tillage, tending cattle, trade, hunting, carpentry, weaving, policing of caravans, archery, driving of carriages, and even snake-charming [ii, 165; iii, 293; iv, 167, 276; iii, 401; iv, 15; v, 22, 471; ii, 200; vi, 170; iv, 207, 457; v, 127] and hold up a Brāhman peasant as a supremely pious man, and even a Bodhisattva [iii, 162]. We also find a deer-trapper becoming the bosom friend of a Seṭṭhi without any social barrier between them [ib., iii, 49 f.]; a weaver turning an archer [ib., ii, 87]; a farmer taking to contemptible rush-weaving [ib., iv, 318]; and a person of high caste turning his hand to any job he finds in distress [ib., i, 120 ff.] till he settles down as a Seṭṭhi's son-in-law! There is an instance of a father, without reference to his own occupation, asking his son to choose between Writing, Accounting, and Money-changing (*rūpa*) [*Vin.*, i, 77 (*Mahāvagga*, i, 49, 1; iv, 128].

There was thus considerable mobility of labour in both directions, vertical and horizontal. But this does not mean that the restrictions of caste did not at all operate in those days. The demand for a girl of certified Śākya birth led to the destruction of the whole Śākya clan by the vengeful Kosala king [ib., iv, 144 f.]. The Brāhman Esukārī of Sāvatthī assigns to Brāhman maintenance by alms, bow and arrow to Kshatriya, village and dairy farming to Vaiśya, and sickle and yoke to the Śūdra [*Majjhima*, ii, 180]. The *Vāseṭṭha-sutta* discussion [*Sutta Nipāta*, iii, 9] of the spiritual content of the term *brāhmaṇa* shows the strength of the current conceptions regarding caste and its ideals. One Jātaka [iv, 363 f.] condemns Brāhmans as losing their caste for taking to unlawful occupations like agriculture, trade, and other callings. Thus the strict Brāhman tradition about caste as defined in the Smṛitis is also recognized in Buddhist canonical works. But that tradition itself allows the pursuit of a lower occupation by a higher caste as " *āpad-dharma* ", in emergencies and distress, as already stated.

Slavery.—Slavery was the consequence of capture [*Jāt.*, iv, 220 ; vi, 135], commutation of death sentence, debt [ib., vi, 521], wilful debasement [*Vin.*, i, 72 (*Mahāvagga*, i, 39, 1) ; *Sum. Vil.*, i, 168], or judicial punishment [*Jāt.*, i, 200]. It could be ended by payment [ib., vi, 547] or by the will of the slave's master [ib., v, 313 ; *Dīgha.*, i, 72]. A slave was liable to be " beaten, branded, imprisoned, and poorly rationed " [*Jāt.*, i, 451 f.], but actual cases of ill-treatment are rarely recorded. On the other hand, a slave working as valet and footman is petted and even taught writing and handicrafts [ib.]. An undischarged slave was not eligible for monkhood [*Vin.*, i, 76 (*Mahāvagga*, i, 46 f.)].

Economic and Social Conditions from Greek Sources.—These throw some further interesting light on the economic and social conditions of the times.

Towns.—The centres of economic prosperity in the Punjab were its numerous towns testified to by the Greek writers, as already stated. Besides the towns which also served as centres of defence or garrisons in the country of the Aśvakas, such as Massaga or Aornus, the Glaussai counted thirty-seven towns to their credit, while the remainder of the Punjab under the Malloi and Oxydrakai and other tribes is stated to have as many " as 5,000 towns ".

Architecture.—Some of these showed creditable design in town planning and architecture. Massaga, for instance, was built as a fort, commanding great natural advantages, on an eminence inaccessible on all sides against steep rock, treacherous morass, deep stream, and a rampart guarded by a deep moat to boot. According to Curtius, the rampart " was thirty-five *stadia* (= about four miles) in circumference, with a basis of stone-work supporting a superstructure of unburnt, sun-dried bricks. The brickwork was bound into a solid fabric by means of stones ". Early Indian architecture was not always, or everywhere and exclusively, wooden. This has been also proved by the Indus Valley discoveries of structures of remotest times. The town of Aornus was similarly planned on a high hill, with its water-supply arranged by tapping a local spring, and food grown with the labour of a thousand men in an adjoining field to render the fort self-contained against a siege.

Manufactures.—But besides the towns, other signs of material progress may be seen in the presents or spoils secured by Alexander at different places. These included quantities of cotton goods, bucklers of ox-hide, skins of lizards, tortoise shells (mentioned as exports in the *Periplus* of first century A.D.), " 100 talents of steel " (*ferri candidi*, " white iron," which Cunningham considers to be nickel). All these came from the Oxydrakai and Malloi. Besides these nickel coins, there were also the silver issues, already referred to, of King Sophytes (Saubhūti), supposed to be imitation Athenian " owls ", showing as they do the king's head on obverse, and a cock and his name in Greek characters on reverse. The King of Taxila presented Alexander with " 200 talents of silver and golden crowns ". Other manufactures of the times are indicated in the equipment described of the Indian soldiery, the iron-tipped arrows, javelins, swords, and lances, and also in the abundance of carts and boats and chariots used for both trade and war.

Live Stock.—Agricultural progress is indicated in the accounts of live-stock. A fine breed of 230,000 oxen was captured by Alexander in the country of the Aśvakas and sent off to Macedonia. He received from Taxila 3,000 fat oxen and 10,000 sheep, from Saubhūti his fighting dogs, and from the Kshudrakas tame lions and tigers. Horses and elephants were of course in great use.

Ascetics.—Regarding social conditions, most interesting information is given about the highest class or caste in society, described as " Philosophers " or " Sophists ". These were divided into two classes, called Brahmans and " Sarmanes ". The Brahmans spend thirty-seven years in studentship, living with their teacher " in a grove near the city, using beds of leaves and skins, living sparely, practising celibacy and abstinence from flesh-food, listening to discourse, and admitting others to discussion". This is the system of *Brahmacharya*. Then the Brahman "departs to his own property", marries, "lives in freedom and luxury, wearing muslins and golden ornaments, eating flesh but not that of the domesticated animals." As to the "Sarmanes" (= Sanskrit *Śramaṇas*, a term applied to ascetics, whether Buddhist or non-Buddhist), "they live in the forests on leaves and wild fruits, wearing barks of trees," and always meditating and worshipping the gods. Some of them were "*Medical* philosophers", "treating people by diet and not by medicines," and preferring "medicines to be applied externally" to "drugs". Others chose to be "diviners and masters of incantations". There was "a higher and finer sort" of them [Megasthenes, Fragment 40 = Strabo, xv, *c.* 711 f.]. Strabo mentions another class of Philosophers called *Pramanai*, who were "argumentative and captious" [xv, *c.* 719]. These may be identified as the *Prāmāṇikas* depending on, and following their own views of, *pramāṇa* or the means of reaching right knowledge. Thus they were not blindly orthodox or superstitious and ritualistic and hence are described by Strabo as laughing at Brahmans, i.e. the formalist priesthood. Strabo further classifies "Brahmans" into (1) those who dwell in the mountains; (2) the naked ones; and (3) those who live in the world.

A point of interest is that "women are permitted to share in the philosophic life" with the ascetics on condition that they "observe sexual continence like the men" [Megasthenes Fragment 40]. This is also observed by Nearchus and Strabo [xv, *c.* 718].

Art and Architecture.—The pre-historic monumental remains, palaeolithic, neolithic, or those of the Indus Valley, have been already noticed. Those for the later periods up to 325 B.C. are comparatively rare and meagre in proportion to the importance of their general history, the magnitude of their achievements in other spheres of learning, culture, and civilization. The reason for this paucity of architectural achievements was the perishable character of the material then used, which was earth or wood, stucco, bamboo, or timber. It was no less due to a philosophy of life which insisted on its simplicity, on " plain living and high thinking ". Architecture, like other arts, had to find a religious origin and justification. It originated in the religious need of constructing *Yajña-vedis* and *Yajña-śālās*, altars and halls for the performance of Vedic sacrifice. The *Vedis* had to be built also in different forms, such as " falcon ", " chariot ", or " man with uplifted arms ", as stated in the *Taittirīya Saṁhitā*, and this gave scope to design.

A Vedic fire-altar is traced in a hollow cave, hemispherical in shape, and with an opening like a chimney at the centre, discovered at Cananore in Malabar. Certain rock-cut tombs discovered near Tellicherry in Malabar are also believed to be of the Vedic age. Vedic burial-mounds are also unearthed at Lauriyā-Nandangarh together with the content of a small gold leaf upon which was impressed the figure of a nude female supposed to be the Earth Goddess of the Vedic burial hymns. We may next mention the walls and fortifications of the old city of Rājagṛiha (Rajgir) and remains of houses, which were all built of rude and rough cyclopean masonry, rare examples of such structures of durable material in that age. As already related, these ruins were of the time of Bimbisāra (*c.* 603–551 B.C.), the founder of *Giribbaja*, " hill-fort." He changed the capital later to new Rājagṛiha. His architect and town planning expert is named as Mahāgovinda. His son, Ajātaśatru (*c.* 551–519 B.C.), as a Buddhist in his later days, is stated to have erected a pandal at the entrance to the Sattapaṇṇi Cave in the hills of Rājagṛiha for purposes of the second Buddhist Council and provided for Bhikkhus all requisites (see references given above).

The next type of buildings for which remains are extant for the period is what is called the *Stūpa*, literally " something raised ", a mound. A mound was raised over the relics of holy persons and was known as a *Chaitya*, from *chitā*, a funeral pile. Later, the sense of the term *Chaitya* was extended so as to mean not merely the *Stūpa* but any temple, or altar, or a shrine of relics. We have already seen how early Jain texts use the term *chaitya* (*cheie*) even in the sense of a park. The *Stūpa* came to be used as a Buddhist architectural term for a mound containing relics of the Buddha, his ashes, bones, hair, or tooth, or relics of famous Buddhist saints or teachers.

The oldest *Stūpa* found up to date is that found in ruins at Piprahwa on the Nepal frontier. It was built in brick and contained an urn bearing the following inscription: "This shrine for relics of the Buddha, the august One, is the pious foundation (*sukiti*) of the Śākyas, His brethren, in association with their sisters, their children, and their wives." When opened, it was almost perfect as a solid cupola or domed mass of brickwork 116 feet in diameter at the base and 22 feet in height, built round and on a massive stone coffer in which were enshrined relics of the body of the Buddha. The bricks were huge slabs, set in mud mortar, of which the largest measured 16 × 11 × 3 inches. "The masonry of the *stūpa* is excellent of its kind, well and truly laid; the great sandstone coffer could not be better made; and the ornaments of gold, silver, coral, crystal, and precious stones which were deposited in honour of the holy relics display a high degree of skill in the arts of the lapidary and goldsmith" [V. A. Smith in *Imperial Gazetteer*, ii, 102–3].

As the inscription on the *Stūpa* attributes its construction to the Śākyas, it may be taken to be one of the original eight *Stūpas* in which, according to *Mahāparinibbāna-Suttanta*, were enshrined the bodily relics of the Buddha by eight different claimants, among whom were included the Śākyas of Kapilavastu. That there were in existence *Stūpas* older than the time of Asoka is stated by Asoka himself in one of his inscriptions (Nigālī Sāgar Pillar Inscription). There he states that he enlarged to double its original size the *Stūpa* of Buddha Koṇāgamana, which thus had been in existence before his time.

Recent excavation at Buxar carried out by Dr. A. Banerji-Sastri have brought to light remains of a very ancient civilization in the Gangetic Valley, disclosing the ruins of a Chalcolithic city (third millenium B.C.) at about 52 feet below the present surface level, and a series of terra-cottas of two types, *Crude*, showing affinity with Sumer and Sindh,

PLATE XI

A
PARKHAM YAKSHA.

B
PIPRAHWA VASE.

and *Subtle* and *Finished*, to be compared with pre-Sumerian Eridu and the Aegean. " These two strata of terra-cotta preceding the primitive stone Yakshas of the fourth century B.C. point to the pre-Aryan culture-currents " [Dr. A. Banerji-Sastri in *Indian Science Congress Handbook to Patna*, 1933, pp. 19–23].

" India, in centuries and perhaps milleniums B.C., was an integral part of an ' Ancient East ' that extended from the Mediterranean to the Ganges Valley. In this ancient world there prevailed a common type of culture, which may well have had a continuous history extending upwards from the stone age. Some of its most widely distributed decorative, or, more accurately speaking, symbolic motifs, such as the cults of sun and fire, may go back to that remote past ; more sophisticated motifs and technical discoveries may have originated in any part of the area ; a majority, perhaps in southern Mesopotamia, others in India or in Egypt " [Dr. A. K. Coomaraswamy in his *History of Indian and Indonesian Art*, pp. 13–14].

Statues.—We have also to assign to this period the colossal statues of figures now identified as those of *Yakshas* or *Yakshīs*. So far eleven examples of these have been discovered, as follows, viz. (1) Parkham (Muttra) Yaksha ; (2) Baroda (Muttra) Yaksha ; (3) Yakshī in another village of Muttra, worshipped as Mansā Devī ; (4) another Muttra *Yaksha* newly discovered (*U.P.H.S.J.*, May 1933, p. 95) ; (5) Patna Yaksha, now in the Indian Museum ; (6) another Patna Yaksha statue in the Indian Museum ; (7) Female Chauri-bearer from Didarganj, Patna ; (8) inscribed Maṇibhadra Yaksha from Pawaya (Gwalior) ; (9) Besnagar Female Statue ; (10) a second Besnagar Female Statue ; and (11) fragments of a Yaksha Statue found at Kosam.

Of these, numbers (1), (3), (6), (7), and (8) bear inscriptions. The inscriptions on numbers (1) and (8) mention the label Maṇibhadra (general of Kubera) for the images. The incription on (3) mentions the label " Yakshi Lāyāvā " together with the name of the sculptor, Nāka, and his teacher, Kunika, who is himself mentioned as the pupil of Gomitaka in the inscription of number (1). The two Patna statues contain inscriptions mentioning " Bhagavān Akshata-nīvika " (Kubera) and the " Yaksha Sarvatra-Nandī ".

As the figures of all these statues are closely alike, we may infer in the light of these inscribed labels that the statues are those of Yakshas or Yakshīs.

These statues may, therefore, be taken as some of the earliest examples of indigenous Indian art, of popular or folk-art, the art of the masses, whose religion meant the worship of minor deities like the Yakshas or Yakshīs, Nāgas or Nāgīs, Gandharvas, Apsaras, Tree- and Water-spirits, and the like. This art may be distinguished from the art of the cultured classes, the official or Court art, which is seen at its best later, in the time of Asoka. We have already seen how Indian art had much earlier origins in the discoveries at Mohenjodaro and Harappa testifying to its capacity for successful treatment of the natural forms of plants, animals, and even of men and women. It is no wonder that the progress registered in later Mauryan art should be the outcome of a long course of evolution of which some evidence may be found in these statues. We have also some literary evidence on the subject. All these statues show in common the use of torque or necklace on which Pāṇini's grammar has a Sūtra [iv, 2, 96] to explain the formation " *graiveyaka* ", " ornament for the neck." Pāṇini also uses the term *Takshan* [v, 4, 95] in the sense of a sculptor or a stone-cutter as distinguished from the *Ratha-Kāra* and *Vardhaki* as woodwrights. He also mentions *Grāma-śilpīs* [ib.] in the sense of " artisans in the employ of the village community ", as distinguished from *Rājaśilpis*, " the Court artists," as mentioned by *Kāśikā*. The former class of artisans may be taken to be the representatives of folk art as contrasted with the aristocratic art of the cities and cultivated society for which the other class of sculptors had catered.

As regards the artistic merits of these Yaksha statues, Dr. A. K. Coomarswamy considers them to be " informed by an astounding physical energy not obscured by their archaic stiffness, and expressive of an immense material force in terms of sheer volume " ; representing " an art of mortal essence almost brutal in its affirmation, not yet spiritualized and without any suggestion of introspection, subjectivity, or spiritual aspiration ". " Stylistically, the type is massive and voluminous and altogether plastically conceived, not bounded by outlines." This type is later represented in examples like the Mathurā Bodhisattva image in the Lucknow Museum, or the image of Bodhisattva Sākyamuni at Sārnāth, which is mentioned in its inscription as being the gift of Bhikshu Bala of Mathurā. These later images were in fact cast into the plastic moulds of the Yaksha forms conceived by the ancient Indian national school of art. Examples of Mathurā work made of the characteristic material of Mathurā, red sand-stone, figures of Buddhas and Bodhisattvas, have been found at many centres outside Mathurā, such as Sārnath, Sahet Mahet, Kusinārā or Bodh-Gayā, while the earlier art of Yaksha statues has left marks of its influence in that of Bharhut and Sanchi in its many figures of minor deities mentioned above, and of floral and other decorative designs [see V. S. Agrawala's article in *U.P.H.S. Journal* for May, 1933].

Sources.—As has been already seen, the chief sources of information for this period of history (650–325 B.C.) are embedded in Buddhist literature.

The growth of this literature has itself a history which may be presented in the following stages as given by T. Rhys Davids (in vol. I, ch. vii, of *Cambridge History of India*): (1) Simple statements of doctrine, stock passages, or Suttas, found repeated in identical words in some of the later works; (2) Episodes similarly recurring; (3) Books no longer existing but traced in quotations in later works, e.g. the *Sīlas*, the *Pārāyana*, the *Octades*, the *Pātimokkha*, etc.; (4) certain poems, ballads, or prose passages similarly recurring in extant anthologies; (5) the four *Nikāyas*, *Dīgha*, *Majjhima*, *Saṁyutta*, and *Aṅguttara* [i.e. " *Suttas* arranged according to a progressive enumeration from one to eleven of the subject with which they deal "]; a supplementary *fifth Nikāya*, comprising smaller works and miscellanea, and called *Khuddaka*; the *Sutta-Vibhaṅga* and the *Khandakas*. All these may be approximately dated

100 years after the Buddha; (6) the *Sutta-Nipāta*, *Thera-* and *Therī-Gāthās*, the *Udānas*, the *Khuddaka-Pāṭha*; (7) the *Jātakas* (verse only) and the *Dhammapadas*; (8) The *Niddesa*, the *Iti-vuttakas*, and the *Paṭisambhidā*; (9) The *Peta-* and *Vimāna-Vatthu*, the *Apadānas*, and the *Buddha-vaṁsa*; and (10) The *Abhidhamma* books, the latest of which is the *Kathā-Vatthu* and the oldest, perhaps, the *Dhamma-Saṅgaṇi*.

It will be seen that much of the history of this period is derived from the four Nikāyas and sometimes from works included in the fifth Nikāya too, as works belonging to that period. They were all composed before Asoka's time. Asoka, in his Bhabrū Edict, selects seven passages from scriptures, four of which are from the four Nikāyas and the fifth from the *Sutta-Nipāta*, now included in the fifth Nikāya. Asoka's seven passages are thus passages selected from a literature which must have been in existence long before his time and his inscription.

Again, in certain inscriptions later than Asoka, but bearing Asokan characters, viz. those of Bharhut, are mentioned names of donors to Buddhist monuments, who are described as being specialists in the Suttantas (*Suttaṁtika* = *Sautrāntika*), or the Piṭakas (*Peṭakī*), or the five *Nikāyas* (*Paṁcha-nekāyika* = *Pañcha-naikāyika*).

Further, according to the evidence of commentators, Moggalīputta Tissa presided at the third Buddhist Council held in the eighteenth year of Asoka's reign (252 B.C.), and composed the *Kathā-Vatthu*, which is the latest book in the three present Piṭakas. It quotes largely from all the five *Nikāyas* and does not contain a single phrase or word which is referable to a later date. Thus the five *Nikāyas* are also proved to be much older than Asoka's time.

It is also to be noted that the four *Nikāyas* quote one another (e.g. *Aṅgu.*, v, 46, quoting *Saṁ.*, i, 126). The quotation does not mention the name of the *Nikāya* but only that of the Sutta quoted. This proves that the Suttas and Suttantas, in their titles found in the four *Nikāyas* in their present form, had been handed down from a much earlier age.

Again, there is a common element in all the four *Nikāyas*, a number of stock passages on ethics recurring in them in identical words. This points to the original material, the accepted formulas of Buddhist teaching, out of which the *Nikāyas* were compiled.

Sometimes, again, we find entire episodes repeated in identical words in the *Nikāyas*, or accounts of events mentioning identical names of persons and places. Nearly two-thirds of the Mahāparinibbāna Suttanta is made up of such recurring episodes and stock passages. The events related sometimes go back very close to the Buddha's death, only two or three years after his death, and, in one case, about forty years after it [as in *Aṅgu.*, iii, 57-62].

Lastly, it is to be noted that the geography of the Nikāyas also points to their age being much earlier than Asoka. They do not know of any place in the east which is south of Kaliṅga, and no place in the west which is south of the Godāvarī. But the Asokan inscriptions know intimately of south India, and even of Ceylon. A long interval must be allowed for this extension of geographical knowledge and horizon.

We have already seen how this old literature throws light on the life of the Buddha in its references to the places at which he was stopping in his ministerial career and delivered a discourse, or to some incidents in his life. It has been estimated that there are about 200 such pages of reference in a total of 6,000 pages of text in the four *Nikāyas*. Two episodes in his life, those treating of its beginning and of its end, have received a more elaborate treatment. The first is described in the *Majjhima*, the period between his assumption of asceticism and "*Nirvāṇa*" or Arhantship under the Bodhi Tree. The *Vinaya* extends this episode and carries it up to the point of his foundation of the Order with his first sixty disciples. This covers about seven years, including one year for the *Vinaya* addition. The other episode is confined to the events and details of the last month of Buddha's life and given in the Mahāparinibbāna Suttanta, as already stated.

INDEX